WILLIAM WORDSWORTH

WILLIAM WORDSWORTH
A BIOGRAPHY

Hunter Davies

F

FRANCES LINCOLN LIMITED
PUBLISHERS

Frances Lincoln Ltd
4 Torriano Mews
Torriano Avenue
London NW5 2RZ
www.franceslincoln.com

William Wordsworth
Copyright © Hunter Davies 1980, 1997, 2003, 2009

First published in 1980 by George Weidenfeld and Nicolson Ltd
This new edition first published in 2009 by Frances Lincoln Ltd

All rights reserved. No part of this publication may be
reproduced, stored in a retrieval system or transmitted in any
form, or by any means, electronic, mechanical, photocopying,
recording or otherwise, without either permission in writing
from the publisher or a licence permitting restricted copying.
In the United Kingdom such licences are issued by the
Copyright Licensing Agency, Saffron House, 6–10 Kirby
Street, London EC1N 8TS.

A catalogue record for this book is available
from the British Library

ISBN 978-0-7112-3045-3

Printed in the UK by CPI Bookmarque, Croydon, CR0 4TD

2 4 6 8 9 7 5 3 1

CONTENTS

Introduction   xi
Prologue   1

1 Cockermouth and Penrith : 1770–1779   5
2 Hawkshead : 1779–1787   16
3 Cambridge : 1787–1790   28
4 France : 1791–1792   45
5 Mainly London : 1793–1795   60
6 West Country : 1795–1798   77
7 Germany and *Lyrical Ballads* : 1798–1799   98
8 Dove Cottage : 1800–1802   110
9 Dorothy and Wedded Bliss : 1802   131
10 Scotland : 1803   148
11 A Death in the Family : 1805   163
12 Coleridge Returns : 1806–1808   177
13 The Great Estrangement : 1808–1813   194
14 Fine Folks : 1813–1817   214
15 Politics and Poems : 1815–1818   228
16 Mary, Dorothy and the Children : 1813–1820   245
17 Friends and Relations : 1813–1820   261
18 Fame : 1820–1830   274
19 Troubles and Triumphs : 1830–1843   300
20 Mellow Moods : 1840–1847   315
21 Last Days : 1847–1850   330
22 Postscript   340

The Family Tree of William Wordsworth   344
Appendix   347
Bibliography   351
Index   355

ILLUSTRATIONS

1 *Wordsworth* House, Cockermouth, from the Art-Journal 1866 (*Trustees of Dove Cottage*)
2 Hawkshead Grammar School (*Sanderson & Dixon Ltd, Ambleside*)
3 An eighteenth-century drawing by William Burgess of Windermere Ferry (*British Museum; photograph by John Freeman Group*)
4 An early portrait of Wordsworth, painted by William Shuter in 1798 (*Cornell University Library*)
5 Caroline Vallon (*Mme Blanchet, Paris*)
6 Dorothy Wordsworth (*Trustees of Dove Cottage*)
7 Dove Cottage (*Trustees of Dove Cottage*)
8 and 9 Contemporary engravings of Windermere, and of Derwent and Bassenthwaite
10 Mary Wordsworth, by Margaret Gillies (*Trustees of Dove Cottage*)
11 Samuel Taylor Coleridge, by P. Vandyke (*National Portrait Gallery*)
12 Robert Southey, by H. Edridge (*National Portrait Gallery*)
13 Greta Hall, Keswick, engraving after a drawing by W. Westall
14 Thomas de Quincey (*Trustees of Dove Cottage*)
15 Sara Coleridge and Edith May Southey, miniature by Edward Nash (*National Portrait Gallery*)
16 Dora Wordsworth, by Margaret Gillies (*Trustees of Dove Cottage*)
17 A contemporary engraving of a room at Rydal Mount
18 Charles Lamb, by W. Hazlitt (*National Portrait Gallery*)
19 William Hazlitt, by W. Bewick (*National Portrait Gallery*)
20 Sir Humphrey Davy, by H. Howard (*National Portrait Gallery*)
21 Sir Walter Scott, by Landseer (*National Portrait Gallery*)
22 Sir George Beaumont, engraving after J. Hoppner (*National Portrait Gallery*)
23 An engraving of Lowther Castle
24 An early version, in Wordsworth's handwriting, of a section of *The Prelude* (*Trustees of Dove Cottage*)
25 An extract from Dorothy Wordsworth's *Journal* (*Trustees of Dove Cottage*)
26 Wordsworth painted by Benjamine Robert Haydon in 1842 (*National Portrait Gallery*)

The author and publishers are most grateful to the copyright holders for permission to reproduce the illustrations.

ACKNOWLEDGEMENTS

I am grateful to the staff, officials and Trustees of the Wordsworth Trust, Grasmere, where were inordinately patient with my questions and requests, and who went on to provide endless information and advice. They cannot be held responsible for my interpreations, but they readily made their scholarship available. I was especially grateful to the late Jonathan Wordsworth of St Catherine's College, Oxford (Chairman of the Wordsworth Trust) for his help, and his good humour throughout the project; to the late Dr Peter Laver, Resident Librarian at the Wordsworth Library, Grasmere, for compiling my original reading list; and perhaps most of all to the late Dr Robert Woof, Director of the Wordsworth Trust for reading and commenting upon my final manuscript, a task well beyond the call of his many duties. Thanks also for help on the present edition to Jeff Cowton, Curator of the Wordsworth Trust.

I would also like to thank the Earl of Lonsdale for his help with the Lowther family records; Beth Darlington of Vassar College, New York, for her guidance on the newly discovered Wordsworth letters; the Librarian of St John's College, Cambridge; the late Mary Henderson of Rydal Mount, and the Curator; the staff at Wordsworth House, Cockermouth, and the National Trust.

INTRODUCTION

This biography first came out in 1980 and so, in the nature of things, you might suspect it could well be dreadfully out of date. The basic facts of Wordsworth's life won't change. How can they, when we know so much and have so many primary sources, manuscripts and first-hand accounts as proof of what we think we all know about him? Of course, as life moves on, minor details get revealed or re-analysed, research is done in associated, sometimes rather peripheral, fields and, more importantly, with any world-class genius, which Wordsworth certainly was, there is always room for new interpretations, new assessments, which reflect our more modern concerns, attitudes and values. As with Shakespeare, every generation can get something new out of Wordworth.

Nonetheless, why repeat the same old book again, the same as it was, except for this new introduction? The simple answer, which I have to admit I find surprising all these years later, is that it is still, arguably, the only general biography of its type available for the general reader. Presumably, that's why it's always been in print here and in the USA, until very recently.

I like to think it is a serious biography, that all the information is correct and agreed upon by Wordsworth scholars, but it is general in the sense that it is aimed at the ordinary, educated member of the public who probably knows only a little about Wordsworth, wants to know, but is not willing or able to take on a 900-page academic study, crammed with footnotes and lengthy analysis of all his poetry. I wanted to tell his life story, from birth to death, in chronological order, without jumping ahead, or assuming detailed knowledge by the reader. I hate it when biographers make references to a wife and children, or later events and dramas, when they are still in the throes of describing our hero's childhood. I also wanted to contain it all in 300 or so pages.

I started to do it because I could find nothing which served my purposes. As a Cumbrian, I knew the basics of his life, learned 'Daffodils' at school, had visited his birthplace in Cockermouth, done a tour of Dove Cottage, read *The Prelude* as a student, but I wanted to know more about his whole life and personality. The standard book at the time was by Mary Moorman, in two volumes, 1,200 pages long. Clearly excellent on his poetry, not to say exhaustive, but it was hard work digging out a clear picture of Wordsworth the man. So I decided to do it myself.

Only a complete outsider would have had the cheek or effrontery to try and cram it all into one, straightforward, easily accessible volume. My mind was so clear in the early stages, when I was sure I could see the patterns of his life. As I progressed, it became cloudier. Wordsworth, as he grew older, did so many things at the same time that I had to be ruthless in separating the sections of his life in order to keep up a simple narrative. Ignorance was a great asset.

I wouldn't attempt such an enterprise again. Not now. I just hadn't realised how bulky his life was. It took three years full time, not one as I'd planned. For a start there was just so much to read. I used to say to myself, 'Oh no, why didn't I pick on someone who'd died young?' Wordsworth was bulky in his life, living until he was eighty, and also in his writings. His life was three times as long as Keats's and he produced about four times as much poetry. (70,000 lines as opposed to Keats's 18,000). With Keats, Shelley and Byron you can hold their life and poetry in your mind, or convince yourself you can, but with Wordsworth, he overwhelms you.

That's therefore the first reason why there have been few, standard-length biographies. The academics either write whoppers or concentrate on one part of his life, usually his early years. A lot of the experts tend to know a great deal about one part of Wordsworth's life, which makes it harder for them to see the whole, and it also makes it difficult for them to communicate what they do know to the general public.

While getting a grip on his whole life is hard for the expert, and more so for the complete outsider, there's also the problem of getting a foothold on the Wordsworth world. Wordsworth has been captured by the scholars, his large body taken away and carved up hungrily into smaller and smaller chunks as they share out the meat amongst themselves. They suspect interlopers and jealously guard their own morsels. It did take me a while to be trusted, but in the end I was allowed loose on the entrails and received nothing but help and generosity.

I will be eternally grateful to the late and wonderful Dr Robert Woof, director and creator of the modern Wordsworth Trust, who died in 2005. When I'd finished my manuscript, I sent it to Robert for his comments. He took weeks to reply, as he was ever on the move, and I began to think he'd never get round to it. Then one night he turned up at our London home clutching my precious pages in a plastic carrier bag. After four hours of what turned out to be an intense tutorial, going through it line by line, he realised he'd missed his train back to Newcastle. 'Not to worry,' he said, curling up on the sofa, where he slept the night. The next day, at dawn, we carried on, till he'd finally given me his considered judgment on every page.

I remember him disliking my use of the word 'hippy' to describe Wordsworth in his post-student years, but I argued it was a phrase present-day readers would understand. He also got upset when I referred to the 'Wordsworth industry'. It just wasn't true, he said, and gave the wrong impression. I was partly doing it to tease. I knew, back in 1980, just how hard he was working to raise money, acquire treasures, expand the work and scope of the Wordsworth Trust.

While working on the book, I did have one bit of luck. A collection of letters between Wordsworth and his wife turned up which revealed a degree of passion and intimacy between them which had not been evident before (see Chapter 16). No one knew where the letters had come from, or how, or to whom they had originally belonged. They were the 'property of a gentleman', according to Sotherby's catalogue. Cornell University bid £38,500 and they were therefore destined to leave the country.

By a sequence of events, I managed to find out who was selling them. It was a man from Carlisle, my home town, a stamp dealer from whom I had bought stamps, as I was at one time a keen collector. He'd acquired a large bundle of old letters and was going through them for their stamp content, looking for Penny Blacks, burning anything which looked boring, when he noticed the name Wordsworth and the address Rydal Mount. He'd heard of Dove Cottage, but not Rydal Mount, and so he sent a colleague to Tullie House, where Carlisle's Reference Library used to be. He discovered that Rydal Mount had indeed once been a William Wordsworth home. He stopped burning, realising he might have stumbled on some valuable literary letters.

Dove Cottage, when I told them all this, quickly started their own investigation into the history of the letters. As a result, they managed to delay their export. They amassed enough funds and were able to pay Cornell and thus keep the letters in Britain, where they are to this day, safe at Dove Cottage.

There hasn't been a similarly exciting find in the subsequent years, though a great many interesting and valuable letters, manuscripts, books, paintings and prints have been acquired. More research is being done all the time, more study undertaken, and every year, about ten new books and studies are published. The Wordsworth industry – sorry, the fascination with Wordsworth – shows no sign of contracting.

In 1998 there appeared a new biography of him called *The Hidden Wordsworth: Poet, Lover, Rebel, Spy*. You have to admit it's a great title, hinting of John le Carré, perhaps a touch of James Bond. Wish I'd thought of something like that instead of the obvious, flat, boring, unadorned title I'd used. It was written by Kenneth Johnston, a distinguished professor of English at Indiana University, an acknowledged expert on Wordsworth and the Romantics. His title might have appeared a bit of a come-hither, but the book was clearly an academic work and ran to 965 pages, including 71 pages of notes.

In it, he spent a lot of time proving, or at least heavily suggesting, that Wordsworth was a lot more sexually experienced than anyone had realised, consorting with prostitutes in Cambridge and dancing girls in Europe. But perhaps his most astonishing claim was that while in Germany, Wordsworth was a paid spy, working for Britain's newly formed Secret Service. Hence the snazzy title. Professor Johnston had studied a hitherto unknown Foreign Office document from 1799 which recorded that Mr Wordsworth had been paid £19-12 for espionage duties. Wow. What a discovery.

However, scholars being as they are – i.e. a mass of sceptics, mockers, know-alls, rivals, just like most professions – it was quickly pointed out that Professor Johnston had got the wrong Wordsworth. It was Robinson Wordsworth, one of his cousins, who'd received the espionage payment.

Two years later, in 2000, the paperback version of his book was published. It was now slightly shorter, cut down to a more manageable 690 pages, and the mistaken identity had been corrected. The original title had also been truncated. Now it was simply *The Hidden Wordsworth*, with the exciting strapline discarded. It can be a rough world out there in academia.

As for Wordsworth's sex life, in later life there was the impression that he was above such things, preferring porridge and cold water, but we all now know about one sexual affair, kept secret in his lifetime, which you will come to in the process of reading this book. Were there others we still don't know about? Possibly. But not even a general biographer should dare suggest it, without at least some fairly solid supporting evidence.

Of all the new biographical studies that have appeared since 1980 there are two which can be heartily recommended, even though they are of an academic nature. Stephen Gill's *William Wordsworth: A Life* came out in 1989 and is still looked upon as probably today's standard biography of Wordsworth, the poet. It is heavily lit crit, as befits an Oxford don, but not too long, just 525 pages. The other, which has exactly the same title, is by Juliet Barker and first appeared in 2000. It's much bigger, with 971 pages, including 120 pages of footnotes, and is very detailed. While Gill's strength is on the poetry, Juliet Barker is particularly good on the historical, social and family background. She also spends as much time and space on the latter half of Wordsworth's life as on the first, which not many biographers do, preferring to concentrate on the dramatic events and wonderful poetry of his first half. So if you have both books, you should find all you might possibly need to know, and more, until the next wave.

I hope many readers will go on to at least one of them, having read my humbler offering, but of course every reader, and every human come to that, should make their own pilgrimage to the Lake District and visit the homes associated with Wordsworth's life – his birthplace in Cockermouth, Dove

Cottage in Grasmere and Rydal Mount, outside Ambleside, where he lived the latter part of his life. There have been huge changes and developments in two of them at least since this book first came out.

Wordsworth House in Main Street, Cockermouth, was reopened in 2004 after being closed for major alterations. It has always suffered slightly in the Wordsworth pecking order by being on the edge of the Lakes, away from the tourist honey traps, and also in not having many original objects or material owned by the Wordworth family. On its reopening, it emerged with some of the staff in period cosumes – working in the kitchen, cooking real food on a real fire. It did sound a bit naff, but they do carry it off well and it does help give the interior a real atmosphere. The house itself is of course a Georgian gem, still the finest in Cockermouth, and with a marvellous garden, beautifully cared for. It's not a place for academic research, and they don't pretend otherwise, but it provides an excellent introduction to Wordsworth's life by seeing where he was born and brought up, getting a feeling of the sort of family he came from. Children love it – especially the dressing-up box where they can put on period clothes and prance around the bedroom. Annual attendance is now 30,000, compared with 20,000 ten years earlier. So the changes worked.

Dove Cottage, by comparison, is All Souls, a place of learning and reverence, though they too have their fun parts and their interactive learning sides. The whole site has been enormously expanded since 1980, mainly thanks to the brilliant work of Robert Woof. Their museum, at the time I used to go there when first writing this book, was in a barn. Now they have two state-of-the-art, architect-designed, award-winning buildings – apart from Dove Cottage itself.

Firstly there's the Wordsworth Museum, which, like Dove Cottage, is open to the public on the same ticket. Then there's the Jerwood Centre, opened by Seamus Heaney in 2005, which is essentially the library, a place of study and research, containing books and original manuscripts. Altogether, the Wordsworth Trust now has 63,000 items related to Wordsworth and his times, ranging from manuscripts and books to paintings, prints and drawings. They have hugely expanded their horizons and now cover the whole Romantic movement, in art and literature, stretching from 1750–1850.

Millions of pounds have been raised to acquire and create all these treasures and most academic and literary folks now believe it is the world's best literary museum. There are always new, handsomely produced books appearing about their treasures and several hundred events are organised each year at Dove Cottage. There is an annual summer school which usually attracts at least fifty of the world's greatest literary scholars, from Japan to the USA.

Dove Cottage now has a permanent staff of over thirty, plus ten interns who come and work, study and live there for a year. Their annual turnover is £1.3 million and they own some twenty properties. Dove Cottage has in fact become a campus.

Academic interest in Wordsworth has never been so high and is still expanding, as can be seen in the quality of their events and the number of scholars arriving from universities around the world – and yet, for some reason, the actual number of visitors to Dove Cottage has recently gone down. It was 80,000 when this book first came out. Now it's 61,000.

It could be that in 1980, most ordinary Brits, and English speakers around the world, did know a little about Wordsworth. They had all learned 'Daffodils' at school, even if it was by rote, getting their knuckles slapped. Now that doesn't happen. Dove Cottage therefore has to work harder to get people in off the street, make them aware and interested in someone they have possibly never heard of.

'I would put it that today we are enjoying an opportunity to bring Wordsworth to people who haven't yet come across his work,' says Jeff Cowton, Curator of the Wordsworth Trust. 'Yes, we do have to work hard, but it is part of our mission as an educational charity to do that very thing.'

There's also the problem of competition for leisure time, people wanting to go abroad for their holidays, as opposed to the rainy old Lake District. Inside Lakeland, rival attractions have greatly increased, especially in the Beatrix Potter industry. (I'm standing by that description – you just have to look at all the BP souvenirs in all the shops, then imagine the factories belting them out.)

The BP tourist industry recently had a huge fillip with a major motion picture, *Miss Potter*, especially when it hit the Japanese market. All the BP sites in Lakeland reported attendances up 20 per cent.

This new edition of WW's biography, which of course will have readers stampeding for it in the nation's bookshops, will help alert the general public to the wonders of Wordsworth, but there is something else which would help even more.

As you read on, you'll soon discover such dramas, plus, deaths, childhood traumas, legal wrangles, visions, warring geniuses, magnificent poetry, awful rows, sex, possible incest, unrequited love, mysteries, spies – OK perhaps not spies. If any producers are interested, the film rights to this book are still available. *Wordsworth: The Movie*: that's clearly what's needed next.

Hunter Davies
Loweswater, 2009

PROLOGUE

WILLIAM WORDSWORTH fell in love with his childhood. He loved it at the time – well, almost all of it – but he loved it even more as he grew older. When he was twenty-eight, and sitting rather cold and homesick in a small town in Germany, he started to write a poem about his life. This vast autobiographical poem, which was later called *The Prelude*, is the account of a man and his mind growing up. It is mainly about his schooldays and early manhood, and in it he recalls in great detail and with great emotion his early experiences and impressions. It is often philosophical, as he tries to interpret and analyse some very strange, almost mystical experiences.

Many of us have had strange experiences as children, strange in the sense that, for no apparent reason, they stick in our minds long after they have happened, long after they have ceased to make any real sense to us. Most of them don't bear repeating. They only have any meaning for ourselves. As we get older, we find it hard to believe that they ever happened, and wonder if perhaps we shaped them to suit ourselves because we were told they happened to us. As we age, they all fade.

Two things distinguish Wordsworth in his obsession with childhood. Firstly, his visions, his moments of mysticism, were unusually deep and clear. He felt not just a communion with nature and the world of the Spirits, but that he was a part of them, beyond normal life, and that he had left his human frame. He often had to touch himself afterwards, or feel a solid wall, to reassure himself that he was back in the real world. These visions were so strong that he could remember them vividly ever afterwards, recall them in tranquillity, re-create at will his original childhood sensations. Secondly, his visions were not restricted to his childhood. These spots of time, as he called them, continued to recur, or so he thought, well into adulthood. They were a mark of his poetic inspiration, and when they started to go, so some would say, his muse began to fade.

Wordsworth knew that his childhood, and his childhood visions, were important to him, which was why he wanted to capture and define them in *The Prelude*. But *The Prelude* is more than simply a list of his mystical experiences. Few poets have ever been so practical, so sane, so healthy, so down-to-earth. In *The Prelude*, he also describes all his everyday, common-or-garden, school and growing-up experiences, the sort we can all identify with, the facts of the matter, such as he remembered them.

Without *The Prelude*, we would know very little about the details of Wordsworth's early years. *The Prelude* is a basic source. It is all written from Wordsworth's point of view, which is to be expected. No-one else was bothering to make notes on an unknown young man growing up in a remote area of the north of England, so we have to rely on it. The mass of letters and diaries and memories, so dense that they can overwhelm an unsuspecting biographer, do not appear till much later. It means, therefore, that the facts of Wordsworth's early life can be simply stated. . . .

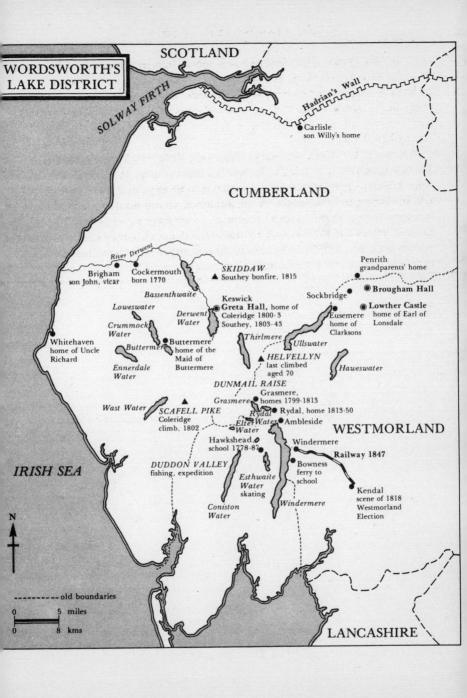

WORDSWORTH'S LAKE DISTRICT

SCOTLAND

SOLWAY FIRTH

Hadrian's Wall

Carlisle
son Willy's home

CUMBERLAND

River Derwent

Brigham
son John, vicar

Cockermouth
born 1770

SKIDDAW
▲ Southey bonfire, 1815

Penrith
grandparents' home

Bassenthwaite

Loweswater

Keswick
Greta Hall, home of
Coleridge 1800-3
Southey, 1803-43

Sockbridge

◉ **Brougham Hall**

*Derwent
Water*

◉ **Lowther Castle**
home of Earl of
Lonsdale

*Crummock
Water*

Eusemere
home of
Clarksons

Whitehaven
home of Uncle
Richard

●**Buttermere**
home of the
Maid of
Buttermere

Buttermere

Thirlmere

Ullswater

▲ *HELVELLYN*
last climbed
aged 70

Haweswater

*Ennerdale
Water*

DUNMAIL RAISE

Grasmere,
homes 1799-1813

Wast Water

▲ *SCAFELL PIKE*
Coleridge
climb, 1802

Grasmere

Rydal
Elter
Water

Rydal, home 1819-50
● Ambleside

WESTMORLAND

Hawkshead
school 1778-87

Windermere

IRISH SEA

DUDDON VALLEY
fishing, expedition

Railway 1847

*Esthwaite
Water*
skating

Bowness
ferry to
school

Kendal
scene of 1818
Westmorland
Election

*Coniston
Water*

Windermere

N

----- old boundaries

0   5 miles

0   8 kms

LANCASHIRE

1

Cockermouth and Penrith
1770-1779

WILLIAM WORDSWORTH was born in Cockermouth in Cumberland on 7 April 1770. It is true, as he subsequently said, that he was 'much favour'd in his birthplace'. Both in the physical setting and in the fortunes of his family at that time, his birth and his begetting were very solid, very professional, very middle-class. It could be argued that in some respects it was more than favoured. For a brief time, before certain unfavourable things occurred, it was rather privileged.

The house, for a start, is still to this day the handsomest house in Cockermouth. It stands in the main street, with seventeen windows at the front, and was built in 1745 by a Sheriff of Cumberland. In those days Cockermouth had only one street and Wordsworth's house was on the northern, the better favoured side, with its rear terrace backing on to the banks of the River Derwent. The opposite side backed on to common lands, lands fast being taken over and gobbled up by the local lordly family.

Cockermouth, then as now, was a clean, cheerful, watery little market town. The name comes from the River Cocker, which flows into the River Derwent not far from Wordsworth's house, though you don't come across the Cocker in many literary remembrances. It's not exactly a poetic name, though the river itself is beautiful enough and arrives at Cockermouth from the Vale of Lorton, flowing up from the heart of the Lakes through Crummock and Buttermere. Wordsworth as a boy played on its banks just as much as he played by the Derwent, but he gives the Cocker only one mention in *The Prelude*, and even then he calls it 'Coker's stream'. The Derwent, on the other hand, he calls the 'fairest of all rivers', and it looms large in all Lakeland literary legends.

Strictly speaking, Cockermouth isn't in the Lake District. It's to the north-west of Lakeland proper, in the coastal plain, more connected in landscape and feeling to the Solway, to Carlisle and the Border country. You can certainly see the heights of Lakeland, to the south and to the east, and Wordsworth was fond of remembering his early views of Skiddaw, but you need to have good eyes and know where to direct them. Today, the Lakeland National Park boundary line takes what looks like a spiteful loop as it approaches Cockermouth, rejecting it, placing it firmly, as it always has been, outside the Lakes.

Wordsworth's father was called John; he was living in Cockermouth at the time of William's birth because his business was directed mainly to the west coast of Cumberland. All his five children were born in Cockermouth, starting with Richard, the eldest, in 1768. William was next, two years later; then came Dorothy, the only girl, in 1771. There was John in 1772 and finally Christopher in 1774. It was a neatly spaced family, with the girl in the middle, though five children in six years would be considered rather impetuous today. There were no still-births, as far as we know, nor any childhood deaths, both of which were unfortunately more than common back in the 1770s.

John Wordsworth was an attorney at law and was employed as an agent for Sir James Lowther. He hadn't been living long in Cockermouth, moving there just a year or so before his marriage in 1766, four years before William's birth, from Penrith on the other side of Cumberland. He was twenty-five when he married and his wife Ann had just turned eighteen. He had been picked out as a bright young man by Sir James Lowther, given a very important job and the equally important-looking house to live in, while still a relatively inexperienced lawyer – in fact, it looks as though he got the job just before he finally qualified. He was helped by the fact that his father, Richard, had also been employed as agent for Sir James Lowther. It always helps, in being spotted early, to have family connections.

Richard Wordsworth (William's grandfather) had been Receiver-General of Cumberland and Clerk of the Peace. During 1745, when Bonny Prince Charlie's men had marched through Penrith, Richard had fled into the hills with the county's money, leaving his wife to guard the family house at Sockbridge, three miles from Penrith. Over the years, he had built up an estate and some property, mainly thanks to his work and his associations with the Lowther family; but he'd done it on his own, from all accounts. He had originally come over the border from Yorkshire, the son of a squire who had invested unwisely in coalmines. In the Wordsworth family, there was a tradition that they'd originated from Wadsworth ('the Woollen Cloth Town') near Halifax.

The important job which John Wordsworth, William's father, was given was to look after the Lowther interests in west Cumberland, particularly his political interests. This was the day of the rotten boroughs, when a local lord could control a parliamentary constituency, putting in his own MP and directing those few freeholders who had the vote. Franchise went with property and it was Sir James's habit to send his representatives round buying up houses and land when he decided to move into a new area, which was how he came to own the Wordsworth house in Cockermouth. At one time, Sir James controlled nine parliamentary seats, a large number even by rotten borough standards. The Younger Pitt first entered Parliament as a Member for Appleby, one of the seats in the Lowther gift. Sir James married a daughter of Lord Bute, who became Prime Minister in 1763, and he was a stout Tory, making sure all his political power and influence were directed to the Tory cause, but he himself was an idiosyncratic Tory, highly independent, going his own way if he thought that would be better for the Lowthers.

The Lowthers have been at Lowther, a village south of Penrith, for almost a thousand years, and the family are still the biggest private landowners in the whole of the Lake District. They dominated life in Cumberland and Westmorland in the eighteenth and nineteenth centuries, running the twin counties like a feudal estate. They certainly dominated Wordsworth's life, for better and for worse. They first became enormously wealthy in the early eighteenth century, when Sir James, and his father Sir John, almost single-handedly brought the Industrial Revolution to the north-west of England, introducing it to west Cumberland decades before it reached Lancashire. They used their landed wealth to move into mines, iron ore and shipping, building up the little inlet of Whitehaven, which had consisted of only three houses in 1680, into a boom town of twelve thousand people when Wordsworth first visited it as a little boy some hundred years later. They created Whitehaven in style, being masters of all they surveyed, bringing in an architect to design the town from scratch, making it one of the earliest examples of town-planning in the world, hiring the best engineers and using the newest developments of the day, such as steam power to pump water out of the coal-mines and developing natural gas.

It is astonishing to realize that Whitehaven in 1780 was, after London, the most important port in the country – far ahead of Liverpool, Bristol, Glasgow or Newcastle. Its wealth came from the coal trade to Ireland, the tobacco trade with Virginia and the slave trade with Africa. It's a rather humbler town today, a left-over town in many ways, though newer industries are now beginning to thrive. Some elegant streets remain and there are Tangier House and Tangier Street in the middle of the town, reminders of the earlier, exotic days.

John Wordsworth rode up and down the coast attending to his master's business – he didn't have a coach, as the roads were so bad, though he did have a liveried servant. One of his positions, which the Lowthers put in his way, was being Coroner of Millom, at the southern tip of the Cumberland peninsula. It was a tough, rather thankless job, exacting the last penny and the last bit of influence on behalf of the Lowther family, though there was some fun at election time. John Wordsworth had to make sure that Lowther voters were well entertained with drinks and hospitality, giving them little gifts and inducements, just in case they forgot where their loyalties lay. On the whole, though, this didn't make him popular. The Lowthers were feared, not loved, for their success: 'provincial monarchs of unmeasured lands', they were called. They were certainly not known for their generous spirits. Sir James Lowther, who was created Earl of Lonsdale in 1784, was mean and grasping. Even today, he is referred to in the family as 'Wicked Jimmy'. But he did at least give John Wordsworth and his young family a rent-free house and there were certain stipends and some status which came with the jobs which he put in Wordsworth's way, such as being Coroner. John Wordsworth, luckily, had some money and property of his own, such as the Sockbridge estate, which he'd inherited from his father.

Not much is known about the personality of John Wordsworth. He was continually away from home and it was said in the family that he had no real friends, but this might have been the fault of the Lowther connection, not of his own character. However, he was an educated and liberal man, knowledgeable about books and poetry, and it was he who first gave William an interest in literature, introducing him to *Don Quixote*, *Gulliver's Travels* and *The Arabian Nights*, teaching him to learn by heart large portions of Shakespeare, Milton and Spenser.

Ann Wordsworth, William's mother, was born Ann Cookson, the daughter of William Cookson, a linen draper in Penrith. On the surface, these origins are definitely 'trade', and professional people, such as lawyers, usually consider themselves a cut above shopkeepers; but the Cooksons were an established Penrith family, albeit petit bourgeois, and owned property and land in and around Penrith. Ann's father had done particularly well for himself by marrying into the county set, the Crackenthorpes of Newbiggen Hall. It looks as if the Crackenthorpes weren't all that excited by their daughter marrying a draper, and his profession wasn't given when they compiled their family tree, but the marriage gave William Cookson some extra social standing and he brought up his own family with definite pretensions, even if they all did live above the shop. Their eldest son Christopher eventually changed his name to Crackenthorpe in order to inherit the Crackenthorpe estates and went to live in Newbiggen Hall; the next son went on to become a Canon of Windsor; and their daughter Ann did well, of course, as John Wordsworth was obviously such a bright young lawyer from a good family with good connections.

Young William, then, and his three brothers and one sister, had some well-off grandparents and some rising and well-connected uncles, not to mention those powerful Lowthers in the background, as they all played happily in that big house in Cockermouth.

One of William's earliest memories was of going to visit an uncle, Richard Wordsworth, Controller of Customs at Whitehaven, with his little sister Dorothy. 'My sister, when she first heard the voice of the sea, and beheld the scene before her, burst into tears.... This fact was often mentioned among us as indicating the sensibility for which she was so remarkable.'

Dorothy was apparently extremely sensitive from an early age, and when William went tearing wildly after butterflies, trying to catch them,

Dorothy was the one who feared for them, lest rough young William should brush the dust from their wings. They roamed the river banks together, with William bathing naked in the nearby mill race from the age of five (so he said), running abroad in wantonness, sporting like a naked savage (so he said). For a conventional, middle-class family of the times, which employed a nurse to look after the children and at least one maidservant, William was allowed a remarkable amount of freedom. From all accounts, he *demanded* a great amount of freedom. Compared with his elder brother Richard, who was solid and conventional, or John, who was very quiet, or Christopher, who was clever but conservative, William was definitely the wild one.

In the early childhood sections of *The Prelude* there are as many references to the beauties of nature, such as the rivers and the mountains, as to times of uproar and tumult. Those periods of silent contemplation were often followed by spells of what sounds like violent tempers and tantrums. It seemed his mother could hardly control him, perhaps with a father so often away, and the family often wondered how she had given birth to such a difficult child. Their Penrith relations, on both sides, told her from the earliest days that they considered William more than a handful. She was a soft and gentle woman, who helped to stir William's more sensitive side, and he was grateful for her good influence over him, whereas his father is scarcely ever mentioned. She worried most about him, of all her five children, and feared for his journey through life, with such a violent and moody personality. She predicted, so William later recalled, that he was destined to be remarkable 'either for good or for evil'.

William went to school in Cockermouth, to the local grammar school, which was then run by the Rev. Joseph Gillbanks, who was also vicar of the parish. He didn't learn much there, and it's not known exactly how many years he attended school in Cockermouth (he was definitely there in 1776, when he was six, as his father's accounts, which have survived, show). The school had a poor reputation; the headmaster had been married four times, which deeply upset the nonconformist element in the town, and was eventually forced to retire.

One of William's contemporaries at Cockermouth was Fletcher Christian, later famous – or infamous – for his part in the mutiny on the *Bounty*. The Christians were a well-known local family, family friends of the Wordsworths, with good connections and with several members who went on to become eminent lawyers. There was a third young man growing up at the same time in the Cockermouth area who went on to achieve national fame – John Dalton, father of the atomic theory – but his path and William's never crossed. It is intriguing, nonetheless, to realize that one small, out-of-the-way town should have three celebrated sons, all growing up in the 1770s.

There was also one contemporary local event which stirred the outside world. It occurred in 1778, during the American War of Independence, when William was eight. This was the raid by John Paul Jones, the Scottish-born American naval hero, on Whitehaven harbour. It is nowhere mentioned in Wordsworth's poems – and he used many local events – which is surprising as he had Whitehaven relations, knew the harbour, was interested in the sea and had relatives who were sailors. One can only assume that he was over on the other side of Cumberland, with his grandparents in Penrith, at the time of the raid, and somehow missed the news.

Throughout these early years, William and his sister and brothers were continually being moved back and forth, between Cockermouth and Penrith. It is not clear why, at least in the very early days, this should have been so. Possibly his mother wanted a stricter upbringing for William, hoping a spell with his grandparents would knock him into shape. Perhaps it was thought that a school in Penrith might do more for him than Mr Gillbanks had done. Perhaps in a bigger town he would have less freedom to roam the countryside and get into mischief. For various reasons, then, Penrith began to play a bigger part in his life than Cockermouth.

Penrith, the home town of each of Wordsworth's parents, was in the late eighteenth century quite a cosmopolitan little town, at least by Cumbrian standards – which, by London standards, would not be saying very much. Unlike Cockermouth, stuck out on a limb in the plain, neither Lakeland nor coastal, Penrith always had a definite identity and a definite character. It is on the main north–south route between England and Scotland, one of the arteries of England, and many invaders have left their mark on Penrith, from Romans, Angles, Saxons and Danes, to marauding Scots, though it was the original Britons who gave Penrith its name: the prefix *Pen*, as in so many Welsh names, is Celtic.

Penrith's little industries and activities, as befits a town used by travellers, were dominated by brewing and by traders of all sorts, cattle-dealers and shopkeepers. Bull-baiting still flourished in the town until about 1790, defended by the burghers as being a good advertisement for the new lot of meat that would soon be on sale, softened up by all the baiting.

The Cooksons' draper's shop was in the market square: a red sandstone building, like almost every house and shop in Penrith. Dorothy used to help out occasionally in the shop and the grandmother did her bit, though there was an ample staff. Dorothy and her brother William (their Cookson grandparents were also called Dorothy and William) were sent to a local dame school run by Ann Birkett, which considered it catered for the quality of Penrith. William even boasted in later years that it taught the 'upper classes' of the town. It didn't in effect teach William much more than the Cockermouth school, but it appears to have been stricter and more old-fashioned.

William first attended this dame school when he was three, so he later asserted, for he maintained that this was when he first played with the Hutchinson girls, the daughters of another local shopkeeping family in Penrith, very close friends and playmates of both Dorothy and William from their earliest Penrith days. Penrith, however, takes up almost no space at all in *The Prelude*, apart from a rather strange incident which happened on the Beacon, the local landmark which towers over the town.

When he was not quite six, he went riding on the hill with an old family servant called James. They became separated and William found himself on the spot where a gruesome murder had been committed some ten years previously – a spot marked with the victim's initials – and where the murderer had been eventually gibbeted, as was the custom of the times. It was a murder well known to everyone in the area and William, being very young, was suitably terrified. Rushing off in a panic, he came across a mysterious young girl, battling up the hill with a pitcher on her head. He admits it was 'an ordinary sight', to see such a girl carrying water, but the little incident had a great mystical and visionary effect on him, which he remembered years and years later. Wordsworth scholars have made much of the incident, searching for hidden psychological insights, analysing every word, dissecting every feeling, researching the details of the murder, but it would seem, to use his own words, an ordinary little incident, of the sort many people would come up with, if asked to search back in their memories for the first occasion on which they were frightened. Its claim to interest, in any study of Wordsworth, is that it is the first recorded event in his life during which he remembered having a visionary 'spot of time'.

William's mother Ann became ill in early 1778 and was confined to bed for about two months, judging by some rather hefty medical bills. The family belief was that she'd caught a cold while sleeping in a damp bed on a visit to London to see a friend. For a shopkeeper's daughter from Penrith, going to London, with or without her lawyer husband, would have been quite an adventure; but nothing else is known of the circumstances. William, in *The Prelude*, hints that someone else was to blame (perhaps whoever lent her the damp bed). She died on 8 March 1778 in her parents' house in Penrith, from what appears to have been pneumonia, and was buried in the parish churchyard, though there is no sign of the grave today. She was only thirty years old. William was aged eight.

I remember my mother only in some few situations [William later recalled], one of which was her pinning a nosegay to my breast when I was going to say the catechism in the church as was customary before Easter. I remember also telling her on one week day that I had been at church, for our school stood in the churchyard, and we had frequent opportunities of seeing what was going on there. The occasion was a woman doing penance in the church in a white sheet. My mother commended my having been present, expressing a hope that I should remember the circumstance for the rest of my life. 'But,' said I, 'Mama, they did not give me a penny, as I had been told they would.' 'Oh,' said she, recanting her praises, 'if that was your motive, you were properly disappointed.'

William's last sight of her was when passing the door of her room as she lay on her death-bed. Her death robbed him of 'the props of his affections' and he was now alone, to be sustained by his own spirit. The five young children felt destitute, left, from then on, to 'troop together'.

The Cookson grandparents had had their daughter's children for months on end, over the previous few years, so they were used to looking after them, but they didn't welcome the idea of having even more to do with William. There were constant clashes between them, and between William and his Uncle Kit, the one who later took over the Crackenthorpe estates and moved to the big house. William appears to have been proud of his defiance and his rebelliousness, and to have been unabashed by any punishments, though on one occasion, after some row, he retired to an attic room where he contemplated suicide, taking hold of a foil as if to end it all.

Upon another occasion [William recalled], along with my eldest brother Richard, we were whipping tops together in the large drawing room, on which the carpet was only laid down upon particular occasions. The walls were hung round with family pictures and I said to my brother, 'Dare you strike your whip through that lady's petticoat?' He replied, 'No, I won't.' 'Then,' said I, 'here goes.' And I struck my lash through her hooped petticoat, for which no doubt, though I have forgotten it, I was properly punished. But possibly from some want of judgement in punishments inflicted, I had become perverse and obstinate in denying chastisement and rather proud of it than otherwise.

Wordsworth, on the whole, glorified all his childhood, and most of his memories are totally happy. He tended in his poems and later recollections to minimize those unhappy early times at Penrith with his grandparents. At the time he probably couldn't grasp why they disliked him so much, or why they made so little effort to understand him. His beloved sister Dorothy, who was always very upset by William being picked upon, was his only real comfort in these early Penrith days, but in June 1778, a few months after the death of their mother, Dorothy was sent away to live in Halifax, Yorkshire, with relations. She didn't see William again for nine years. William didn't find it as easy to troop together with his brothers, though all the boys usually spent Christmas together with their father in his Cockermouth house. Dorothy had been the only one completely in tune with his moods and personality.

Not long afterwards, in 1779, when he was nine years old, it was decided that William in turn should be sent away, not to a relation as with Dorothy, but to a school on the other side of the Lake District. It was yet another change. The cultural, rather liberal base of his father's big house had been replaced early in his life by the more stifling, bourgeois, shopkeeping mentality of the Penrith family home. The change had not helped his naturally rebellious, wilful nature. As for the death of his mother, who knows what scars that created. But, perhaps surprisingly, the next nine years turned out to be the years of his genuinely happy childhood.

To a Butterfly*

Composed 14 March 1802, it deals with one of Wordsworth's earliest memories of his Cockermouth childhood. Emmeline stands for Dorothy, his sister.

STAY near me – do not take thy flight!
A little longer stay in sight!
Much converse do I find in thee,
Historian of my infancy!
Float near me; do not yet depart!
Dead times revive in thee:
Thou bring'st, gay creature as thou art!
A solemn image to my heart,
My father's family!

Oh! pleasant, pleasant were the days,
The time, when in our childish plays,
My sister Emmeline and I
Together chased the butterfly!
A very hunter did I rush
Upon the prey; – with leaps and springs
I followed on from brake to bush;
But she, God love her! feared to brush
The dust from off its wings.

---

* The poetry which comes at the end of each chapter is not necessarily meant to be an example of Wordsworth's finest work but more of biographical interest, either being written during the period dealt with in the preceding chapter or somehow related to the mood or content of that particular chapter.

2

Hawkshead
1779-1787

HAWKSHEAD is a little town in south Lakeland, between the lakes of Windermere and Coniston. It was the home town of Ann Tyson, a lady not known today to the world at large but still remembered in Hawkshead for her connection with young William Wordsworth. She was married in 1749, aged thirty-six, to a local carpenter called Hugh Tyson. They had no children and, when his business declined, she opened a little shop which sold foodstuffs and clothing materials. They did a good line in luxury goods, such as tea at up to eight shillings a pound, though the most popular brand was something called Bohea, a dark tea which sold at 4s 4d a pound. Tea and coffee were relatively new in England at the time, but very popular with those who could afford them. Those who couldn't drank ale. Mrs Tyson also sold sugar, brown or white, and a crystallized sugar which she referred to as Candy, which was popular with local schoolboys. This is mentioned in her accounts in 1762, seven years before the first known example of the word 'candy' appeared in print, according to the *Shorter Oxford Dictionary*.

The good townspeople of Hawkshead could certainly afford their little luxuries. It was a thriving town, back in the eighteenth century, a centre for the woollen trade, an ancient activity in southern Lakeland which had gone on for centuries and had been famous in Shakespeare's day. (He refers in *Henry IV* to a well known cloth called Kendal green.) There were no roads as we know them in the area, not till towards the end of the century, and no carriages until 1792, but the rough tracks were alive with pack-horses, carrying on their backs the raw wool, the finished materials, or the products of other local industries, such as charcoal-burning. The charcoal was used for iron-ore smelting in little bloomeries which dotted the surrounding forest areas, right down to the Furness coast. Pedlars, very often Scotsmen, moved from town to town, hawking their wares. Sad soldiers, also often Scotsmen, trudged along the pack routes, limping with their wounds, back to their homeland. England was at war almost ceaselessly for about forty years, starting in the 1770s, with America struggling for its independence, and continuing with the long war with France which followed the Revolution.

By 1779, the Tysons, now well into their sixties, had given up the shop and had decided instead to take in boarders, boy pupils from the local grammar school. Amongst their first batch were two young Cockermouth boys, Richard and William Wordsworth.

Mrs William Cookson from Penrith, the boys' grandmother, paid the Tysons ten guineas for their board and lodgings for the half year, plus 10s 6d extra for Ann Tyson to do their washing. It is not known who rode down with them from Penrith to settle them in. Perhaps the family groom, James, brought them. Their father, John Wordsworth, was apparently too busy with his Lowther affairs to take them down personally, though he did pay their grandmother for having settled their bills.

William was nine and Richard eleven. They spent their entire Hawkshead schooldays with Dame Tyson, as did the two younger Wordsworth boys, who soon followed. She became a mother figure to them, a substitute parent for four displaced boys, the most constant adult figure in Wordsworth's growing-up years, a loved figure whom he always cherished. She hadn't been educated, nor had she read any books, though her ledgers show that she was at least literate. She had once worked in Scotland as a servant and was full of her experiences. Some people thought she tended to go on somewhat, when she started on her old tales, but William loved to hear them. The most surprising thing about her was the enormous freedom she allowed William. Even at the age of nine, when he had just arrived to lodge with her, he was out roaming the fields and the fells almost half the night. It was in general a very good school, which was no doubt why John Wordsworth had chosen it for his sons. Mrs Tyson, an old lady unused to children, was informal and permissive. She was a church-goer, but she didn't try to indoctrinate young William. She allowed him to be himself.

If you stand in the middle of Hawkshead today, carefully avoiding the hordes of tourists, it is easy to see what a prosperous business town it once was. The wool merchants have gone, but their houses remain, handsome buildings, grouped in small squares, or overhanging little cobbled lanes. Hawkshead is the prettiest town in the whole of the Lake District today, and by far the best preserved.

But it is hard to imagine the former prosperity of the modest little building which was Hawkshead Grammar School. The town's ancient school building is still there, neatly painted and preserved, with the original desks still in rows, the books on the shelves, but, alas, the pupils all gone. It is such a little building, yet it held a hundred boys when Wordsworth attended it, which is difficult to believe. Even more surprising, Hawkshead Grammar School was one of the north of England's most successful and distinguished schools, sending several boys to Cambridge every year, many of whom went on to become prize-winning Fellows. It had been founded in 1585 by Edwin Sandys, Archbishop of York, who'd been born locally. All lessons were free, although boys who came from outside the immediate neighbourhood (including the Wordsworth boys) had to pay cockpennies, an entrance fee of about a guinea a year. (It was called cockpenny because originally the headmaster collected the pennies and awarded a prize for the boy with the best fighting cock. Cock-fighting, which was particularly strong in Cumberland, Westmorland and north Lancashire, was not made illegal until 1849.) The school allowed up to twelve charity boys to get their lodgings free, as well as their education. It was in many ways typical of English grammar schools of the day. Even at the great public schools, boys lodged with dames. Boarding houses, run by masters, didn't take over until the nineteenth century, which was when public schools generally became the way they are today.

In the eighteenth century, the poor boys at Hawkshead, as at most schools, sat side by side on the crowded benches with the sons of the local gentry and professional people. The real nobs, of course, usually had their children educated at home by tutors. The successful, popular schools – and a school could lose its pupils and masters in just a decade, if it fell out of favour – were enormously crowded. There was only one large classroom at Hawkshead, plus two smaller ones above, and so the classes must have been large. (The big popular southern schools of the day, such as Sherborne and Shrewsbury, had at times seventy-five in a class and Eton once had two hundred in a class.)

The basis of the education was Latin – hence the name grammar school. It was the world of Rome and grammar of Latin which had been the sign of the educated man and the entrance to all professions since medieval days. Most of all, Latin got you into the Church. Schoolmasters were clerics and a common route to becoming a bishop was to be a headmaster first.

Hawkshead drew boys from all over the Lakeland area, from Carlisle, which had its own perfectly good grammar school, even more ancient than Hawkshead's, down to Furness and north Lancashire. During Wordsworth's days, judging by a list of names of those who donated library books before going up to university, the range was even wider, with boys coming from Edinburgh, Sheffield, Liverpool and Manchester. The Edinburgh boys, two brothers, appear to have been the only sons of an aristocratic family (one of them later became ninth Earl of Stair). The ten or so charity boys were usually sons of local craftsmen (Mrs Tyson boasted that her husband Hugh had been a charity boy, though this is in doubt), but the majority had fathers who were clerics, lawyers or army officers, with the occasional woollen mill owner or even landscape painter.

School, it seems, started at six o'clock in the morning in the summer, and at seven in the winter, which meant that old Mrs Tyson had to get them up in summer time at about five fifteen for breakfast, which more often than not was porridge. Just after eleven, they broke for lunch, which was boiled mutton, if they were lucky; then back for afternoon school from one till five. William used to get up even earlier than he needed in order to walk round the shores of Esthwaite Water, Hawkshead's local lake, before school.

He'd been at the school only two weeks, so he recounts in *The Prelude*, when one evening, in the twilight, hardly able to see the shore in the gloom, he came across a pile of clothes, left by someone who had apparently gone bathing. Next day, in the light, he came back and watched some men in boats, with grappling irons and long poles, fish out a drowned body. A rather nasty experience for a young boy, but the fact that he was only nine, and being allowed out at all hours of night and day, is also significant.

It was what he loved, of course, wandering the countryside or taking part in all the rural activities. Hawkshead, unlike either Cockermouth or Penrith, is right in the heart of Lakeland, surrounded by fells and lakes. William skated every winter on Esthwaite Water, a shallow lake which freezes quickly, though in those days every winter seemed to be freezing. Today, our winters seem positively Mediterranean by comparison. Even Windermere, Lakeland's biggest lake, just four miles from Hawkshead, was often hard enough for skating. William joined in the hunt, and went searching for raven's eggs, all of which makes very lyrical reading in *The Prelude*, though the incentive was probably monetary gain as much as anything else. Rewards were given for killing vermin, such as foxes (which could net five shillings a time) or ravens, though well-brought-up grammar school boys were not supposed to do this, under school rules. William loved fishing, and there's a nice account of him persuading a fisherman to take him angling in the Duddon valley, which was a good ten miles away. They were away a whole day, crawling back late at night, with little William, exhausted, being given a piggy-back by the fisherman. The furthest he went, along with some schoolfellows, was down to Furness Abbey, some twenty miles away, but this time they hired horses. He also loved boating, racing his schoolfellows on Windermere or, on one occasion, stealing a boat on Ullswater for an evening row across the lake, till he came face to face with a huge, dark mountain, towering over him, and retreated, terrified, just as he had terrified himself imagining all sorts of horrors on Penrith Beacon.

For well over a century, scholars and interested amateurs have had great fun trying to identify the people, such as pedlars, fellow schoolboys or discharged soldiers, described by Wordsworth in *The Prelude*, and many of them have been traced – even ones whom the poet admitted later had been amalgamations of several characters.

William was very fond of sitting on the benches round the centre of Hawkshead, especially at the church, and of talking to the old men of the town, listening to their tales of the old days. Research has shown that a surprising number of old men lived in Hawkshead in those days. In 1785, for example, while Wordsworth was a schoolboy at the grammar school, nine of the twenty registered burials were of people aged from eighty to eighty-nine. In those days, of course, if you survived birth and early childhood – and in many towns up to half the new-born population died – then you had a good chance of living to a reasonable age.

The struggle to identify Wordsworth's cottage in Hawkshead, the one where he lived with old Mrs Tyson, has been one of the most popular searches for easily a hundred years. Tradition for a long time pointed to a little cottage right in the middle of the town, and it is named as Wordsworth's cottage on the local picture postcards. Ernest de Selincourt, the great pre-war Wordsworthian scholar, believed this was where William had lived with Mrs Tyson, but a discovery by Mrs Heelis, a local sheep farmer who lived nearby at Sawrey, showed that Ann Tyson had in fact lived at Colthouse, about half a mile away. Mrs Heelis found Mrs Tyson's old ledgers, now an invaluable source for all Wordsworth scholars, and traced her home to Colthouse. (Mrs Heelis is better known to the public as Beatrix Potter.) Mary Moorman, in the first volume of her classic study on Wordsworth, published in 1957, based on this discovery, and on clues in *The Prelude*, her belief that Wordsworth had spent *all* his school-days with Mrs Tyson in Colthouse. Today, a compromise appears to have been reached amongst the experts, though naturally new evidence, or new fashions, might change all this. It is now thought that Wordsworth lived with Mrs Tyson in the middle of Hawkshead for his first few years, but that he moved with her to Colthouse by 1784, when her husband died. So, both places are correct. The post-cards needn't be scrapped.

William's life with Mrs Tyson was fairly frugal. Though other boys who lodged with her occasionally had cakes or bottles of wine on their bill, William lived the simple life, most of it in 'pennyless poverty'. Candles and coals were extras which they could rarely afford, though he usually had a few shillings to spare for such luxuries at the beginning of each term on his return from the school holidays. The summer holidays were probably spent in Penrith, while Christmas was spent with his father in Cockermouth.

The Cockermouth connection ceased, and a more frugal life began, with the death of William's father in 1783. He had been about his Lowther business in the southern part of the Lakes, in the Millom area, where he was Coroner, when he lost his way in bad weather while riding home from Broughton-in-Furness to Cockermouth. He was forced to spend the night without shelter on the slopes of Cold Fell. He suffered a severe chill from which he never recovered. William said later that his father had never kept his usual cheerfulness of mind since the death of his wife. The official cause of death was given as dropsy.

William's father died on 30 December 1783, aged forty-two, during the boys' Christmas holidays. William remembered afterwards how he'd waited impatiently at Hawkshead for the ponies to arrive. Transport was always a source of trouble at Hawkshead, with everyone dependent on horses to take them home. This time, the horses sent by his father did not turn up, though William had been sitting on the road for a long time, moaning about their absence – only to arrive home and find his father mortally ill, much to his anguish and mortification.

John Wordsworth's death merited only one line of appreciation in the weekly *Cumberland Pacquet*: 'Jan 6, 1784. Last Tuesday, about half past 12 o'clock, Mr Wordsworth, Attorney, of Cockermouth, departed this life after a short confinement. He lived deservedly esteemed and died universally lamented.' Dorothy said later that it was 'mortifying to my Brothers and me to find that amongst all those who visited at my father's house he had not one real friend'.

Worst of all, he left no real money. His estate, in theory, was handsome enough, even though he died before his prime earning years: it totalled £10,485, an impressive amount for those days. But, on investigation, it turned out that almost all of it was made up of debts people owed him – chiefly his employer, Sir James Lowther. He did leave a bit of property, but the rents were exceedingly modest. His immediate effects and belongings were sold for £328 and the cash in hand proved to be £225. What was missing was the large sum of £4,625, owed by Lowther. It turned out that he had never been paid for his Lowther work, a mysterious state of affairs which has never been satisfactorily explained. There was virtually nothing to split between the five children, though the family began legal proceedings against the Earl of Lonsdale, as Sir James Lowther became later that year. This legal action, which proved very costly in itself, became a huge, dark cloud, a veritable albatross, which hung over the Wordsworth children from then on, blighting their lives in many ways.

They were now truly orphans, though they had felt as if they were ever since the death of their mother, with the added embarrassment of poverty and complete dependence on their relations for survival. The children found themselves under the guardianship of two uncles: Uncle Richard Wordsworth and, worse still, Uncle Kit, the Penrith uncle

William had never liked. They'd always looked upon William as a bit of a burden anyway, because of his personality. Now they would have to pay for his education too. Poor William. He and the two elder boys attended the funeral. Christopher, the youngest, was still at Penrith, being too young for Hawkshead Grammar School. Dorothy missed attending the funeral as well, being away in Yorkshire with relations.

She had felt hardest done by of all, being separated from her brothers, but was finding that her life with her Halifax relations wasn't as bad as she'd feared it would be. They were kind and considerate, unlike the Penrith relations, and she made many good local friends, though all the time she was wondering what was happening to her brothers. During her father's lifetime, they'd usually managed to be at home in Cockermouth for those Christmas holidays, but Dorothy never made it, which was very sad, especially as her birthday was on Christmas Day:

I can almost tell where every Birth day of my life was spent, from a very early time. The Day was always kept by my Brothers with rejoicing in my father's house but for six years, the interval between My Mother's death and his, I was never once at home, which I cannot think of without regret for many causes and particularly that I have been thereby put out of the way of many recollections in common with my Brothers of that period of life which, whatever it may be actually as it goes along, generally appears more delightful than any other when it is over. . . .

Back in Hawkshead, William was indeed having a delightful time and could forget the unpleasantness of the Penrith household. His night-and-day wanderings continued throughout his school-days, though he doesn't appear to have neglected his school work. He never won any prizes, but at this period of his life he was a keen reader, when he wasn't out roaming the lakes and fells. 'Had I been born in a class which would have deprived me of what is called a liberal education, it is not unlikely that, being strong in body, I should have taken to a way of life such as that in which my "Pedlar" passed the greater part of his days.'

He had quite an active social life as well, as he got into his late 'teens. He spent many a wet evening with the other boys in his lodgings, playing cards round the peat fire, and he became very fond of dancing. The school didn't arrange this, but a Mr Mingay had for a time a dancing academy in Hawkshead which all four Wordsworth boys attended. Mr Mingay, a gentleman of several talents, also taught fencing and

French. In *The Prelude* there are several references to late-night dances, parties with strawberries and cream and other jollifications. But were there any girls? William did go out walking during at least one school holiday in Penrith with Mary Hutchinson, one of the Hutchinson sisters who'd been at the Penrith dame school with him, but he doesn't appear to have had any lady friends in Hawkshead. The local county girls certainly looked to Hawkshead School to produce suitable beaux for their dances, but William seems not to have become attached to any girl in particular. The scholastic sleuths have been through every possible Hawkshead record over the last hundred years, but still no girls have yet been turned up.

William's first poetry was written in 1784, when he was aged fourteen, as a school exercise, on a subject beloved by schoolmasters to this day – what I did in my summer holidays. The lines don't survive, which is probably just as well, but some verses which he wrote the following year do survive; again, these were written as a school exercise to celebrate the school's bicentenary.

After that, William started to write verses on his own account. The first poetry which he composed spontaneously, he later recalled, was written after walking home late from a dance. Most of his visions, his dream-like trances, occurred on his walks, even on the half-mile or so walk from his lodgings in Colthouse to school, though he usually extended this to a five-mile walk by going round the lake. 'I was often unable,' he said years later, 'to think of external things as having external existence and I communed with all I saw as something not apart from but inherent in my own immaterial nature. Many times while going to school have I grasped at a wall or tree to recall myself from this abyss of idealism to the reality.'

The great reunion with Dorothy was due to take place in the summer holidays of 1787, after William had finished his final term at Hawkshead School. She'd recently been sent back to Penrith from Halifax, to live with her grandparents and help out in the shop. Dorothy wasn't at all pleased at this, as she'd enjoyed her years at Halifax, apart from the separation from her brothers, and had friends whom she was to keep all her life. It is lucky for us, however, that she did go back to Penrith, for, from now on, the best running commentary on the activities of William Wordsworth is the one supplied by Dorothy: an incessant letter-writer who, almost every day of her life, sent off two or three huge letters to her friends, keeping them in touch with what she was doing.

As the summer holidays approached, Dorothy was in a fearful state, waiting and longing to see her long-lost brothers; it would be her first meeting with them for nine years.

I was for a whole week kept in expectation of my brothers who staid at school all that time after the vacation begun owing to ill nature of my uncle (Kit) who would not send horses for them because when they wrote they did not happen to mention them, and only said when they should break up which was always before sufficient. This was the beginning of my mortifications for . . . indeed nobody but myself expressed one wish to see them. At last however they were sent for, but not till my Brother William had hired a horse for himself because he thought some one must be ill.

The brothers at last turned up and Dorothy had many happy hours together with them, especially with William. They read some newly published poems by Robert Burns, which had just come out in the Kilmarnock edition. A friend had recommended them to Dorothy, and William got the book for her from a local book club in Penrith.

A few weeks later, in a letter to a friend, Dorothy gave an interesting pen portrait of her four brothers and their characters. She was sixteen at the time.

They are just the boys I could wish them, they are so affectionate and so kind to me as makes me love them more every day. Wm and Christopher are very clever boys at least so they appear in the partial eyes of a Sister. No doubt I am partial and see virtues in them that by everybody else will pass unnoticed. John, who is to be the sailor, has a most excellent heart, he is not so bright as either Wm or Christopher but he has very good common sense and is very well calculated for the profession he has chosen. Richard, the oldest, I have seen, he is equally affectionate and good but he is far from being as clever as William, but I have no doubts of his succeeding in his businesses for he is very diligent and far from being dull. Many a time have Wlm, J, C and myself shed tears together, tears of the bitterest sorrow, we all of us, each day feel more sensibly the loss we sustained when we were deprived of our parents and each day we do receive fresh insults.

The insults were long and hurtful and Dorothy always felt mortified (one of her favourite words) by the servants, who obviously took the lead from the uncle and grandparents and continually abused them, especially about their poverty, pointing out that they were living on charity. They had been hoping that Lord Lonsdale would at least pay some of his debts on account, but they'd just learned that he refused to pay anything at all. Dorothy's letters are full of references to their troubles:

I daresay our fortunes have been weighed thousands of times at the tea table and I have no doubt but they always concluded their conversations with 'they have nothing to be proud of'....

We are found fault with every hour of the day both by the servants and my Grandfather and Grandmother, the former of whom never speaks to us but when he scolds which is not seldom. We have been told thousands of times that we are liars....

My Uncle Kit has taken a dislike to my Brother Wm and never takes any notice of any of us....

William, at the time, was apparently thinking of going into the law, like his father and grandfather before him, and as Richard was going to do. Dorothy, however, did have her little worries about him: 'He wishes very much to be a Lawyer if his health will permit, but he is troubled with violent head aches and a pain in his side, but I hope they will leave him in a little time.'

Dorothy was naturally very upset when they all left Penrith at the end of the summer holidays. 'I cannot paint to you my distress at their Departure. I can only tell you that for a few hours I was absolutely miserable, a thousand tormenting fears rushed upon me, the approaching Winter and the ill nature of my Grandfather and Uncle Christopher.'

In the autumn of 1787, William was due to take up residence at St John's College, Cambridge. He was a liberal and well-educated young man of the times, well ahead for his years in mathematics and Classics, a noisy, sociable fellow with his friends, but given to strange periods of introspection and silences. There is no doubt he had enormously enjoyed the freedom of his days at Hawkshead, a great relief from the constraints of Penrith. The strange visions, the sudden feelings of being at one with nature, could possibly have contained an element of escape, subjugating the deeper fears and insecurities caused by the deaths of his mother and father, the lack of love from his relations and his worries about the future. His guardians still found him moody and ill-tempered, hard to like, hard to control and with a definite streak of rebellion in him. They made it plain that they considered they were doing him a great favour by continuing to pay for his education. And they made it even plainer that he had better curb his wayward ways and work hard at Cambridge.

SKATING

These lines are taken from The Prelude, *begun early in 1799 and finished in 1805, and are about one of his greatest pleasures from his Hawkshead school days, a sport he continued throughout his life.*

> All shod with steel,
> We hiss'd along the polish'd ice, in games
> Confederate, imitative of the chace
> And woodland pleasures, the resounding horn,
> The Pack loud bellowing, and the hunted hare.
>
> Not seldom from the uproar I retired
> Into a silent bay, or sportively
> Glanced sideways, leaving the tumultuous throng,
> To cut across the image of a star
> That gleam'd upon the ice: and oftentimes
> When we had given our bodies to the wind,
> And all the shadowy banks, on either side,
> Came sweeping through the darkness, spinning still
> The rapid line of motion; then at once
> Have I, reclining back upon my heels,
> Stopp'd short, yet still the solitary Cliffs
> Wheeled by me, even as if the earth had roll'd
> With visible motion her diurnal round;
> Behind me did they stretch in solemn train
> Feebler and feebler, and I stood and watch'd
> Till all was tranquil as a dreamless sleep.

3

Cambridge
1787-1790

WORDSWORTH set off by coach for Cambridge in October 1787, accompanied by his uncle, the Rev. William Cookson, and his cousin, John Myers, who was also going up to St John's College. His Uncle William was his mother's younger brother, a young man of thirty-three who'd done very well for himself, considering he was a draper's son. He'd had a brilliant career at Cambridge, was now a Fellow of St John's and had for a time been a tutor to three of the royal children. He was obviously destined for a nice living somewhere, one of the plum country rectories which his college controlled, a step which would no doubt in the end lead to even higher things. He'd been in Penrith most of the summer holidays, which had been a welcome surprise for Dorothy and William. He'd taken a great interest in Dorothy, helping her to learn French and arithmetic, a pleasant change from shirt-mending and serving in the shop. He'd even been kind to William (unlike his elder brother, the horrid Uncle Kit) and was keen to help him at Cambridge and with his future career, outlining the various stages ahead for a bright but impecunious young gentleman like William. Do well at the books, my boy, get a good degree and then a fellowship. That will give you an income till you get ordained, and then you'll be secure for life. William at least must have considered this advice, during those long hours as the coach rolled south, for he very soon gave up all thoughts of a legal career.

William had with him in his trunk some new clothes, which Dorothy had made for him. Ann Tyson, before he had left her in Hawkshead, had also got a few things ready for him. She'd charged him 4s 1½d for velvet, which she'd had made into a jacket for him, and some silk at 4s 9d for a waistcoat and stock. He might have been a simple country boy, but he didn't want to look a complete bumpkin when he arrived in Cambridge.

They'd gone about two hundred miles on their coach trip when William had a rather nasty experience – quite shocking really, for a country boy who'd led a secluded life. In the town of Grantham, or it may have been Stamford, neighbouring busy little coaching towns on the Great North Road, both of which must have appeared equally wicked to William, he heard for the first time in his life the distinct sounds of women swearing and blaspheming. Even worse, he saw 'abandoned women', given over to 'open shame' and 'public vice'. Goodness knows what the Rev. William said. Perhaps he was more used to such sights than his seventeen-year-old nephew. England at the time supported a 'great army of prostitutes', according to G.M. Trevelyan, and the harlot's cry was heard in almost every town. William, as he observed rather sadly in *The Prelude*, saw worse later: 'Afterwards a milder sadness on such spectacles attended.'

It was all excitement in those first few weeks at Cambridge, a mad whirl of new sensations, as William, the archetypal fresher, did the introductory rounds, accepting invitations, suppers and teas, conversations and counsel. He looked up all the old Hawkshead boys he knew; nine of them were there, which shows how well his little grammar school was doing in those days. Some of them were now terribly important, swaggering fellows, but they were all very friendly to the new boy from their old school. He paid a call on his tutor, hastened to a tailor, arranged to have his hair powdered (as the style then was for young Cambridge gentlemen), ordered silk stockings and turned himself into a dandy over-night, though one hardly old enough to shave, hardly able to disguise his lack of manhood. He roamed the famous colleges, proud of the spectacle, proud of himself, admiring the views, admiring himself. St John's is not, architecturally, one of Cambridge's finest colleges, and his room turned out to be little more than a cell above the kitchens, but, by pulling his bed to the little window, he could see an avenue of splendid elm-trees, and, by craning hard, he could see Trinity College and the statue of Newton, then the dominant influence in Cambridge teaching.

Wordsworth couldn't have had a better or happier start at Cambridge. It was true he arrived as a sizar, a sort of charity boy, one who paid reduced fees, but he later received a small scholarship. At one time, sizars had been forced to serve at table to pay their fees, but this had ceased by the time Wordsworth arrived. All the same, if only his father had lived, then he might not have needed to take the social status of a sizar. His uncles, who begrudged his small fees anyway, were sending him to Cambridge on the cheap.

His good start was due to his schooling and to his connections. William Taylor, the young and brilliant headmaster at Hawkshead, whom William said was the person who had first encouraged him to write poetry, had only recently come down from Cambridge, where he'd been Second Wrangler in 1778 (second in the BA honours list), and therefore knew the Cambridge system. It was he who'd pushed the Hawkshead boys ahead in mathematics, knowing that was Cambridge's obsession. Taylor had died, aged only thirty-two, in William's second last year at school. William, with some other senior boys, had been called into his room, where he lay on his death-bed, and they'd each kissed him on the cheek. Years later, when William visited Taylor's grave at Cartmel, he'd cried real tears, imagining he could hear his voice. One of the many things William owed to Taylor was that, when he arrived at Cambridge, he found himself a year ahead of everyone else in Euclid.

As for good connections, having your uncle as a Fellow is naturally an asset, but there was also Edward Christian, another Fellow of St John's, who, for one year, early in Wordsworth's school days, had been headmaster at Hawkshead. He was also from Cockermouth, the brother of Fletcher Christian. At Cambridge, he was lecturing in law, and was soon to become Professor of Law. A year or so later, while still quite young and relatively unknown, he was chosen by the Wordsworth family to carry on their lawsuit against the might of the Lowthers. Northerners generally were in powerful positions in Cambridge at the time, and were prejudiced in favour of boys from their old schools or counties.

At the end of his first term, William was placed in the first class in his college examinations, despite dashing round Cambridge and enjoying himself, soaking up all the dazzle and novelty – a Dreamer who thought that Cambridge was a Dream. But by the end of his first year, in June 1788, he suddenly dropped to the second class. He had become completely disillusioned with Cambridge and had given up all attempts to follow a proper course of study, dropping his honours course and ignoring lectures, to the absolute bewilderment of his Uncle William and all his other well-wishers. Wilfully, he was throwing away every advantage. What had gone wrong? Had those fancy clothes and fancy life gone to his head?

For the rest of his life, Wordsworth looked back on Cambridge with a mixture of anger and melancholy – when, that is, he looked back on it at all. In truth, he wrote and talked little about it, save to dismiss the Cambridge of his time as being wild and dissolute. His attack on it in *The Prelude* is, in parts, extremely savage. He tinkered around with this bit of *The Prelude* in later years, toning down his criticisms, blaming himself a bit more; but it is still very violent, describing the dons, for example, as 'grotesque in character'.

Cambridge, in those days, was indeed in a pretty sad state. There were two extremes of Cambridge life, each of which Wordsworth inspected in turn, observing at first hand their different degradations (though he didn't really join in, so he says), and then he rejected both of them, one after the other.

One of these extremes, the academic race, was followed by only a small proportion of the students. At the top, it was crumbling and corrupt, with absentee professors and non-lecturing Fellows, who mainly sat around, waiting for some 'perk' to come their way. Cambridge was still basically a training-ground for Anglican clerics, but most livings were in the hands of the politicians or of members of the landed aristocracy, such as the Lowthers, who had not only parliamentary boroughs, but clerical livings, in their gift. It was the Prime Minister who personally appointed bishops; so, when Pitt visited Cambridge, the Fellows positively crawled before him. Fellows would even curry favour with their pupils, if they were rich enough. One example was William Wilberforce, a particularly wealthy young student from Yorkshire, who was about to inherit greatness and therefore didn't need to earn it. He'd recently been at St John's, where he was a fellow-student of William's

Uncle William, and he was still his close friend (which shows how well the Rev. William had done). While there, the Fellows had actively encouraged Wilberforce to be idle, considering him to be a talented young man of fortune who did not need to work to earn his bread.

The professors and masters of colleges were quick to follow any political wind, favouring the Whigs or the Tories, depending on who was in power. Dr Watson, Bishop of Llandaff, an important Cambridge figure of the day, managed to be reformer and reactionary in turn. At one and the same time, he held down his see in South Wales, the professorship of Divinity at Cambridge and a rich living in Leicestershire, while spending most of his time at his house on Windermere. He had previously been Professor of Chemistry, before procuring himself a DD and moving into Divinity, adroitly securing for himself the best clerical endowment of its kind.

However, to get started on this road to riches and preferment, it was vital for a bright but less affluent or less well connected boy to do well in his examinations. The main examination at Cambridge, upon which everything depended, was the Mathematical Tripos. This may seem rather a strange speciality, and it infuriated many great Cambridge men before and after Wordsworth. Thomas Gray, the poet, had protested some fifty years earlier about the ridiculous emphasis on mathematics; and Thackeray, some fifty years afterwards, felt he would never master algebra and geometry, and left after only one year. The tradition dated back to Newton, Cambridge's favourite son. There were separate college examinations (as St John's, which held them every year), and there were other specialist chairs, such as History; but these were almost extras, for graduates or dilettantes. The Mathematical Tripos was what counted, and in the final BA honours examinations everyone who took part was listed in order of merit, from first to last. The top fifteen or so were called Wranglers, from Senior Wrangler down to Fifteenth Wrangler. The secondary honours were similarly graded, and there were many prizes and medals to be won. Cambridge was centuries ahead of the meritocratic society.

It was vital to be high on the honours list and so get a fellowship. There were mental breakdowns, just as today, as people felt themselves slipping out of the race, but there was also a bit of fiddling, as wealthy or well-connected students were 'huddled' through their disputations (examinations on philosophical questions which were part of the Mathematical Tripos). You couldn't actually fiddle your way on to the Wranglers' part of the list, but to get a respectable position further down wasn't difficult, either for the reasonably clever or for the wealthy but indolent. The Tripos included moral philosophy and logic, as well as geometry, algebra and arithmetic. Cambridge considered itself rather advanced – its pre-eminence in science dates from these days – whereas at Oxford, where they were firmly bedded in Classical literature, it was as if Newton had never been born.

William hated the syllabus, and felt it had nothing to do with him. If this was how you became a cleric, then he didn't want to be one; and who would want to be a cleric anyway, once one had seen how they fought and crawled for sinecures and positions. He hated examinations and competition of all sorts. Such a view is more fashionable today, but in Wordsworth's day the Church almost deified competition, usually referring to it as Emulation. By emulating your betters, you did better yourself. Wordsworth only ever remembered twice in his life being envious of someone. As a little boy, in a foot race in some sports, he'd tripped up his brother when he saw him getting ahead. The second time was at Cambridge, when for a moment he felt jealous of a fellow-student who was better at Italian than he was. Looking back as an old man, he could remember no other occasions. 'I can sincerely affirm, that I am not indebted to emulation for my attainments, whatever they may be. I have from my youth cultivated the habit of valuing knowledge for its own sake.'

The other extreme at Cambridge – and the one more widely pursued – was the social life. Even the studious did most of their studying in the vacation, as many do today, and looked upon the term as a time for fun. Wordsworth in *The Prelude* maintains he 'observed', not shared, the dissolute pleasures, but they were there and were well recorded by many of his contemporaries.

Thomas Gray had had a few coarse tricks played on him as a Cambridge student, and he was horrified to see the young bucks place 'women upon their heads in the streets at noon, break open shops and game in the coffee houses on Sundays'. The Tuns Tavern was 'the scene of nightly orgies in which professors and Fellows set an example of roistering to the youth of the University'. Another poet, William Cowper, reported in 1785 that the universities contained nothing but 'gamesters, jockeys, brothellers impure, spendthrifts and booted sportsmen'. Coleridge, referring to the 1790s, said that both the universities and the public schools were the homes of 'vicious habits, unstained acts of intemperance or the degradations akin to intemperance'. Wordsworth was never as specific, apart from referring to 'rioting, rotting and dissolute pleasures'. He must have been more appalled by Cambridge life than those students who came from the big, southern public schools, where brutality and other vices were almost as commonplace. Hawkshead, in every sense, had been a haven of innocence.

The 'bucks', the wealthy undergraduates and those who tried to ape them, followed a life that was a mixture of effeminacy and violence. It was the fashion of the day for gentlemen to be obsessed by their clothes, and in Cambridge, as elsewhere, the trend-setters would spend the whole morning dressing. Little wonder that Wordsworth, despite his handful of home-made smart clothes, rushed straight out to get his hair done and order some more clothes, self-conscious about his home-spun northern dress and manners.

In those years, the only meal taken in college was dinner, which was at 2.30 in the afternoon; the undergraduates ate breakfast and supper in their rooms, or in the rooms of friends. As dinner was the social peak of the day, everyone made a big attempt to dress their best for it. Even Christopher Wordsworth, William's younger brother, who soon followed him to Cambridge, spent forty minutes getting dressed for dinner, despite being the family swot. Christopher kept a diary of his Cambridge days; like almost everyone else, he went on from dinner in college to wine parties, which lasted all afternoon, in the rooms of his friends. He usually managed to sober up enough to start working again at about six o'clock, reading the Classics for three or four hours before bed. As for the bucks, since dinner was immediately followed by afternoon wine parties, that meant no more work was done for the rest of the day. Thackeray, when he was up at Cambridge, admitted that there was literally no time for work, what with dressing all morning and drinking all afternoon and evening. As the day wore on, their smart clothes must have begun to suffer – which was no doubt why they had to spend so much time the next day getting ready again. The violence of those days was terrifying. The bucks, rioted in the colleges, breaking down people's doors, roughing up sizars or anyone they felt like picking on, then going into the streets, breaking down shops and cracking the heads of anyone who got in their way. During Wordsworth's first year a local drayman of the town was murdered by a gang of rioting students. As Coleridge and others remarked, once you'd seen the vice current amongst the privileged undergraduates, the streets of London could never shock you.

Wordsworth admitted that in his first year he 'sauntered, play'd, rioted' along the streets and on one occasion, after a particularly heavy afternoon wine party, got drunk. How shocking. He was actually toasting Milton's name at the time, so it was excusable, and he did manage to pull himself together and was able to race back to his college before the bell went at nine and the doors closed. But his brain had definitely reeled and it was 'never so clouded by the fumes of wine before that hour or since'. Wordsworth was in fact virtually teetotal throughout his adult years, as is well recorded, but notice that he says 'never *so* clouded'. If he'd literally never touched a drop again, he would simply have said 'never clouded', so perhaps he did have a few jars on other occasions in his Cambridge days.

Throughout that first year, he felt himself very much the innocent abroad, the simple country lad. After a year's excitement and novelty, he was rather glad, when the holidays came, to get back to his former innocent life. When he returned to Hawkshead for his first summer vacation in 1788, he doubtless needed a good rest as much as anything else, after his contact with the wild goings-on at Cambridge.

What a welcome he got from old Mrs Tyson, his motherly dame, who insisted straight away that he should parade round the village, and walk round the fields and along the paths, to let everyone see what a fine young gentleman her little orphan lodger had turned into. He was a bit embarrassed, knowing what some of the locals would think of his gay attire, but he quite enjoyed going the rounds, shouting curt greetings to the farmers, half-way across a field, knowing they'd be amazed when they'd straightened up and taken it all in, but also knowing they wouldn't say much, not being given to such social ceremonies. He was particularly pleased to see again the old ferryman on Windermere, one who had taken him across the lake so many times over the years, going back and forth to school. Naturally, he went to see his school friends, regaling them with his adventures and his dazzling Cambridge life.

Above all, it was easing himself into his old physical surroundings that pleased him most – to be in the only place he knew of as home, rushing upstairs to stretch himself out on his old bed, joining the other student lodgers at Mrs Tyson's big communal dining-table, feeling the garden and the trees, walking round Esthwaite Water, luxuriating in nature, returning to his real self again. Or was it his real self? He was a trifle confused, worried by the new pleasures he'd seen and enjoyed. He realized his imagination had slept, while he'd sauntered and idled round Cambridge. He half blamed himself for his rather hedonistic year, his vanity and his weakness, for enjoying the gaudy nights – and some of them, he had to admit, he *had* enjoyed.

As he explored his old haunts, he felt a conflict of pleasures, wondering what was true or false, real or affected. He started to write some verse again, which he hadn't done at Cambridge, and began a poem called *An Evening Walk*. His habit then, which continued throughout his life, was to compose aloud, trying out the lines in the open air as he strode along. There's a nice, lightly humoured section in *The Prelude* about walking with his dog, or at least Mrs Tyson's household dog, on his return to Hawkshead. (Everything to do with Hawkshead in *The Prelude* is joyful – a joy to read and a pleasure to realize his joy – whereas other sections, such as that in Cambridge, are confused and melancholy.) The dog always walked with him, but a few paces ahead, and when it saw someone coming, it always turned and gave William notice, time to compose his face and gait, so that no-one would see and hear him in full spate and suspect he was crazy.

He bought an umbrella during his summer holidays in Hawkshead, putting it on his bill at Mrs Tyson's, along with £2 17s for nine weeks' board and 1s 6d for the hire of a horse. Even to this day, a man carrying an umbrella in the Lake District is thought a bit soft, but in 1789 it was positively effeminate. It must have been a habit he'd picked up in Cambridge, though even there it was something of a novelty. (The first man to carry an umbrella in the streets of London was Jonas Hanway in 1750; he was ridiculed by passers-by and abused by cabmen.) We don't know if William took it with him around Hawkshead, which would seem very strange for an open-air boy. Perhaps he'd just bought it to stun them when he got back to Cambridge. It shows that even in his dress there was a conflict of styles.

He entered once again into the spirit of the rural social life, always having fancied himself when it came to dancing, and went to several 'promiscuous routs', whatever that meant. One assumes it referred to drinking rather than anything else, though one of his first impressions, on returning to Hawkshead, was to notice which pretty girls had gone plain and which plain ones were now pretty. The local yeomen farmers had barn dances, with the village fiddler doing his bit, and Wordsworth went to these. There was no social discrimination. The boys at the grammar school were still very much village boys, part of the community. But now he was a Cambridge buck, as far as the local quality could see, he also got invited to the smarter parties in the smarter houses by some of the smart, new people. Perhaps that was when he took his umbrella.

It is strange to realize that the Lakes were already attracting visitors. We tend to think of Wordsworth's Lakes as being pre-trippers and pre-holiday homes, an undiscovered sylvan paradise, but the discovery of Lakeland coincided almost exactly with Wordsworth's birth. The first guide-books, by people like West and Gilpin, appeared in the 1770s and were very successful. Wordsworth read them avidly. The poem he was now writing, *An Evening Walk*, showed the current fashion for landscape descriptions. The guides were meant for gentlemen, those with taste and discrimination, who were looking for the picturesque, who could be led to certain beauty spots and there feast their eyes or get out their paints and pencils and record the picturesque scene. These spots were called 'stations' and there was one not far from Hawkshead, overlooking Windermere, which Wordsworth was very fond of visiting.

Along with the gentlemen trippers came the first of the second-homers, the first wave of Lancashire industrialists who were already building or buying lavish holiday homes on the slopes of Windermere. They brought a completely new social class to Lakeland life. It had always been a fairly classless life anyway: the central dales were dominated by small-scale yeomen farmers ('statesmen', as they were called, because of their small estates), whereas the local aristocracy (feudal overlords, such as the Lowthers) lived on the fringes, in the plains of the Eden valley, well away from the mountains. The new, wealthy summer visitors gave big parties, regattas and hunts, organized fancy-dress balls and competitions for the best-decorated boats, and their daughters looked forward avidly to the holiday festivities. They weren't all complete strangers to the area. Several families who lived in industrial west Cumberland, for example the Curwens from Workington, had for years possessed a country home in the Lakes. The Curwens had theirs right in the middle of Windermere, on Belle Isle.

There's a nice contemporary letter, written in 1786, by a young lady living over in Bassenthwaite, Mary Spedding of Armathwaite Hall, whose brother John was at school with William, to a girl friend in Hawkshead with whom she'd spent a previous summer holiday. In the letter, she is complaining about the lack of suitable men for dances in her area. 'So little Hawkshead still retains its superiority. I believe so great a majority of Beaux can seldom be boasted of in this part of the world.'

William enjoyed the parties and dances and many a time spent all night at them, returning home in the early hours. It was after one such party, perhaps with the Curwens on Windermere, full of the usual dancing, gaiety and mirth, of maids and youths enjoying themselves, dancing the night away, that he had a strange experience as he walked home, with the cock crowing, the birds wakening and the labourers going to their fields. It was a beautiful sunrise and the mountains looked as bright as clouds. During this walk, it came to Wordsworth that what he had to do in life was be a 'Dedicated Spirit'. An unknown bond was given to him, one which it would be a sin to ignore. It wasn't a great mystical experience, like others he describes in *The Prelude*: just a simple realization of his duty in life. He doesn't even say it meant he had to be a poet, though everyone accepts that's what is meant. This dedication section has been scrambled over by countless scholars, looking for clues, and those who think it refers to Windermere have always been foxed by a line which says the 'sea was laughing at a distance'. You would have to have had quite a few drinks to hear the sea from Windermere. Wherever the revelation took place, and however Wordsworth shaped the details afterwards, he suddenly saw clearly what he must do. Confused by these new conflicting experiences and sensations, Wordsworth made his choice for the conduct of his future life.

Back in Cambridge, he decided to create his own pattern of study for the next two years. From now on, he devoted his time to his own reading, including modern authors and modern subjects, and to learning foreign languages. It's not clear how much he actually read, though he told everybody that was what he was doing, but he definitely took instruction in Italian from an old gentleman called Isola, who had been a friend of Thomas Gray at Cambridge. This was about the only teacher at Cambridge Wordsworth had any respect for. He seems to have despised the rest.

It was a brave thing to do, for an impoverished student: deliberately ruining all his chances of a proper and secure career. But from his early days William had been a rebel, headstrong and determined, whether he was defying his Penrith grandparents or his Cambridge teachers, demanding to be free to go his own way. Why did he not just leave, as many disenchanted students have done, before and since? The answer must be that, though he disliked the place, there was no money and nothing else for him to do. The future was obscure, so he might as well make the most of the present. He says in *The Prelude*, rather arrogantly, that he decided he was a Chosen Son, so why grieve or be cast down or even feel guilty?

Dorothy worried on his behalf, being most upset when she heard that he'd opted out of the Tripos course. In his second year he was 'unplaced', which meant he had not sat the full examination, though he had taken a paper in Classics and done quite well in that. In her regular letters, Dorothy reassured her friends, who were equally concerned about her wayward brother, that he was reading quite a lot and was 'acquainted' with French, Spanish and Italian.

The uncles were more than upset. They were furious. William had called in at Penrith, as he had done during his first long summer holiday from Cambridge, but hadn't stayed long. Uncle Kit, after one of William's brief visits, wrote complaining about his conduct to his elder brother Richard, now a young lawyer in London. 'I should have been happy if he had favoured me with more of his company, but I'm afraid I'm out of his good graces.... I am sorry to say that I think your Bro. William very extravagant. He has had very near £300 since he went to Cambridge which I think is a very shameful sum for him to spend, considering his expectations.'

His family wanted him to stick to the Tripos and become a Wrangler, and that way his life would be secure, and his family and all his well-wishers happy; but William took no notice. Even his kind Uncle William, the Fellow of his college, began to despair of him.

The Master of the college died in March 1789. As was the custom of the day, literary-minded students from the college pinned on the coffin some nicely composed verses of appreciation. William, however, refused, saying he had had no connection with the dead man, nor any interest in him, so why should he write something. His uncle couldn't understand it. Here was his nephew, who had given up all proper study because he was supposedly only interested in poetry, not taking an opportunity to distinguish himself by having his verse read by the Cambridge public.

William had become positively anti-clerical by this time. There is no evidence, either way, of any interest in religion while he was at school, nor in his early poetry, but at Cambridge he actively despised the old clerics and deans of the university, finding more wisdom and goodness in the old shepherds back in Hawkshead. Daily chapel attendance was compulsory at Cambridge, and the rules were strict in this, if in few other departments of Cambridge life. William found it all a mockery, a disgraceful and empty gesture, and he attacked it vociferously in *The Prelude*.

Perhaps William's most defiant gesture during his Cambridge years was to go off in his last summer vacation, just a few months before the final examinations, on a holiday across France to the Alps. His relations still had hopes that he would come to his senses in his final year, see the light at last and catch up with some frantic holiday revising, as others had done, and in the end get some sort of respectable honours degree, enough for his good connections to ease him into a comfortable niche. He didn't even tell Dorothy, his beloved sister, he was going, not until he'd set off. He knew that even she would think he was absolutely mad....

We left Dorothy still having a hard time with the Penrith grandparents, but Uncle William came to her rescue, just as he had tried to come to William's.

In William's second year, Uncle William got married to the daughter of the vicar of Penrith and resigned his Fellowship to take up a rather well-appointed living in Norfolk, a gift of St John's. The newly-weds asked Dorothy to come with them, to be a kind of housekeeper, and Dorothy jumped at the chance of leaving Penrith. On their way to Norfolk, they spent a few hours in Cambridge, and William was able to show Dorothy round the sights. Later on, he went to visit them in Norfolk, but it was by this time that his uncle was beginning to realize that William was not going to be the scholar he'd expected. Dorothy and William went for long walks, up and down the huge garden of the vicarage, discussing their idealistic plans for the future, their worries about the Lowthers and about whether they would ever get their rightful inheritance. Dorothy loved such visits, but eventually her uncle made it clear that William was no longer a welcome visitor.

Dorothy made her home with her uncle and aunt for the next seven years, acting as a nurse to their children when they started to arrive, but she had to keep her contact with William as quiet as possible. Not only had he become unwelcome: it looks as if he was now thought to be an undesirable influence on young Dorothy, and someone of whom the family had become ashamed.

William's and Dorothy's joint fantasy at the time, which they discussed together and which Dorothy continually mentioned in letters to her close friends, was that one day they would set up house together, sharing life in a beautiful village – Grasmere is mentioned as one possibility – and be happy ever after, just the two of them.

Dorothy kept in touch with all her brothers – even Richard, a very tardy letter-writer, now in London – and with young John, now a sailor, who had just taken up a junior position on the *Earl of Abergavenny* and had gone on a voyage to the West Indies; but she was always closest to William. She did feel that, as five stranded orphans, they had to huddle together for protection, especially herself and the unloved William. It is not surprising that she should have created fantasies of a future life with her favourite brother. As a woman, she had no possibility of a career of her own. Her destiny lay either in going into service, getting married or living with one of her brothers.

There's no record of any boy friends in her life, though one of her friends did tease her about the possibility of romance with Mr Wilberforce – yes, William Wilberforce, the great anti-slavery philanthropist. He came to spend a month with her uncle, being an old Cambridge friend of his, and was very impressed by a little class that Dorothy was running at the time for local poor children, teaching them reading, spelling and knitting. Mr Wilberforce gave her ten guineas a year, to spend for the poor children in any way she wanted.

'My heart is perfectly disengaged,' she replied to her friend Jane Pollard in Halifax, who'd obviously made certain hints in her letter, on hearing what Mr Wilberforce had done. 'I would make a confidante of you, had there been any foundations for your suspicions. Mr W would, were he ever to marry, look for a Lady possessed of many more accomplishments than I can boast. . . .'

There had still been only one girl in William's life: the girl from his early Penrith schooldays, Mary Hutchinson; but she already seems to have become more an old friend than a *girl* friend – someone he just happened to have grown up with. He did visit her during those first two Cambridge holidays when he went to Penrith. After all, he did like parties and dancing and was not unaware of girls being plain or pretty. But she, apparently, was on the plain side.

During his final year at Cambridge, he seems to have turned his back on thoughts of Mary, not visiting her any more, never contemplating a life with anyone else, apart from Dorothy. Was he simply being kind to Dorothy, stuck away in the country parsonage, or did he mean it? He certainly didn't discuss everything with her, or she would have known beforehand about his final Cambridge holiday in France. Perhaps he feared she might worry about his future, as much as everyone else seemed to be worrying, and want him to devote his final vacation to his books.

He came back to Cambridge in October 1790, after his summer holiday in France and before the time to sit for his final examinations. 'I am very anxious about him just now,' wrote Dorothy, 'as he will shortly have to provide for himself; next year he takes his degree, when he will go into orders I do not know, nor how he will employ himself. He must when he is three and twenty either go into orders or take pupils.'

In January 1791, William received his degree, an unclassified BA. He had not sat for the full examinations and so couldn't get an honours degree. There was no possibility of a fellowship, which would have seen comfortably to his needs for the next three years, till he could be ordained – that is, if he was still going to be ordained. He had no idea what he wanted to do. The one or two remaining friendly relations talked of putting a curacy in his way, when the time came, and in her letters to her friends, Dorothy's little dreams now took place in a parsonage, not a cottage, as she visualized the snug little parlour and bright little fire by which they would sit and converse together; but William had no such clear or clerical thoughts. Once he'd been admitted to his BA, he was on the road to London.

He was glad to get Cambridge behind him. From the very beginning, he had realized he was a stranger there. 'A feeling that I was not for that hour, not for that place.' That's probably one of the best-known lines in *The Prelude*, though he has another phrase about Cambridge which is equally apt. Describing his last two years and his feeling of detachment, he says he decided to live like a 'lodger in that house of Letters'.

It could be argued that Wordsworth was the failure at Cambridge – rather than Cambridge failing him, which is how it is often described. There is not one contemporary account of him at Cambridge by any of his fellow-students, which is surprising, considering how people usually manage to dig up and produce yellowing memories of people, once they are famous. He didn't impress anyone sufficiently at the time for them to rush to their notebooks or diaries and jot down a few impressions. The only known reference is by an anonymous contemporary some three years later, who remembered Wordsworth as that chap who went on and on about the beauties of the Lake District.

He *was* a failure at Cambridge, in the sense of not passing the right examination. Even as a poet, he did very little, except for starting *An Evening Walk*, most of which he wrote in the holidays at Hawkshead. Cambridge was very much a fallow time. He might have felt secretly that he was a Chosen Son, but nobody else seems to have noticed. It has been suggested that he was discriminated against for his country ways and bucolic dress and manners, and that this could be one reason why he disliked Cambridge so much and why he was driven in upon himself. But there's not much evidence for this and in *The Prelude* he does try to tell the truth, as he remembers it. We have to believe, therefore, his evidence which points to him *choosing* to turn Cambridge down. He tested it and found it wanting. In any case, quite apart from Wordsworth's own reminiscences, there is overwhelming evidence of the low state of almost everything at Cambridge at that time. His wasn't an isolated experience. Wordsworth's often quoted remark about being in the wrong place at the wrong time is, with hindsight, peculiarly true. If he had gone to Cambridge a couple of years later, this might have made all the difference. But he was there at the nadir of eighteenth-century thinking and eighteenth-century dissipation. The ruling cliques, though corrupt and tottering, were still in control.

It was while Wordsworth was at Cambridge, after his second year, that the French Revolution broke out. On the actual day the Bastille was stormed, 14 July 1789, it looks as if he was on his way to Norfolk, to see Dorothy at his uncle's parsonage.

Rousseau's writings had a great effect on the whole of Europe, not just on France. Dissidents, in religion and in politics, had already started pressing independently for reform. Wordsworth, being a rebel at heart, judging from his boyhood and his Cambridge days, would have been attracted to any student radical movement or radical teachers, if he'd met any. Nothing and no-one of that sort appear to have come his way at Cambridge. They were there, in a minor form, but the heady days were to come a year or so later. As far as he was concerned, he was just passing through.

But Cambridge did have one good effect, albeit a negative one, on Wordsworth. It showed him what he wasn't. It let him see he didn't want to be a lawyer or a cleric, though it remained to be seen what form his dedicated spirit would take. It was a great revelation to him, being exposed to the world of Cambridge – a veritable culture shock for a young innocent from the hills to go amongst the wicked and the dissolute, so different from the world of nature. He was now able to see the value of Hawkshead. By going away, he was beginning to arrive.

CAMBRIDGE

Some lines from Book 3 of The Prelude *about his early impressions of Cambridge.*

Strange transformation for a Mountain Youth,
A northern Villager. As if by word
Of Magic or some Fairy's power at once
Behold me rich in monies, and attir'd
In splendid clothes, with hose of silk and hair
Glittering like rimy trees when frost is keen,
My Lordly Dressing-gown I pass it by,
With other signs of manhood which supplied
The lack of beard. The weeks went roundly on,
With invitations, suppers, wine and fruit,
Smooth housekeeping within, and all without
Liberal and suiting Gentleman's array!

We saunter'd, play'd, we rioted, we talked
Unprofitable talk at morning hours.

Such was the tenor of the opening act
In this new life. Imagination slept.

Some fears
About my future worldly maintainance,
And, more than all, a strangeness in my mind,
A feeling that I was not for that hour,
Nor for that place. But wherefore be cast down?
Why should I grieve? I was a chosen Son.

[44]

4

France
1791-1792

WILLIAM made two trips to France within the space of about a year. The first one, during that last vacation from Cambridge, was fascinating in its own way. The second one, not long after he'd come down, was sensational. That's the only word for it, considering the character of the young man we have got to know so far. It is still one of the least explicable events in his whole life.

The first trip can be explained in several ways. It was a defiance of Cambridge, an open slight to the system. Secondly, he had always loved travelling and wandering, right from the earliest days. And thirdly the whole civilized world was agog with the news and excitement of the Revolution. It never struck him for one moment as being dangerous, to venture across a foreign land at such a time. He never thought of personal danger anyway, even when lost all night on a Lakeland fell. In those first heady days, the Revolution seemed so welcoming, a breath of fresh air; the horrors came later. There's a fourth, minor reason. Mrs Tyson had shut up shop. She had become too old to take in boarders any more. For the first time, William had nowhere else to go for his summer holidays. No-one else, after all, would have him.

All the same, it was a strange adventure, one which his relations thought was crazy, which was why he didn't tell them beforehand. It was common enough in those days for young gentlemen to go on a Continental tour, though sensible ones waited till after university. Rich ones went in their own coaches. Less rich ones went in someone else's coach, getting a job as a companion. William Wordsworth went on foot – a pedestrian tour right across Europe.

His companion was another student from St John's, Robert Jones, a jolly, roly-poly Welshman. He made a good counterfoil to William, who, by his own confession, tended to be irritable when travelling. William was tall and spare and already looked older than his years, in manner and in his awkward gait. His face was long and his expression was usually rather serious. Most people found him reserved on first acquaintance, but there were strong feelings and passionate enthusiasms bubbling away just below the surface. The two young men had a common background: both were sons of country lawyers, both had gone to local country grammar schools and both had grown up in mountainous regions.

They must have made a funny-looking pair, as they set off from London to walk across Europe on the morning of 11 July 1790, each man's belongings tied up in a pocket handkerchief. Between them, they only had £20 to keep them going for the three months ahead. Those friends at Cambridge, who knew about their plans, said they'd never make it. But a long letter to Dorothy, written after they'd been on the road for two months and had reached Switzerland, shows that William was obviously thrilled with himself:

Our appearance is singular and we have often observed that in passing thro' a village, we have excited a general smile. Our coats which we had made light on purpose for our journey are of the same piece; and our manner of bearing our bundles which is upon our heads, with each an oak stick in our hands, contributes not a little to that general curiosity which we seemed to excite. I expect great pleasure on my return to Cambridge in exulting over those of my friends who threatened us with such an accumulation of difficulties as must undoubtedly render it impossible for us to perform the tour. Everything however has succeeded with us far beyond my most sanguined expectations.

They'd been greeted with affectionate amusement on their journey through France. Each village was in the throes of revolutionary celebrations and they were invited to join in the festivities, the dancing and the singing. As Englishmen, from the land of liberty, or so the French believed, they were welcomed as brothers. 'During the time which was near a month which we were in France, we had not once to complain of the smallest incivility of any person, much less of any positive rudeness. But I must remind you that we crossed it at a time when the whole nation was mad with joy in consequence of the revolution.'

They had many adventures and encounters, several of which Wordsworth relates in *The Prelude* and in a long poem about the tour, *Descriptive Sketches*. None was particularly dramatic. They got lost a few times, slept out in the open when they couldn't find an inn, met pedlars and horsemen. Crossing the Alps by themselves turned out to be an anti-climax. They lost their way going over the Simplon Pass only to find that when they thought the top was yet to come, they'd got over the summit of the pass and were now going downhill. The discovery at first made Wordsworth dejected and deflated, as if he'd been cheated.

Switzerland was a disappointment on the whole, which surprised William, as Switzerland was then a fashionable country for English travellers, who normally rhapsodized about its natural beauty, the sturdiness of its inhabitants, the idealism of its political system. Mont Blanc had just been climbed, in 1787, and Thomas Gray was one of the many English writers who had recently visited the country and written about it. Wordsworth had probably read some of the current travel books about Switzerland, as his school library had contained several. Perhaps he had expected too much.

Had we been able to speak the language, which is German, and had time to insinuate ourselves into their cottages, we should probably have had as much occasion to admire the simplicity of their lives as the beauty of their country. My partiality to Swisserland excited by its natural charms induces me to hope that the manners of its inhabitants are amiable, but at the same time I cannot help frequently contrasting them with those of the French and as far as I have had the opportunity to observe they lose by the comparison.

William gave Dorothy a blow-by-blow account of their route so far, boasting how they'd walked twenty miles a day, and how several times they had managed twice that, which seemed a slight exaggeration; but they were strong chaps, with very little to carry. On their way back, they were very enterprising and bought a little boat which they sailed down the Rhine, from Basel to Cologne. When they'd finished with it, they sold it. They came back through Belgium, where they ran into more stirring events, as the Belgians had risen against the Emperor Joseph II.

The scenery throughout had captivated William, and he spent a long time trying to describe it, and trying to describe the problems of trying to describe it – a difficulty which all travellers face:

Ten thousand times in the course of this tour have I regretted the inability of my memory to retain a more strong impression of the beautiful forms before me, and again and again in quitting a fortunate station have I returned to it with the most eager avidity, with the hope of bearing away a more lively picture. At this moment, when many of these landscapes are floating before my mind, I feel a high enjoyment in reflecting that perhaps scarce a day of my life will pass in which I shall not derive some happiness from these images.

But it was the passions of the Revolution that had the most immediate effect on him. The natural rebel in him, the lover of freedom and liberty, rejoiced in what was happening, and for the next few years this dominated a great deal of his mind and energies. As with the natural beauty, he got an extra pleasure by realizing *at the time* that he was witnessing something momentous. So often in life, it is only when we look back that we realize what was happening, that we recognize later we were happy then. Wordsworth knew.

> Bliss was it in that dawn to be alive,
> But to be young was very Heaven!

William returned to Cambridge, took his poor degree and then spent the next four months in London, bumming around. No details are known of how he lived or where he lived. Presumably he sponged off old Cambridge friends, perhaps those with some sort of job and some sort of accommodation. He idled the days away, watching the passing show, going to the law courts and watching the trials, which he described as 'brawls', and to churches, where he heard sermons which were 'light follies'. It all sounds so contemporary, except that now an unemployed graduate can at least claim social security. William, however, had no income, though it looked as if soon the Lowther case might come to court.

'My times passed in a strange manner,' he wrote to a friend. 'Sometimes whirled about by the vortex, and sometimes thrown by the eddy into a corner of the stream where I lay in almost motionless indolence. Think not, however, that I had not many pleasant hours; a man must be fortunate indeed who resides four months in Town without some of his time being disposed of in such a manner, as he would forget with reluctance.'

He managed to muster enough energy to move out of London when the weather got better and he spent the four summer months, from about May to September 1791, staying in North Wales with his pedestrian friend Robert Jones. They did some walking round Wales together, climbed Snowdon in the dark, and Wordsworth got into an argument with a Welsh priest who pulled a carving knife on him. (It's not clear what the row was about: possibly William started on his anti-clerical theories.)

But one of the big attractions of staying with Jones was the fact that three of Jones's sisters were all at home. There's a nice nudging reference in a letter from Dorothy to her friend Jane in Halifax. It's the only reference I can find, in almost four thousand pages of published Wordsworth letters, in which William is teased about girls, though, as teases go, it's a very harmless one.

'William is now in Wales where I think he seems so happy that it is probable that he will remain there all summer,' wrote Dorothy in June 1791. 'Who would not be happy enjoying the company of three young ladies in the Vale of Clewwyd without a rival? His friend Jones is a charming young man and has *five* sisters, three of whom are at home at present; then there are mountains, rivers, woods and rocks, whose charms without any other inducement would be sufficient to tempt William to continue amongst them as long as possible.' Is there perhaps just a little hint of jealousy on Dorothy's part...?

During this summer, the big Lowther trial was at last heard at the Carlisle Assizes. The Wordsworth family had been trying for seven years, since the death of John Wordsworth, to get the Earl of Lonsdale to pay up the money owing. It was estimated to be about £5,000. Divided amongst five of them, it would give them £1,000 each and would solve all William's problems. There had been endless litigation and stays of proceedings and other nonsense, while Lowther kept them at bay, but at last the case was tried before a full court. Lowther had engaged forty counsel, brought forward a hundred witnesses and produced a mass of evidence. The Wordsworths could only afford four counsel, the leading one being Mr Christian, the new Professor of Law at Cambridge. 'We have got a very clever man on our side,' wrote Dorothy, 'but he is young and he will not have much authority. I hope that what he wants in experience will be made up in zeal for our interests.'

The Wordsworths won – but Lord Lonsdale refused to pay. The case went to an arbitrator in London. Proceedings dragged on all winter, with more witnesses being called, and the case eventually slid to a halt, the Wordsworths having to take out mortgages to get them started again.

It is not hard to see why William had such a violent hatred of the aristocracy. They had blighted his whole life, ruined his present and clouded his future. He hated their power and their corruption, their friends and their influence. It would be unfair to say that his passionate support for the French Revolution, and for the toppling of the French aristocracy, owed everything to his personal prejudice, but this certainly played a part.

During the summer he had idly contemplated becoming a tramp, taking to the road for the rest of his life. All he would need would be £100 a year, and he'd be a free man. But the Lowther disaster meant he had to think again, and when his distant cousin, an MP, said he was still holding a curacy in Harwich for him, William went to London to see him face to face, no doubt pushed into such courtesies by Uncle William and his guardians, who may have advised him at least to *look* a gift horse in the eye. William half promised that he would take the curacy, when he turned twenty-three and could be ordained. In the meantime, said his cousin, get some useful experience, instead of just wandering the countryside. So poor William trudged back to Cambridge, where he enrolled to attend a series of lectures on Hebrew and Oriental languages, a preparation for a clerical life.

In a letter to a friend, dated 23 November 1791, William privately ridiculed this plan, saying that he hardly knew any Latin and scarcely any Greek, so what was the point of him starting a new language, like Hebrew?

A pretty confession for a young gentleman whose whole life ought to have been devoted to study. And thus the world wags. I am doomed to be an idler throughout my whole life. I have read nothing this age, nor indeed did I ever. Yet, with all this I am tolerable happy. But away with this outrageous Egotism. Tell me what you are doing, and what you read. What authors are your favourites and what number of that venerable body you wish in the red sea? I shall be happy to hear from you. My address, Mon, Mons? W. Wordsworth, Les Trois Empereurs, Orleans. . . .

This rather sprightly letter was not written from Cambridge, as his uncles would have expected. The address was Brighton. After only a few weeks of Hebrew in Cambridge, William had thrown up his course, though he'd promised himself that he would do what his relations wanted, *after* he returned. In the meantime, he was bound once more for sunny France.

William's reason for going to France again, so he told his long-suffering relations, was to improve his French so that he could get a job as a tutor. Then he would come back and, at twenty-three, get himself ordained, settle down and do the right thing for a change. He was now twenty-one, and, as far as they were concerned, he had loafed around for long enough. For the last four years, since he was seventeen and had first gone up to Cambridge, he had completely disobeyed them, ruining all his chances, making a mess of his life, letting down the family and himself. He did want to improve his French, but wanting to return to France was basically part of his wanderlust. He'd loved France best of all on his previous year's pedestrian tour to the Alps and wanted to go back. He decided to do it in rather more style this time, so he got his brother Richard, the London solicitor, to extract £40 from his guardians to finance the trip. This was a large sum, when you consider that William and Jones had survived for three months on half as much. He did well to get it out of his guardians, as the Lowther money still seemed to be stuck. If and when his £1,000 or so did materialize, there would be £300 in Cambridge expenses to pay back, plus all the other bits he'd had over the years.

He was going alone this time, using coaches, and he made plans beforehand to get himself introduced into the local society at Orleans when he got there. It is not clear why he should have chosen to go to Orleans. Had he already met somebody from there he wanted to see again? For some years it had been a popular centre for English people abroad, so perhaps he had been told he would enjoy himself there.

In Brighton, while waiting four days for favourable winds, William went to see a local literary lady who gave him an introduction to a Miss Helen Maria Williams, a well-known writer of the day who was living in Orleans. William had for a long time been a fan of hers. While in his last year at school at Hawkshead, he'd written a sonnet about her ('On seeing Miss Helen Maria Williams weep at a Tale of Distress') which he'd had published anonymously in a London magazine in 1787 – his first published work. She was a poet and journalist and had just published a book on France, which showed her in favour of the Revolution. It was probably this introduction to Miss Williams which made William finally decide on Orleans.

He spent only a few days in Paris on the way there, just enough time to visit the National Assembly, wander round the arcades and gape at the taverns, brothels and gaming houses, and go and look at the Bastille and pocket a piece of stone as a relic, just like any other rubbernecking tourist. In Paris he changed £20 into French money, receiving 643 *livres* in exchange. Then he headed straight for Orleans and found himself some lodgings there.

On 19 December 1791, two weeks after he had reached Orleans, he wrote to his brother Richard in London, telling him he'd arrived safely but that he'd missed Miss Williams after all. She'd already left Orleans. However, he had found some nice lodgings which he was sharing with some cavalry officers. He didn't know anybody else in Orleans so far, except a family nearby whom he found very agreeable and had spent several evenings with. He idled away the first few weeks in Orleans, living a 'loose and disjointed' life, so he says in *The Prelude* – a very tranquil existence, considering what was going on around him: '... careless as a flower / Glassed in a green-house, ... When every bush and tree, the country through / Is shaking to the roots.'

William's first enthusiasm for the Revolution had been a fairly adolescent response, an emotional reaction to a joyful uprising. He hadn't so far been actively interested in politics. It was one of the cavalry officers who really made him appreciate intellectually what was going on. This officer, Captain Beaupuy, was from a noble family, but had left the army for a while and had been involved in Revolutionary politics. He'd then come back to his regiment, much to the disgust of his fellowofficers, who were mostly royalists and considered him a traitor. Beaupuy was fifteen years older than Wordsworth, a much experienced and well travelled man, something of a womanizer in his youth but now a great idealist with an interest in politics and philosophy. He became a firm friend of William's, spending several months in his company, teaching and talking to him about France and about the world in general. According to William, he was the biggest single influence in his life up till that time. It was mainly thanks to Beaupuy that William, so he said, moved on from a love of nature to a love of man.

In *The Prelude* he recalls walking with Beaupuy in the country one day, when they came across a poor, half-starved girl with a cow, both bowed down and defeated-looking. "'Tis against *that* which we are fighting,' declaims Beaupuy. William became passionately involved in the Revolution, fired by the ideals of equality, the need to abolish cruel laws and to make the people free. He felt himself suddenly to be a patriot – which was something of an exaggeration, considering he was an English tourist, but his heart was certainly in the right place.

He'd also fallen passionately in love, a fact which he doesn't mention in *The Prelude*, for all that it is supposed to be an autobiographical poem. Her name was Annette Vallon and he first met her in Orleans, where she was staying at the time with her brother. They were probably the nearby 'family' William had been visiting. She gave him French lessons – free, it would appear – and the lessons led on to love-making. She was very soon pregnant.

It must have been a most dramatic and exciting courtship, a sudden and intense physical passion, each of them swept off their feet, carried away blindly, ignoring all the dangers and problems surrounding such a relationship. It is hard to fit it in with the character of Wordsworth as the world at large later knew him. It is almost as difficult to reconcile it with the facts of his life recounted so far. We know he had been a rebel – wayward, headstrong and disobedient to his guardians, refusing to conform, a drifter and a procrastinator, irresponsible even – but he was supposedly a dedicated spirit, one who had so far avoided the sins of the flesh, as far as we know. What came over him?

Annette was from a respectable, middle-class family and came from Blois, not far from Orleans. Her father, now dead, had been a surgeon in Blois, as had his father and grandfather before him. Surgeons in those days didn't have quite the esteem they enjoy today, having not so long before been little more than clever barbers; but they were of some social standing nonetheless. Annette's mother had remarried, so perhaps Annette had rather moved away and was no longer completely under parental control. However, like the rest of her family, she was a devout Catholic and a strong royalist. She was twenty-five, four years older than William, so there's a temptation – though absolutely no evidence – to suppose *she* might have been the dominant partner, the woman of the world who was amused by this young, serious but passionate young foreigner who chanced to walk into her life. He also happened to be a penniless foreigner, with no job, no training or prospects, a non-

Catholic, an anti-royalist and a strong republican. What, then, was *she* doing? It could only have been passion.

Annette moved back to her home in Blois, and William followed her. It's not known what her family thought, but there's a hint of secret meetings, so no doubt they were not best pleased.

On 19 May 1792, when Annette must have been pregnant for about a couple of months, William wrote from Blois to a friend in England, saying he still intended to come home in the winter and take holy orders. He wished he could defer it, but it wasn't in his power, as he'd made a promise to his uncle. In September, still at Blois, with Annette now heavily pregnant, he wrote to his brother Richard in London, asking for a further £20 to be sent out to him urgently. In the same letter, he repeats his intention to return in the winter, saying he'll probably stay with Richard for a few weeks in London while he sees about the publication of his *Descriptive Sketches*, which he'd been completing while in France. He expected to be back in October. In neither letter is his connection with Annette mentioned, nor the slightest hint of it given.

Not long afterwards, William and Annette both returned to Orleans. Perhaps Annette's family had refused to shelter her any more, now the birth was imminent. William, as he'd planned, left Orleans in October. This would seem a callous thing to do, leaving the mother-to-be on her own, but it was now dangerous to be an Englishman in France and he needed to go home to England and get some money, so he said. But he promised to return to Annette and the baby. He had no intention of abandoning them. He left someone with legal powers to register the birth, and his name was entered on the baptismal certificate as father. Annette's child – a girl, Caroline – was born on 15 December 1792.

But William did not go straight home. For about a month, at least, he was lingering in Paris, and was possibly still there at the time of the birth, despite having no money and being in danger. It was obviously a most exciting time to be in Paris, and no doubt it proved hard for a young idealist to drag himself away, even with personal commitments and responsibilities elsewhere. The King had been deposed after the mob had stormed the Tuileries in August and he was now locked up, for his own safety. Some allied forces were marching into France, threatening to put down the Revolution. In reply, the Commune, led by Danton, Marat and Robespierre, had encouraged the September Massacre. Over three thousand royalist sympathizers had been taken out of prison and publicly murdered. William arrived just a few weeks after the massacre, and could feel and smell the blood and the bodies still in the street. He was horrified and frightened, but still he didn't leave. He watched and heard the reaction against Robespierre, in the streets and in the newspapers, as some sections blamed him and the Jacobins for the excesses. William, like many of the idealists, felt more sympathy with the Girondists: the more moderate, more peaceful of the Revolutionary groups. But in November, Robespierre routed his critics, denied responsibility for the September Massacre, and went on to take charge of the Revolution – until his own head rolled off the guillotine. It was, indeed, a dramatic time. No student of the human race would want to have missed it.

William eventually arrived back in England by late December 1792, and immediately confessed all to his sister Dorothy. He did intend to return to Annette, but very soon war between England and France officially broke out and it was then not possible for him to go back to Orleans. He definitely planned to marry Annette, judging by a series of very touching love-letters, as well as many letters to Dorothy, which Annette wrote, and which were discovered earlier this century. Dorothy, the perfect sister, immediately understood what had happened, blamed no-one, and from then on addressed Annette as her own sister. William, never a great letter-writer, let Dorothy do most of the corresponding, even though, in theory, he could now speak French, whereas Dorothy, who'd never been abroad or been educated, had to teach herself.

In Wordsworth's lifetime, the public never knew about the Annette affair and his French daughter, though he told his immediate family and closest friends. After his death, the official biography, written by his nephew, made no reference to the affair and it was all hushed up. (The nephew, who knew the truth, simply says he was 'young, impetuous, encompassed with strong temptations'). The story only emerged in the 1920s after an American scholar (Harper) and a French one (Legouis) had done some brilliant detective work and tracked down letters from Annette, still lying unread, 130 years later, in local departmental archives in the Loire district. At the time the letters were written, England had been an alien power, at war with France, and so they had never been delivered. Imagine the scandal! Imagine the shock to Wordsworth scholars, as they all rushed to read the love-letters and to reassess their theories about who or what had been the great influences in the poet's life.

The letters are utterly charming. Annette never threatens or blackmails William, morally or financially. Whatever else William was at the time, he prided himself on being a young man of principles. If Annette had been wicked and scheming in the first place – as some people believed when the news first came out, unable to reconcile the facts with the later, Victorian image of Wordsworth as the stern man of God – then surely she would have tried to force him to marry her before the birth of the child. She might well have managed it, if that had been her wish. It is interesting to wonder why he didn't marry her in Orleans, before the war had started. What held him back, in that first mad passion, when nothing else in his life seemed to matter? His staying on in Paris, while she was about to give birth, is also mysterious, since he was supposed to be going home for money. However, when he left her, Annette was convinced that they would soon be together again, as man and wife. After he'd arrived in London, she wrote to him:

My distress would be lessened were we married. Yet I regard it as almost impossible that you should risk yourself. You might be taken prisoner. But where do my wishes lead me?

I speak as though the instant of my happiness were at hand. Write and tell me what you think and do your very utmost to hasten your daughter's happiness and mine, but only if there is not the slightest risk to be run. I think the war will not last long ... but find some way by which we can write to each other in case the correspondence between the two kingdoms were stopped.

In a letter to Dorothy, Annette sympathized with the problems of telling the uncles and said she did not want William to be unhappy. But her biggest concern was for Caroline's happiness. She even considered it would be enough if only William could come across to France for a short while, marry her and make Caroline legitimate, thereby taking away the shame which she and her family feared Caroline would have to bear for ever.

William was in great distress, contorted with guilt and worry, confused by his emotions, caught up in events which were now out of his control. The following summer he spent about a month on the Isle of Wight, for no apparent reason, just sitting around, watching the English fleet preparing to fight the French. Did he half hope or half try to get on a boat bound for France? Annette's letters had certainly become very emotional:

Often when I am alone in my room with his [William's] letters I dream he is going to walk in. I stand ready to throw myself into his arms and say to him: 'Come my love, come and dry these tears which have long been flowing for you, let us fly and see Caroline, your child and your likeness; behold your wife, sorrow has altered her much; do you know her? Yes! by the emotion which your heart must share with hers. If her features are altered, if her pallor makes it impossible for you to know her, her heart is unchanged. . . .' Ah, my dear sister, such is my habitual state of mind. But waking from my delusion as from a dream, I do not see him, my child's father; he is very far from me. These transports occur again and again and throw me into a state of dejection. . . .

But the war went on, and William could do nothing; he learnt to live with the situation and waited for the war to end. Although he put no reference to Annette in *The Prelude*, in the middle of the French section there is a long and extremely tedious story about a blighted love affair between a nobly born French boy and a humble local girl. It appears to be a rather pointless, sudden interlude, though Wordsworth has inserted a few similarly sudden interludes elsewhere in *The Prelude*, dragging in stories and incidents, out of context, from other periods of his life.

Until the Annette story was revealed, the Wordsworth scholars, while admitting that this was a boring interlude, decided it was meant to be a political metaphor, illustrating one of the iniquities of the *ancien régime* in France, since it showed a noble family being oppressive and dogmatic. But once they knew about Annette, they suddenly decided it was obviously meant to be a metaphor for William's own love affair! It makes one wary of all deductions based on a handful of letters or facts, when we never know what has not survived. It also shows how easy it can be to find things, once you've decided what it is you're trying to find. However, and nonetheless and notwithstanding, the saga in *The Prelude* of Vaudracour and Julia, as told in Wordsworth's words, does bear some striking relationships with the poet's love affair such as it was eventually revealed to have been. The differences between the two lovers, the obstacles put in the way of their marriage, and then the birth of Julia's baby, are very similar to the facts of William's and Annette's affair. The most revealing lines are the early ones about their passion:

> He beheld
> A vision, and he loved the thing he saw.

> Arabian Fiction never filled the world
> With half the wonders that were wrought for him.

We know, because Wordsworth has told us earlier in the poem, that as a boy he adored reading *The Arabian Nights*: the first book to stir his imagination. So, that could be a clue. He later describes the girl's fears in words which have echoes of Annette's own letters, though, admittedly, you would never think of the connection, unless you'd just read Annette's letters:

> A thousand thousand fears and hopes
> Stirred in her mind; thoughts waking, thoughts of sleep
> Entangled in each other.

The end of the story is all highly dramatic. The nobleman locks up his son – and no doubt Wordsworth felt he too was in a prison, being locked in England – but then the son kills a servant while trying to escape. He has to agree to give up all thoughts of marriage, to appease his father, and is then allowed out. He sees Julia briefly again, but she goes into a convent and he goes off with the child, living on his own in a forest, talking to no-one, wasting his days, becoming an imbecile.

We will probably never know how serious William was about marrying Annette, though she certainly wrote like a woman who knew that her lover planned to marry her. It had been a moment of ecstasy and grand passion, but it all ended in sadness, a harrowing experience for both of them, one that clouded his thoughts and life for many, many years.

The bare facts can make him appear rather callous, but doubtless Annette urged him to leave her, agreeing that he should go back to England to get some money, wait for the Lowther case to be settled, and then return when it was safe.

It was a sudden thing, done in the heat of passion. William hadn't been completely unaware of girls till then, as Dorothy's barbed remark about the three Jones sisters indicates, but it doesn't look as if he had had any sexual experience. He'd been appalled by the sight of prostitutes and by the dissolute life of the wild bucks at Cambridge. There were no real ladies at Cambridge for the young men: it was either women of the street or nothing. William surely wouldn't have fallen in that way. But in France – a headstrong, rebellious young man, passionate and excited about everything that was happening to him, fresh from Cambridge, where morals had been extremely lax – he was a long way from home and far from normal conventions and restraints. And he did love Annette. There's no doubt about that. But, oh, the remorse and moral turpitude he must now have experienced. Until then, he had been sinned against rather than sinning. The Lowthers, his hateful Penrith relations, the corrupt and distasteful Cambridge system – with them all, he felt he was in the right. Now, in his darker moments, he felt he had done wrong.

THE PRELUDE

From The Prelude, *Book 10, the end of his residence in France.*

> In this frame of mind,
> Reluctantly to England I return'd,
> Compelled by nothing less than absolute want
> Of funds for my support, else, well assured
> That I both was and must be of small worth,
> No better than an alien in the Land,
> I doubtless should have made a common cause
> With some who perish'd, haply perish'd, too,
> A poor mistaken and bewilder'd offering,
> Should to the breast of Nature have gone back
> With all my resolutions, all my hopes,
> A Poet only to myself, to Men
> Useless, and even, beloved Friend! a soul
> To thee unknown.

Mainly London
1793-1795

WORDSWORTH loved London, but he also hated London. Even when he loved it, he hated himself for loving it. He knew he could never really live there, but its loveliness and its hatefulness always fascinated him. It is an archetypal provincial reaction, one that is still with us, but Wordsworth at least put his impressions on paper. His descriptions of wandering round London, observing street life, the theatres, the shows, the public spectacles, are some of the finest passages of observation in *The Prelude*. Poets of the day, when they described London, saw only its grandeur. Wordsworth, like Dickens later on, saw only too clearly its seamy side as well.

As a young boy in Hawkshead, he'd been mesmerized by the idea of London, like most country folk. He once fell eagerly upon a crippled boy at his school who had been on a visit to London, pumping him for information, but unfortunately the boy couldn't remember anything. He didn't even *look* different. Wordsworth was most disappointed. His own images of London consisted of processions, the Royal Palace, dukes, kings, Dick Whittington and the notion that next-door neighbours in the same street don't know each other's names. Some images never change.

The reality of the crowds, the squalor, the freaks, the cheap entertainment, the maimed and the beggars appalled him when he eventually saw them, but even so, the city at night, when the great tide of human life stood still, had almost a hypnotizing effect on him. He clearly saw the follies of the public men, the postures of the politicians, yet in the vast receptacle of London, 'living amid the same perpetual flow of trivial objects, melted and reduced to one identity', he managed to feel the Spirit of Nature come upon him.

London drew from Wordsworth, in *The Prelude*, one of his few pieces of humorous – well, faintly satirical, or perhaps gently teasing – writing. It was about a vicar in a fashionable church who had a particularly fruity accent, the sort of contorted, affected voice which is still common in fashionable London churches.

However, William didn't have so much time for standing around listening and staring as he'd had on his previous visit. He was now fired with revolutionary fervour, and with a desire to get his two poems published: *Descriptive Sketches*, which he'd finished in Orleans and which contained a lot of pro-revolutionary writing, and his Lakeland landscape poem, *An Evening Walk*. These two poems, his first published volumes, appeared on 29 January 1793. They seem to have been rather rushed through the press, considering he'd only been back in London a little over a month, but perhaps he knew beforehand that he had an interested publisher and this was probably one of the reasons he had given Annette for having to come back to London, hoping to get some money from his poems and so help her and the baby. The publisher, Joseph Johnson, had radical leanings and introduced Wordsworth to others of the same inclination.

'It was with great reluctance that I huddled up those two little works,' William wrote to a friend. 'But as I had done nothing to distinguish myself at the University, I thought these little things might show that I could do something.' They were exceedingly thin. *An Evening Walk* ran to twenty-seven pages, and was priced two shillings. *Descriptive Sketches* was fifty-five pages long, price three shillings.

An Evening Walk was addressed to Dorothy, but William doesn't appear to have let her see the book before publication, completing it in London while she was still in Norfolk. (It was his practice later to listen to criticisms from Dorothy, and from other close friends, and he was for ever rewriting his verses.) When she did read these first published poems, Dorothy was very honest and forthright in her opinions, considering she was missing her beloved William so desperately and was longing to be with him: 'The poems contain many passages exquisitely beautiful, but they also contain many Faults, the chief of which are Obscurity . . .' She picked upon the word 'moveless' as an example of a fairly meaningless word which William had used three times, describing the motion of a swan gliding. Many years later, in a reprint, William removed the offending word.

The poems didn't get much public attention. Only two magazines reviewed them in 1793, over six months after publication, and in each case the anonymous reviewer was pretty savage. 'More descriptive poetry!' complained the *Monthly Review*. 'Have we not had enough? Must eternal changes be rung on uplands and woodlands, and nodding forests, and brooding clouds, and cells, and dells and dingles? Yes: more; and yet more; so it is decreed.' The reviewer did end by saying there were passages which showed imagination and hope for the future, if the poet managed critically to question every line.

A third review appeared the following year, by a former Cambridge contemporary of William's who happened to be visiting the Lakes, and this was much more complimentary; but the poems were indeed rather derivative in style, showing the influence of Pope and Goldsmith and with heavy eighteenth-century overtones, though in *Descriptive Sketches* William had broken some new ground. But that hint of ridicule by that first critic followed Wordsworth for the rest of his life, whenever his poems were reviewed. At the same time, unknown to him, there were several young people who heard in the poems a new voice and a new attitude. Unfortunately, their interest didn't show in the sales or in public appreciation. The two slim volumes made hardly a ripple and brought William little money, certainly not enough for him to contemplate a career as a poet.

For the next two years, as with the previous six, he had no idea what he was going to do with his life. He would probably have taken holy orders, now that he was twenty-three, despite having put it off for so long, and having complained about and generally disapproved of the Church; but his relatives now stopped trying to persuade him and finally withdrew their offer of a curacy. It is not clear if William himself told them about his affair with Annette, or whether he got Dorothy to do it, but it looks as if it was this news that caused them finally to wash their hands of him and William was henceforth banned from visiting his reverend uncle in Norfolk. He'd had to tell them, because his uncles controlled the purse-strings and he needed money, some for himself and some to send to Annette, which he planned to do as soon as he had any and as soon as he could get it through. They were horrified at the very idea of him marrying Annette, a Catholic, and then moving, along with the bastard child, into some little parsonage which they themselves would have to provide. This was Dorothy's latest little romantic notion, which she outlined in letters to Annette. Her dream cottage now contained herself, William, Annette and the baby Caroline, though the wish was no nearer fulfilment than it had ever been.

William thought for a while of becoming a soldier, as he had delusions that he was meant to command people, but that didn't last long. He thought, over the next couple of years, of beginning a literary magazine, with a London friend putting up the money. He saw himself writing nice little articles about moral philosophy, politics, the arts and gardening. Apart from commanding people, he also fancied he had a talent for telling people how to lay out their gardens. On one occasion he made enquiries about being a political reporter, though he had few delusions about this, being well aware that he was without knowledge or experience of newspaper work. 'There is still a further circumstance which disqualifies me for the office of parliamentary reporter, viz, my being subject to nervous headaches which invariably attack me when exposed to a heated atmosphere or to loud noises and that with such an excess of pain as to deprive me of all recollections.' Very true. All reporters know that feeling.

He had hopes of becoming a tutor to some young gentleman, for which he was reasonably well qualified, with his Cambridge degree, such as it was, and his first-hand knowledge of Europe and of the French and Italian languages. He considered going to Ireland to be tutor to Lord Belfore's son in the summer of 1793, but the post had gone before his letter of application arrived.

It is impossible to know exactly how he lived over these two years, as he wandered around, with no fixed abode. He was based in London for about half of the time, but he made long tours elsewhere. There's a theory that he went on a secret visit to Paris at the end of 1793, perhaps trying to see Annette. It's based on the fact that he told Thomas Carlyle, many years later, that he'd seen with his own eyes the guillotining of Gorsas, which took place on 7 October 1793, but Wordsworth was never completely reliable on dates and no firm evidence has come to light.

During the first six months of 1793, on his return from France, he was seriously involved in radical politics, a cause which obsessed him for the next three years, but at the same time confused and confounded him and added to his general feeling of unhappiness and depression.

In the same week as *Descriptive Sketches* was published, Louis XVI and Marie Antoinette were executed, and a few days later England was officially at war with France, a war which went on, apart from one brief period of peace, for the next twenty-two years. William's guilt about Annette was now mixed up with guilt about England. The terror of the Revolution, and all the bloody excesses, had alarmed and disappointed the more romantic, peaceful radicals in Britain, though they still supported the theory of revolution and pressed for reforms in England. But the announcement of war was a great shock. Could they now betray their own country? The government of the day certainly considered the pro-French agitators as traitors. Young men down from the universities were suddenly inflamed by ideas of equality; they wanted the abolishment of the monarchy in England, the repeal of oppressive laws and an end to the power of the Church and of the aristocracy. The government was sufficiently worried about the possibility of revolution at home to suspend the Habeas Corpus Acts. Several agitators were arrested. Richard Wordsworth, William's brother, advised William in a letter to be very careful about his associates.

William attended a lot of meetings, sat up all night arguing, and avidly read the radical pamphlets and books which were being produced in London, such as Tom Paine's *The Rights of Man*, and in the early stages he did actively support the idea of an English revolution. He didn't actually *do* much about it. He was there in spirit rather than deed, though he did produce one piece of political invective, a strange but powerful piece of writing which was addressed to the Bishop of Llandaff, the notorious Cambridge absentee professor and bishop. The bishop had printed one of his sermons with the unbelievable title of 'The Wisdom and Goodness of God in having made both Rich and Poor' – at least, it was unbelievable to young radicals like Wordsworth. The bishop defended all English rules and traditions, saying that parliamentary reform was unnecessary, the peasants were quite happy, and what had happened in France was disgusting.

The basis of William's long letter was an attack on the British monarchy and constitution, and it is interesting, in view of his personal problems, to see him attacking the legal system: 'I congratulate your Lordship upon your enthusiasm for the judicial proceedings of this country. I am happy to find you have passed through life without having your fleece torn from your back in the thorny labyrinth of litigation ... or the consuming expense of our never ending process, the verbosity of unintelligible statutes and the perpetual contrariety in our judicial decisions.' Down with the Lowthers, in other words.

William had evidently moved away from thoughts of war or of active revolution as a means of bringing about reform, which he appears to have supported earlier. He'd now decided that war was a disaster because it was the poor who always suffered most, as he'd seen in France. In his letter, there's a strain of puritanism which was to grow stronger as the years went on. He attacked the system which allowed prostitution to deluge the streets, though he appears to be defending the poor, who are driven to 'that promiscuous intercourse to which they are impelled by the instincts of nature, and the dreadful satisfaction of escaping the prospects of infants ... whom they are unable to support'. Was he thinking of Annette and his own child?

The letter was never published. Perhaps Johnson, his radical publisher, saw the harm it could do Wordsworth and for his sake refused to print it. It would have been easy enough to have become a martyr in 1793.

William already had enough problems. He had no job, no training, no money, no home. The only person he could have turned to was living with relatives who had disowned him. His first attempt to realize his self-professed spirit of dedication had failed. Nobody appeared to want his poems. He was a staunch republican, a friend of France, in love with a French royalist girl by whom he'd had a child; but there he was, stuck in England, forced to watch helplessly while his own country went to war with France. Yet, while despising his own country, he was beginning to worry about what was happening in France, his newly adopted country. It certainly wouldn't ease his confusions and depressions if his left-wing, republican pamphlet was published – and if he ended up in prison.

Meanwhile, Dorothy was cut off, in splendid rural isolation, ensconced in the comfortably old-fashioned eighteenth-century clerical life, safe in the sleepy Norfolk parsonage, away from such horrid modern topics as revolution, political agitation and war. But she wasn't happy either. William was not just banned from the house – even talking about him was discouraged. They couldn't have such a good-for-nothing, disgusting character mentioned in the house, not when such respectable friends as William Wilberforce, now a great Evangelical reformer, might arrive to see them.

Dorothy was busy enough. Her aunt and uncle now had four young children whom she helped to care for. She had her endless letters to write, to her old friend Jane in Halifax, or to dear William and her other brothers. The Reverend William Cookson's clerical career was advancing steadily, and he was given a temporary position at Windsor, where he was soon appointed a canon. The whole family, together with Dorothy and two maids, moved to Windsor for three months. The Reverend William, of course, had had royal connections when, as a young Fellow of St John's College, he'd been a tutor to some of the royal children.

Dorothy wrote some delightful letters about her impressions of Windsor. She used to hang around the terrace at Windsor Castle, watching George III (not long recovered from his first attack of apparent insanity) and the other members of the royal family coming in and out, when she was walking with the children. She was delighted by the friendliness and informality of the King and Queen. 'I say it's impossible to see them at Windsor without loving them, because at Windsor they are seen unattended by Pomp or State.' On two occasions the King stopped to admire Dorothy's little charges. 'Mary he considers a great Beauty and desired the Duke of York to come from one side of the Terrace to the other to look at her. The first time she appeared before him she had an unbecoming and rather shabby hat on. We then got her a new one. "Ah," he says, "Mary, that's a *pretty* hat!"' While Dorothy was basking in these royal contacts, William was of course dreaming of bringing the royal family down.

Although William couldn't visit Dorothy in Norfolk, their youngest brother Christopher, still at Cambridge, did come to see her there. 'He is like William; he has the same Traits in his Character but less highly touched; he is not so ardent in any of his pursuits. William has a sort of violence of Affection if I may so term it which demonstrates itself every moment of the Day when the objects of his affection are present with him, in a sort of restless watchfulness which I know not how to describe. . . .'

Dorothy's vision of herself and William being together one day was still very clear to her, and in this same letter she again describes the sort of winter evenings she will one day have with William – closing the shutters, setting the tea table, reading books by the fire:

Oh Jane, with such romantic dreams as these I amuse my fancy during many an hour which would otherwise pass heavily along. I cannot help heaving many a sigh of reflection that I have passed one and twenty years of my life and that the first six years only of this time was spent in the enjoyment of the same pleasures by my brothers. We have been endeared to each other by early misfortune. We in the same moment lost a father, a mother, a home; we have been equally deprived of our patrimony by the cruel Hand of lordly Tyranny. These afflictions have all contributed to unite us.

The image of life with William never goes from Dorothy's letters, though it fades now and then: 'I cannot foresee the Day of my Felicity, the Day which I am once more to find a Home under the same Roof with my brother. All is still obscure and dark and there is much ground to fear that my Scheme may prove a shadow, a mere Vision of Happiness.'

During these years, she never appeared for one moment to think of life with another man, of being married: 'I am very sure that Love will never bind me closer to any Human being than Friendship binds me to you my dearest female Friend and to William my earliest and my dearest Male Friend.'

Dorothy's love for William, whom she now hadn't seen for over two years, since before he went to Orleans, is absolutely total, yet at the same time, as with his poetry, she is not blind to his faults:

Do not expect too much of this brother of whom I have delighted to talk so much. In the first place, you must be with him more than once before he will be perfectly easy in conversation; in the second place, his person is not in his favour, but I soon ceased to discover this, nay I almost thought that the first opinion that I formed was erroneous. He is, however, certainly plain than otherwise, has an extremely thoughtful countenance, but when he speaks it is often lighted up with a smile.

It makes one wonder what Annette thought of William when she first saw him, if he took such getting to know.

It looks as though Dorothy had plans to tell her confidante Jane about William's scandalous affair: 'I have not time or room to explain to you the foundation of the prejudices of my two Uncles against my dear William. The subject is an unpleasant one for a letter, though I must confess that he has been somewhat to blame ... it will employ us more agreeably in conversation.'

Dorothy was hoping to see Jane soon, for she'd worked out a plot with William. She'd got permission from her uncle to be away from Norfolk for a while in the summer and had made secret plans to meet William at Halifax, though Jane had to say nothing about this in her letters and had to keep it all secret. It wasn't to be known by anyone that she was also going to see William again.

William wanted to see Dorothy, the only person who had ever stood by him, through thick and thin, ever since he'd been born, who without question understood and sympathized with his moods and his views and his problems, yet who had a mind of her own, a critical yet constructive mind, who saw flaws and sensed feelings he often missed. He shared her romance of that little country cottage. He too wanted to be with her. Since Annette, no-one had come along, either male or female, to share his soul. But, things happened. He put off the secret meeting in Halifax for a month, then another month, and so it went on for six months.

The first thing that happened was a piece of luck. His hopes of talking some lord into letting him tutor his son had failed, but an old school friend from Hawkshead, William Calvert, suddenly asked him to accompany him on a tour of the West Country, all expenses paid. William Calvert, and his young brother Raisley, had inherited a sizeable fortune on the death of their father, who had been steward of the Duke of Norfolk's properties at Greystoke, near Penrith. (The same Howard family is still there, but the duke lives elsewhere.) It is an indication of how well off the young Wordsworths might have been, as their father had had a similar job with the Earl of Lonsdale. William jumped at the chance. His political life in London was becoming very intense. No jobs, or opportunities for publication, had come his way. Inviting William on a tour of anywhere was like offering a drunkard a drink.

First, they dallied on the Isle of Wight for a month, where he watched the boats go by, and then they headed west. While near Salisbury, Calvert's whisky, the coach in which they were travelling, was involved in an accident and broke into smithereens – or 'shivers', as Dorothy described it. Calvert decided to return north on the horse, while William, ever the adventurer, set off north on foot, a wander which he managed to spin out for weeks. He had a three-day visionary experience on Salisbury Plain, imagining all sorts of terrifying sights: human sacrifices, Druids and blood-stained altars. The vision probably owed a lot to the terror of the Revolution – the guillotining and massacres – allied with the personal horrors throbbing round his mind at the time.

William worked his way along the Welsh border, visiting Tintern Abbey (though he didn't write about it on this visit), and then went to North Wales and the valley of the River Clwyd, to visit his old walking friend Robert Jones, now a cleric. Despite frittering his time away at Cambridge, along with Wordsworth, Jones had now settled down. He had taken a respectable teaching job till he was twenty-three and able to be ordained. William also had Jones's delightful sisters to see once more. In such a hospitable atmosphere, he sat down and wrote his poem, 'Salisbury Plain'.

He eventually got going again, and met William Calvert back on the Calvert family farm, Windy Browe, near Keswick, on the slopes of Skiddaw, where Calvert was staying with his brother Raisley. William also visited a few other old friends, such as the Speddings of Armthwaite (the family of another old schoolfellow, who also had charming sisters), and visited his Wordsworth relations down the coast at Whitehaven. It wasn't until February that William finally managed to get across to Halifax and have his long-awaited secret reunion with Dorothy.

'Oh my dear sister, dear sister, with what transports of delight shall I again meet you, with what rapture shall I again wear out the day in your sight. I assure you so eager is my desire to see you that all obstacles vanish. I see you in a moment running or rather flying to my arms.' These had been William's pretty words, in a letter to Dorothy some eight months earlier, when the secret meeting was first planned, but of course the Calvert trip had intervened. There may have been other obstacles which kept them apart, such as that possible trip to France. In a letter sent after his arrival in Halifax to a friend in London, he wrote, 'I have been doing nothing and still continue to do nothing; what is to become of me I do not know.' There is no doubt, however, that his feelings for Dorothy were sincere and that after all the delays and procrastinations he did rush to her arms, when at last they did meet again.

William and Dorothy spent about six weeks with their relations and friends in Halifax and then, in the spring of 1794, they ran away together. That might seem rather an emotive phrase, considering they were siblings, and perhaps even an unnecessary one, as they were both adults; but there is a hint of an elopement. Dorothy did have obligations to her Uncle William who had taken her in and saved her from her awful life in Penrith. Her role as an unmarried, impecunious member of a large family was to stay at home and help those relations, such as her clerical uncle, who had children or large houses or both. Her uncles were her guardians and she was beholden to them for help and money, till the Lowther debts were settled. She had had a little windfall on the death of her grandmother, and her big brother Richard, the only brother so far with a proper career, was kind and sent her occasional presents. Young John was doing well at sea, sailing round the world on various ships, but he'd still only risen to fifth mate. She had to heed her uncles, who certainly didn't want her running around with a ne'er-do-well like her brother William.

Nonetheless, William and Dorothy went off, on foot, heading for the Lake District. In those days, it was considered an extraordinary sight for a young lady to be seen walking anywhere. 'I walked with my brother at my side, from Kendal to Grasmere, eighteen miles, and afterwards from Grasmere to Keswick, fifteen miles, through the most delightful country that ever was seen.' Unlike William, Dorothy had never lived in the Lakes, having spent her adolescence in Penrith, Halifax and then Norfolk. They were aiming, once they got to Keswick, for the Calverts' farm, which had been put at their disposal. They spent an idyllic two months in and around the Lakes, with endless walks and visits to old friends of William's, like the Speddings. Dorothy found the Spedding daughters absolutely charming. 'They have read much and are amiable and engaging in their manners. We have been staying there three nights and should have stayed longer if Mrs Spedding had not been going from home.' It wouldn't of course have been proper in those days for young men to be in the same house overnight with unattended young ladies, even if they were over twenty-one.

While Dorothy and William were in their Keswick retreat, staying at the Calvert farm, one of her aunts, Mrs Crackenthorpe, the wife of the disagreeable Uncle Kit, wrote what must have been a pretty strong letter of censure, judging by Dorothy's reply:

I am much obliged to you for your frankness with which you have expressed your sentiments upon my conduct and am at the same time extremely sorry that you should think it so severely to be condemned. In answer to your suggestion that I may be supposed to be in an exposed situation, I affirm that I consider the character and virtues of my brother as a sufficient protection, and besides I am convinced that there is no place in the world in which a good and virtuous young woman would be more likely to continue good and virtuous than under the roof of these worthy uncorrupted people.

The Calverts and their tenant farmers were indeed good and worthy people; but the Calverts themselves weren't there, having left William and Dorothy, with their own quarters, to fend for themselves.

'I am now twenty-two years of age,' continued Dorothy, 'and such has been the circumstances of my life that I may be said to have enjoyed his company only for a very few months. An opportunity now presents itself of obtaining this satisfaction, an opportunity which I could not see pass from me without unbearable pain.'

It was during their stay at Windy Browe that Dorothy began copying out 'Salisbury Plain' for William – the first time she'd acted as his secretary and copyist, a job she eventually turned into a lifetime's occupation.

They left Windy Browe after about a month and went down the coast to see their Whitehaven relations, paying a visit to their old Cockermouth home on the way. 'All was in ruin, the terrace walk buried and choked up with the old privet hedge which had formerly been so beautiful – the same hedge where the sparrows used to build their nests.' How typical of that beastly Lord Lonsdale to have let the house become empty and overgrown, almost as another slight to the Wordsworth family.

William still hadn't found any employment, though he was again in correspondence with his London friend about a possible new magazine. Their money, such as it was, eventually ran out. Dorothy was forced to return to living with relations once again, this time near Barrow, while William went back to the Calvert house, where young Raisley Calvert was seriously ill and needed a companion.

Raisley, though not of a literary inclination himself, had been most affected to learn from William of his struggles and of his attempts to write poetry. He'd obviously heard many times about the awful Lowthers and about how William was penniless and would never be able to dedicate his life to poetry in the way he wanted. To all intents and purposes William had so far been something of a failure. Nevertheless, Raisley saw in William a spark of genius, or at least a spark of something out of the ordinary – enough for him to promise William that he would share his income with him. Few people until this time had seen such a spark in William, apart from Dorothy, and all she got for her devotion was a severe ticking-off from her relations.

But Raisley Calvert had promised more than to share his income with William. He vowed to leave him a legacy of £600: enough for him to live on without having to follow a profession. No wonder William hurried back when he heard he was ill.

It was thought that after a holiday abroad, with William as his companion, Raisley would soon recover. This plan greatly appealed to William. Lisbon was chosen, well away from all the awful troubles in France. William had never visited Portugal, a country which was also very popular with English people at the time, and he relished the prospect of being Raisley's paid companion on such an exotic tour. They set off from Keswick in October 1794, but had only got as far as Penrith, not exactly a glamorous town in William's eyes, when they had to turn back because of Raisley's health. For the next three months, William was stuck at Keswick, morally obliged to nurse Raisley.

William looked after Raisley, who had just turned twenty-one, with care and attention, but in his letters to his London friends he betrays signs of definite irritation. He obviously felt trapped. He couldn't leave Raisley, his benefactor-to-be, not when he was so needed, but at the same time, Raisley had never been an intimate friend. It was his first chance for years, since leaving Cambridge, of having enough money to be able to do what he really wanted. At least he now knew what he wanted, to write poetry and be with Dorothy, but there seemed little chance of achieving it, without some amazing piece of luck, such as Raisley Calvert dying ... His thoughts and motives must have been very mixed and very morbid.

William found himself in something of a panic when he discovered that, if and when the money was left to him, he might have it immediately taken away from him. His Uncle Richard in Whitehaven, one of his two legal guardians, had just died, and his uncle's children claimed that William owed them £460, the money their father had advanced to him at Cambridge. It was a topic which was to split the family for years, and William could clearly see the terrible possibilities. While he was impoverished, they would simply have to wait. But if he came into £600 from Raisley, they could legally claim almost all of it for themselves at once.

William wrote desperate letters to his brother Richard, who had now assumed responsibility for handling the Wordsworth family affairs. He asked Richard if he would make a bond to pay the debt of £460 for him, out of his own money, so that when William received Raisley's £600, he could have all of it to live on and be free. One of these years, when he had *more* money, he promised he would pay Richard back. It was a large favour to ask his brother – a shadowy figure in life, except when it came to financial matters – but Richard handsomely agreed.

Then there was a further panic when Raisley Calvert, now on his death-bed, became fed up with his local family solicitor and decided to write out a new will by himself. Raisley talked of increasing his promised legacy from £600 to £900, which must have pleased William, but it could all go wrong, right at the last moment, if Raisley, so William wrote in great agitation to his brother, made his new will in an irregular manner: 'What I have further to say is to ask whether it would not be proper for you if possible to come down immediately so as to see that the will is executed according to form. At all events no time is to be lost as he is so much reduced as to make it probable he cannot be on earth long.'

The situation had now become macabre, with William hovering in a panic around the dying youth, but eventually Raisley managed somehow to make his will to William's satisfaction, and William was able to tell his brother there was no need after all to come up from London. Raisley died in January 1795, and the sum of £900 was left 'to my friend William Wordsworth'. It took some time for the money to come through, and it did so in dribs and drabs, but William's immediate financial future was now assured.

It was a rather eerie episode, which, if examined closely, doesn't show William in all that wonderful a light. He didn't scheme or in any way precipitate the legacy, but he made sure that matters worked out to his advantage. 'I had had but little connection,' he admitted later about his relationship with Raisley, 'and the act was done entirely from a confidence on his part that I had powers and attainments which might be of use to mankind.'

There's another interesting sidelight on William's feelings and opinions at that time, as revealed in his letters to London, stuck as he was up in Keswick, wondering how he'd got himself into such a position, sitting by the death-bed of someone he hardly knew:

I begin to wish much to be in town; cataracts and mountains are good occasional society, but they will not do for constant companions, besides I have not even much of their conversation as I am so much with my sick friend and he cannot bear the fatigue of being read to. Nothing indeed but a sense of duty could detain me here under the present circumstance. This is a country for poetry it is true, but the muse is not to be won but by the sacrifice of time, and time I have not to spare.

He was a young, impatient man, it is true, caught in an emotional situation, but who would have thought you could catch William Wordsworth ever criticizing the Lakes? But, when life is in a state of flux, you can float many ways and all ways, and display feelings and inclinations which later you might not care or be able to remember.

William didn't immediately rush to Dorothy to set up their dream cottage somewhere, as one might have imagined, now that he had some money. Instead, he went straight back to London, where another stroke of good luck soon befell him, though at first he was caught up again with his old radical friends, which brought him only more worries and confusions. He became a disciple at this period of William Godwin, the political philosopher whose work and books he had admired since his return from France. He sat at his feet for several months, talking with him into the night with other young Cambridge graduates. Godwin's complicated philosophy of reason appealed to him. He believed, for example, that good people could sin, could do wrong, yet still be good. This notion attracted William, thinking perhaps of Annette or of the tortuous thoughts he must have had by Raisley's bedside. Godwin was also anti-marriage, which must have sounded attractive, though in 1797 Godwin himself got married, to Mary Wollstonecraft, the writer and early feminist. (Their daughter Mary was the future wife of Shelley and the author of *Frankenstein*.) Much has been made of the many influences Godwin had over William during these few months, but once a chance appeared to get away, William took it immediately and was gone.

It came through his friendship with an old Cambridge contemporary, Basil Montagu, with whom William went to live on his return to London. Montagu was the natural son of the Earl of Sandwich and his mistress, Martha Ray, a singer who'd been shot dead some years earlier outside Covent Garden Theatre by a former lover, a vicar from Norfolk. It was a great scandal of the time – of any time – and James Boswell is said to have accompanied the vicar in the mourning coach on his way to his execution at Tyburn.

Basil Montagu was studying for the bar, but was also taking in pupils to pay his way as his wife had died and he was trying to combine work with bringing up his two-year-old son, also called Basil. He had been a great and good friend of William's for many years, though a slightly eccentric, disorganized, impulsive one. He was constantly hard up, and William gave him £300 of his Raisley Calvert legacy in a lump sum, in return for an annuity which Montagu promised to pay him at ten per cent. It sounds a foolhardy thing to have done, but William was looking for some way to invest his money and give himself a regular income.

Through Montagu, William got to know two of his pupils, the Pinney boys, who, like young Raisley Calvert, were very impressed by William's spark of originality and his efforts as a struggling poet. They offered William the use of their country home, Racedown Lodge in Dorset, for him and his sister to live in rent-free. Their family home was a big house in Bristol where their father lived, a prosperous sugar merchant, with plantations in the West Indies.

Dorothy was absolutely thrilled when she heard that William was being offered a country cottage – and wanted her to join him. She had gone to visit her old friend Mary Hutchinson and her family in Durham, and had then moved back to the Halifax relations. She never returned to her clerical uncle and his family in Norfolk. Perhaps he'd washed his hands of her, as well as of William.

At last, her long-held dream was about to come true. Not only had they got a rent-free cottage, even if only for a short time, but they had also two sources of income. Basil Montagu was arranging for his young son to go with William and Dorothy to Racedown. For looking after him, he was going to pay them £50 a year. They were also going to have another child in their care, a natural daughter of one of their Myers cousins – a love child, as they called them in those days.

With the money paid them to look after the two children, plus the income from Calvert's legacy, Dorothy calculated that they would have about £170 a year. To William and his sister this seemed a fortune. Their luck had turned. The years of wandering and indecision, and of being dependent on the ill grace of others, seemed over. Dorothy could already see the parlour, the cosy fire. Together, at last.

The London Vicar

From Book 7 of The Prelude, *Residence in London.*

These are grave follies: other public Shows
The capital City teems with, of a kind
More light, and where but in the holy Church?
There have I seen a comely Bachelor,
Fresh from a toilette of two hours, ascend
The Pulpit, with seraphic glance look up,
And, in a tone elaborately low
Beginning, lead his voice through many a maze,
A minuet course, and winding up his mouth,
From time to time into an orifice
Most delicate, a lurking eyelet, small
And only not invisible, again
Open it out, diffusing thence a smile
Of rapt irradiation exquisite.

This pretty Shepherd, pride of all the Plains,
Leads up and down his captivated Flock.

6

West Country
1795-1798

THERE was in the city of Bristol in 1795 a group of young gentlemen, educated young gentlemen, clever and ambitious and very radical young gentlemen, who had decided that England was reactionary and corrupt, and, as there seemed no likelihood of reform, let alone revolution, they were going to emigrate and found their own Utopian community on the banks of the River Susquehanna in America. They'd never been there, nor were they quite sure where the Susquehanna flowed, but they liked the mellifluous sound of its name. The scheme was called Pantisocracy. 'The equal government of all' was their paraphrase of the title. Twelve young gentlemen, with twelve young ladies, would set up an agricultural commune where everyone was equal. Each man would have to labour for only three hours a day. According to their reading of the latest economic theories, by Adam Smith, who maintained that only one in twenty men was productive anyway, this would be sufficient to support the whole community. Everyone could hold his own religious and political beliefs and all children of the community would be educated together. They hadn't quite decided on whether marriages could be dissolved at will by any one partner, but they were working on it. The sum of £125 each, they calculated, would be enough to get a boat, sail out of Bristol and start their brave new life together.

It is hard not to smile at the idealism of it all, though, if you too happen to be young and idealistic and radical, you perhaps won't smile but think it perfectly wonderful – the sort of thing you might at this very moment be looking for. Two hundred years later, such notions still attract and similar communities, with a few modern refinements, are still being set up. The leaders of the Pantisocratic scheme were two struggling young poets: Samuel Taylor Coleridge, aged twenty-three, and Robert Southey, aged twenty-one. In their lives and hard times and rebellious attitudes, they were very similar to each other – and to another struggling young poet who, that very summer, was making plans to travel to the West Country to await his sister.

Coleridge was born in Ottery St Mary in Devon in 1772, the tenth child of the Vicar of Ottery, who died when Samuel was seven. When he was nine, he was sent away to school in London, to Christ's Hospital, where he remained for the next eight years. He was a brilliant scholar, something of a child prodigy, but he was lonely and unhappy for much of his time at school, though he began a life-long friendship with a boy some three years younger than himself, Charles Lamb, and fell in love with a girl called Mary Evans, who was the sister of another school friend.

He went up to Jesus College, Cambridge, as a sizar, in 1791 – the year that Wordsworth went down – and started off there in excellent style, winning medals and prizes; but his enthusiasm for Cambridge soon waned. He devoted his time to talking, not working, to parties, radical politics and running up debts; then, when his girl friend Mary rejected him, he ran away from Cambridge and enlisted in the 15th Regiment of Light Dragoons, under the name of Silas Tomkyn Comberbacke. It was a defiant, melodramatic gesture of a sort which Coleridge increasingly took to when, as he often believed, the world and his friends didn't quite understand him or had let him down. He was in the Dragoons as a private for several months, puzzling the officers by speaking Greek and pleasing his fellow privates by writing their love-letters, until at last his family tracked him down and persuaded him to return to Cambridge.

He didn't stay long at Cambridge, leaving at the end of the summer term in 1794 without taking a degree. He set off on a walking tour to Wales with a friend, stopping first of all at Oxford to see some old school friends. This stop stretched to three weeks, because in Oxford he met Robert Southey, then a student at Balliol. This was when they first became inflamed with their wonderful joint scheme of Pantisocracy....

Robert Southey was born in Bristol in 1774, the second of nine children of a local linen draper. When he was two, Robert was taken off by an aunt, Miss Tyler (his mother's half-sister), a wealthy, snobbish, eccentric lady who decided she could give him a better home than his own impoverished father. He spent most of his childhood with this strange lady, sleeping in her bed with her till he was six years old. As she didn't rise till about eleven, and he usually awoke at six, he was forced to lie for hours, staring at the ceiling. She wouldn't let him play in the garden, for fear that he got dirty. It made for a rather dreary, lonely childhood, but it is supposed to have encouraged in him self-sufficiency and a sense of duty.

Another relation, an uncle who was a clergyman, paid for Southey's education. Like Coleridge, he was sent away to a London public school, Westminster, which, along with Eton, was considered the best of the day. Compared with the homely comforts of Hawkshead Grammar School, it sounds frightening. Older boys poured cold water in his ears when he was asleep and then held him out of a window by one leg. The curriculum was very old-fashioned, consisting mainly of Latin and Greek learned by rote, and the whole school of 250 boys was taught in one big room, divided down the middle by a curtain. Like Coleridge, Southey didn't like his school, but made some good friends there.

Southey's memory of the news of the French Revolution – which happened when he was at Westminster – is very typical of young, idealistic youths of the day: 'Few persons but those who have lived in it can conceive or comprehend what a visionary world seemed to open up. Old things seemed passing away and nothing was dreamt of it but the regeneration of the human race.' He became a fierce radical, anti-Church, anti-government and against most forms of discipline, particularly his school's. In 1792, he was expelled from Westminster for writing a violent attack on the school in a magazine he'd helped to found, the *Flagellant*. It was a full frontal attack on corporal punishment, saying that those who practised it (his reverend teachers) were worse than heathens and unfit to instruct youth. His headmaster not only expelled him but warned Christ Church, the Oxford college about to take him. 'I will never submit,' wrote Southey. 'Should I be rejected at Oxford the grave is always open – there at least I shall not be molested.' Ah, the passions of youth!

Balliol took him instead, in a fit of liberalism, but just as he went up, in 1792, he had some family misfortune which clouded his next few years, just as happened with Wordsworth. His father, who'd never been much of a success as a draper (he really wanted to be a farmer), was arrested for debt. Miss Tyler, the dreaded aunt, rescued his father financially, but he fell ill and died within a few months. Southey's mother was forced to start taking lodgers to survive.

Southey was already a committed radical when he arrived at Oxford. One of his first acts of protest was to go into a formal dinner with his hair unpowdered. As we know from Wordsworth's undergraduate days, powered hair was *de rigueur*. Barbers were on duty for two hours every morning, just to see to the young gentlemen. Pitt, whom all the radicals hated, had put a tax on powder, and this was the specific cause of complaint. (Next door, at Trinity, Walter Savage Landor, known to his contemporaries as the 'Mad Jacobin', also chose the same means of protest, though he and Southey never met till much later in life.)

During the next two years, Southey continued to indulge in radical politics, refusing all pleas from his uncle, who was paying for his education, to go into the Church and settle down. He hated the Established Church. But he knew he would have no money whatsoever, unless he somehow kept in with his uncle, so he tried medicine one term, but gave up. He then tried the Civil Service, with no more luck. He'd been writing poetry at a furious rate since school and had started writing a dramatic epic poem, then the fashion with literary-minded undergraduates, based on the story of Joan of Arc but really a pro-Revolution diatribe. He fancied a literary career, but, with no private income, he had decided it was impossible. When Coleridge chanced into his life, during that summer vacation, Southey, with his final year looming up, had just resolved that the only solution was to emigrate. There seemed nothing else he could do in life.

The finding of a kindred spirit, when Southey thought he was alone against the world, was a revelation. It all fitted in. They would set up their ideal community together. Coleridge, after three weeks of incessant chat, went off to complete his tour of Wales with his friend. Southey decided he might as well leave and not take his degree. As he was going off for ever to the New World, what was the point of a boring Oxford degree?

He went home to Bristol, where Coleridge joined him, and they worked on plans for their new life in America. Southey introduced him to his Bristol friends, such as Robert Lovell, with whom he was writing a book of poems, and the three Fricker sisters. Mrs Fricker, the widow of a failed sugar-pan manufacturer, was a family friend. Robert Lovell was engaged to one of the Fricker girls. Southey started going out with another, Edith, and was soon about to become engaged. Coleridge became friendly with the third one, Sara. All six of them, the three young men and their three Fricker girls, declared themselves passionate Pantisocrats, all bound for America.

It was a very fertile time for Southey and Coleridge. They sparked each other off and wrote numbers of poems and articles, sometimes literally together, doing alternate sections. Southey completed a dramatic poem about Wat Tyler, the early radical, which was accepted for publication but never appeared. Perhaps his publisher thought, wisely, that it would damage his reputation and his future.

They went on walking tours together round the West Country. On one jaunt, to visit a wealthy tanner called Thomas Poole, an older, republican friend of Coleridge's in Somerset, they were forced to spend the night sleeping in a garret. 'Coleridge is a vile bed fellow,' wrote Southey to a friend, 'and I slept but ill. In the morning I rose – and lo! we were fastened in. They certainly took us for footpads and had bolted the door on the outside for fear we should rob the house.'

They were a pretty alarming couple, in their political passions as much as in their appearance. Poole decided that, of the two young men Coleridge was the more fluent and talented, with striking abilities, but that he wasn't very prudent, though he promised to be 'as sober and rational as his most sober friends could wish'. He found Southey less splendid in his abilities, but 'more violent in his principles than even Coleridge himself'. Coleridge was at least a Unitarian, and believed in God, but Southey, so Poole found, had no religious views. 'In religion, shocking to say in a mere Boy as he is, I fear he wavers between Deism and Atheism.'

Towards the end of the year, 1794, Coleridge went off to London, to try and place some of their poems and to drum up interest and customers for Pantisocracy. He went back to his old school to see some of the senior boys, and spent a lot of time hanging around the 'Salutation and Cat' in Newgate Street, which meant that he wasn't as sober as he might have been, spending many hours in 'that nice little smoky room', as Charles Lamb described it, 'with all its associated train of pipes, tobacco, egghot, Welsh rarebit, metaphysics and poetry'.

Coleridge tried to make contact again with Mary Evans, the girl who'd already rejected him – an occurrence which, in Coleridge's case, always spurred him to greater protestations of love – but got nowhere. Instead, or perhaps at the same time, he started a flirtation with another young lady, a Miss Brunton – purely of course to help him get over the first love. 'Her exquisite beauty and uncommon accomplishments might have cured one passion by another.'

When Southey heard, he was most upset. Southey might not have held any religious views, but he was certainly a most moral young man, very keen on duty and principles. He wrote a severe letter to Coleridge, reprimanding him for his behaviour, telling him to come back to Sara Fricker, to whom he was as good as betrothed.

Coleridge in turn accused Southey of being self-righteous: 'Having never erred, you feel more indignation at error than pity for it. O Southey! Bear with my weakness. Love makes all things pure and heavenly like itself – but to marry a woman whom I do not love, to degrade her whom I call my wife by making her the instrument of low desires, and on removal of a desultory appetite to be perhaps not displeased with her absence! Enough. Mark you, Southey! *I will do my duty.*' But still he didn't return, so Southey in the New Year went to fetch him. He came back quickly, and Southey and Coleridge moved into lodgings together in College Street, Bristol, where they remained for the next seven months, their friendship, their writing and their Pantisocracy as strong as ever.

The numbers were growing and by now they included Mrs Southey (Robert's mother) and Mrs Fricker, as well as Miss Tyler's manservant, Shadrach Weeks, though Coleridge protested when he discovered that the others were proposing that 'Shad' should also be their servant in America, ridiculing the idea of 'unequal equals'. However, that difference was settled and they each got down to the final business of getting their £125 together.

A local bookseller, a young and enterprising man called Joseph Cottle, who'd already agreed to publish some of Coleridge's and Southey's poems, arranged a series of public lectures for them in Bristol, on politics and theology. Coleridge was a brilliant public speaker, immensely knowledgeable and fluent, and his lectures were very successful amongst the young radicals of Bristol. Southey was competent rather than sparkling but his lectures also did well. Coleridge asked to give an extra lecture in the series Southey was running, on the 'Rise, Progress and Decline of the Roman Empire', as he said it was a subject he had particularly studied. Southey agreed he could do it, but on the evening in question, Coleridge didn't turn up and no lecture was given.

The next day, they happened to be going on a little excursion to Tintern Abbey, given by Cottle for his two young protégés and their respective fiancées, Edith and Sara Fricker. After dinner, Southey brought up the subject of the missing lecture, and the most heated argument ensued. It went on for hours, with the two poets shouting at each other, the Fricker sisters hanging on to and defending their respective fiancés, while Cottle tried to calm things down. They lost their way coming home, as it was so late. Coleridge tried to go off on horseback for help – after all, had he not been a dragoon at one time – but they ended up having to spend the night in Tintern.

This then was the state of play between the two young men when Wordsworth chanced to arrive in Bristol – and into their lives. William stayed at the house of Mr Pinney, the rich sugar merchant, for five weeks, and either met them there or perhaps attended their lectures. He was drawn to both of them, in just a few brief meetings, particularly to Coleridge, who had read, it turned out, his *An Evening Walk* and *Descriptive Sketches* and praised them highly. Coleridge had, coincidentally, discussed them at Cambridge with young Christopher Wordsworth, not knowing that he was eventually going to meet his brother.

William wrote to a young London friend, Matthews, who already knew the two of them:

Coleridge was at Bristol part of the time I was there. I saw but little of him. I wished indeed I had seen more – his talents appear to me very great, I met with Southey also. His manners pleased me exceedingly and I have every reason to think very highly of his powers of mind. He is about publishing an epic poem on the subject of the Maid of Orleans. From the specimens I have seen I am inclined to think it will have many beauties. I recollect your mentioning you had met Southey and thought him a coxcomb. This surprises me much, as I never saw a young man who seemed to have less of that character....

Wordsworth, of course, didn't know about the growing differences and rows between the two friends, which very soon afterwards led to the collapse of Pantisocracy. This took place during that summer, though there was no actual date when the scheme was called off. The two just drifted apart, as most of the participants began to realize that the whole idea was slightly mad and that temperamental differences, especially between Coleridge and Southey, would never allow it to work.

Coleridge put the blame on Southey for the final collapse. Southey's aunt, Miss Tyler, was absolutely furious when she heard about the scheme and about his engagement to the Fricker girl, whom she dismissed as a mere seamstress, not fit for her nephew, to whom she had devoted so many years and so much money. She said she would cut him off completely, would give him no more money and that she never wanted to see or hear from him again – and she never did.

But Southey's uncle, the cleric, still took an interest and suggested that he should now accompany him for a few months to Lisbon, where he was chaplain to the British community. This would enable him to get over his ridiculous schemes. Southey, surprisingly, agreed to the plan. At the same time, he was offered an annuity from a wealthy school friend which would start being paid the following year, when he came of age, and provide him with £160 a year.

Coleridge cut Southey in the street in Bristol when he heard he was going to Portugal, but Coleridge nonetheless married his Fricker sister. He must have been keen enough on her by this time to be more than just doing his duty, but he later blamed Southey for forcing him into the marriage. Southey married his Fricker girl the next month, November 1795, and then left straight from the church doors for Portugal. So they became brothers-in-law just at the time when they'd ceased to be friends.

Coleridge moved to a Somerset cottage with his bride and began work on a new magazine, feeling let down by Southey, whom he now considered even more of a self-righteous prig: 'You are lost to me, because you are lost to Virtue.'

Wordsworth, therefore, had come along at the perfect time, at least for Coleridge. Coleridge now had a new friend to take Southey's place, someone equally radical, equally interested in poetry and literature, but without all that moralizing and censoriousness. It was true they'd hardly met in Bristol, but Coleridge got Wordsworth's Dorset address and started corresponding. Coleridge was one of nature's enthusiasts, a man of instant passions, who enjoyed all the pleasures. After those first brief meetings, he'd already decided that in Wordsworth he'd met a giant.

Racedown Lodge is a square-built house near the hamlet of Birdsmoor Gate, about half-way between Lyme Regis and Crewkerne in the rolling Dorset downs. The coast is about six miles away – within sight, if you pick a good day and a reasonable mound. The country isn't wild, like the Lake District fells, and in fact today the hills seem positively cosy and suburban, with the influx of retired gentlefolk and a summer stream of Cortinas on all the roads. But in 1795, when the Wordsworths arrived, it was wild in the sense of being isolated and undeveloped. The scattered farming communities led a rather lonely, impoverished life. William and Dorothy were both much struck by the poverty of the local peasants, many of whom lived in primitive huts, begging or stealing to keep themselves alive. In the Lake District valleys, surrounded by the high fells and forced to be self-sufficient, the people of the small towns and villages somehow coped better with their poor and deprived.

We are now at Racedown [wrote William], and both as happy as people can be who live in perfect solitude. We do not see a soul. Now and then we meet a miserable peasant in the road. The country people here are wretchedly poor; ignorant and overwhelmed with every vice that usually attends ignorance in that class, viz, lying and stealing.

We plant cabbages and if retirement, in its full perfection, be as powerful in working transformations as one of Ovid's Gods, you may suspect that into cabbages we shall be transformed. . . .

They got no newspapers and, worst of all for Dorothy, considering her passion for letter-writing, they were miles from a post office. All provisions had to come from Crewkerne, seven miles away. But they were together, sharing the same simple pleasures, walking, gardening, hedging, reading and, most of all, working. William had written very little poetry in the previous two years, what with all his radical agitation in London, and, fuelled and cosseted and inspired by Dorothy, his secretary and kindred soul, he now set to work with a renewed energy. Unfortunately, his head was still full of turbulent ideas about revolution and violence, all mixed up with his own mental and moral dilemmas, and the poetry of this period suffered in consequence. It seemed to be something he had to work out of his system, though Dorothy, who had little interest in philosophical topics, was gradually weaning him back to nature.

William started work on a full-length tragedy which was called *The Borderers* and was set in thirteenth-century England. This was his only attempt at a play. It doesn't seem to have been much of a pleasure to write – nor is it much pleasure to read. It would seem that at several stages he suffered severe depressions at Racedown, perhaps even teetering on the verge of a mental breakdown; but Dorothy pulled him through.

They had only one child with them, little Basil, as the other one had not arrived after all, and they discussed his upbringing endlessly, worrying about how to stop him telling lies (they decided that, because they asked him silly, unsuitable questions, he told lies in return), and how to stop him crying (putting him in a room on his own till he stopped, which they said worked in the end). There was an old caretaker who lived on the premises, a servant of Mr Pinney, who kept a rather suspicious eye on them, though they looked after themselves completely. 'I have lately been living upon air and the essence of carrots, cabbages, turnips,' wrote William.

The Pinney boys brought them news of life in the big city of Bristol, especially news of Coleridge, who was also working on a play which Sheridan, at Covent Garden in London, had commissioned. When the Pinneys came, the caretaker unlocked the best glasses and crockery from a cupboard and they had big, jolly meals. After that, the Wordsworths went back to carrots.

During his stay at Racedown, William wrote his only signed letter to a newspaper (he later wrote some anonymously). It was to the *Weekly Entertainer* in Sherborne and was in defence of Fletcher Christian, his Cockermouth school contemporary, whose actions during the mutiny on the *Bounty* were then a source of great public discussion. Christian's brother, the professor of law, had organized a pamphlet in his support, and it was noticeable that amongst those who signed it were several members of the Wordsworth and Cookson families – old friends sticking together.

William went to Bristol once or twice on his own, to see Cottle, who was interested in publishing his poems, and to look up 'those two extraordinary young men, Southey and Coleridge'. He couldn't have seen Southey on this occasion (20 November 1795), as Southey had by then gone to Portugal, but he saw Coleridge again and Cottle sent him a copy of Southey's *Joan of Arc* which Cottle had just published. When William read it, Southey rather went down in his estimation, though he might have been influenced in this by Coleridge: 'You were right about Southey,' William wrote to his old friend in London, Matthews. 'He is certainly a coxcomb, and has proved it completely by the preface to his *Joan of Arc*, an epic poem which he has just published. This preface is indeed a very conceited performance and the poem, though in some passages of first rate excellence, is on the whole of a very inferior execution.'

Several visitors came to stay with them during their two years of seclusion at Racedown, such as Basil Montagu – who had run out of money and wasn't keeping up his payments on the annuity – and Mary Hutchinson, their old Penrith friend, now living in Yorkshire with relations. She stayed several months and provided invaluable company for Dorothy – and for William as well, no doubt, though he went off on one of his Bristol trips just as she arrived. 'My friend Mary Hutchinson is staying with us,' wrote Dorothy. 'She is one of the best girls in the world and we are as happy as human beings can be; that is when William is at home, for you cannot imagine how dull we feel and what a vacuum his loss has occasioned, but this is the first day; tomorrow we shall be better.'

The two girls weren't completely unoccupied while William was away. There was Basil to look after, plus a lot of gardening and cooking. Dorothy was also sewing shirts, for relations and friends, to make some money, and both she and Mary worked on William's poems, copying them out for him. In those days, before the invention of typewriters and copying machines, a writer had to be a writer in every sense, unless he could persuade someone to take dictation, which Dorothy often did, walking with him as he spouted and making notes for him. Once a poem had been taken down to the poet's satisfaction, it was vital to get as many copies made as possible, before it could be lost or destroyed. A publisher needed at least one copy, and Wordsworth, like Coleridge and Southey, was always sending off hand-written copies of his poems, or chunks of his latest writings, to friends, or likely friends and contacts, for their comments and appreciation.

William was soon sending samples of his poems to Coleridge, and getting back copious and excellent critical advice. Coleridge was as clear and decisive as Dorothy in his instinctive observations, but, unlike

Dorothy, he had an educated mind, a powerful intellect, great knowledge and insight, and, as a writer himself, could creatively help Wordsworth to improve or alter his work. Wordsworth was tremendously impressed. As a young man, he was never verbally very fluent; even on paper, his prose wasn't as succinct at expressing his reactions and opinions as Coleridge. Most of all, he didn't have the critical faculty of Coleridge, especially when it came to his own work. Like many writers, he took outside criticism very badly.

But he could see that Coleridge was his friend, his fan even, who criticized him only for his own good. It was the combination of Dorothy and Coleridge – one settling him down as a person, the other sorting out his creative problems – that was the making of William. This period, when they both came together intimately into his life, two lifeboats upon which he could depend, enabling him to cruise majestically forward, was the most crucial in his whole writing life. Who is to say which was the greater influence? Who is to say exactly what each gave him? But after the turbulence and indecision and wrong turnings, the isolations and depressions, of the previous ten years, his genius now began to flower.

The great meeting between all three came in June 1797, a momentous day in each of their lives, when Coleridge came out to Racedown to see William at his home and meet Dorothy in the flesh. They'd corresponded for two years and he and William had had occasional meetings, but it was the first time all three came face to face.

'We both have a distinctive remembrance of his arrival,' William recalled more than forty years later. 'He did not keep to the high road but leaped over a gate and bounded down a pathless field by which he cut off an angle.'

Coleridge was living about forty miles away, at Nether Stowey in Somerset, in a cottage provided by Thomas Poole, his wealthy patron, who lived next door. He was in the first flush of marriage, and seemed happy and content with Sara and their first child, Hartley, who'd been born the previous year. His differences with Southey had partly been forgotten. As brothers-in-law, they were in occasional contact once more, especially when Southey, and his Fricker wife, returned from Portugal and moved to London. Southey had decided to read for the bar and get himself a proper profession, not relying on odd pieces of writing in the way Coleridge and Wordsworth were both trying to do.

Coleridge stayed with the Wordsworths for three weeks, then persuaded them to come back with him to his Nether Stowey cottage. They all somehow managed to cram into the little cottage, with Mrs Coleridge and the baby, and were joined a week later by another visitor, Charles Lamb, Coleridge's London friend.

The Wordsworths never moved back to Racedown. Such was the excitement of life with their new friend, that when he found them a house to rent, some four miles away, they decided to take it immediately. This was Alfoxden House, a much larger house than Racedown, standing on the edge of the Quantock Hills (it is now a hotel).

'Here we are,' wrote Dorothy, 'in a large mansion, in a large park, with seventy head of deer. The woods are as fine as those at Lowther and the country more romantic; it has the character of the less grand parts of the neighbourhood of the Lakes.'

Thomas Poole vouched for their respectability and finances – both of which were in doubt, according to most people who met them – and they got the house for the very low rent of £23 a year.

The neighbours were indeed suspicious. A young man with his sister, so he said, looking after someone else's child, so he said, wandering round the countryside at all hours of the night, looking at nature. Well, no wonder tongues wagged.

With Coleridge so near, and his constant stream of London and Bristol radicals and writers coming to see him, they tended to live a communal life. It was almost as if Pantisocracy had happened – but at home in England, not in America. The theory that one could get rid of one's spouse if one wanted to, which had been one of the Pantisocrats' original ideas, now came true as Coleridge more and more preferred the company of William and Dorothy to that of Sara his wife, leaving her for days and weeks on end, either while he stayed with the Wordsworths in their house or accompanied them on long walking tours round the West Country.

'He is a wonderful man,' so Dorothy described Coleridge to Mary Hutchinson, just after the first meeting, saying what a sad loss it had been for Mary to miss meeting him. 'His conversation teems with soul, mind and spirit. Then he is so benevolent, so good tempered and cheerful, and like William, interests himself so much about every trifle.'

On first sight, she hadn't thought Coleridge all that handsome, which is a surprise, judging by a contemporary portrait which makes him look very much the romantic young poet, though his lips are noticeably heavy, as Dorothy was quick to spot:

I thought him very plain, that is, for about three minutes; he is pale and thin, has a wide mouth, thick lips and not very good teeth; longish, loose-growing half curling rough black hair. But if you hear him speak for five minutes, you think no more of them. His eye is large and full, not dark but grey. It speaks every emotion of his animated mind. It was more of the 'poet's eye in a fine frenzy rolling' than I ever witnessed.

Coleridge was equally impressed by Dorothy:

If you expected to see a pretty woman, you would think her ordinary; if you expected to see an ordinary woman you would think her pretty, but her manners are simple, ardent, impressive. In every motion, her most innocent soul outbeams so brightly that who saw her would say, guilt was a thing impossible to her. Her eye watchful in minutest observation of nature and her taste a perfect electrometer. It bends, protrudes and draws in, at subtlest beauties and most recondite faults.

Dorothy had quickly shown Coleridge she had a mind of her own. He had let her see some of his journalism, expecting her instant admiration: 'Some half a score or more of what I thought clever and epigrammatic and devilishly severe reviews ... but a remark made by Miss Wordsworth to whom I had, in full expectation of gaining a laugh of applause, read one of my judgements, occasioned my committing the whole batch to the Fire.'

As for William, Coleridge's opinion of him was pure hagiolatry. 'Wordsworth is a very great man, the only man at all times and in all modes of excellence, I feel myself inferior.... The Giant Wordsworth. God love him! Even when I speak in terms of admiration due to his intellect, I fear lest those terms should keep out of sight the amiableness of manners.'

This worship of Wordsworth's genius never faltered. For years, Coleridge did little else but rave about Wordsworth to all his friends, which they thought was very strange. And it was strange. Although they were alike in their radical views, in their undergraduate experiences and in their wandering impecunious life since university, they were in so many ways quite different people. Coleridge was very much a southerner, Devon-born but brought up in the middle of London. He had disliked his school-days, when he had retreated from being bullied and beaten into books and learning, arming himself with knowledge gained from the Classics, though in later life still imagining in his dreams that masters had returned to thrash him. Coleridge was gregarious and impetuous, loved parties and social activites, was always with a crowd of friends, rushing from one thing to another. He had already dazzled everyone he met by the brilliance of his conversation and he was very much the golden boy, the centre of his own circle, attracting people, young and old, to seek out his company and his friendship. His contemporaries, such as Charles Lamb, William Hazlitt and Charles Lloyd, young and talented people themselves, made special journeys to be with him, to bask in his company, enjoy his mind. Cottle the bookseller and Poole the wealthy farmer and tanner were deeply impressed by him, far more than by Southey or Wordsworth. They gave him money, presents and free accommodation, and helped him in any way they could.

Wordsworth, on the other hand, had many typical northern qualities: he was solid, slow, unpolished, careful, dour, but with hidden depths. His totally happy schooldays, in the rural isolation of Hawkshead, where he lived much of his life in the open air, couldn't have been more different from Coleridge's. So far, his main fan had been Dorothy, and he'd had only one real patron: young Raisley Calvert, the dying youth. Yet when this awkward, ungainly northerner, with little sophistication of manner or appearance, arrived in Coleridge's gilded life, Coleridge immediately subordinated his personality and his talents to Wordsworth's. Coleridge's friends couldn't believe it. They were slightly jealous of Wordsworth's arrival, resentful of the time and space and attention he was getting. When they tried to see where William's genius lay, some of them found it very hard. Coleridge's sudden passion for Wordsworth's apparently simple rustic poems, made a few of them eager to tease William, to ridicule him when they got a chance. And they got their chances. Like Coleridge, they were the sort of smart, clever young men who were in the set which was asked to write those smart, sharp, clever reviews in the magazines. Wordsworth's talents and inclinations never lay in that direction. He didn't care for their cutting observations. They thought this was because he was too self-obsessed, which indeed he was – another reason to tease him, when given the opportunity.

Lamb had great fun, amongst his London friends, in describing William's big heavy shoes, displaying them once, when he happened to have them in his possession, as provincial curiosities. Hazlitt, on his first meeting with William, when Coleridge introduced him and read out his poems, could at least sense a new style of poetry, but thought his appearance most strange:

He answered in some degree his friend's description of him but was more gaunt and Don Quixote-like. He was quaintly dressed ... in a brown fustian jacket and striped pantaloons.

There was something of a roll, a lounge in his gait.... There was a severe worn pressure of thought about his temples, a fire in his eye (as if he saw something in objects more than the outward appearance); an intense, high forehead, a Roman nose, cheeks furrowed by strong purpose and feeling, and a convulsive inclination to laughter about the mouth, a good deal at variance with the solemn, stately expression of the rest of the face.... He talked with a mixture of clear gushing accents, a deep guttural intonation, a strong tincture of the Northern burr....

Although Coleridge praised everything about Wordsworth, going on about his genius in letters to his friends, such as William Godwin and the chemist Humphry Davy, Wordsworth hardly ever reciprocated in the same terms, taking all the praise as his due, though he did admire Coleridge's mind and his learning and his conversation. In his quieter, more restrained way, he was just as devoted to his friend.

Intellectually, they disagreed on only one minor point. Whereas Coleridge was a Unitarian, Wordsworth professed no formal religious faith; Coleridge took this as being on God's side, as Wordsworth wasn't *against* religion: 'I have now known him a year and some months and my admiration, I might say my awe, of his intellectual powers has increased even to this hour and, what is more important, he is a tried good man.'

That reference to him being *tried* is interesting. Coleridge was not known for his punctuality, his reliability or his sober habits, though Wordsworth, if he was then aware of such failings in Coleridge, dismissed them. They were all three in love with each other – or, as Coleridge remarked to several acquaintances, they were 'three people, but one soul'. That rather leaves Mrs Coleridge out of account.

Wordsworth and Coleridge finished their respective dramas about the same time and sent them off to Covent Garden, though of course Coleridge was the only one who'd been offered a commission. However, he heard nothing from the theatre for six weeks, much to his fury, and eventually got a curt reply from Sheridan, rejecting it because of the 'obscurity of the last three acts'. Wordsworth got better news. One of the principal actors at Covent Garden loved his play and asked William to do some alterations. Both William and Dorothy went up to London in great excitement. 'If the play is accepted,' wrote Dorothy to brother Christopher, keeping him abreast of family news, 'we shall probably stay a fortnight or three weeks longer.' Alas, it too was rejected and Wordsworth never tried to write another play.

While in London, they saw a good deal of Southey. Dorothy, who hadn't met him before, wasn't very impressed, though no doubt Coleridge had already given her some of his opinions. 'I know a good deal of his character from our common friends. He is a young man of the most rigidly virtuous habits and is, I believe, exemplary in the discharge of all Domestic Duties, but though his talents are certainly very remarkable for his years, as far as I can judge, I think them much inferior to the talents of Coleridge.'

The failures of their respective plays left William and Coleridge free to concentrate on their poetry. William was working on 'The Recluse' and on the section on the ruined cottage in *The Excursion*. Coleridge was writing 'The Ancient Mariner' (a work he and William had originally planned to write together), 'Christabel', 'Frost at Midnight' and 'Kubla Khan'. The idea for the last-named poem came to Coleridge in a dream. He'd gone away for a few days on his own, because of ill health, taken some grains of opium 'to check a dysentery', and in a dream (unfortunately interrupted by the arrival of a visitor) had a vision which he later wrote down as the unfinished poem 'Kubla Khan'. It's interesting to realize how often the use of visions – either natural ones like Wordsworth's, or drug-induced ones, like Coleridge's – influenced the writings of the Romantic poets. Research has been done to show the recurrence of certain images in their poetry, such as waves and flying, which occur in hallucinations. Wordsworth of course never took drugs and, after Cambridge, appears never to have indulged in strong drink, apart from the occasional glass of ale. His favourite drink was water. His favourite mental stimulus was nature. All the same, his visions, as on Salisbury Plain, could be just as awesome as those caused by drugs.

However, Coleridge at the time was in no sense dependent on drugs, taking them only on isolated occasions when he didn't feel well. They were all living a healthy outdoor life, extremely active in every sense, not just in their walking tours in the surrounding countryside, but in their creative writing. It was for Coleridge a meteoric year – a never-to-be-equalled year of abundance, when poems and ideas flowed from his pen. Wordsworth had also been ignited, but he had always been a slower burner. He was by now almost twenty-eight – an old man by poetic standards, when you consider how many young poetic prodigies there have been. But though, in his careful northern way, he was slow to start, the meeting with Coleridge coincided with the beginning of a much longer spell of inspired creation than that enjoyed by his friend.

Amongst the radical friends who came to see the Wordsworths and Coleridge was John Thelwall, who had been tried in London on a charge of high treason, but acquitted. They talked noisily and heatedly long into the night with him, about revolution and the state of the war and the latest happenings in poor old France. What with their strange nocturnal habits, the north-country accents of the Wordsworths and Dorothy's dark complexion, it is not surprising that some locals decided they were not just English Jacobins, but French spies. It is all rather laughable now, but it has to be remembered that England was at war, a known radical element was stirring up insurrection, and thoughts of invasion were in everyone's mind.

In August 1797, a local doctor sent the following account of his suspicions to the Duke of Portland, the Home Secretary:

On the 8th instant I took the liberty to acquaint your grace with a very suspicious business concerning an emigrant family who have contrived to get possession of a mansion house at Alfoxden. I am since informed that the Master of the house has no wife with him but only a woman who passes for his Sister. The man has Camp Stools which he and his visitors take with them, when they go about the country upon their nocturnal or diurnal excursions which they have been heard to say were almost finished. They have been heard to say they should be rewarded for them, and were very attentive to the River near them.... These people may possibly be under-agents to some principal in Bristol.

The plot thickened, so much so that a Home Office secret agent, a Mr G. Walsh, was sent down to keep an eye on the suspected spies and write a full report on their activities. The official Home Office correspondence is proof that all this happened; the details have been invaluable to literary students in furnishing details of William's,

Dorothy's and Coleridge's life at the time and of the visitors who came to see them.

Walsh took up his quarters in the local inn at Stowey and began to spy on them, lying behind sand-dunes when they were on the sea-shore, listening to Wordsworth and Coleridge discussing someone called Spy Nozy – which convinced him he was on the right track, since he did not realize they were discussing Spinoza. Walsh took a statement from a man who'd waited at their table one evening when they had a large party of guests at Alfoxden, 'There was a little stout man with dark cropt hair and wore a white hat and glasses [probably Thelwall] who after dinner got up and talked so loud and in such passion that I was frightened and did not like to go near them since.' Such a large dinner did take place, though it doesn't sound their normal style to have someone waiting, but Thomas Poole was there and perhaps paid for the dinner.

Walsh sounds rather like a down-trodden John le Carré secret agent, sent from London to trail round after some rural eccentrics for no apparent reason. In the end, he realized they weren't either French or 'immigrants', though they might be harmful, all the same: 'I think this will turn out no French affair but a mischiefous gang of disaffected Englishmen.'

Although the scare blew over, it was probably one of the reasons why the Wordsworths' lease on Alfoxden was not renewed at the end of the year. They had certainly worried and distressed the local people and the owners didn't want them back. The Wordsworths had nowhere else to go, as they couldn't afford another cottage, unless it was very cheap. Basil Montagu had not been paying the money he owed them and not all the funds from the Calvert legacy had yet materialized. The only thing that tied them to the West Country was Coleridge's presence. 'What may be our destination I cannot say. We have no particular reason to be attached to the neighbourhood of Stowey,' William wrote, 'but the society of Coleridge.'

Coleridge had also been having problems over money, since his own magazine had failed. However, Tom and Josiah Wedgwood, of the pottery family, offered him an annuity of £150 a year. All three poets, Wordsworth, Southey and Coleridge, had now been presented with handsome annuities by friends – people of their own age who, though not especially interested in literature, had been persuaded by the poets' talents and worthiness to give them enough money to save them from the ordinary mundane problems of earning a living. There were no public patrons in those days: no Arts Councils or writers' fellowships. The only way for a young man of no means to get a helping hand was to find a patron. All three of our poets achieved this without having published anything of public note – certainly without having made names for themselves. It says a lot for their personal magnetism.

Coleridge's annuity, the Wedgwoods said, would release him from the need to become a Unitarian preacher, which had been his latest plan, as a way of providing an income to support himself, his wife and now their two children. But hardly had he received the money when he devised another plan. 'We have come to a resolution, Coleridge, Mrs Coleridge, my Sister, and myself of going to Germany,' William wrote to an old friend, James Losh, inviting him and also his wife to join the party. 'We propose to pass the two ensuing years in order to acquire the German language and to furnish ourselves with a tolerable stock of information in natural science. May I venture a wish that she [Mrs Losh] would consent to join this little colony?'

To earn enough money for their trip to Germany, Wordsworth and Coleridge got down to compiling a book of poems which they then sold to Cottle. It was Cottle's offer of thirty guineas for the book which was their specific reason for producing it, and for making them hurry to complete enough poems in time. The volume was *Lyrical Ballads*, the single most influential book of poetry in the history of English literature. By the time it came out, in September 1798, they were already in Germany.

Expostulation and Reply

These verses are from 'Expostulation and Reply' and 'The Tables Turned' which were written in June 1798 and appeared in the first edition of Lyrical Ballads. *It was based on a conversation Wordsworth had with Hazlitt when he was visiting Coleridge in the West Country, though Wordsworth transposed the setting to the Lake District. They 'got into a metaphysical argument' with Hazlitt extolling the virtues of books while Wordsworth replied, 'Let Nature be your teacher.'*

Why, William, on that old grey stone,
Thus for the length of half a day,
Why, William, sit you thus alone,
And dream your time away?

One morning thus, by Esthwaite lake,
When life was sweet, I knew not why,
To me my good friend Matthew spake,
And thus I made reply:

'The eye – it cannot choose but see;
We cannot bid the ear be still;
Our bodies feel, where'er they be,
Against or with our will.

One impulse from a vernal wood
May teach you more of man,
Of moral evil and of good,
Than all the sages can.

Enough of Science and of Art;
Close up those barren leaves;
Come forth, and bring with you a heart
That watches and receives.'

7

Germany and 'Lyrical Ballads' 1798-1799

MRS COLERIDGE didn't go to Germany. She was dropped from the party at the last moment, though Coleridge set off with William and Dorothy, half promising to send for his wife and the two children later on, when he'd got settled. Instead, a local friend of Coleridge's from Stowey, John Chester, made up the foursome.

'Chester was ill the whole time,' wrote Coleridge about the voyage in his notebook. 'Wordsworth was shockingly ill! Miss Wordsworth worst of all – vomiting and groaning and crying the whole time – and I neither sick nor giddy but gay as a lark.' And that's roughly how it all went during the whole of their German adventure.

The Wordsworths had very little money, and, before leaving, they tried to sell William's copy of Gilpin's *Guide to the Lake District* – a treasured possession, as William loved all travel books. Even so, the Wedgwoods had to advance them a loan of £110 so that they could go at all. Coleridge, on the other hand, now had his Wedgwood annuity and was able to enjoy every minute of his stay in Germany, getting himself lots of invitations and throwing himself fully into German life. One of the attractions of Germany for English people was that they could roam anywhere in that country in safety, whereas most of the rest of Europe was being overrun by Napoleon.

The English Channel being too dangerous because of the war, they sailed from Yarmouth to Hamburg, where they all spent a few days, meeting some local poets, being upset by the bad smells, looking at the sights and wondering in amazement at a street full of prostitutes (already a great attraction for all visitors to Hamburg). Then Coleridge and Wordsworth separated. It seems a strange decision, but as the relevant letters have disappeared, the reasons can only be guessed at. It could be that they thought they would learn more German by separating. Together, they would be speaking English all the time. Perhaps they just wanted to see different places. Anyway, Coleridge and his friend went off to the university town of Ratzeburg, where they had letters of introduction, while the Wordsworths moved a bit further south to the small town of Goslar, near Hanover, not far from the present East German border.

Goslar was an old imperial town, where the royal courts had once been held, and was supposed to have romantic associations and be very pretty, situated right on the edge of the Hartz Mountains. William and Dorothy found it decidedly unromantic, unbearably cold, very dull, very cheerless. They wanted to live with a German family and take part in local life, but could find only a lodging-house where they were ill fed, ignored and lacked any books, as there turned out to be no library in the town. There's one remark in passing by Dorothy, describing how she 'carried Kubla to a fountain where I drank some excellent water', which shows that some sense of humour (Kubla Khan = water can) was retained, despite all the disappointments.

Most of the time, they were exceedingly poor and one of William's constant worries was that innkeepers and shopkeepers were just waiting to cheat him, a feeling which he always had when travelling abroad. They were in fact too poor to be worth cheating. On one occasion, when they'd been wandering the German countryside, they were taken for vagrants and Dorothy was arrested and put inside a tower at the gates of a town, till William returned and was able to prove their identity. In general, their life in Germany seems to have been totally isolated. 'My hope was that I should be able to learn German as I learn'd French,' wrote William. 'In this I have been woefully deceived. I acquired more French in two months than I should acquire

German in five years living as we have lived.' Of course, in France he had enjoyed the advantage of living *en famille*.

Coleridge, meanwhile, was amongst the nobs, dining out with counts and countesses, jabbering away in German, having a good time. He was in correspondence with the Wordsworths, and so he soon knew how badly William was faring. 'He might as well have been in England as at Goslar, in the situation which he chose and with his unseeking manners. His taking his sister with him was a wrong step.... Sister here is considered as only a name for mistress. Still, male acquaintances he might have had, and had I been at Goslar I would have had them; but W, God love him! seems to have lost his spirits and almost his inclination for it.'

Dorothy herself realized she might be a handicap to William – not because people might think she was his mistress, or because she put off potential girl friends for him, but because, as a single person, William might have got more invitations. 'There is no society at Goslar, it is a lifeless town and it seems that here in Germany a man travelling alone may do very well but if his wife or sister goes with him, he must give entertainments. So we content ourselves with reading German ... plenty of dry walks. William is very industrious; his mind is always active, indeed too much so; he overwearies himself and suffers from pain and weakness in the side.'

William's pain in the side was a familiar symptom, indicating that he was working hard, usually revising. It is difficult to know whether he imagined the pain or not, as it never led to any serious illness, but once he started on the poetry, his side started hurting. Coleridge suspected it was hypochondria. We are, incidentally, well supplied with copious information about their little ailments from now on, as Dorothy had begun a daily journal in Alfoxden, which she continued for a short time in Germany, though her letters anyway always gave the latest details of the state of their bowels, as well as headaches and assorted pains in the side. Blinding headaches were Dorothy's speciality: and they were often so bad that she had to lie down.

Starved of books to read, William decided to write his own, and these four months in Germany were an enormously active and fertile time for him. Going to a foreign country made him write about his native land – about the Lake District, his school-days, his childhood memories. It is a common reaction. You realize what you had, once you've left it.

The poems about Lucy are perhaps Wordsworth's best-known work which he did in Germany, along with 'Nutting' and the Matthew poems, but the most *important* work was the beginning of *The Prelude*. He was stuck in that freezing cold lodging-house, forced to wear an overcoat constantly to keep warm, with no friends and no social or intellectual contacts, apart from Dorothy. It was 1799, the last year of the century. His thirtieth birthday was in the offing. It seemed a good time to take stock. Coleridge had suggested some time before that he should write a philosophical poem, and so William started writing it for Coleridge, addressing it to him personally.

Dorothy also appears a lot in the other poems he started writing in Germany and she is often thought to have been an element in the origin of Lucy. 'Strange fits of passion have I known' and 'She dwelt among the untrodden ways' were both written in this year. Strange stuff to write about your sister, but the Lucy figure in the end dies, which is equally bizarre. Perhaps Lucy was part-based on some unknown girl who had died. One possible friend (who had died three years earlier, in 1796) was Mary Hutchinson's sister, Margaret, a friend from the Penrith days. Literary scholars are still turning over these Lucy poems, looking for clues, tracking down the influences.

William and Dorothy left Goslar in February 1799, heading for England. Germany had proved excellent for work, if dreary for their personal life; but while William was there he at last decided where he would like to live. He wanted to go back to the north of England, preferably the Lake District.

Lyrical Ballads had come out while William was away, but there was no crowd of worshippers at Yarmouth quayside to greet them on their return from Germany, no gentlemen with green eye-shades from the *Morning Post*, eager for some suitable comment.

Joseph Cottle, their young Bristol bookseller, born in 1770, the same year as William, was the publisher of the first works of Southey, Coleridge and Wordsworth, a distinction which in later years he managed to boast about, though at the time it ruined him as a publisher. As far as he was concerned, *Lyrical Ballads* was a failure. At first, he wrote vaguely hopeful notes to William, giving no details, but saying things looked encouraging, and William wrote back, demanding to know exactly how many copies had been sold. In the end, Cottle had to admit that he had already remaindered most of the five hundred copies which he'd published: 'The sale was so slow and the severity of most of the reviews so great, that its progress to oblivion ... seemed ordained. I parted with the greatest proportion of the 500, at a loss, to Mr Arch, a London bookseller.'

Cottle then ceased publishing and transferred all his copyrights in the books he'd published to Longmans. The value of the copyright of *Lyrical Ballads* was assessed as nil. When William heard this, he asked Cottle to recover the copyright and transfer it to him and Coleridge, which Cottle did.

Three reviews had appeared after publication, all of them poor; it was probably the earliest, which was very critical, that caused Cottle to sell out. This review was by Southey, of all people; but then Coleridge had fallen out with him and Wordsworth had been rather horrid about him and his *Joan of Arc*. Southey thought that the poems had failed, 'not because the language of conversation is little adapted to the purposes of poetic pleasure, but because it has been tried upon uninteresting subjects'. He was particularly harsh about Coleridge's 'Ancient Mariner', calling it absurd and unintelligible.

William wrote to Cottle:

> Southey's review I have seen. He knew that I published those poems for money and money alone. He knew that money was of importance to me. If he could not conscientously have spoken differently of the volume, he ought to have declined the task of reviewing it.
>
> The bulk of the poems he has described as destitute of merit. Am I recompensed for this by vague praises of my talent? I care little for the praise of any other professional critics, but as it may help me to pudding. Believe me, dear Cottle, your affectionate friend, W. Wordsworth.

The big thing, the particularly original thing, about *Lyrical Ballads* was their conversational style and content, at least by the standards of the day. All the poems weren't like this, but those that were, by contemporary standards, were considered either aggressively modernistic or brutally banal. Wordsworth and Coleridge, as William outlined in a foreword note, were attempting to do two things: firstly, to write poems about nature, emphasizing the romantic and the imaginative; secondly, to write about 'matter-of-fact' subjects. William later added a lengthier preface, expounding rather didactically, almost coxcombly, his views and aims as a poet, elaborating on his theme that the convention of poetry of the time bore no relation to the real languge of men. He explained that the poems were meant to be experiments, and so the reader had to expect to be shocked by a certain awkwardness: 'Readers of superior judgment may disapprove of the style in which many of the pieces are executed. It will perhaps appear to them that the author has sometimes descended too low and that many of his expressions are too familiar, and not of sufficient dignity.'

It is hard today for the layman to see how the poems could in any way be called experimental, or even shocking. They appear, in the main, to be simple rustic poems, some of them little more than doggerel; but it has to be realized that eighteenth-century conventions were very rigid. Language was flowery, the form was strictly metric, there was a heavy Classical influence and the subject-matter was meant to be equally Classical and flowery. Reviewers admired perfect hexameters or iambic pentameters. Birds were 'feathered songsters'. It is true that poets like Burns were writing about ordinary subjects, but usually as regional poets, writing in a dialect. Educated gentlemen like Wordsworth were meant to follow the literary rules. Wordsworth had indeed read and admired the accepted eighteenth-century poets, but now, so some critics thought, he was slumming and deliberately letting down the side. As in so many other matters, he had decided to revolt, throwing the accepted standards over in order to go his own way.

It has to be understood what Wordsworth, and many young men like him, had been going through in the last decade. The French Revolution had had a profound effect on all aspects of life and thought. In his own little revolution, Wordsworth was not only reacting against the eighteenth-century style of poetry, with all its embellishments and rules, but against the eighteenth-century intellectual obsessions, such as the cult of Reason. Even people like Godwin, whose philosophical teaching he'd now rejected, put the intellect first, denying the power of the senses and emotions. Wordsworth, in his revolt, was deliberately writing about people with no intellect, no knowledge of classical logic – in fact, in many cases about people with no reason at all, being stark, raving mad.

To find poems in *Lyrical Ballads* called 'The Idiot Boy', 'The Mad Mother' or 'The Female Vagrant' was indeed shocking to people of superior tastes. One just didn't write about village imbeciles or deranged women. Pedlars and shepherds could conceivably be written about, but they had to be idealized and romanticized. One didn't want some old shepherd blathering on in a conversational style about how he'd lost his flock and ended up with one dead lamb, as Wordsworth did. Poetry should be written by an educated *élite*, for an educated *élite*. It had no connection with folk ballads, passed on by peasants by word of mouth and most of which were either very rude, in every sense, or simply meant to be humorous. Wordsworth, without being humorous or saucy, was taking rustic subjects and trying to get the *educated* people to read about them. He never wrote in dialect. He didn't in fact write for ordinary people, which is ironic, considering he thought he was writing about ordinary subjects. The ordinary people, whoever they are, never read his poems, and still don't. He is the poet of the Lake District, but you don't find Lake District shepherds reading his stuff. Wordsworth, despite his experiments, was still hoping to be read by the traditional, poetry-reading, educated public.

Naturally enough, most educated people were put off by Wordsworth's rustic topics, which are certainly very easy to ridicule, and only slowly did they get round to realizing that it was his *reactions* to such topics or such people that was new and interesting. That was where his message lay. He was leading readers to see a wisdom and a morality in ordinary people and in ordinary, natural things that had been dismissed and ignored, not just in poetry but in life, by the so-called superior people. Often, when the message as well as the medium is very simple, then the result can appear totally simplistic, not to say pointless. It is always easier to hide behind complications, to cover yourself in style. Doing or saying the simple thing leaves you open to groans and heavy sighs, or, as happened with Wordsworth in many quarters, to laughter and ridicule.

The most ridiculed passage has usually been from the poem 'The Thorn', where Wordsworth did take his matter-of-fact style to extremes, writing more like a surveyor than a poet:

> And to the left, three yards beyond
> You see a little muddy pond
> Of water – never dry,
> I've measured it from side to side
> 'Tis three feet long, and two feet wide.

'The Idiot Boy' was also much abused, for its subject-matter and style:

> 'Tis eight o'clock – a clear March night,
> The moon is up, – the sky is blue,

> The owlet, in the moonlight air,
> Shouts from nobody knows where;
> He lengthens out his lonely shout,
> Halloo! halloo! a long halloo!

One of the simplest poems in *Lyrical Ballads* is called 'We are seven', in which the poet meets a little girl and asks her how many brothers and sisters she has. It turns out there are five living, and two buried in the churchyard, but she still insists 'we are seven'. That's about all there is to it. No wonder people scoffed at the banality of the subject – and the style is no better.

> I met a little cottage girl:
> She was eight years old, she said;
> Her hair was thick with many a curl
> That clustered round her head.

It could be a nursery rhyme, or a poem written by a child of eight, but there's a certain haunting beauty in its simplicity and starkness – at least, I think there is, having read it a few times, at first preparing to scoff.

William wrote this poem at Alfoxden, walking up and down in a little wood outside the house, remembering a conversation he'd had a few years earlier with a little girl while walking up the Wye valley. Coleridge and Dorothy were waiting inside for him, with the tea all set, but William, who'd composed the last lines first, couldn't think of an opening stanza.

'When it was all finished,' William later recalled, 'I came in and recited it to Mr Coleridge and my Sister and said "A prefatory stanza must be added and I should sit down to our little tea meal with greater pleasure if my task were finished." I mentioned in substance what I wished to be expressed and Coleridge immediately threw off the stanza....'

Not all the poems were as simple as that – notably 'Expostulation and Reply' and 'The Tables Turned'. They were the ones written at Alfoxden, based on conversations which had taken place between William and young William Hazlitt, then only nineteen years old. He had heard Coleridge lecture at Shrewsbury the previous year – he had walked ten miles through mud to get there – and got himself invited to Coleridge's cottage. 'I got into a metaphysical argument with Wordsworth,' wrote Hazlitt, 'while Coleridge was explaining the different notes of the nightingale to his sister, in which we neither of us succeeded in making ourselves perfectly clear and intelligible.'

Hazlitt had a highly developed critical brain, even at nineteen, and he later held some strong opinions on Wordsworth, but he remembered ever afterwards that first meeting with the poet and how Dorothy had allowed him free access to the manuscripts of *Lyrical Ballads*. 'I dipped into a few of these with great satisfaction. I was not critically or sceptically inclined. I saw touches of truth and nature ... and the sense of a new style of poetry came over me. It had to me something of the new effect that arises from the turning up of fresh soil, or the first welcome breath of Spring.'

Coleridge also read out to him some of Wordsworth's ballads, in a sonorous and musical voice, and told Hazlitt, as he told all his friends, about the greatness of Mr Wordsworth. 'He strides so far before you that he dwindles in the distance.'

The best known and the best received of William's poems in the first volume of *Lyrical Ballads* was 'Lines composed a few Miles above Tintern Abbey'. This was written by William *after* the rest of the book was at the printers, which was why it became the last poem in the collection. Having finished the book, so he thought, he went on a four- or five-day walking trip up the Wye valley with Dorothy. On the road back from Tintern, he was suddenly inspired to write the poem and composed it in three days, rushing it straight to the printers without making any alterations – a rare occurrence for him. His feelings of spontaneous joyfulness shine through: 'No poem of mine was composed under circumstances more pleasant for me to remember than this.'

There were twenty-three poems in the book, nineteen by Wordsworth and only four by Coleridge, including the first one, 'The Rime of the Ancient Mariner'. This was obviously not a matter-of-fact, colloquial poem, but it represents the supernatural side of *Lyrical Ballads*. As a narrative poem, it is now considered one of the finest in the English language, though by 1799, even Wordsworth turned against it, disliking the archaic language, putting the blame on it for their poor reviews and suggesting to Cottle that it could be taken out, if there was ever another edition.

Coleridge even agreed with this, willing as ever to subjugate his muse to Wordsworth's. By the time the book came out they realized they were different sorts of poet anyway, though still the most passionate of friends. Their attempt at complete collaboration had been brief –

Wordsworth thought of the albatross for 'The Ancient Mariner', but little else. Wordsworth was never as keen as Coleridge was on the supernatural or the legendary, preferring to start on the ground, with hard, observed incidents or topics, mundane sights, ordinary people, and then build his poem up from there, rising into the mind and the spirit, rather than starting off from some fanciful, surrealistic, hallucinatory images.

Coleridge was probably the first to realize that what in fact Wordsworth was trying to do was give poetry higher aims than it currently had. Through the images of poetry, Wordsworth was doing nothing less than teaching men about his relationship with his fellows and with the universe. Even when Coleridge could see when it didn't work, he still recognized the giant in Wordsworth, struggling to get out.

As we have seen, *Lyrical Ballads* was mainly Wordsworth's production. Coleridge hadn't produced much new material: of his three other poems (apart from 'The Ancient Mariner'), one had already been published in the *Morning Post* and the other two were taken from his play. However, the book was published anonymously with neither poet's name appearing anywhere. 'Wordsworth's name is nothing,' said Coleridge, when Cottle suggested their names should appear, 'and mine stinks.' The first reactions, as they learned when they returned from Germany, seemed to prove Coleridge's point.

William came straight back from Germany and headed for the north of England. Coleridge stayed on for a few more months, despite the death of his baby son Berkeley. He worried about William hiding himself away in the North, if indeed that was what he finally intended to do. 'I think it is highly probable that where I live, there he will live, unless he should find in the North any person or persons who can feel and understand him, and reciprocate and react on him. My many weaknesses are of some advantage to me; they unite me more with the great mass of my fellow-beings but dear Wordsworth appears to me to have hurtfully segregated and isolated his being.'

William thought differently. He and Dorothy went first of all to Sockburn on Tees, the home of their old friends the Hutchinsons, where they based themselves for several months. 'We have spent our time pleasantly enough in Germany,' wrote William. 'But we are right glad to find ourselves in England for we have learnt to know its value.'

Coleridge eventually dragged himself away from Germany and

joined William in the north of England, going with him on a tremendous walking tour, right round the Lakes, in the autumn of 1799. Cottle, their erstwhile publisher, who had now gone back to bookselling, joined them for a while, and so did John Wordsworth, William's sailor brother, who was between voyages. But mostly they were on their own. They climbed Helvellyn and toured the outlying valleys – ones, such as Ennerdale, that even the hardiest travel writers of the day never ventured into. William proudly showed his native land to Coleridge, who'd never been there before, and Coleridge was suitable enthralled.

It was on this trip that William revisited Grasmere Vale, and he chanced upon a little cottage that was available to rent. He decided it would be perfect for himself and Dorothy, just the two of them together again. It was up to Coleridge this time to decide if he wanted to live with them there. William's roving days were over.

TINTERN ABBEY

Some lines from the final poem in Lyrical Ballads, *1798.*

For I have learned
To look on nature, not as in the hour
Of thoughtless youth; but hearing oftentimes
The still, sad music of humanity,
Nor harsh nor grating, though of ample power
To chasten and subdue. And I have felt
A presence that disturbs me with the joy
Of elevated thoughts; a sense sublime
Of something far more deeply interfused,
Whose dwelling is the light of setting suns,
And the round ocean and the living air,
And the blue sky, and in the mind of man:
A motion and a spirit, that impels
All thinking things, all objects of all thought,
And rolls through all things. Therefore am I still
A lover of the meadows and the woods,
And mountains; and of all that we behold
From this green earth; of all the mighty world
Of eye, and ear, – both what they half create,
And what perceive; well pleased to recognise
In nature and the language of the sense
The anchor of my purest thoughts, the nurse,
The guide, the guardian of my heart, and soul
Of all my moral being.

8

Dove Cottage
1800-1802

IT was ten years since Wordsworth's home had been in the Lakes, ten years of wandering round England and Europe; but, at the time, his return was not as inevitable as it might now appear. The world at large thought of him later as purely a Lake District poet. Yet there was an element of chance in his decision to move to Grasmere when he did. If he hadn't lost the lease of the Alfoxden house, thanks to his radical friends and radical habits, he would have stayed there much longer. He was happy enough in the West Country, living with Dorothy at last, writing away excitedly with Coleridge. Even when they lost that house, their thoughts had turned to Germany, not to the Lakes.

William was homeless, in the sense of no longer having a family home or any family ties in the Lakes, and free to go anywhere. The original plan had been for a two-year stay in Germany. Coleridge, at least, thought they would eventually all end up back in the West Country. It was William's dreadful homesickness in Germany, which turned his mind back to his youth, that seems to have decided him to return to the north of England. He'd never felt like that in France, but then he had other things to occupy himself with in Orleans and Blois. But if any other suggestions or possibilities had turned up after Germany, who knows where he might have gone.

He returned to the Lakes on the very stroke of a new century and spent the rest of his life there, but for several years, as can be seen from his letters, he did not believe he had returned to the Lakes for good and ever. He had now definitely decided that his purpose in life was to write poetry (unlike Coleridge, who was still involved with differing projects), but he didn't necessarily consider that the only place he could write his poetry would be the Lakes. It was events which kept him there, till he realized, deep down, that this was where he belonged.

He had been led into the West Country and into the German adventure by other people's whims. The Lakes had been his personal choice. Now, in his thirtieth year, though he might not have been aware of it, he was beginning, just ever so slightly, to settle down. . . .

William did not approve of some of the things he saw on his return. On his tour of rediscovery with Coleridge in the autumn of 1799, he was appalled by the new developments and the growth of tourism in the previous ten years. Almost two hundred years later, when people go back to the Lakes after a short absence and see more cars and more people, they are still being appalled, maintaining things have been ruined. In Wordsworth's case, he could make such statements with even greater truth, since he had seen the Lakes in their virgin state.

'Went on the ferry – a cold passage – and were much disgusted with the New Erections and objects about Windermere,' William wrote to Dorothy. 'Thence to Hawkshead – great change amongst the People since we were last there.'

Although Coleridge had never seen the Lakes before, he agreed with his companion's opinion that the vandals had arrived. Coleridge always kept a notebook on his journeys, and though most of the entries are little more than rough jottings, his comments are often lively and amusing. 'The Damned Scoundrel on the right hand with his house and barn built to represent a Chapel. His name is Partridge from London. This *Fowl* is a stocking weaver by trade. . . .' On Derwentwater, they heard about a wealthy eccentric called Colonel Pocklington who'd built himself a mock ruin on an island in the middle of the lake, following the contemporary fashion for Gothic follies. Coleridge noted: 'Pocklington has taken off the steeple of the mock church. Ey! Ey! Turned my church to a Presbyterian Meeting. Pocklington shaved off the Branches of an oak, whitewashed and shaped it into an Obelisk. Art Beats Nature....' When they got to the prehistoric Castlerigg Stone Circles near Keswick, they found that some hooligans had beaten them to it. The stones had been painted with whitewash, so that they looked like 'an assembly of white-vested Wizards'. As Coleridge commented, 'The Keswickians have been playing Tricks with the stone.'

Coleridge was nonetheless genuinely enthralled by the Lakes and his notebooks are scattered with comments like 'O, God, what a scene!', which might not be very original but was heart-felt. He noticed one day some lady tourists deep in their copy of Gilpin – one of the earliest travel books on the Lakes, which Wordsworth and most educated people had read: 'Ladies reading Gilpin while passing by the very places instead of looking at the places....'

As well as introducing Coleridge to the sights of Lakeland, Wordsworth also fitted in visits to some of their old friends. They went to see the Clarksons at Ullswater, where they'd recently built a house. Thomas Clarkson was a leader of the anti-slavery movement, while his young wife Catherine became one of Dorothy's closest correspondents.

'I must tell you that we had a visit from Coleridge and W. Wordsworth who spent a whole day with us,' wrote Mrs Clarkson in a letter to Priscilla Lloyd, sister of Charles Lloyd, Coleridge's friend. 'C. was in high Spirits and talk'd a great deal. W. was more reserved but there was neither hauteur nor moroseness in his Reserve. He was a fine commanding figure and looks as if he was born to be a great prince or a great general. He seems very fond of C. laughing at all his jokes and taking all opportunities of showing him off and to crown all, he has the manners of a gentleman.'

Wordsworth was delighted by Coleridge's genuine enthusiasm for the whole Lake District and it reinforced his own desire to live in the Lakes. 'Coleridge enchanted with Grasmere and Rydal,' William explained in a letter to Dorothy. 'You will think my plan a mad one, but I have thought of building a house there by the Lakeside. John [their sailor brother] would give me £40 to buy the ground and for £250 I am sure I could build one as good as we can wish. We shall talk of this.... I have much to say to you.'

They never did build a house for themselves, but instead they took the little cottage in Grasmere which they had seen some time earlier; a modest little dwelling (available at a rent of only £8 a year, a third the rent of Alfoxden) which the world now knows as Dove Cottage.

William and Dorothy never knew it as Dove Cottage. It didn't have a name. Their address was simply Town End, Grasmere, the name for a little group of cottages on the road outside the village itself, at the end of the town. Much earlier, their cottage had been a pub, the 'Dove and Olive Branch', which is where its later name came from. It must have been a good spot for a pub, being on the main route from Ambleside, part of the last group of cottages which the traveller heading for Keswick would pass before he starts hitting the high land over Dunmail Raise. The Wordsworths were for ever getting beggars and old soldiers and pedlars calling at their door, hoping for a crust or a few pennies, and they were usually lucky.

It was their first unfurnished premises – Racedown and Alfoxden were furnished – so Dorothy, determined to make it into *her* home, had good fun buying furniture and materials at Kendal. 'We were young and healthy and had obtained an object long desired, we had returned to our native mountains, there to live; so we cared not for any annoyances that a little exertion on our parts would not speedily remove.'

The cottage was basically three up and three down, plus a buttery downstairs and a little box-room upstairs. Dorothy's bedroom was downstairs, next to the front parlour-kitchen, a panelled room which you entered straight from the front door. William slept upstairs, next door to their sitting-room, used for entertaining, which had been chosen as such because it had the best fire. 'The chimney draws perfectly,' wrote William, 'and does not smoke at the first lighting of the fire.' Keeping warm and draught-free was the biggest bugbear of every Lakeland house – and still is – and as the cottage's heat came from the fire, it meant that if by chance you were stuck with a bad fire, which didn't draw or smoked, you might as well leave home. Dorothy lined the little box-room with newspapers, as it didn't have a fire or a proper ceiling, hoping that would help to keep it warm. She did most of the decorating and made most of the furnishings herself, sewing and cleaning all day long, and was scarcely out of doors during the first few weeks. 'One evening I tempted her out,' wrote William, 'but I had reason to repent of having seduced her from her work as she returned with raging tooth ache.'

Dorothy loved the house, and wrote ecstatic letters to her old Halifax friend Jane, now Mrs Marshall. 'The only objection we have to our house is that it is rather too near the road and from its smallness and the manner in which it is built, noises pass from one part of the house to the other.' However, they planted roses and honeysuckle against the cottage walls and enclosed the few yards of open ground at the front, roping it in as their front garden and separating themselves a bit more from the road. Their greatest success was their back garden. Even today, you can imagine what an exciting challenge it must have been. Basically, it is little more than the bottom of a hill, a steep slope which goes straight up from the back door. It contained a few old trees, which they grandly referred to as the orchard, and at the top Dorothy could see in her mind's eye a little summer-house where they would sit of a summer's evening. Together, they eventually built a little hut, made of moss, and planted the whole back garden, despite the slope, with wild mountain flowers, ferns and plants. From the hut, they got perfect views over the roof of their cottage, right across Grasmere to the lake and the surrounding fells, such as Silver Howe.

William's main contribution in the first few weeks was to go and buy himself some ice skates, determined to relive his boyhood fantasies. They'd moved in during the last few days of December 1799, and their two adjacent little lakes – Grasmere and Rydal – were both frozen. 'Rydal is covered with ice, clear as polished steel, and tomorrow I mean to give my body to the wind.' They also had the use of a boat on Grasmere, which, when the ice melted, made possible other outings, such as fishing, which William loved, or picnicking on the little island in the middle of the lake.

Although William didn't do much inside the house, where Dorothy was in charge of all cooking, baking, sewing, washing and ironing, he was quite useful outside, digging the garden, planting runner-beans, cleaning the well, fetching and cutting firewood. Together, with their domestic duties done, they went for walks round the two little lakes opposite, up the slopes of Nab Scar behind them, or through the village of Grasmere and up the secret valley of Easedale, past the waterfalls and up to the tarn. It was a huge delight when they discovered Easedale, which remained for ever a favourite walk. Morning and evening they would go on such two- and three-hour jaunts as part of their daily routine, but they also did longer walks, over the mountain slopes of Helvellyn to Keswick, to Ullswater to see friends, or just to look for a particular sheep fold, because William wanted to describe one in a poem. Their meals were simple, porridge being the most regular item, plus boiled mutton now and again or home-made pies. As Dorothy often remarked, their life was 'plain living and high thinking'.

Their neighbours were friendly: local craftsmen and small-time statesmen, few of them educated or middle-class, except for one, a retired clergyman. 'We are very comfortably situated with respect to neighbours of the lower classes,' wrote Dorothy. 'They are excellent people, friendly in performing all offices of kindness and humanity and attentive to us without servility – if we were sick they could wait upon us night and day.'

They don't seem to have had any of the Alfoxden problems; nobody wondered whether they really were brother and sister or whether they were secret, radical agitators. The locals far exceeded William's expectations; he pronounced them 'little adulterated'. Being unsophisticated, they took Dorothy and William at face-value and welcomed them, noting their thrifty habits and their outdoor activities. No doubt the Wordsworths soon made it known that they were in fact natives of Cumberland, despite their wanderings in the south, which must have helped their acceptance. They took on a daily woman, Molly Fisher, partly inheriting her, and keeping her on out of charity as she was a bit simple and not much good in the house, but they became devoted to her, and she to them.

Many of the local families still did home weaving and spinning (these were the last of the cottage-industry days, before it all moved south to the Lancashire factories), and in the evenings, coming back from their twilight walks, they would see their neighbours' daughters, sitting at their spinning-wheels by candlelight. There wasn't much affluence, as the Industrial Revolution was having a bad effect on the little farmers, taking away their labourers and their side-lines, like weaving; but most of the neighbours still managed to employ a servant or two, as the Wordsworths did with their Molly. Domestic servants rarely earned above £2 a year, or up to £5 for a man, so they were cheap to hire, though they had to be fed. All the local families, servants included, ate round one communal oak table, a table so big that the carpenter had usually built it inside the room. All the men wore clogs and homespun coats for their everyday life, farmers and servants alike. They'd gather in the evening round the peat or log fires – coals, if they could afford it and if the carrier had got through – with their mobcaps on. Even if your fire didn't smoke, you could still get covered with soot and smutty drops. Local ale, usually home-brewed, was drunk with most meals, including breakfast. Though William drank water rather than ale, he would take a glass if he was out visiting and the host pressed it upon him. The front room, the parlour which you entered from the front door, was the focal point in all these Lakeland farmhouses, where the fire was kept on, night and day. The Wordsworths were a bit different in allocating an upstairs room as an extra sitting-room, making it more a withdrawing room in the Southern style. But then, in the early days at Dove Cottage there were often just the two of them, before the visitors and others arrived and so they could apportion the rooms as they liked.

They had visitors almost from the beginning, their first being their brother John who came in January and stayed till September, though he went off elsewhere on occasional visits. He had joined William and Coleridge on part of their Lakeland tour the previous autumn – Coleridge had been very impressed by him. 'Your brother John is one of you; a man who hath solitary musings of his own intellect, deep in feeling, with a subtle tact, a swift instinct of truth and beauty, he interests me much.' He was the quiet, introverted one of the family, with Dorothy's sensitivities though without her effervescence and liveliness, and so it's surprising, in a way, that he should have taken up such a tough and brutal life as a sailor's. These were the days of press-gangs, lashings and ill treatment, though the officers were naturally of a more gentlemanly breed than hitherto. John was now approaching twenty-eight and had proved a great success in his chosen career, having climbed from fifth mate up to first mate. He was about to take up the captaincy of the *Earl of Abergavenny*, an East Indian ship which had had family connections. Their cousin, another Captain Wordsworth, had previously been the master.

Despite his naval success, John's ambition was to make as much money as quickly as he could by investing in his cargoes, as was the custom of the time, and then to retire to Grasmere. He'd already done well, having saved enough money for William to contemplate borrowing £40 from him for the plot for his proposed house, but he wanted to have sufficient to build his own house, near to theirs. Most of all, he wanted to be able to give money to William to help him devote himself to poetry. With his new and important position, he looked well set to achieve these ambitions.

Mary Hutchinson and then her sister Sarah came next, while John was still there, and stayed for several weeks. John was very close to both of them. William himself was friendly with both sisters, and although he and John went in turn to visit them at their farm in Yorkshire, William at least had 'no thoughts of marrying'.

Charles Lloyd and his wife became their neighbours, not completely welcome ones, moving into a house near Ambleside not long after the Wordsworths had arrived in Grasmere. He was the wealthy young friend and pupil of Coleridge whom they'd first met in the West Country. (He was a member of the Lloyds banking family.) Lloyd had rather fallen out with Coleridge after he'd published a novel, dedicated to Lamb, in which Coleridge felt he'd been ridiculed. Lloyd, Lamb and Southey felt Coleridge had started it all by parodying their poetic style in some sonnets. Lloyd was something of a lame duck, suffering from epilepsy and mental depressions, but he and the Wordsworths kept up a regular if lukewarm connection for many years, visiting each other's homes for tea and literary conversations. There weren't after all many literary people in their immediate neighbourhood in the early days. They had a further connection when the youngest Wordsworth brother Christopher – who had done brilliantly at Cambridge, where he'd become a Fellow and was now ordained – became engaged to Lloyd's sister Priscilla.

'We have not any society except the Wordsworths,' wrote Lloyd to a friend in January 1801. 'They are very unusual characters – indeed Miss Wordsworth I much like – but her Brother is not a man after my own heart – I always feel depressed in his society.'

The most important visitor, the number one friend in their life, was of course Coleridge. He had returned to his family in the West Country but came in April to visit them at Dove Cottage and decided then to live in the Lakes. Dorothy found him a house to let at Keswick, Greta Hall; he brought his pregnant wife and son Hartley up from Somerset and they moved in.

Greta Hall was, and is, a large, handsome mansion on high ground, overlooking Derwentwater. The Coleridges rented only half of it, the rest being occupied by its owner, a wealthy carrier; but the accommodation was vastly superior to their little Somerset cottage – an old hovel, as Coleridge had described it. The positions were now reversed, with the Wordsworths living in a humble cottage and Coleridge having the smarter address. Not that it mattered, since Coleridge was hardly ever

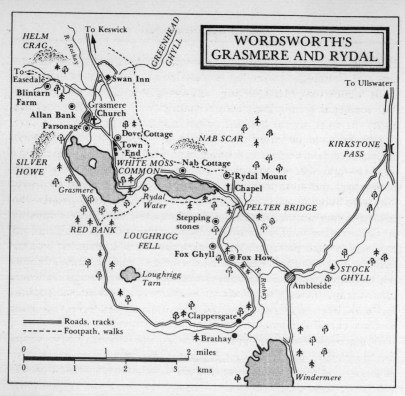

there. He was constantly walking the thirteen miles from Keswick to Grasmere – a long and steep walk at the best of times, even without taking in Helvellyn on the way, as he sometimes did. He'd come to Dove Cottage for tea, or arrive late at night when they were all in bed, and stay for weeks. He'd bring some poem or other piece of writing, and Dorothy would get up and make some porridge while William put on his dressing-gown and listened, then in turn read his own latest pieces of poetry.

During these early years at Dove Cottage, they often lived and moved like one close-knit little club, with their own jokes and references. They had their own names for special places, such as Sarah's seat or John's grove. On one rock, on the road across to Keswick, which all of them frequently used, they carved their initials: WW, MH, DW, STC, JW, SH. They stood for William Wordsworth, Mary Hutchinson, Dorothy Wordsworth, Samuel Taylor Coleridge, John Wordsworth and Sarah Hutchinson. (The rock was dynamited during road-widening, and only fragments survive, but a painting of it hangs in Dove Cottage today.)

This shows the strong friendship between the Wordsworths, Hutchinsons and Coleridge – three ladies and three men, a perfect little unit – but notice that Mrs Coleridge is missing. She didn't go in for all this nocturnal wandering, these romantic musings, poetry readings under the trees, by the lakeside or behind rocks. It's hard to be sure how the sixsome paired off, if they ever did – Dorothy was very fond of Coleridge, who was especially fond of Sarah Hutchinson, who in turn was very fond of John Wordsworth. They were really all in love with each other, and all in love with themselves. As in the West Country, they were living an early version of a drop-out life: young people who refused to take up the conventional middle-class occupations, moving around, staying in cheap rented premises, living off the land and off their wits (and off pieces of writing when they could manage it), getting hand-outs from their friends or relations, endlessly discussing and arguing about their philosophical or political views. There was also the overtone of drugs – at least, with Coleridge, who had started off using opium for illness, but now increasingly took it to make himself feel better when he was generally depressed.

William and Coleridge had been living this sort of embryo hippy life for the previous ten years, since they'd left Cambridge, but in William's case it was beginning to seem a little unreal. Coleridge was still full of plans for further moves, new settlements and re-groupings in Europe or the West Indies, but William's life at Dove Cottage was becoming much more regular than it had been in the West Country. He had rushed his first two publications through to earn money for a specific purpose and had then turned to other activities, but now he was writing all the time. He'd become a professional poet. From the first months at Dove Cottage, he decided to be more wary of spongers and his rule became: 'If you like to have a cup of tea with us, you are very welcome; but if you want any meat, you must pay for your board.'

Coleridge wasn't exactly a sponger, though he was very keen on people sharing according to their means. (When he and Southey had shared lodgings in Bristol, he had paid only a third of the rent, on the grounds that Southey was earning twice as much as he was.)

Coleridge's health, however, was becoming a serious problem, and he would often spend weeks ill in bed in Dove Cottage, with Dorothy having to nurse him, fearing for his life. One of his complaints seems to have been rheumatism, the causes of which he traced back to his childhood. He once spent the night alone in some damp fields, having had a row with his brother and run away. He still took silly risks with his health, like swimming rivers and then keeping on his wet clothes, or deliberately spending nights on misty hillsides. He also suffered from gout and neuritis. When his health was good, which it certainly was for long spells, he did the most amazing walks and mountain climbs all round the Lakes single-handed. He was in effect the first of the modern fell walkers, the first known outsider to set out to climb the mountain tops, just for the pleasure of doing so. His ascent in 1802 of Scafell Pike, the highest Lakeland peak, is the first recorded climb of that magnificent mountain. He took pen and ink up Scafell, and wrote in his notebook and composed a letter to Sarah Hutchinson, and then rushed madly down again, avoiding the easy ways.

His marriage, alas, was finally collapsing. Yet he loved his children. Two others were born after he moved to Greta Hall: Derwent in 1800 (named after the river) and Sara in 1802. He got it into his head that he was passionately in love with Sarah Hutchinson, and she, for a time, seems to have returned some of his affection, though one has to presume, for want of any evidence, that the affair was completely chaste. One of her sisters, Joanna, was very disappointed when she met Coleridge, having been given a glowing description of him by Sarah. She much preferred William, finding him much more 'canny a man', even if he wasn't handsome.

Sara Coleridge usually comes out of all this very badly. The Words-worths, especially Dorothy, tended to give her a bad press, agreeing with Coleridge's opinion of her as a shrew and a complainer, interested only in her domestic life and her babies, and not interested in him, his writing or his friends. (Incidentally, to avoid confusion, I've spelt Sarah Hutchinson throughout this book with an 'h', which is how the name appeared on her gravestone, though it was often spelt Sara as well.)

'She would have made a very good wife to many another man, but for Coleridge!!,' so Dorothy wrote about Sara Coleridge after she and William had been to stay with the Coleridges at Greta Hall. 'Her radical fault is want of sensibility and what can such a woman be to Coleridge. She is an excellent nurse to her sucking children – I mean to the best of her skill, for she employs her time often foolishly enough about them. Derwent is a sweet lovely Fatty – she suckles him entirely – he has no other food. She is sure to be a sad fiddle faddler.' Almost every remark about Mrs Coleridge in Dorothy's letters is either bitchy or critical; at one point she calls her 'the lightest weakest silliest woman'. Considering Dorothy hadn't experienced childbirth herself, she had rather set herself up as an expert on child-rearing. Dorothy was always forthright in her private letters, but rarely nasty and unfair, so perhaps Mrs Coleridge did deserve some of the blame for the collapse of the marriage. But, though she did seem unable to nurse Coleridge through his mental and physical troubles, imagined or otherwise, she was by no means stupid or uneducated. Coleridge and Southey, after all, wouldn't have chosen completely unsuitable partners for their Susquehanna enterprise. As her children grew up, Sara Coleridge proved an excellent mother, teaching them French and mathematics and providing some of the intellectual stimulus which Coleridge would have given them, had he stayed at home.

Mrs Coleridge has to be pitied slightly – left behind while they were all in Germany, then dragged up to the Lakes, away from her home area and friends, with no personal desire to follow the Wordsworths, whose life style, nocturnal wanderings, shabby clothes, uncivilized habits, lack of gentility and unpunctuality she disapproved of. When she got to the Lakes, she had babies to suckle and could not suddenly be available for three-day hikes over the mountains. It was all right for Dorothy. She could up and go when asked.

Coleridge was planning a great philosophical book, while being employed, ostensibly, as a journalist. He'd managed to get a retainer of sorts from the *Morning Post*, writing reviews, articles and poetry, though William often helped him, contributing some anonymous verse when Coleridge fell behind with his commitments. Daniel Stuart, editor of the *Morning Post*, was a personal friend of both William and Coleridge, and William might have made a little money that way, if he'd wanted to. Dorothy was against William doing any such journalism, and even fretted when William started 'wasting his mind in the magazines'. Coleridge was an excellent journalist, able to turn his hand to most sorts of article, and was in demand as a 'writer-up' of parliamentary debates. It was a legal rule of the day that speeches could not be reported verbatim, but it was Samuel Johnson who had perfected a system of rewriting the main points of a speech in new words, doing it so elegantly that the speakers themselves were pleased to acknowledge them as their own.

Coleridge was an expert at this and could produce a Pitt speech often better than Pitt himself. He tended to do this sort of journalism in the winter, when he usually spent a few months in London, away from the worst of the Lakeland weather, but he was a little ashamed of his facility. His old West Country friend Poole was very disapproving. Being a clever journalist had no more social standing then than it has today – though it could pay well, for the right people.

Coleridge decided to try to persuade Southey to follow him to the Lakes, an arrangement which he thought would help with his own family commitments. They'd patched up their quarrel and were now friends again. Southey had abandoned his idea of reading for the bar and getting a steady job, and he too was now concentrating full-time on being a writer. Coleridge wrote glowing letters and reports of the marvellous life they were all having in Keswick: the terrific views from the windows, the marvellous walks. He even got Southey to go off on a three-day exploratory hike across Skiddaw and round the northern fells, but Southey gave in after the first night, when they'd only reached Caldbeck. However, he eventually moved into Greta Hall with his family in 1803, soon finding that he was also expected to be responsible for Coleridge's family, as Coleridge wandered off to be with his real friends.

Coleridge's devotion to William's genius didn't waver, but it began to have a negative effect on his own poetic ambitions. 'I abandon poetry altogether,' he eventually wrote to a friend. 'I leave the higher and deeper kinds to Wordsworth, the delightful, popular and simply digni-fied to Southey, and reserve for myself the honourable attempt to make others feel and understand their writings, and they deserve to be felt.'

It was a mark of true friendship and devotion, to subordinate his own aspiration to a friend's. In the long run, he did more than anyone else to give Wordsworth the reputation he has today, forcing people to think carefully about his poems, leading them to a proper under-standing, defending him, in books and articles, letters and conversa-tions, against the mockers and the ridiculers. But Coleridge's immediate help took a practical form. He threw himself into the task of helping Wordsworth see through the press a new edition of *Lyrical Ballads*.

Cottle had miscalculated, as publishers so often do. He'd been too quick to sell off the bulk of the first edition of five hundred copies of *Lyrical Ballads* as remainders – and at a loss. The first three reviews were so bad that they would have put off any likely buyers. But about a year after publication, in the summer and autumn of 1799, two more reviews suddenly appeared, both of them very long and very fulsome, talking of the poet's 'genius and originality ... and many excellences'. The books had also been advertised by the new distributor; sales started to jump and the whole stock was quickly sold.

The first of these good reviews, in the *British Critic*, appears to have been written by one of William's friends, but whatever the personal background, there had been a slight public unease at the viciousness of the early reviews – although being vicious was part of the style of the times – and many people thought the reviewers had gone too far, especially when it was known that Southey had a personal grudge against Coleridge. Even Southey himself had begun to regret being so harsh.

The delayed success proved what Dorothy had thought all along. 'The first volume sold so much better than we expected and was liked by a much greater number of people; not that we had ever much doubt of its finally making its way; but we knew that poems so different from what have in general become popular immediately after publication, were not likely to be admired all at once.'

Longmans came to William and offered him £80 for a new two-volume edition of *Lyrical Ballads*. They planned to reprint seven hundred and fifty copies of the first edition and a thousand copies of a second volume (which would contain new poems), bringing them out as companion volumes, although the second volume could be bought separately. It was a handsome offer, the best William had received so far, and he was hard at work throughout 1800, producing enough new poems. Coleridge originally planned to finish his poem 'Christabel' in order to include it; but he didn't after all, concentrating instead on helping Wordsworth to get ready about forty of his new poems for the second volume, and insisting that only Wordsworth's name should appear in either volume, even though his own work, 'The Ancient Mariner', was still to be included in the first volume.

The volumes were printed in Bristol, though they were to be published by Longmans in London, and Coleridge got their young Bristol friend, Humphry Davy, still only twenty-two, to do the final proof-checking and seeing through the press. Davy, though emerging as a brilliant chemist, was also an amateur poet and writer. William gave him instructions to keep an eye on the punctuation, saying that he could make any changes to it that he thought fit, since William himself wasn't very good at punctuation.

The new poems in the second volume included 'Strange fits of passion', and some other Lucy poems (the ones written in Germany); 'The Brothers' (a poem based on the story of the death of a shepherd in Ennerdale, told to William and Coleridge during their Lakes tour); 'Nutting', 'Michael', 'Ruth' and others.

The new edition of *Lyrical Ballads* appeared in January 1801, and received limited but very warm acclaim. There was a short review in the *Monthly Review* and then an enormously long and favourable one in the *British Critic*. This again appears to have been written by a friend, but it was a most professional review, going through almost every poem, point by point. Literary circles are always fairly small, in every age, and when a writer has had a few works published, he knows, or knows of, most other people in the same field, which of course can either be a help or a hindrance. Wordsworth and Coleridge, closely followed by Southey, had apparently cut themselves off in the wilds of Lakeland, but, by their university education and early London life, they were known to many people in the London literary world.

Although only two reviews appeared, there was a great deal of talk and excitement, with people telling their friends which poems they liked best. Even Southey had now come to appreciate them, writing to a friend that he found 'The Brothers' and 'Michael' 'to my taste excellent.... I have never been so much affected and so well, as by some passages there.'

It is a little harder to decide what Charles Lamb thought, as he wrote rather teasing letters to friends, poking fun at William and Coleridge behind their backs. William, Dorothy and Coleridge all valued Lamb's opinion, as he was a vital and influential member of the younger literary circle, and William had at once sent him a copy. Lamb replied at great length, giving his detailed criticisms, and deciding that on balance he preferred the first volume. William at once jumped to the defence of the new poems, which highly amused Lamb. Writing to another friend in February 1801, he describes the whole affair with typical Lamb wit.

So you don't think there's a Word's-worth of good poetry in the great L.B.? I daren't put the dreaded syllables at their just length.... Between you and me the L. Ballads are but drowsy performances....

I had need be cautious henceforward what opinion I give. All the North of England are in a turmoil. Cumberland and Westmoreland have already declared a state of war. I lately received from Wordsworth a copy of the second volume, with excuses owing to an 'almost insurmountable aversion from Letter-writing'. This letter I answered in due form and time, and enumerated several passages which had most affected me, adding, unfortunately, that no single piece had moved me so forcibly as the 'Ancient Mariner', 'The Mad Mother' or the 'Lines at Tintern Abbey'. The Post did not sleep a moment. I received almost instantaneously a long letter of four sweating pages from my Reluctant Letter-Writer, the purport of which was that he was sorry his 2nd volume had not given me more pleasure. (Devil a hint did I give that it had *not* pleased me) and was 'compelled to wish that my range of sensibility was more extended, being obliged to believe that I should receive large influxes of happiness and happy thoughts' (I suppose from the LB)....

This was not to be *all* my castigation. Coleridge, who had not written to me for some months before, starts up from his bed of sickness to reprove me for my hardy presumption; four long pages equally sweaty and more tedious, came from him; assuring me that when the works of a man of true genius, such as W. undoubtedly was, do not please me at first sight, I should suspect the fault to lie 'in me and not in them', etc, etc, etc, etc, etc. What am I to do with such people? I shall certainly write them a very merry letter.

Lamb might have been having sport with William and Coleridge and their heavy seriousness, but he genuinely admired much that William had written, as did many of their contemporaries. So much so, that the two volumes were reprinted the following year, 1802, and again in 1805.

There was no recognition of these early editions of *Lyrical Ballads* in the *Edinburgh Review*, which was founded in 1802 and quickly became the most powerful voice in English literary criticism. It was begun by a group of young Edinburgh liberals, notably Francis Jeffrey (its famous editor), Sydney Smith and Henry Brougham, and built its reputation on its savage reviews. Many of the great nineteenth-century writers, such as Scott, Macaulay and Matthew Arnold, later became contributors. The editors were well aware of the growing success of *Lyrical Ballads*, but chose to ignore it, apparently because of what they considered the conceit of William's Preface.

He had written a short introduction, which he called an 'Advertisement', for the first edition, back in 1798; it was here that he described the poems as 'experiments'. But he went to town with the two-volume edition, producing a six-thousand-word Preface which in the end did him, and his poems, more harm than good. On their walks, Coleridge had spent hours and hours discussing the philosophy of poetry with William, as had other literary friends, like Hazlitt, but these conversations usually ended in some acrimony, with William laying down the law on what poetry should be all about. Coleridge knew about the new Preface, but he later said it was all Wordsworth's doing – while William later said he'd written it out of good nature, because of a request from Coleridge.

The Preface made William many unnecessary enemies, prejudicing several writers against him for ever, just because he was foolhardy enough to try to dictate what was and what was not poetry, but it is a document which has endless fascination for all students of Wordsworth. This is not the place to discuss it properly, as our concern is with the main narrative of William's life, but it can't be ignored completely, as it is considered the first example in the history of English literature of a creative artist trying to analyse his own creative methods. Here Wordsworth was in many ways a hundred years ahead of his time – as he was in his self-analysis in *The Prelude*, which in many of its childhood insights pre-dated Freud.

Today, the study of 'creative writing', and all the analysis that goes with it, is seen as a serious and proper subject, especially in the American universities. But back in the 1800s, the majority of young literary men thought William's analysis, in his Preface, was the height of pretension and conceit, not to say gibberish. Byron, after he had read it, considered Wordsworth an idiot, as daft as his 'Idiot Woman with her Idiot Boy'.

The most quoted line in the Preface concerns his definition of poetry as 'emotion recollected in tranquillity'. On reading the passage fully, I realized that I, for one, had never fully understood Wordsworth's meaning. Over the passage of time, only the first half of his theory has survived to be quoted. But in fact Wordsworth goes on to include several more stages in the act of creation:

Poetry takes its origins from emotion recollected in tranquillity: the emotion is contemplated till, by a species of reaction, the tranquillity gradually disappears, and an emotion, kindred to that which was before the subject of contemplation, is gradually produced, and does itself actually exist in the mind. In this mood, successful composition generally begins ... so that in describing any passions whatsoever, the mind will, upon the whole, be in a state of enjoyment.

In other words, if I now understand Wordsworth correctly, the tranquil stage *disappears* when the moment of writing begins, with the original excitement and enjoyment being recaptured in the act of writing. A great many creative writers today would agree that this is true, though there are examples of different writers going through different stages of composition, experiencing different creative processes.

It is an indication of Wordsworth's character that, when he did come to his conclusion, he should think it defined the nature of all poetry, once and for all. What it defined was Wordsworth's creative process. For that alone, we should be grateful.

William did something else that was new for him with this two-volume edition, something almost all writers have done at some stage, though it was rather surprising in William, considering what we know of his character and habits so far. He sent off a series of complimentary copies of the edition to eminent people of the day, such as the Duchess of Devonshire, William Wilberforce and Charles James Fox. With the presentation copies went a signed letter from William, full of the most toadying sentiments, flattering the recipients in a desperate bid for their favour and patronage. Apparently this idea had come from Coleridge, who wanted to act as William's public relations man, and Coleridge actually dictated many of the letters. But the letter to Fox was definitely written by William himself and was utterly obsequious in tone: 'In common with the whole English People I have observed in your public character a constant predominance of sensibility of heart. . . . This habit cannot but have made you dear to Poets; and I am sure that if since your first entrance into public life there has been a single true poet living in England, he must have loved you.'

It is hard to imagine William having written such a letter just ten years previously – William, the young rebel who went his own way, who hated the wealthy and powerful (especially aristocrats and politicians), who had actively refused all help, all contacts with people who might do him some good. He was older now, approaching thirty-one, either wiser or perhaps more worldly, knowing that, though your heart might be in the right place and that ideally you want your work to be taken only on its own merits, every little helps, every string is worth pulling. A professional poet has to be willing to be professional in every sense and push his product. It was the first time that William deliberately made an attempt to keep in with the rich and famous – a significant, but perhaps inevitable, reversal of previous attitudes.

Every little did help. Even the Queen bought a copy of *Lyrical Ballads* and gave it as a present to a friend – so William was told when he was taken out to dinner one evening, at the 'Royal Oak' in Keswick, by a visiting lordling. It also resulted in what appears to have been his first fan letter, in May 1802, from a seventeen-year-old Glasgow University undergraduate, John Wilson, who said that he and the rest of mankind were indebted for such poetry as *Lyrical Ballads*, though he did gently suggest that the subject of 'The Idiot Boy' wasn't quite to his own personal taste. William wrote back, starting off by saying that he didn't write letters: 'Partly from a weakness in my stomach and digestion and partly from certain habits of mind I do not write any letters unless upon business, not even to my dearest Friends. Except during absence from my own family, I have not written five letters during the last five years.' Having cleared his chest, and his conscience, of all that, William then went on to write a 2,500-word letter, putting the unknown young man right about 'The Idiot Boy' and about poetry in general.

William was pleased by the many praising comments he received, especially from young people, but even with adverse comments, he could always comfort himself by saying he was writing for posterity, which was true. He never wrote for immediate fame, though he might have written for immediate money. He agreed with Coleridge, who saw him as a figure striding so far ahead of his contemporaries that they could hardly see him in the distance. *The Prelude*, which he returned to at Dove Cottage, was from the very beginning planned to be published after his death. You can look upon that as the height of conceit, or as the ultimate in modesty.

Lyrical Ballads did at last make his name in many important circles, though he was still not known nationally. By the standards of the day, the book had a good reception, was well loved by many young people, and the new edition quickly sold out, with Longmans eager for not just another reprint but for more new poems – poems which William was already busily writing.

These early Dove Cottage years, from 1800 until about 1805, were Wordsworth's greatest creative years. He was working at high speed and in a state of great excitement, producing scores of poems of unarguable genius, such as the 'Immortality' ode, or nature poems of a simpler, less philosophical nature, such as 'Daffodils'.

Although the *Edinburgh Review* did not review *Lyrical Ballads* directly, they took the opportunity to have a side-swipe at Wordsworth, and especially his Preface, when ostensibly reviewing Southey's *Thalaba* in October 1802. They lumped Southey with his brother-in-law Coleridge, and with Wordsworth, and together christened them dismissively as the Lake Poets. It was something of a literary liberty, as Southey at the time had no connection with Wordsworth – least of all in his poetry – nor could Coleridge's poetry be said to be similar to Wordsworth's. However, this was the first time the phrase was used – and it stuck for ever.

Southey didn't mind. 'I am well pleased to be abused with Coleridge and Wordsworth. It is the best omen that I shall be remembered with them.' Two years later, he went further. 'Wordsworth will do better than Coleridge and leave behind him a name, unique in his way; he will rank among the very first poets and probably possess a mass of merit superior to all except only Shakespeare.'

LUCY

Some verses from the Lucy poems, written in Germany in 1798–9 and published in the 1800 edition of Lyrical Ballads.

STRANGE fits of passion have I known:
And I will dare to tell,
But in the Lover's ear alone,
What once to me befell.

When she I loved looked every day
Fresh as a rose in June,
I to her cottage bent my way,
Beneath an evening-moon.

What fond and wayward thoughts will slide
Into a Lover's head!
'O mercy!' to myself I cried,
'If Lucy should be dead!'

SHE dwelt among the untrodden ways
  Beside the springs of Dove,
A Maid whom there were none to praise
  And very few to love:

A violet by a mossy stone
  Half hidden from the eye!
– Fair as a star, when only one
  Is shining in the sky.

She lived unknown, and few could know
  When Lucy ceased to be;
But she is in her grave, and, oh,
  The difference to me!

A SLUMBER did my spirit seal;
  I had no human fears:
She seemed a thing that could not feel
  The touch of earthly years

No motion has she now, no force;
  She neither hears nor sees;
Rolled round in earth's diurnal course
  With rocks, and stones, and trees.

9

Dorothy and Wedded Bliss
1802

DOROTHY WORDSWORTH was a remarkable woman. Most
remarkable women, even the wealthy, lived unfulfilled lives in the nineteenth century. There was no formal education for girls; and no careers
were open to them. Their duty was to be subservient – to their husband,
or, if they didn't marry, to their own families. There are countless
examples, as Miss Austen has shown us, of exceedingly talented and
intelligent women who, purely because they were women, were forced to
live in the shadows of stupider, untalented brothers, depending on them
for money and support. Some ladies did manage to become people in
their own right, writing elegant novels or acting on the stage but
they were the exceptions. Most women withered away, doomed to a
life in the background, forever discussing trivialities.

Dorothy devoted her life to her brother, putting herself, strictly
speaking, in the subservient role; yet, without Dorothy, would William
have been the same person? Coleridge had an exceptional intellect,
and a store of learning which helped William to form his own philosophy; his mind was like a stone on which William could sharpen his own,
rather rough-hewn mental blades. Dorothy was a spirit, a child of

nature, an unformed, inspirational, intuitive being. William discussed the abstractions of literature and life with Coleridge, benefiting from his ability to quote chapter and verse from almost every known writer from the Greeks to the moderns, from the East to the West. With Dorothy, he could share the pleasures of the humdrum – children playing, birds singing, a rainbow, a distant cuckoo, a glowworm on a leaf, the cock crowing, a butterfly, the sun rising, the sun setting – the ordinary things we all see and hear and feel every day. Dorothy was all feelings, almost extra-sensory in her perceptions, often leading William to notice things and joys which otherwise he would have missed. No brother could in turn have been more grateful to a sister:

> The Blessing of my later years
> Was with me when a boy:
> She gave me eyes, she gave me ears;
> And humble cares, and delicate fears;
> A heart, the fountain of sweet tears,
> And love, and thought, and joy.

Although Dorothy had had no education, and didn't pretend to be an intellectual, she was a great reader, assiduously improving her own mind by going through the plays of Shakespeare. When William was away, she always settled down to some edifying work, such as teaching herself French or German. She took over the correspondence with Annette, to whom she must have written in French, as Annette couldn't speak English.

Dorothy always felt deeply involved in her brother's poetry. One of those first two published volumes, *An Evening Walk*, was dedicated to her, and though she could be critical with William himself, pointing out obscure words and passages, she stoutly defended him when others dared to criticize his work. Sarah Hutchinson, for example, once ventured her opinion that she found his poem 'The Leech-gatherer' tedious. 'When you happen to be displeased with ... any poem which William writes,' wrote Dorothy in reply, 'ask yourself whether you have hit upon the real tendency and true moral, and above all, never think that he writes for no reason but merely because a thing happened – and when you feel any poem of his to be tedious, ask yourself in what spirit it was written. ...' This was the sort of defence which Lamb had mocked; but, even today, it is a good guide-line when approaching all Wordsworth's poetry.

Was Dorothy a poet herself? Many experts consider her as one. Ernest de Selincourt, the great Wordsworth expert, said she was probably 'the most remarkable and the most distinguished of English writers who never wrote a line for the general public'. He was thinking of her private *Journals* which she kept at Alfoxden and in the early Dove Cottage years, a work not published as a book until as recently as 1958. It is a book greatly loved by all Wordsworth enthusiasts, lay and professional, and until now it has usually been the best-selling book every year at the Dove Cottage bookshop. It is a pleasure to read, but, personally, I prefer Dorothy's letters. You see her thoughts and her opinions in her letters, as she sits down to tell her friend Jane, for example, about some incident, a journey, or people she has met. She has great insight into character, a strong narrative drive, a sense of humour and of the ridiculous, always vivid and colourful in her descriptions. Jane must have loved receiving the letters, and it is not surprising that she kept them, years and years before anybody was interested in knowing about Dorothy or her brother.

So much of Dorothy's *Journals*, however, is unsatisfactory. She often lists events, but rarely stands back to comment on them. Nothing is explained. You have to know what was really happening in the Wordsworths' lives to understand the sudden changes of location or of mood. The *Journals* were basically a diary, jottings written for Dorothy herself, and of course for William – not for the illumination or pleasure of outsiders. 'Dullish, damp and cloudy – a day that promises not to dry our clothes. We spent a happy evening – went to bed late and had a restless night. Wm better than expected.' That's a typical entry, picked at random, describing their activities on Friday, 13 November 1801. What was so happy about that particular evening? What made the night restless? Why had she expected William not to be better? She doesn't say. In a letter, she would have filled pages, describing such an evening's activities, even if they had turned out to consist of only a game of whist by the fireside or of more worries about William's bowels.

In her staccato style, she can go from some event we now know was vitally important, straight on to something completely mundane: 'Monday, July 28, 1800. Received a letter from Coleridge enclosing one from Mr Davy about *Lyrical Ballads*. Intensely hot. I made pies in the morning. Wm went into the wood and altered his poems.'

Fortunately, in her *Journals* she records many days which merit more than two or three disjointed lines – days in which she sits writing for longer and goes into fuller descriptions, if still without any real explanations. It is these entries that make the *Journals* so special, such a joy to read, and are endlessly fascinating, for two important reasons.

Firstly, the *Journals* provide factual evidence of how important Dorothy was to William, the poet. When William came to write a poem (having gone through his tranquil stage of reflection, which could last for anything from a few hours to a few years), he very often used the same words that Dorothy had used originally in her *Journals* to describe an incident they had both witnessed. She wasn't just a separate tool, but part of him, his amanuensis, sharing his creative force. Writers get a lot of help these days, from dictating machines to electric type-writers and computers, but it is going to be a while before someone invents a machine as efficient as Dorothy. As everyone who ever met Wordsworth always observed, lucky William. There are countless examples, but the best known is probably also the easiest to give. Here is Dorothy describing their walk along the shores of Ullswater on Thursday, 15 April 1802: 'I never saw daffodils so beautiful they grew among the mossy stones about and about them, some rested their heads upon these stones as on a pillow for weariness and the rest tossed and reeled and danced and seemed as if they verily laughed with the wind that blew upon them over the lake, they looked so gay ever glancing ever changing.'

Now compare it with the first two verses of the poem William eventually wrote, two years later:

I wandered lonely as a cloud
That floats on high o'er vales and hills,
When all at once I saw a crowd,
A host, of golden daffodils;
Beside the lake, beneath the trees,
Fluttering and dancing in the breeze.

Continuous as the stars that shine
And twinkle on the milky way,
They stretched in never-ending line
Along the margin of a bay:
Ten thousand saw I at a glance,
Tossing their heads in sprightly dance.

The second element in the *Journals* which has provided equal fascination is the light they throw on the relationship between William and Dorothy. She wasn't simply his secretary, his note-taker, his copyist; she wasn't just his pie-maker, his bed-maker, his health-watcher, his walking companion. Dorothy was more even than his critic and creative inspiration: she was his best friend. Their love for each other is what makes the relationship so extraordinary.

In those early years at Dove Cottage, they did have all those visitors, but, even so, the basic unit was William and Dorothy, sharing all the ordinary domestic pleasures. There's a nice letter from William to Coleridge – an unusually light-hearted letter, describing the more ordinary aspects of their domestic life:

It is now past ten and we are both tired so that it is an absolute *contest* of politeness, with a little brotherly kindness interspersed, which of us walk up to Fletchers [the carrier] with this Letter and the accompanying parcel. We cannot *both* go as we have suffered Molly to retire and little Hartley [Coleridge's son] cannot be left. These several displays of presence of mind in this antithetical way are highly entertaining. Dorothy is packing up a few small loaves of our American flour which I promised. It died of a very common malady, bad advice. The oven must be hot, perfectly hot said Molly the experienced, so into a piping red-hot oven it went, and came out black as a genuine child of the coal hole. In plain English, it is not a sendable article. . . .

Their life together in domestic bliss was obviously very happy. I nearly wrote 'wedded bliss'. If you didn't know they were brother and sister, the *Journals* would make you think they were married, judging by so many of Dorothy's descriptions.

After dinner I read him to sleep. I read Spenser while he leaned upon my shoulder. . . .

I went and sate with W and walked backwards and forwards in the orchard till dinner time. He read me his poem. I broiled Beefsteaks. After dinner, we made a pillow of my shoulder. I read to him and my Beloved slept. I afterwards got him the pillows and he was lying with his head on the table when Miss Simpson came in. . . .

Read Wm to sleep after dinner and read to him in bed till ½ past one. . . .

After we came in and we sate in deep silence at the window. I on a chair and William with his hand on my shoulder. We were deep in Silence and Love, a blessed hour. . . .

When William was away, Dorothy was greatly distressed, missing him dreadfully, as if her whole world had collapsed. It was on such a day, at Grasmere in May 1800, when William and their brother John had gone off on a three-week trip, that she first began her *Journal*. She decided to take refuge in it, as a means of continuing their joint life; William could read it all when he came back: to catch up on their visitors and on her impressions:

Wm and John set off into Yorkshire after dinner, cold pork in their pockets. I left them at the turning of Low wood bay under the trees. My heart was so full that I could hardly speak to W when I give him a farewell kiss. I sate a long time upon a stone at the margin of the lake, and after a flood of tears my heart was easier.... I resolved to write a Journal of the time till W and J return and I set about keeping my resolve because I will not quarrel with myself and because I shall give Wm Pleasure by it when he comes home.

Dorothy often went twice a day to Ambleside, over six miles there and back, and sometimes even further down the road, looking for the postman with letters from William. 'The post was not come in. I walked as far as Windermere [the lake, not the town] and met him there. No letters! No papers. Came home by Clappersgate [on the northern shore of the lake]. I was sadly tired, ate a hasty dinner and had a bad headache. Went to bed and slept at least two hours.' There was the utmost joy when William did return, and they sat up till four in the morning, just the two of them, and then slept till ten o'clock the next day.

On another occasion, when William was away, her desire for him was so strong that she went to his bedroom. 'Went to bed at about 12 o'clock. I slept in Wm's bed and I slept badly, for my thoughts were full of William.' He came home rather unexpectedly and when someone told her he'd been seen on the road, 'I believe I screamed.'

She was obsessed by William and he was devoted to her, loving her dearly, though his letters, such as they are, don't furnish much evidence of passion. It is in his poems that his love for Dorothy shines through, even when William is using another girl's name, such as Emmeline or Lucy, as was his normal habit. 'Strange fits of passion,' as we have seen, was written while he and Dorothy were alone together in Germany. 'Among all lovely things my Love had been ...' was inspired by Dorothy and was about an incident, the finding of a glowworm, which they experienced together.

Was there more to it than a brother–sister love? Dorothy was certainly an emotional woman, given to outbursts, laughter and tears, and great shows of affection. There are references in her letters which show she loved Coleridge, or her brother John, almost as much as William. She addressed Annette effusively, as a dear and beloved sister, without having met her.

Accepted habits and signs of affection are bound to have changed in nearly two hundred years, and we would do well not to translate everything too literally into modern terms. William and Dorothy were orphans, after all. They only had each other. Physical contact between brother and sister was more normal then than it is today.

Nonetheless, and making all allowances, it was a rather strange, not to say intense, relationship. Their love appears almost suffocating at times, though there are no references in her *Journals* to any rows, or even a cross word. We can only guess at the climaxes, the highs and the lows, from the strange clues, but there are enough of these to indicate that at times the relationship verged on the unhealthy.

Dorothy was a virgin – of that there is little doubt – and there's no reference to her ever having had a serious boy friend, in the courting sense. Coleridge loved her, calling her Wordsworth's 'exquisite sister', and so did all William's friends, each impressed by her mind and personality. Hazlitt was so enchanted by her, De Quincey later alleged, that he proposed to her, but Dorothy turned him down. Not even those who eventually fell out with William had anything nasty to say about Dorothy.

She was not physically very attractive, but in her early days that does not appear to have mattered, because her sheer physical presence was so striking. 'Her face was of Egyptian brown,' De Quincey recalled, 'rarely in a woman of English birth had I seen a more determined gipsy tan. Her eyes were not soft, but wild and startling, and hurried in their motion. Her manner was warm and ardent; her sensibility seemed constitutionally deep; and some subtle fire of impassioned intellect apparently burned within her.'

One or two friends detected similarly ardent, even animal, feelings in William himself, though the only known incident in his life involving animal passion was his sudden and passionate love affair with Annette. He at least wasn't a virgin.

Today, in this permissive, uninhibited, fully contracepted age, it would be hard to imagine a healthy, attractive young single man staying celibate for ten years, from the age of twenty-two to thirty-two, unless he was a monk who'd taken vows or was homosexual. In ten long years, in the prime of his life, when he'd already had one passionate sexual affair, how could he have managed it? would be the modern reaction. He certainly met girls, entertained girls, visited houses where girls were living, admired a pretty face, and was well aware of the sisters of his male friends; but there's not the slightest sign, so far, of any serious relationship since the Annette affair. We have to believe, then, that for ten years he was chaste. We have to believe that in those days young men – and young ladies – found it much easier to resist. Morals and methods were different, and it simply wasn't considered a hardship. You might say this is how it should be. What's so hard or reprehensible about being sexually pure? Why judge others by our shocking, decadent standards? All the same, one does wonder.

In the 1950s Mr F.W. Bateson, a well-known Wordsworth scholar and a Fellow of Corpus Christi College, Oxford, raised a suggestion that could help to explain William's behaviour. William and Dorothy were lovers. If the discovery of the Annette letters caused a furore in the 1920s, it was nothing to the scandal caused by the theory of incest, which Mr Bateson discussed in his book *Wordsworth, a Reinterpretation*. This is a serious psychological study of Wordsworth's poetry, suggesting that he was a much more subjective writer than is usually thought – just as much as Keats or Shelley. In his early life, writes Mr Bateson, Wordsworth was subject to strong sensual passions and emotions, which are in his poetry, if you look for them, though most readers have missed them (such as Shelley, for example, who called Wordsworth a 'solemn and unsexual man'). Bateson cites as evidence one of Wordsworth's two earliest books, *Descriptive Sketches*, where the poet experiences 'voluptuous dreams' by Lake Como and sees 'shadowy breasts', just like many a normal twenty-year-old. Wordsworth, however, expurgated these references when the poem was reprinted in 1820.

As for the possibility of incest, Mr Bateson pointed to Dorothy's love-letters, the descriptions of physical contact between the pair, certain actions which would indicate panic (as things perhaps became too hot for William to deal with), and others which might betray guilt; but his main evidence rests on the fact that someone, at some later date, removed crucial passages from Dorothy's *Journals*. This evidence is all rather circumstantial, and somewhat negative in that two missing pages from the original text, which Mr Bateson considers might contain evidence of incest, could be harmless. (In a later edition of his book, Mr Bateson rather softens some of his assertions.)

One day, some letters, at present unknown, might suddenly turn up, as with Annette, throwing completely new light on the whole relationship with Dorothy, revealing more precisely William's true feelings. In the meantime, all that can honestly be said is that he and Dorothy were a very devoted and very loving brother and sister.

There then occurred an important event which spoils the incest theories, though no doubt someone could argue that it provides proof of guilt. In 1802, after two very devoted, intimate, domestic years alone with Dorothy in Dove Cottage, William got married.

If you relied solely on Dorothy's *Journals* for enlightenment, you wouldn't know what was going on. It is only when you look back, having got to the end and found that a wedding has taken place, that you can understand little remarks, half references, trips and letters which must obviously have been part of the build-up to the marriage. But Dorothy never says at any time that William has become engaged and that a marriage will take place.

One morning in July 1802, according to the *Journals*, we find that Dorothy and William have got up and are heading south for London. In a roundabout way, they turn out to be *en route* to France, which must come as a big surprise to any innocent reader. You've guessed, of course, where they are going. To see Annette.

If William is to get married, he must first disentangle himself from Annette, tell her face to face what he plans to do, discuss it with her and make appropriate arrangements. It sounds very much the sort of thing William would want to do, though no doubt his bride-to-be, who had been told about Annette, had also insisted. It was an interlude in his life which had preyed on his mind for many years. It needed a meeting to close it for good.

Because Dorothy offers no preparatory explanations in her *Journals*, the exact sequence of events can only be guessed at, though, from her letters to friends, it looks as if William had become engaged earlier in the year, probably in February. By good fortune, this year, 1802, turned out to be the only year for ten years that William could possibly have got back to France. In March 1802 the Peace of Amiens was signed, and for a brief period – it lasted for little over a year – England and France were not at war. Perhaps *knowing* that peace was coming encouraged William to get engaged. If the war had not halted, would he have got married without first seeing Annette? As recently as 1800, William had said he had no thoughts of marriage.

There was another event connected with his marriage – connected in the sense that it eased the thought of marriage and eased the separation from Annette, though whether it was in any way a cause or just a coincidence is again not clear. In May 1802, the bad Earl of Lonsdale, who had ruined the Wordsworths' early years by his meanness, died. By July 1802, when William set off, the family knew that the new Earl planned to pay off all the old debts, and that the Wordsworth children should at last get their inheritance.

In London, while they were crossing the river on their way to the coast, Dorothy, as usual, made a note of their impressions. William later turned them into one of his best-known sonnets, that on Westminster Bridge. 'We mounted the Dover Coach at Charing Cross. It was a beautiful morning. The City, St Pauls, with the River and a Multitude of little boats, made a most beautiful sight as we crossed Westminster Bridge. The houses were not overhung by their cloud of smoke and they were spread out endlessly, yet the sun shone so brightly with such pure light that there was even something like a purity of Nature's own grand spectacles. . . .'

They were on their way to Calais, where they'd arranged their appointment with Annette. She was travelling up from Blois to meet them. Perhaps they thought it could have been dangerous for an English couple to venture too far into the heartland of France, just in case war should break out again. Perhaps they wanted a half-way, neutral, anonymous rendezvous. Their meeting took place on the sands at Calais, within view of the English coast – emotionally comforting no doubt, just in case things went too far.

We left Annette Vallon in 1792 – heavily pregnant, waving a sad farewell to her lover, having come back to Blois in readiness for the birth. Before William left, she'd got him to touch and feel the baby clothes which she'd already bought. Judging by her subsequent letters, Annette could be as emotional and sentimental as Dorothy. William seemed to like emotional ladies.

During the previous ten years, other elements in her character had appeared, such as courage and strong beliefs. The Terror had been just as violent in the French provincial towns as in Paris, and in Orleans, which had been a noted royalist centre, the local Jacobins conducted a witch-hunt of royalist sympathizers. Annette's brother, Paul Vallon, who stood godfather to William's child, was one of thirty arrested for allegedly assaulting a local republican politician. Nine went to the scaffold, but Paul managed to escape and went into hiding. Annette helped to protect him and from then on became actively involved in the underground movement, hiding priests and royalists, organizing escapes, plots and hiding-places. She was constantly in danger of losing her own life, but though her name appeared in various records as a known royalist, working for counter-revolutionary movements, she managed to escape being put in prison. On one police file she was described as 'Widow Williams of Blois; gives shelter to Chouans'.

She obviously had a great deal more to think about than her departed lover during these ten years, but it is interesting that she should have remained unmarried and called herself either Madame William or Veuve William. Her daughter had been christened Anne Caroline Wordwodsth (sic). William still appears to have been the only man in her life.

None of her letters appears to have got through to William after 1795, but they started arriving in late 1801, when negotiations for the Amiens peace were under way. Dorothy refers to letters arriving from 'Poor Annette', no doubt telling of her sufferings and dangers, but they are simply mentioned in passing, along with letters from other friends, such as Sarah Hutchinson.

William and Annette now had in common a hatred of Napoleon, who was then in Paris, having taken over control of France. It was on 15 August 1802, while the one-time lovers were walking up and down the Calais sands, that Napoleon made himself Consul for life. Many English people did go to Paris to catch a glimpse of the new hero, including Charles Fox and Thomas Poole, Coleridge's friend, but doubtless William and Annette couldn't face Paris and such celebrations. Annette hated Napoleon because her long years of work and sacrifice for the restoration of the Bourbons had now been ruined. William had had hopes after the collapse of the Terror that a true and liberal republican government would return, but now a new tyrant had arisen.

They also had in common nine-year-old Caroline. She romped and played on the beach while her mother and father went on their incessant walks. William wrote several sonnets in Calais and in one he refers to Caroline, calling her 'Dear Child', though it wasn't known when the sonnet was published that he had such a child.

They spent four weeks in Calais, which seems an enormously long time for a simple farewell, while William's bride-to-be was waiting at home for the wedding to take place. What could have taken up all their solemn talks? They would have had a lot of adventures to tell each other; but a gap of ten years imposes barriers, changes relationships, changes people. William's French must have been quite rusty, while Annette knew no English. Did he still love her in any way? She was now thirty-six and had been through ten tough years. Was Dorothy there as a sort of chaperon, just in case?

Dorothy gives no clue to their conversations: 'We lodged in tolerably decent sized rooms but badly furnished and with large store of bad smells and dirt in the yard and all about. The weather was very hot. We walked by the sea shore almost every evening with Annette and Caroline or Wm and I alone. I had a bad cold and could not bathe at first but William did....'

Talk of the impending marriage probably didn't take up much of their conversation, as Annette probably knew all about that already by letter, but Caroline and her future must have been discussed at length. William might even have offered to take her back to England. Dorothy would have enjoyed being a foster-mother. But after four weeks, they parted, Annette and Caroline going back to Blois. William did not see them again for eighteen years.

You may have guessed by now the name of the lady William was coming home to marry: Mary Hutchinson. Where his relationship with Annette had been short and ecstatic, had begun and ended in a matter of months – an exciting, if brief, moment of passion – his relationship with Mary had gone on slowly, and with little apparent passion, for years – in fact, for almost the whole of his life, if you remember that he first met her, when they were both about three, at Dame Birkett's school in Penrith. Why did it take so long? What made him marry her when he did? These questions hardly troubled the scholars, until very recently. The discovery of Annette, and all the new possibilities that emerged from this, have been a much more exciting field for speculation. Few questions have been raised about Mary during the last hundred years because it has been thought that the answers would be fairly boring and unimportant. There has been so little evidence of her having had any influence on William's life or poetry that she has tended to be dismissed as just a mother and housekeeper – someone he happened to marry, when he decided it was time to get married and to be the father of children.

Most people who knew Mary found her very quiet, and one observer remarked that she appeared to have a squint, which wasn't very kind. Dorothy's dark complexion, when that was remarked upon, was always seen as something wild and attractive. Wordsworth's nephew, when he came to write the official family memoir, is strangely silent about Mary, giving no descriptions of her.

It is Dorothy who has left all the valuable letters and journals; Dorothy whom all visitors were impressed by; Dorothy who got written about by other people; Dorothy whom William wrote and talked so much about. This has been so much the case that it is thought by some people that William went to Mary on a complicated rebound from Dorothy – as an escape or release from the insulated, hot-house atmosphere of the two Dove Cottage years. It need not necessarily have been incest that brought about the change. Some sort of climax might have been reached with Dorothy, and William just didn't want it to go on.

William and Mary had certainly been friends for many years, but, at the same time, he'd left her for many years, going his own way with other people, treating her simply as an old family friend. Even when she came to visit the Wordsworth household in the West Country, he'd left to go to Bristol on her arrival. From the letters, Mary would appear to have been Dorothy's friend, not William's, at that stage. He had no thoughts of marriage, to her or anyone else, just two years before the wedding. By 1802, Mary was thirty-two, the same age as William (he was just four months older), and, by the standards of the day, something of an old maid, presumed by all to be destined to spend her life as some sort of housekeeper to one of her brothers, just as Dorothy was doing.

The Hutchinsons had originally come from County Durham to Penrith, where Mary's father had lived all his life. He was a fairly prosperous tobacconist in the town, which meant that she came from the same sort of shopkeeper stock as William's mother's family. He had eight children (plus two who appear to have died young), all of them orphaned while they were still growing up. (Mary's mother died in 1783, the same year as William's father died, and her father two years later.) The Hutchinsons felt they had a lot in common with the

Wordsworths and, despite family separations, with both sets of children being sent away to relations, they kept in contact.

There were four Hutchinson sisters, all near in age to William and Dorothy – Mary, Sarah, Joanna and Margaret, the one who died – and four brothers, John, Henry (who went to sea), Tom and George. Mary was particularly close to Tom, who was a farmer. Tom had little money and was always trying to buy himself land and moving about; for a time he lived at Sockburn on Tees – where William and Dorothy visited them on their return from Germany – and then he moved to Yorkshire, where Mary was now living. Those trips by John and William to Yorkshire, referred to by Dorothy in her *Journals*, therefore have deeper significance, when you realize that William must have been courting Mary.

Dorothy was a dear and beloved friend of Mary's and it was she who had kept up the letters over the years, much more than William; but she was genuinely upset when William was away visiting her, especially during 1801 and 1802. She need not necessarily have felt personal jealousy; perhaps she just feared for his muse, if he took on the responsibility for a wife and family.

In June 1802, when the marriage had been arranged, and William and Dorothy were about to set off for France, Dorothy wrote to her brother Richard, answering questions that he must have asked her about her own future with William:

His marriage will add to his comfort and happiness. Mary Hutchinson is a most excellent woman – I have known her a long time and I know her thoroughly; she has been a dear friend of mine, is deeply attached to William and is disposed to feel kindly to all his family.

As you express a desire to know what are my expectations, I have every reason to rely upon the affection of my Brothers and their regard for my happiness. I shall continue to live with my Brother William – but he, having nothing to spare nor being likely to have, at least for many years, I am obliged (I need not say how much he regrets this necessity) to consider myself as boarding through my life with an indifferent person. Sixty pounds a year is the sum which would entirely satisfy all my desires. With sixty pounds a year I should fear not any accidents or changes which might befall me. I cannot look forward to the time, when with my habits of frugality, I could not live comfortably on that sum....

How reassuring not to have to take inflation into account! In those far-off days, one could see £60 supplying the same needs for forty years ahead. Dorothy's financial hopes rested on her brothers Richard, John and Christopher, all now pursuing their respective careers; she hoped they would be kind enough to allow her £20 a year each, which they readily agreed to do. She had of course no job or income of her own, though that horrid Uncle Kit, the one who'd blighted William's early Penrith years, had died, leaving nothing to William or any other Wordsworth son, but £100 to Dorothy. She apparently did not know at the time she wrote the letter quoted above (though she came to know soon afterwards) that she would be getting her share of the Lowther money.

Dorothy's agitation of course did not spring from solely financial causes, and we can only guess at her real emotions. She'd welcomed Mary's visits over the last few years, firstly at Racedown and then during those early months at Dove Cottage; Mary had been part of their circle. But Dorothy must have believed William when he'd said he had no thoughts of marriage. However, when it was decided, she immediately addressed Mary in all letters as her sister, as she'd done with Annette, accepting her as William's bride-to-be. But underneath, what did she feel?

'I have long loved Mary as a sister,' Dorothy wrote to her old friend Jane, just a few days before the wedding was due to take place. 'She is equally attached to me, this being so you will guess that I look forward with perfect happiness to this Connection between us, but, happy as I am, I half dread that concentration of all tender feelings, past, present and future, which will come upon me on the wedding morning....'

The wedding took place at Brompton Church, near Scarborough in Yorkshire, on 4 October 1802, and Dorothy was right about the confusion of her feelings. Her description of the day is one of the strangest and most revealing accounts in the whole of her *Journals*.

She and William had arrived a few days before the wedding, and Dorothy had felt ill most of the time. The night before, she had slept with William's wedding-ring on her finger. In the morning, when the time came to go to the church, she couldn't face it:

At a little after 8 o'clock I saw them go down the avenue towards the church. William had parted from me upstairs. I gave him the wedding ring – with how deep a blessing! I took it from my forefinger where I had worn it the whole of the night before. He slipped it again onto my finger and blessed me fervently.

I kept myself as quiet as I could but when I saw the two men [Mary's brothers] running up the walk, coming to tell us it was over, I could stand it no longer and threw myself on the bed where I lay in stillness, neither hearing or seeing anything, till Sarah came upstairs to me and said 'They are coming'. This forced me from the bed where I lay and I moved I knew not how straight forwards, faster than my strength could carry me, till I met my Beloved William and fell upon his bosom. . . .

It was a very quiet wedding, apart from Dorothy's hysterics. There were no senior members of the Hutchinson family there, just three of her brothers and two sisters. The Hutchinson children, like the Wordsworths, had been placed under the care of guardians when their parents died, including a wealthy, landed uncle, from whom Mary had high hopes of some financial help, but they cut her off when she married William. One of them described him as a 'vagabond'. Like William's own guardian uncles, they considered William a waster, a rebel with no proper employment. They might possibly have heard rumours about his French affair. Whatever the reasons, the couple received not one single wedding present. William even signed a marriage bond, in which he agreed to pay £200, should it ever come to light that there was any impediment to his marriage. Did someone suspect that perhaps he might even be married already?

After the wedding, all three came straight back to the Lakes, William with his bride Mary and his sister Dorothy, where all three lived happily ever after. . . .

WESTMINSTER BRIDGE

*William and Dorothy crossed Westminster Bridge on 31 July 1802,
on the way to Calais. Dorothy made notes of their impressions.
William later wrote a sonnet.*

EARTH has not anything to show more fair:
Dull would he be of soul who could pass by
A sight so touching in its majesty:
This City now doth, like a garment, wear
The beauty of the morning; silent, bare,
Ships, towers, domes, theatres, and temples lie
Open unto the fields, and to the sky;
All bright and glittering in the smokeless air.
Never did sun more beautifully steep
In his first splendour, valley, rock, or hill;
Ne'er saw I, never felt, a calm so deep!
The river glideth at his own sweet will:
Dear God! the very houses seem asleep;
And all that mighty heart is lying still!

10

Scotland
1803

FIVE days after the marriage of William and Mary, there appeared
a most curious announcement in the *Morning Post* – a gentle bit of teasing, no doubt the work of a close friend, which greatly upset William,
who wasn't quite in the mood for such jokes:

Monday last, W. Wordsworth, Esq., was married to Miss Hutchinson of
Wykeham, near Scarborough, and proceeded immediately, with his wife and
his sister, for his charming cottage in the little Paradise Vale of Grasmere.
His neighbour, Mr Coleridge, resides in the Vale of Keswick, 13 miles from
Grasmere. His house (situated on a low hill at the foot of Skiddaw, with the
Derwent Lake in front, and the romantic River Greta winding round the hill)
commands perhaps the most various and interesting prospects of any house
in the island. It is a perfect panorama of that wonderful vale, with its two
lakes, and its complete circle, or rather ellipse, of mountains.

William had sent the usual sort of curt and formal wedding
announcement to the local paper in Yorkshire, which appeared the
same day (9 October 1802), but had no knowledge whatsoever of the
publication of the *Morning Post*'s purple prose. The reference to his
sister, and to the fact that all three went back to his charming cottage,

must have been rather hurtful. It was the first of a long series of such sly digs at him and his female household, that went on for years. The suggestion that he and Coleridge were setting themselves up as some sort of tourist attraction complete with estate agent's flowery descriptions, also upset him, especially as most people would think he'd been responsible for it. It was worrying for him, anyway, setting up a new household, without having outsiders being malicious about a very sensitive subject.

Dorothy was just as furious, though other members of the family couldn't quite see what all the fuss was about. 'It is not quite so bad as I thought it would have been from what you said,' wrote brother John, the captain of the *Earl of Abergavenny*, who'd recently returned from another voyage.

Dorothy was still smarting three years later, putting the blame upon Daniel Stuart, editor of the *Morning Post*: 'Upon my brother's marriage, he inserted in the Morning Post the most ridiculous paragraph that was ever penned.' It is still not definitely known who wrote the offending paragraph. It could have been Stuart himself, perhaps based on gossip from Charles Lamb, who had recently visited Dove Cottage (while William and Dorothy had been away in France) and had stayed at Keswick. The paragraph indicates first-hand knowledge of Greta Hall – and was couched in Lamb's style of humour.

It could of course have been Coleridge, mentioning himself in the paragraph by way of a double bluff; but Coleridge, though he did have a keen sense of humour, wasn't at that time in the mood for such fun. On the wedding-day itself, the *Morning Post* had published his 'Dejection: an Ode'. It was the seventh anniversary of his own marriage and he saw this happy event in William's life as confirmation of his own unhappy state. The 'Dejection' ode was sparked off by his complicated relationship with Sarah Hutchinson. He felt very much alone, compared with William, who had so much – not just his exquisite sister Dorothy, but now a loving wife in Mary and also her sister Sarah, who was equally devoted to William.

Coleridge was at home in Keswick on the eve of the wedding, having been on a marathon ten-day solo tour of the Lakes while the Wordsworths were away, and had some rather strange dreams, according to the entry in his notebook for 3 October 1802:

I dreamt that I was asleep in the cloysters at Christ's Hospital [his old school] and had woken with a pain in my hand from some corrosion. Boys and nurses daughters peeping at me. On their implying that I was not in the School, I answered yes I am. I then recollected that I was thirty and of course could not be in the school. So dreamt of Dorothy, William and Mary – and that Dorothy was altered in every feature, a fat, thick-limbed and rather red haired – in short, no resemblance to her at all – and I said, if I did not *know* you to be Dorothy, I never should suppose it. Why says she, I have not a feature the same. I was followed up and down by a frightful pale woman who, I thought, wanted to kiss me, and had the property of giving a shameful Disease by breathing in the face.

There's some good raw material for an analyst here – and there's a lot more of the same; it all gives an indication of Coleridge's mental state. The Wordsworths, despite what Coleridge might in his blacker moods have thought about them, were full of pity and sympathy for him. He was their first guest when eventually all three returned to Dove Cottage after the wedding, and they all followed him back to Greta Hall for a three-day visit. They consented to stay with him, so Dorothy remarks rather heavily in her *Journals*, 'Mrs C not being at home'. Coleridge for a while had hopes that they might all move in with him at Greta Hall, but Dorothy's antipathy for Mrs Coleridge was one of many factors which prevented this.

Coleridge was still a welcome guest at Dove Cottage – still popping back and forth, despite his bouts of ill health – but jealousy was eating into his soul, as he watched William having all that love and attention. 'I saw him more and more living wholly among Devotees, having the minutest thing, almost his very eating and drinking, done for him by his Sister, or Wife and I trembled less a Film should rise and thicken on his moral Eye.'

The Wordsworth household was indeed extremely happy. Dorothy's half-dreads were ill founded. She doesn't appear to have been usurped in William's affections and her place at his side was not affected. 'Wm fell asleep, lying upon my breast and I upon Mary,' she wrote in her *Journals* about the ride home to Grasmere after the wedding. Her domestic routine, as described in her *Journals*, was now being shared by all three of them:

William is now sitting by me. I have been beside him ever since tea running the heel of a stocking, repeating some of his sonnets to him, listening to his own repeating. Mary is in the parlour below attending to the baking of cakes and pies. Sarah is in bed in the toothache – beloved William is turning over the leaves of Charlotte Smith's sonnets, but he keeps his hand to his poor chest pushing aside his breast plate. Mary is well and I am well and Molly is as blithe as last year at this time. Coleridge came this morning with Wedgwood. We all turned out of Wm's bedroom one by one to meet him. He looked well. . . .

William, as ever, was the centre of attention. A very cold day. Wm promised me he would rise as soon as I had carried him his breakfast but he lay in bed till between 12 and one . . .

When William was away, Mary and Dorothy had each other for company, and Dorothy didn't feel as lonely as she would have done before the marriage, though she was by no means happy at her brother's absence. 'After dinner we both lay on the floor. Mary slept. I *could* not for I was thinking of so many things.'

The *Journals* come suddenly to a halt in January 1803, just a few months after the wedding, the last entry being about William of course. He wanted some gingerbread – a great speciality in Grasmere – so Dorothy put on her cloak and went off to buy some. A few days previously, in her *Journals*, she had been vowing to herself to write regularly in the future, having neglected to write anything for several weeks over the Christmas period; but she never did. Thus we leave her for ever in her Grasmere *Journals*: going out to get gingerbread for her beloved, never to return to her daily domestic notes and thoughts, though she did keep a diary when she was away from home. Subsequent household journals might have been lost of course, or destroyed, but we have to assume there were no more. She had Mary to discuss William with, night and day, and didn't need the outlet of writing any more. Or perhaps she was just too busy.

William was not just fortunate in his domestic life – and all three women, Dorothy, Mary and Sarah, were completely happy with each other, with never a hint of disagreement – his financial affairs also began to improve. The Lowther money, £8,500, for the whole Wordsworth family, started to be paid. As they were living together, William and Dorothy got their share jointly; it eventually came to about £3,000 and made a big difference to their household budget. They invested some of it jointly with their brother Captain John, buying shares in his cargo for his next long voyage to China. He returned safely from China in August 1804, so that investment must have improved their finances still further. They left it to their brother Richard to administer the money and they were, as before, always writing to him to settle debts. In December 1803, for example, twelve years after he'd left Cambridge, William got a bill from his college tutor for £10 15s 3½d. William also loaned money to Coleridge, even though old friends, like Montagu, still hadn't paid back money he'd loaned them years before.

William also acquired a new and wealthy patron, one who became one of his closest friends and a very influential figure in his life. This was Sir George Beaumont, an amateur painter of some note in his day and a great patron of the arts. Sir George encouraged many young artists, such as Constable, and was one of the founders of the National Gallery. He owned a large house in Grosvenor Square and several estates, including a large one in Leicestershire. He and his wife were a middle-aged couple, some sixteen years older than William, but, despite the age gap, they became great personal friends of William, lavishing presents upon him even before they had met him. It was Coleridge who got to know them first, when the Beaumonts spent a holiday in Keswick. They already knew William's poetry and were 'half-mad' to meet him, so Coleridge said. Coleridge told them about all their joint plans and problems, his own ill health, the long journeys back and forth to Grasmere to visit each other, their difficulties with their respective writings. Without telling William, Sir George bought a little property near Keswick – at Applethwaite, on the slopes of Skiddaw – and, through Coleridge, presented it to William. Sir George's idea was that William could build a house there, or modernize an existing old cottage, and would therefore have a home near Coleridge's, where they could write happily together. William was rather embarrassed by the gift, but Sir George wouldn't hear of him declining, and he graciously accepted. He never used the property, being uncertain about Coleridge's future and realizing that difficulties could arise from the proximity of Mrs Coleridge; but he was soon boasting about his good luck in letters to friends, particularly as the property made him a freeholder of Cumberland and thus able to vote at elections. It was eight weeks before he wrote a thank-you letter to Sir George, but when he did, complaining of pains in his chest, which handicapped his writing letters, he was suitably grateful.

The Wordsworths' first child was born in June 1803, just nine months after their wedding. He was christened John, after William's father. The godparents were Dorothy, Coleridge and their brother Richard. Dorothy was delighted, and her letters from now on are filled with endless details of 'our little babe'. You would think, from her descriptions, that she was the mother:

He has blue eyes, a fair complexion, a body as fat as a little pig, arms that are thickening and dimpling and bracelets at his wrists, a very prominent nose, which *will be* like his Father's, and head shaped upon the very same model. I send you a lock of his hair sewed to this letter.

I wish you could see him in his Basket which is neither more nor less than a Meat basket which costs half a crown. In this basket he has floated over Grasmere water asleep and made one of a dinner party at the Island. We often carry it to the orchard seat where he drops asleep beside us.

William added a note to this paragraph, which shows how carefully he must have read Dorothy's letters, checking her accounts of their joint family news. Beside the reference to the babe crossing Grasmere in his basket, he makes it clear the baby hadn't floated off alone: 'Not like Moses in his cradle of rushes but in a boat, mind that. W.W.'

One can imagine William reading all Dorothy's letters, tut-tutting at her endless chatter, but enjoying it, and too lazy to do much himself to keep up contact with their family and friends. In William's own letters, when of course the pain in his side allowed him to write any, he either discusses business and financial affairs, or lays down the law about poetry or the world in general.

There's further evidence that William read Dorothy's letters in an amusing P.S. at the end of a letter from her to Mrs Clarkson, one of their closest friends, in which she's been going on about the family illnesses, including troubles with her own bowels and a 'violent looseness' that has lasted four days: 'William after reading over my letter is not half satisfied with what I have said of myself – he bids me add that I *always* begin with sickness and that any agitation of mind either of joy or sorrow will bring it on. Anything puts me past my sleep, for instance being in much company and hot rooms. Ever since I can remember, going into company made me have violent aches....' The P.S. rather proves William's point.

Coleridge had by now a third child in his family, his only daughter Sara, who was born just six months before the Wordsworths' first babe. All of the Coleridge children became constant visitors to Dove Cottage, often being left with the Wordsworths for many weeks at a time. When Dorothy is describing their own little Johnny, she can't avoid including some digs at the Coleridge household: 'He likes dearly to be laid upon his back on the floor, kicking and sprawling like a Merry Andrew such as they make for children and hang against the wall with strings to pull up their legs with a jerk. We bathe him every morning – he sobs bitterly but never cries yet in dressing after it he sometimes screams lustily and is in a violent passion. I believe Sara Coleridge was never in a passion in her life, she is the very soul of meekness.'

Dorothy rather disapproved of the Coleridge methods of child care. All three Coleridge children were highly precocious and advanced, with little Hartley appearing to be a child prodigy, already being known by some as 'The Philosopher' at the age of only six. Dorothy thought the children were rather repressed, with too much learning and not enough outdoor life, though she was very fond of them personally and enjoyed looking after them at Dove Cottage.

Just two months after the birth of John, William, Dorothy and Coleridge set off on a six-week tour of Scotland. This would appear to have been hard on Mary – left behind while they had a good time – but neither she nor they seemed to think so. They considered they'd done well to wait until after the birth, when they made special arrangements for Joanna Hutchinson, Mary's younger sister, to move in and keep her company. (They had panicked slightly when Sarah, their first choice, couldn't come, but Joanna had agreed to help instead.)

William had been to Scotland on a very brief visit a couple of years previously, when his friend Montagu had re-married, but the other two had never been there. Dorothy was very excited, but Coleridge was worried, wondering if six weeks in bad weather in the north might bring on all his illnesses again. The tour was in fact planned for the good of Coleridge's health, as much as anything – a change of scene to buck him up, though he was convinced that only the Mediterranean sunshine would do that.

The Wordsworths bought an Irish jaunting car, a sign of their improved financial position, though the horse that was sold with it was rather old and awkward, as was the vehicle itself. William sat at the front on a sort of dicky box, doing the driving, while Dorothy and Coleridge sat behind, their backs to the centre of the road, with all the luggage stored beneath. There was no protection from the elements – no enclosed space where they could shelter – but it was better than being a pedestrian, carrying your belongings in a handkerchief on your head, as William had done when he'd gone off on his first tour, thirteen years before. It was an interesting and important trip, both stimulating and depressing, which brought several things into the open.

In Carlisle, they witnessed a strange event, the culmination of a story that had kept the whole nation agog for several months. A gentleman calling himself the Hon. Augustus Hope, MP, had married the daughter of an innkeeper in Buttermere, Mary Robinson, a young girl of eighteen, known as the 'Beauty of Buttermere'. He took her on a lavish spending spree, staying at all the best places in the Lake District, such as the 'Royal Oak' at Keswick, flashing his smart visiting-card and travelling in his smart carriage, until the police caught up with him and the cultured lordling turned out to be a downright blackguard, a confidence trickster from the West Country called Hatfield, who had left a string of broken hearts and fatherless children all over the country.

Hatfield was tried at the assizes in Carlisle on several fraud charges, including one of defrauding the Post Office – he'd been franking his own letters without authority, which was a capital offence in those days – but the jury might have been fairly lenient if all his personal letters hadn't been produced in court, especially the tear-stained letters from his many conquests, left despairing in his wake. The whole nation was on the side of poor Mary of Buttermere, including William, who later used her story in *The Prelude*: 'Unfaithful to a virtuous wife, / Deserted and deceived, the spoiler came . . . / And wooed the artless daughter of the hills, / And wedded her, in cruel mockery.'

Coleridge also subsequently wrote about her. What struck him particularly was that Hatfield had had the taste and talent deliberately to seek out the most picturesque places and pleasures of the Lake District, despite 'the litany of anguish sounding in his ears from despairing women.'

It happened to be the final day of Hatfield's trial when the three of them arrived in their jaunting car in Carlisle, and naturally they went to see. Coleridge rather disgraced himself by shouting in court: 'I alarmed the Judges, Counsellors, Tipstaves, Jurymen, Witnesses and Spectators by hallooing to Wordsworth who was in a window on the other side of the Hall – *Dinner*! . . .'

'This day Hatfield was condemned,' wrote Dorothy in a travel note-book she had started, just for the Scottish tour. 'I stood at the door of the gaoler's house where he was; Wm entered the house and C saw him. I fell into conversation with a debtor who told me, in a dry way, that "he was far over-learned"; and another man observed to Wm that we might learn from Hatfield's fate "not to meddle with pen and ink" '.

The saga later appeared in several forms on the London stage and a great deal was written about it. Mary went back to Buttermere and turned out not to be so artless as Wordsworth made her appear in *The Prelude*, becoming a great tourist attraction and bringing in shoals of well-known visitors, including Southey. Meanwhile, leaving Hatfield to his execution, William, Dorothy and Coleridge got into their jaunting car and headed for the Scottish border.

It's interesting to compare the two accounts of their trip: Dorothy, writing away in her notebook of the journey about the people they met and their conversations; Coleridge, in his notebook, concentrating more on the scenery, making little drawings of buildings and slopes of hills, bringing in chunks of Scottish history and assorted philosophical thoughts. William, on the other hand, kept no diary or notebook.

They did the things that most visitors to Scotland still do, stopping at Gretna Green (which they found very depressing), then visiting Burns's house and grave in Dumfries. They hoped to see his widow, all of them being great lovers of Burns's poetry, but she was out when they called. They then went up the Nith Valley to the River Clyde and through Glasgow; by this time they were all getting depressed, disappointed by the dreary Lowlands scenery, upset by the naked and dirty feet of the Glasgow poor and resigned to the low quality of Scottish inns. 'We must expect many of these Inconveniences during the Tour,' wrote Coleridge, 'we wanting three beds for 3 persons.'

The rains set in and Coleridge had to sit all day, soaked through and very miserable, while the old horse slowly stumbled on. The other two were equally unprotected, but William was concentrating on the driving and Dorothy was concentrating on keeping William cheerful; so Coleridge was left concentrating on his ills, feeling very much the outsider. 'I went to sleep after dinner and reflected how little there was in this world that could compensate for the loss or diminishment of the Love of such as truly love us and what bad Calculators Vanity and Selfishness prove to be in the long run.'

Despite these bouts of self-pity, Coleridge could still produce some nice observations, as in Glasgow, when he stood beside an asthmatic town crier – 'a ludicrous combination' – and then watched a lady at work in a barber's shop: 'A Woman-Shaver and a man with his lathered chin, most amorously ogling her as she had him by the Nose....' Matters improved when they reached Loch Lomond and the first glimpses of the Highland scenery, which delighted them greatly, though they all thought Ullswater was probably prettier than Loch Lomond. The weather didn't improve, but their humour did. They ended up one evening, soaked through, sheltering in a very primitive hut belonging to a ferryman on Loch Lomond – a hovel, black inside with peat smoke – but instead of being even more depressed by their surroundings, they all collapsed in a fit of giggles. 'We caroused our cups of coffee,' wrote Coleridge, 'laughing like children at the strange atmosphere; the smoke came in gusts and spread along the walls and above our heads in the chimney where the hens were roosting like light clouds in the sky; we laughed and laughed again, in spite of the smarting of our eyes.' However, on the whole, Coleridge didn't find much to laugh about on the tour.

According to Dorothy's account, the weather never seemed to get her down, and there's no sign of her being at any time depressed. Her stories and observations are all sweetness and light. As for William, the tour was having a great spiritual effect on him, and from it came later some fine poems, such as 'To a Highland Girl' and 'The Solitary Reaper', as well as several not so good poems in praise of Burns. Dorothy's notebook provides a record of William's thoughts as well as of their experiences:

While we were walking forward, we all stopped suddenly at the sound of a half articulated Gaelic hooting from the field close to us. It came from a little boy whom we could see on the hill between us and the lake wrapped up in a grey plaid. He was probably calling home the cattle for the night. His appearance was in the highest degree moving to the imagination: mists were on the hill-sides; darkness shutting in upon the huge avenue of mountains; torrents roaring; no house in sight to which the child might belong; his dress, cry and appearance, all different from anything we had been accustomed to: it was a text, as William has since observed to me, containing in itself the whole history of the Highlander's life; his melancholy, his simplicity, his poverty, his superstition and above all, that visionariness which resulted from a communion with the unworldliness of nature.

William got lost one day, so Dorothy recounts, walking up some rocks on his own, but another little boy found him and offered to guide him:

His guide was a pretty boy and Wm was exceedingly pleased with him. He conducted Wm to the other falls and as they were going along a narrow path they came to a small cavern where Wm lost him and, looking about, saw his pretty figure in a sort of natural niche fitted for a statue, from which the boy jumped out, laughing, delighted with the success of his trick. Wm told us a great deal about him while we sate by the fire and of the pleasure of his walk, often repeating 'I wish you had been with me.'

They were all more than willing to look at any famous place, such as Rob Roy's birthplace or William Wallace's cave. 'There is scarce a glen in Scotland,' remarks Dorothy, 'that has not a cave for Wallace or some other hero.'

All three of them were most taken by two girls from a ferry house who helped them one evening. 'The two little lasses did everything with such *Sweetness* and one of them, 14, with such native Elegance,' wrote Coleridge. 'O, she was a divine Creature.' Dorothy was equally struck by their beauty, and also by their voices: 'I think I never heard the English language more sweetly than from the mouth of the elder of these girls while she stood at the gate answering our inquiries, her face flushed with rain; her pronounciation was clear and distinct, without difficulty, yet slow, as if like a foreign speech.'

They were still wandering around the bonny banks of Loch Lomond when, on 29 August, just two weeks after they'd left home, Coleridge went off on his own. A few days before he had sunk again into one of his pathetic moods: 'Tho' the World praise me, I have no dear Heart that loves my Verses. I never hear snatches from a beloved Voice, fitted to some sweet occasion, of natural prospect, in winds at night....' All the same, the details of their parting, in either diary, are sparse and no real explanation is given. 'Here I left W and D, returned myself to Tarbet, slept there,' wrote Coleridge, though above that note, some ten years later, when he was feeling truly bitter, he added the Latin tag *utinam nonq vidissem* ('Would that I had never seen them'). Dorothy, in her notebook entry for that day, says that the rains had set in heavily again, 'so poor C., being unwell, determined to send his clothes to Edinburgh and make his way thither, being afraid to face so much wet weather'.

However, in letters which Coleridge sent to his wife while on the tour – an indication that they were still friends, despite his wanderings and his passion for Sarah – Coleridge had for some time been complaining about William: 'This was the pleasantest evening I had spent since my Tour for W's Hypochondriacal Feelings kept him silent.'

Wordsworth's version of the tour, which he gave years later to his nephew, was that the separation was all Coleridge's fault: 'Coleridge was at that time in bad spirits and somewhat too much in love with his own dejection and he departed from us, as is recorded in my sister's journal, soon as we left Loch Lomond.'

The separation itself seems to have been calm and amicable. There doesn't appear to have been any row, or a particular disagreement over any one topic: just a general realization that things hadn't gone well for Coleridge on the tour, and that he might as well leave his companions and go home on his own. Travelling as a threesome is often difficult; tensions creep in, as one member can easily feel that the other two are siding against him. William had previously travelled best with only one person: with Jones to the Alps, with Coleridge in the Lakes, with Dorothy to Calais. Their earlier attempt at travelling together, when the three of them (plus Chester) had gone to Hamburg, had also resulted in a parting.

They divided up the money, and off Coleridge went, though he felt a little hurt, so he wrote to his wife, at the smallness of his share: 'The worse thing was the money – they took 29 guineas and I six – all our remaining Cash.' This division seems fair, however, as Coleridge was leaving them to return home, whereas William and Dorothy had another four weeks planned, plus the expense of the horse and jaunting car.

Once on the open road, walking by himself, free of the cursed jaunting car, removed from William and his ever-attentive sister, with the weather clearing up and his spirits beginning to soar, Coleridge decided not to go straight to Edinburgh to take the coach home, as had been his plan. Why should he not see the rest of the Highlands after all, 'having found myself so happy alone, such blessing is there in perfect liberty'.

This is so typical of Coleridge. One moment he is at death's door, taking twenty-five drops of laudanum every five hours to ease his pain, and the next he is off up the nearest fell, not returning home for days. In all his passions and pleasures, friendships and fancies, he tended to swing from one extreme to another. No wonder he could be exhausting, both as a companion and as a husband – yet at other times so stimulating and exciting.

Coleridge continued on his one-man Scottish tour, walking four hundred miles in the next two weeks, overdoing things, as usual, wearing out his shoes, having nightmares and hysterical attacks, vomiting, getting lost, using up all his money, but most of the time enjoying himself tremendously. He nearly bumped into the Wordsworths again (they presumed that by this time he was safely home), when by chance they stayed in an inn which Coleridge had just vacated. In the end, he saw more of Scotland than they did in their jaunting car. They stuck mainly to the Trossachs, working their way slowly round the little roads and lochs in an arc to Edinburgh, while Coleridge struck much further north, reaching Fort William and Inverness, before coming down to Edinburgh just two days before the Wordsworths arrived there.

The Wordsworths devoted the final week of their tour to the Border country, mostly in the company of Walter Scott, who conducted them on several trips round the countryside, which he knew so well and later wrote about in his poems. He couldn't be with them all the time, as he had his legal work to do. Scott and William had never met before, but they had friends in common and were aware of each other's works. The Wordsworths arrived at Scott's home early one morning, armed with an introduction, while Scott and his wife were still in bed, but were invited to stay for breakfast.

Scott wasn't yet known as a poet – not until *The Lay of the Last Minstrel* appeared in 1805 – and it was another ten years before he published his first novel, but his first book, a collection of Border ballads, had just appeared. He and Wordsworth, each the son of a lawyer, born within a year of each other, though on different sides of the Border, had many interests in common, such as nature and the countryside, travelling and walking, but they had differing personalities. Scott had none of the austereness of Wordsworth and was more like Coleridge in his sudden passions and excitements. Like Coleridge, he was a great reader and knowledgeable on many subjects. He was generous and kind-hearted – one of the many reasons why he was so loved by all who knew him – and immediately went out of his way to help and guide William and Dorothy. He took them to Melrose Abbey, read his unpublished *Lay of the Last Minstrel* to them, and found them suitable inns.

'Dined with Mr S at the inn,' wrote Dorothy in Melrose. 'He was now travelling to the assizes at Jedburgh, in his character of Sheriff of Selkirk, a small part of which was vouchsafed to us as his friends, though I could not persuade the woman to show me the beds or to make any promise till she was assured from the sheriff himself that he had no objection to sleep in the same room with Wm....'

William was worried that *The Lay of the Last Minstrel*, when published, would put in the shade Coleridge's 'Christabel', whenever that should be published, as the two poems were in similar styles. Scott had already heard parts of 'Christabel', from a friend of Wordsworth and Coleridge, but Dorothy was convinced that the resemblance was a coincidence and that any imitation on Scott's part was unconscious.

One of the subjects they discussed was royalties and sales, as all good authors do when they get together, and William was surprised by Scott's assertion that he could earn a lot more money from books, should he choose to do so. His profession, the law, was, by comparison, not very profitable. This was the opposite of Wordsworth's own experience: making little or nothing from his writings, while watching people like his brother Richard do very well at the law. Scott, of course, went on to make a veritable fortune from *The Lay* when it was published and became the best-selling poet in the land.

William and Walter Scott became good friends, and William wrote to Scott very warmly on his return, sending some poems inspired by Scott and the Borders and inviting him to the Lakes. Scott visited the Wordsworths several times over the ensuing decades, though he wasn't at ease in William's rather frugal accommodation, preferring the comfort of hotels or of bigger, smarter houses.

Almost immediately after their return to the Lakes, Wordsworth went round to see Coleridge at Greta Hall – a sign that there was no real ill feeling between them. He also met Southey again, and, as he told Walter Scott in his letter of thanks for his hospitality, was much impressed by him: 'I had the pleasure of seeing both Coleridge and Southey at Keswick last Sunday. Southey whom I never saw much of before, I liked much better than I expected; he is very pleasant in his manners, and a man of great reading.'

Wordsworth came back glowing from his Scottish tour, and it is only in retrospect that the tensions between him and Coleridge become significant. It is also in retrospect that we note another important feature of the Scottish tour: that it was the last of its kind for the Wordsworths, the last of wandering about, roughing it, taking things as they came. William went on many other tours in the years ahead, as he always loved travelling, but they were rather different.

The stimulus of the Scottish tour lasted William for many years, and he was continually drawing on its reserves; but he felt his visionary experiences were becoming rarer even before Scotland. Both in frequency and in quality they began to fade. As he approached thirty-five, certain changes appeared to be taking place, both in his character and in his attitude to life.

THE SOLITARY REAPER

Wordsworth included this poem as one of those he described as a Memorial of a Tour of Scotland, 1803. It is set in the Highlands he saw on that journey, but the image which sparked off the poem came from a sentence in a travel book he later read.

BEHOLD her, single in the field,
Yon solitary Highland Lass,
Reaping and singing by herself;
Stop here, or gently pass.
Alone she cuts and binds the grain;
And sings a melancholy strain;
O listen! for the Vale profound
Is overflowing with the sound.

Will no one tell me what she sings?
Perhaps the plaintive numbers flow
For old, unhappy, far off things,
And battles long ago:
Or is it some more humble lay,
Familiar matters of today?
Some natural sorrow, loss or pain,
That has been, and may be again?

Whate'er the theme, the Maiden sang
As if her song could have no ending;
I saw her singing at her work,
And o'er the sickle bending;
I listened, motionless and still;
And, as I mounted up the hill,
The music in my heart I bore,
Long after it was heard no more.

11

A Death in the Family
1805

NOT long after they were back in Dove Cottage, there was a knock on the door one evening at about midnight and there was William Hazlitt, their young artistic friend, the admirer of Coleridge, whom they'd first met in the West Country. He was exhausted and rather agitated.

William had had several meetings and some serious disputations with Hazlitt since their first meeting at Alfoxden had resulted in 'The Tables Turned'. Hazlitt had been in the Lakes earlier that summer, when he'd painted both William's and Coleridge's portraits – William had paid three guineas for his – but Hazlitt took them away with him and they haven't survived.

Hazlitt was exhausted because he had run and walked all the way from Keswick, and in an agitated state as a result of an incident with a local girl with whom he had attempted to have his wicked way. A mob of some two hundred local men had come out looking for him, determined to have his blood, or at least throw him in the river, but Coleridge and Southey had hidden him in Greta Hall. As the mob got angrier, they decided it wasn't safe for him to stay in

Keswick any longer, so they got him out of the house, wearing a pair of Coleridge's walking shoes, and sent him over the mountains to Grasmere.

Hazlitt probably didn't tell Wordsworth the whole story, if he had any sense. He was still a young buck of twenty-five, while Wordsworth was some eight years older and now a respectable married man, his more dissolute days fast fading into the distance, and in his memory. Whatever Hazlitt told Wordsworth had the desired effect, and William took him in, sheltered him, gave him clothes and money, and eventually helped him to make his way south. Hazlitt never returned to the Lakes again, which was probably wise, and it was only much later that William heard the full details of the unsavoury incident. Hazlitt had apparently spanked the girl, so William related many years afterwards, when she had 'refused to gratify his abominable and devilish propensities'.

William and Hazlitt eventually grew apart, but Hazlitt already realized that Wordsworth was, morally and politically, moving along different lines. William had become a patriot, joining the local Volunteers on his return from Scotland, much to the disgust of Hazlitt, who admired Napoleon and hated people like William and Southey for turning against France, the country they had at one time publicly admired so much. Many young people, who'd been drawn to William by his revolutionary poetry, felt betrayed when he appeared to them to be changing sides. But they hadn't suffered the moral and political agonies which William and Southey had suffered, when, step by step, they had seen their youthful republican ideals being gradually ruined and now, so they believed, perverted.

Beethoven – born in 1770, the same year as Wordsworth – tore out the dedication to Napoleon in his Third Symphony, the 'Eroica', in 1804 when he heard the news that Napoleon had crowned himself Emperor. (He later substituted the words 'for the memory of a great man'.) Like Wordsworth, Beethoven had been inspired by the early ideals of the French Revolution, as were most of the artists who were later to be loosely termed Romantics, but his idealism turned to disgust with the rise of Napoleon.

England was under serious threat of invasion, now that Napoleon was sweeping through Europe and it was expected that he would attack Britain next. Throughout the country, local squires and lords set up little groups of Volunteers of the Home Guard type, often clothing and arming them at their own expense; these men were drilled and attended camps, as they prepared to defend their homeland.

Dorothy and Mary were half amused and half apprehensive when William decided to do this little bit for King and Country. Dorothy wrote to her friend, Mrs Clarkson:

William has gone to volunteer his services with the greatest part of the Men of Grasmere. Alas! Alas! Mary and I have no other hope than that they will not be called upon out of these quiet far off places except in the case of the French being *successful* after their landing, and in that case, what matters? We may all go together. But we wanted him to wait till the Body of the people should be called. For my part I thought much of the inconvenience and fatigue of going to be exercised twice or thrice a week, however if he really enters into it heart and soul and likes it, that will do him good, and surely there never was a more determined hater of the French nor one more willing to do his utmost to destroy them if they really do come.

It was a complete reversal. In his early letters and poems, William had expressed love for France and contempt for his own country, and also his opposition to war and fighting of any sort. Now he was writing sonnets in which he exhorted young men to arms, even if it led to bloodshed and death. Sir George Beaumont, his new landed friend, congratulated him on these fine sentiments and on his work with the Volunteers: 'I am delighted with your patriotic lines, they are animating to a degree.' Sir George was a Tory, a political state of mind which William appeared to be fast approaching as he became increasingly conscious of his position and his responsibilities.

In January 1804, Coleridge left the Lakes, heading for Malta, where he hoped the sun would improve his health. No one knew when, or even if, he would return. He'd been seriously ill all winter and this now seemed his only hope. Wordsworth loaned him £100 for his proposed voyage, and, before he left, the women of the Wordsworth household settled down to copy out all William's unpublished manuscripts, so that Coleridge could take them with him. It was a labour of love, because they knew they would miss poor Coleridge desperately.

William then got down to some hard work on *The Prelude*, or the poem of his life, as he called it, spurred on by Coleridge's departure. He had hardly touched it during the last three or four years, when he was working on shorter poems, but, as it was written for Coleridge and addressed personally to him, he now decided to finish it while his friend was away, which he did by May 1805.

Having his women around him was of course a great source of comfort and encouragement for William, as Coleridge always bitterly observed. They provided a secure and attentive domestic setting in which he could carry on with his work. As ever, he composed most of his lines in the open air, either striding up and down the back orchard, with Dorothy not far away, and making notes when necessary, or beside the lakes, along the fells. He recited his words aloud – as he'd done back in Hawkshead when walking with his dog, often frightening strangers and children who didn't know his eccentric ways.

At present he is walking [wrote Dorothy in a letter to Lady Beaumont in May 1804] and has been out of doors these two hours though it has rained heavily all the morning. In wet weather he takes out an umbrella; chuses the most sheltered spot, and there walks backwards and forwards and though the length of his walk be sometimes a quarter or half a mile, he is as fast bound within the chosen limits as if by prison walls. He generally composes his verses out of doors and while he is so engaged he seldom knows how the time slips away or hardly whether it is rain or fair.

The second Wordsworth child, a girl, was born on 16 August 1804 and was christened Dorothy. 'The name of Dorothy, obsolete as it is now grown, had been so devoted in my own thoughts to the first Daughter that I could not break this promise to myself,' William wrote to the Beaumonts, 'though the name of Mary, to my ear the most musical and truly English in sound we have, would have otherwise been most welcome to me, including as it would Lady Beaumont and its mother.' Lady Beaumont was a godmother and sent £10 for the new baby, who was hardly ever called Dorothy, even obsoletely, but was eventually known by all as Dora.

Once again, William and Dorothy went off on a trip after the birth of the new baby, though this time it was just the two of them and it was only a five-day local tour, down the Duddon valley. They missed poor Coleridge, forgetting his unhappiness the last time they'd all been together, and became more and more worried by the lack of letters from him. Dorothy of course was writing continually to him, keeping him up to date with all the family and local news, but they heard little from Coleridge in return.

The Wordsworth household was growing bigger all the time, with two children and four adults (including Sarah Hutchinson, who was there for very long spells), plus the Coleridge children, who were regular all-the-year-round visitors. In the summer, they also received non-Lakes visitors: friends from the south, such as Humphry Davy, who came for a couple of nights.

Walter Scott visited the Lakes at the same time as Davy, and all three men – William, Scott and Davy – travelled from Patterdale and climbed Helvellyn together, which must have been an interesting sight. They had to go slowly, because of Scott's limp and his continuous stories and anecdotes. Davy got bored with all the literary talk and, when they finally reached the top, came down quickly on his own.

William had taken Scott on a little tour of the Lakes, just as Scott had shown him the Borders, and they spent the night at a little inn at Patterdale. There wasn't a bedroom for them, so they were offered the sitting-room to sleep in, but this was occupied till after midnight by four ladies, who seemed set to gossip all night, despite William and Scott shouting out the time every half-hour through the window, pretending to be London nightwatchmen.

Scott also took Southey on his Lakes tour, and became a close friend of his, but he found Wordsworth the more impressive. 'Wordsworth in particular is such a character as only exists in romance,' wrote Scott to a friend after his visit, 'virtuous, simple and unaffectedly restricting every want and wish to the bounds of a very narrow income in order to enjoy the literary and poetical leisure which his happiness consists in.'

Dove Cottage had become too small for so many visitors, but the Wordsworths were uncertain about whether to move. They had decided to fit in with Coleridge's plans, if only Coleridge would write and tell them what his plans were. 'His returning to *live* in the North of England is quite out of the question,' Dorothy wrote to Lady Beaumont in October 1804. 'Therefore we intend to keep ourselves unfettered here, ready to move to any place where he may chuse to settle with his family. We find ourselves sadly crowded in this small Cottage since the Birth of the Little Girl and we are looking about for another house but we should only take it from year to year, that we may have nothing to bind us down.' Later, in a letter to Mrs Clarkson, she was contemplating a move to Kent: 'It is a dry county – perhaps we might all settle there. But oh, it will be a hard thing when we leave these dear Mountains without having some home to draw us back from time to time.'

Over at Greta Hall, the Southeys and Coleridges got themselves into a mild state of panic when the owner, Mr Jackson, announced that he was selling the house. A gentleman called Mr White inspected the building with his wife and a boy servant – a boy who later turned out to be a girl dressed in boy's clothes, to disguise the fact that she was the man's mistress. (Keswick seems to have been the place for scandals.) But the deal fell through, and Southey and his many relations were able to stay in Greta Hall.

William's own income must have been in a slightly healthier position than before, judging by a call the taxman made on him in December 1804. 'I have just had the Tax Gatherer with me,' he wrote to his brother Richard. 'We should have less contributions to pay if Dorothy and I had the money which I suppose you pay for in the funds or elswhere parcelled out between us. I am anxious that this should be done against the next assessment.' It is not clear what sort of financial arrangement he was hoping to achieve, but it is the mark of the middle class, and of established man in modern times everywhere, to be making plans to take any tax advantages that were on offer.

That winter, the lakes were frozen over once again, and this time, William, the family man, was out and about on his skates with his family in tow, or at least in front of him. 'We had been taking our pleasures upon the ice,' so Dorothy wrote to Lady Beaumont, 'my sister and I sitting upon our chairs with the children on our knees while my Brother and Mr H [Mary's brother George] in their skates drove us along.' It must have made a very attractive family picture. Such a pity photography hadn't been invented.

The happy family circle was missing two people they longed desperately to have with them again in the Lakes – poor Coleridge and dear John, William's sailor brother, whom Mary loved just as much as her own brothers. John had had two long voyages as Captain of the *Earl of Abergavenny*, and in January 1805 was waiting to set sail again, this time to China. He'd lost several thousand pounds on the first voyage, by investing in a cargo that didn't sell, but if this voyage was as successful financially as he hoped, it might be his last one, enabling him to retire and live near them.

John wrote from Portsmouth:

My investment is well laid in and my voyage thought by most persons the first of the season and if we are fortunate as to get safe and soon to Bengal – I mean before any other ship of the season – I have no doubt that I shall make a very good voyage of it, if not a *very great* one – at least this is the general opinion. I have got investments upon the best of terms, having paid ready money for great part of it, which I was enabled to do by one gentleman lending me £5,000. It amounts to about £20,000 in goods and money.

The passengers are all down and we are anxiously expecting to sail. We shall muster at my table 36 or 38 persons. In ship's company we have 200 and soldiers and passengers 200 more, amounting all together to 400 people, so that I shall have sufficient employment on my hands to keep all these people in order.

John then went on in his letter to discuss his favourite poems in the latest edition of *Lyrical Ballads*, and also some of the unpublished poems which he'd been sent. He was a loyal reader of his brother's poetry, and his letters were always full of intelligent comments and criticisms. He loved all poetry and took a large stock of books with him on every voyage. 'Remember me most affectionately to Mary and Dorothy,' he concluded. 'Give my little namesake and his sister a kiss from me, and believe me to be, Your affectionate brother, John Wordsworth.'

Alas, John died only a few days after this letter was written, on 5 February 1805. The ship was caught in a gale off Portland Bill and, despite the presence of a pilot on board, she drifted on to some rocks and then sank. Captain Wordsworth was one of the three hundred crew and passengers who died a cold and icy death.

The *Earl of Abergavenny* was the leading East Indiaman of its day – a large, well-known ship – and all prominent politicians were appalled by the accident. It was treated as a national catastrophe and all the newspapers were full of the story for many months.

Nothing like the death of John ever struck Dove Cottage, either before or after. Dorothy was heartbroken, physically ill with the anguish, and so was Mary. William was forced for once to do the letter-writing, informing all friends and relations of the tragedy, while trying at the same time to comfort Dorothy and Mary and to fight back his own tears.

'They are both very ill,' William wrote to Richard. 'Dorothy especially on whom this loss will long take deep hold. I shall do my best to comfort her; but John was dear to me and my heart will never forget him. God rest his soul!

'We wish you were with us. God keep the rest of us together. The set is now broken.'

William had always looked upon his three brothers and sister as a tight little unit, isolated by the early deaths of their parents and forced to struggle alone against the wicked world, and he saw the death of John as a terrible omen, convinced that more was bound to follow. The whole household went into a great emotional decline.

William's friends rallied round in a most heartening way, even those who might previously have poked fun at him behind his back. Walter Scott sent his condolences and Southey wrote a most touching letter: 'I scarcely know what to say to you after the thunderstroke, nor whether I ought to say anything. Only – whenever you feel or fancy yourself in a state to derive any advantage from company – I will come to you or do you come here.' William at once invited Southey over: 'If you could bear to come to this house of mourning tomorrow, I should be forever thankful. We weep much today – and that relieves us.' Southey came over at once and stayed several days with them, comforting them in their distress. 'He wept with us in our sorrow,' wrote Dorothy, 'and for that cause I think I must always love him.' It is often said that Wordsworth and Southey, for all their geographical nearness, were not really close friends, but at this time they certainly were, forming a bond in grief which was never broken.

Charles Lamb, who had often mocked Wordsworth in his letters, proved of invaluable help. A rumour had been circulating that John Wordsworth had somehow mismanaged the ship, and then, in guilt and shame, had made little effort to save his own life. Lamb was employed by the East India Company and he used his position to clear up the mystery of John's death, personally interviewing survivors, and finally proving, after two months of investigations, that John had in no way been to blame for the disaster.

Coleridge was at a public reception in Malta at the Governor's house when a guest casually told him the news and he was instantly taken ill, collapsing and hurting his neck in the fall. His notebooks show the depth of his feeling, recalling all the joyous times he'd had with John: 'O dear John Wordsworth. Ah that I could but have died for you, and you have gone home, married Sarah Hutchinson, and protected my poor little ones. O how very very gladly would I have accepted the conditions.' It's not known how definite John was in his intention to marry Sarah one day, or whether Coleridge had turned their friendship into marriage in his own imagination; but others in the family had also thought the union possible.

When William began to recover from the first emotional shock, he realized that he'd probably also suffered a financial one, a blow which could prove just as crippling. John's £20,000 worth of investments also included William's own personal savings and those of Dorothy.

In a long, rather self-pitying, almost begging letter to Sir George Beaumont, William went into the details of his finances, describing how he'd managed somehow to live on the £900 Calvert legacy, plus £100 from *Lyrical Ballads*, throughout the last eight years. But to provide for their future well-being, he and Dorothy had risked £1,200 of their Lowther money on John's voyage. John had died, trying to ensure a secure life for William. Now all was lost.

Sir George immediately sent William some money by return – a noble and very typical gesture. It turned out to be unnecessary, as Richard Wordsworth soon afterwards informed William that the ship and cargo had been fully insured, so their investment would not be lost after all. William was naturally rather embarrassed by what he'd written and Sir George's generosity, but he decided to keep the gift after all, to buy some books.

The death of his brother stopped William writing any poetry for over two months, but long after that they were still all silently weeping whenever John's name was mentioned. The tragedy had a profound effect on all of them, despite the fact that John hadn't been to Grasmere for over four years – though William had met him in London two years previously, when he and Dorothy were returning from Calais. His death seemed to make them suddenly aware of their own lives, as all the memories which he had shared with them, even back to childhood, flooded back. 'My father in an allusion used to call him Ibex, the shyest of all the beasts.' (This is one of the few references in all William's writings to his father.) William felt from now on that he had to live his life for John's sake, doing his best to produce something worthy of John's memory. As a physical memento, he asked Richard to retrieve for him any personal remains found on the ship, such as John's telescope, or perhaps his box writing-desk. John's sword was eventually salvaged and sent to William – and is still in the Wordsworth family today.

John was almost perpetually in our minds [wrote William], was always there as an object of pleasure; in this he differed from all our friends, from Coleridge in particular, in connection with whom we have many melancholy, fearful and unhappy feelings, but with John it was all comfort and expectation and pleasure. We have lost him at a time when we are young enough to have been justified in looking forward to many happy years to be passed in his society, and when we are too old to outgrow the loss.

Grasmere contained so many memories associated with John that it confirmed them in their intention to move. 'This Vale is changed to us,' wrote Dorothy. 'It can never be what it has been and as we cannot spend our days here the sooner we remove the better.' In any case, they were upset by changes in Grasmere, by the tourists and by the new buildings, particularly one being built by an attorney from Liverpool called Crump. Mr Crump must have been a man of some means, because he was one of several people whom Hatfield (the Beast of Buttermere) had defrauded, using his name on bills. 'A temple of abomination,' wrote William, 'this house will stare you in the face from every part of the Vale and entirely destroy its character and simplicity and seclusion.'

The problem about moving was Coleridge. As we have seen, the Wordsworths couldn't make definite plans without knowing what he was going to do. 'We have entirely made up our minds upon quitting Grasmere,' wrote Dorothy, 'as soon as ever Coleridge has fixed upon and procured a residence for himself.'

Throughout the summer of 1805 they waited, expecting Coleridge every month, but they were still there when Christmas came. As usual on Christmas Eve, her birthday, Dorothy had suitably maudlin thoughts: 'Six Christmases have we spent at Grasmere and though the freshness of life was passed away even when we came hither, I think these years have been the happiest of my life.'

It is always tempting, though dangerous, to see what others never saw at the time, to stand back with the benefit of hindsight, presuming to detect patterns, pinpointing changes, encapsulating the strands of other people's lives. Yet one can't always rely on the participants to do it for us, since they are rarely aware themselves that they are changing.

William Wordsworth as a young man was different from William Wordsworth as a middle-aged man. Few people would argue about that. When and how and why the changes came about are much more difficult to agree upon, but it seems to me that in about 1805 he reached a watershed in his life. William at thirty-five held rather different views from William at twenty-five though he himself never seems to have remarked on it, which is strange, considering the degree of introspection with which he analysed his poetic development. His close family, his domestic partners, don't seem to have remarked on it either – but then, when you are close to someone, it's hard to see the changes. It was the younger writers coming up in the world, the new commentators and activists, who realized that William wasn't the person he once was – or wasn't, at least, the person they'd led themselves to believe he once was.

Marriage had a big effect on him; that was certainly one clearly defined staging post in his life. He had now taken on hostages to fortune and become very conscious of his responsibilities and duties as a family man. In all his letters, he now seems suddenly so obsessed by money, not in a greedy, avaricious way – greedy people wouldn't choose to be poets – but seeing money as a means of safety and security. He was the least spendthrift of men, a master of frugality, with no expensive luxuries or vices. Perhaps it was the Lowthers who did it. He saw how they had ruined his early life and he didn't want it to happen with his own family. He'd been so carefree in those wandering, post-Cambridge days, with only himself to think about. Now it was as if his childhood insecurities had arrived to haunt him.

He was not only married to Mary – he still had Dorothy and to a lesser extent Sarah Hutchinson; thus there were three women looking after so many of his needs, domestic and secretarial. Ten years earlier he'd walked alone, a rebel without any real close friends, refusing help and guidance, going his own way, but insecure, not sure of his aims. Now, he was becoming insulated, surrounded by attentive women – if not always doting ones, as Coleridge alleged. It wasn't surprising that he became more self-opinionated, not having outsiders to put him down. When they did, in the way of bad reviews, the women were there to protect and comfort him.

His male friends had changed. Coleridge had gone abroad, and although the Wordsworths still longed for his return, and were planning their future life around him, the things that he had meant to them could never be recaptured. Coleridge now made them melancholy, just as much as they made him happy. William's new male friends were older, like Sir George Beaumont, or becoming establishment figures, like Walter Scott and Humphry Davy, both eventually to be knighted for services to their respective professions. William often called himself a recluse, which was untrue, but for some years he had been cut off from regular London contacts and all the new movements and influences.

Politically, there had been drastic changes in William's outlook. His new friends tended to have Tory views and, like Southey, he was losing his radical fervour. The war with France had a confusing and complicating effect on his politics, one which is hard to appreciate fully today.

William didn't think he had basically changed, still loving liberty and democracy as he always had done. It was the revolutionaries who had changed. They had let him down. They'd turned to excesses, creating a tyranny, and were in turn being replaced by a tyrant. England, whose institutions, such as the aristocracy, the Church and the government, he had once despised, now seemed the home of fairness and freedom and all the best moral values.

The death of John had a very sobering effect, hardening William's resolve to live a moral, upright life and to be worthy of his calling. He'd never cheated or prostituted his art for immediate gain or fame, but at the same time he hadn't castigated those who did fall to such temptations. Now, he started telling others how to behave, moralizing and sermonizing. His own shortcomings as a young man were almost forgotten, or he forced himself to forget them, perhaps out of guilt, putting the whole Annette saga out of his mind, becoming almost a puritan in his attitudes to life as the years went on.

As for his poetry, most experts agree that his genius was fading by 1805, though he still had a great deal of fine verses in him. In his great Immortality Ode, which he completed in 1804, he himself mourns the changes brought with age. 'Whither is fled the visionary gleam? Where is it now, the glory and the dream?' He finished *The Prelude* in 1805, and worked on some new poems, which included work from his Scottish Tour. It also included 'Ode to Duty'. It is hard to imagine him writing that back in his Cambridge days.

One of the dangers in seeing watersheds, and attempting to define changes in someone's personality, is to forget that the young man is still inside the middle-aged body, if rather deeper down, hiding away. William might on the surface have become more reactionary and conservative in these middle years, but he was still liable to surprise.

Here he is in 1806, in a letter to Sir George Beaumont, making some witty, rather *risqué* observations, the sort of light descriptive writing we don't normally associate with Wordsworth, either in youth or middle age:

I am now writing in the Moss hut, a place of retirement for the eye and well suited to my occupations. I cannot however refrain from smiling at the situation in which I sometimes find myself here; as for instance the other morning when I heard a voice which I knew to be a male voice, crying out from the road below, in a tone exquisitely effeminate, 'Sautez, sautez, apportez, apportez; vous ne le ferez pas, venez donc Pandore, venez venez.' Guess who

this creature could be, thus speaking to his Lap-dog in the midst of our venerable mountains? It is one of the two nondescripts who have taken the Cottage
for the summer which we thought you might occupy, and who go about parad-
ing the valley in all kinds of fantastic dresses, green leather caps, turkey half-
boots, jackets of fine linen, or long dressing gowns, as suit them. Now you
hear them in the roads; now you find them lolling in this attire, book in hand,
by a brook-side – then they pass your window in their Curricle. Today the
Horses tandem wise, and tomorrow abreast; or on Horseback, as suits their
fancies. One of them we suspect to be painted, and the other, though a pale
cheeked Puppy, is surely not surpassed by his blooming Brother. If you come
you will see them, and I promise you they will be a treat.'

You never see that letter quoted in any literary study of Wordsworth.
It makes a pleasant change after all the gloom and melancholy.

Intimations of Immortality from Recollections of Early Childhood

Some early stanzas from Wordsworth's greatest ode, completed in 1804. He was thinking back to his childhood days in Hawkshead and his early visions, now beginning to fade.

The Child is father of the Man;
And I could wish my days to be
Bound each to each by natural piety.

There was a time when meadow, grove, and stream,
The earth, and every common sight,
        To me did seem
        Apparelled in celestial light,
The glory and the freshness of a dream,
It is not now as it hath been of yore;—
        Turn wheresoe'er I may,
            By night or day,
The things which I have seen I now can see no more.

The Rainbow comes and goes,
And lovely is the Rose,
The Moon doth with delight
Look round here when the heavens are bare,
    Waters on a starry night
    Are beautiful and fair;
The sunshine is a glorious birth;
But yet I know, where'er I go,
That there hath past away a glory from the earth.

Our birth is but a sleep and a forgetting:
The Soul that rises with us, our life's Star,
        Hath had elsewhere its setting,
            And cometh from afar:
        Not in entire forgetfulness,
        And not in utter nakedness,
But trailing clouds of glory do we come
        From God, who is our home.

12

Coleridge Returns
1806-1808

WILLIAM decided he would give himself a spring holiday in early 1806: go off on his own for once, buck himself up with a change of scenery. He went to London, his first visit there for almost four years, knowing that this time he would be rather welcome in many literary circles. As the author of the successful *Lyrical Ballads* – four editions so far, and still selling well – many people now wanted to meet him. He could move around freely and easily on his own. Mary couldn't come with him, as she was pregnant, yet again. Dorothy stayed at home, worrying if William should travel all that way, having just been 'tormented with the piles'.

It had been a rather claustrophobic winter in Dove Cottage – all cramped in the tiny bedrooms, sleeping two to a bed, babies doubling with adults, everyone restless and unsettled, still not knowing where or when they were moving, waiting for Coleridge's return. The depression of John's death hadn't yet fully lifted. William, naturally enough, longed for a little excitement in his life: 'I am chiefly come to crowd as many people and sight seeing as I can into one month with an odd sort of hope that it may be of some use both to my health of body and mind.'

He had seen himself as something of a recluse when he'd returned to his native hills six years previously, and that was certainly how he was regarded by his old London friends; but his household had grown enormously in a very short time. It's hard to be alone with a young family about, or with three ladies ministering to their needs, or with endless visitors requiring amusement. And although he disliked towns, and never wanted to live in one, there was scarcely a year from now on in which he didn't visit London. In the spring of the next two years, he made similar trips, though for different reasons.

He stayed two months in London this time – not one month, as he had planned – and went to several smart literary parties and society *soirées*, including a party given by the Marchioness of Stafford, where he wore his hair powdered and carried a cocked hat, and a ball given by Mrs Charles James Fox, where he met Fox himself, just a few months before his death. As a young man, Fox, the great liberal, had been one of William's heroes, so it was worth getting his hair done, and they had a little chat about poetry. Wordsworth's name didn't appear in the VIP guest list in the *Morning Post* for either of these functions, as he was very much a passing entrant in society, but he was moving around and even met Lady Holland for the first time, the leading Whig hostess of the day.

Many people who felt in touch with the literary world, especially with its *avant-garde* elements, wanted to have a glimpse of the man behind what was now being referred to as the new school of poetry, as much because it was disliked and had annoyed as because it was popular. It had in fact been overtaken as the number one literary topic by *The Lay of the Last Minstrel*, which had just appeared, hot from the presses (they actually did advertise volumes as being 'hotpressed'), and William graciously wrote to his friend Scott to tell him so: 'I heard of your Last Minstrel everywhere in London; your Poem is more popular and more highly spoken of than you can possibly be aware of.'

However, William was doing better in society than Southey, who was also in London at the time. They'd travelled part of the way down in the same coach, Southey leaving when they were near Lincoln, to visit Cambridge. 'Wordsworth flourishes in London,' wrote Southey. 'He powders and goes to all the great routs. No man is more flattered by the attentions of the great, and no man would be more offended to be told so.' This was rather bitter, coming from Southey, who in his domestic life was a kindly man, but he'd just had the depressing

1 William Wordsworth was born in this house in Cockermouth, West Cumberland in 1770, the second oldest of five children. His father, John, a lawyer, was agent for Sir James Lowther, later Earl of Lonsdale. The house – which went with the job – is still the handsomest in Cockermouth.

2 Hawkshead Grammar School where Wordsworth was sent from the age of nine.

3 Windermere Ferry, with Belle Isle in the background, often used by Wordsworth when going to and from school in Hawkshead.

4 William Wordsworth, an early portrait by William Shuter, done in 1798 when Wordsworth was twenty-eight.

7 Dove Cottage, Grasmere. Wordsworth returned to the Lake District in 1799, after travels in France and the West Country, and moved into Dove Cottage with his sister Dorothy.

5 *Opposite above* Caroline Vallon, Wordsworth's illegitimate daughter. While in Orleans in 1792, at the height of the French Revolution, Wordsworth fell in love with Annette Vallon by whom he had one child.

6 *Opposite below* Dorothy Wordsworth, William's sister and lifelong inspiration.

8 and 9 Wordsworth lived the rest of his life in the Lake District, the subject and the source of much of his poetry. *Above* Windermere. *Below* Derwentwater and Bassenthwaite.

10 Mary Wordsworth, the Poet's wife, whom he married in 1802. She died in 1859.

11 Samuel Taylor Coleridge, co-author with Wordsworth of the *Lyrical Ballads* in 1798. They met in the West Country, and Coleridge then followed Wordsworth to the Lakes in 1800.

12 Robert Southey, the third of the Lake Poets. He in turn followed his brother-in-law Coleridge to the Lakes in 1803, and stayed there till his death in 1843.

13 Greta Hall, Keswick, home of the Coleridge and Southey families from 1800–43.

14 Thomas de Quincey, author and opium-eater, wrote a fan letter to Wordsworth in 1803 and subsequently took over Dove Cottage from the Wordsworths.

15 *Daughters of the Poets:* Sara Coleridge and Edith May Southey.

16 Dora Wordsworth, William's beloved daughter who died in 1847, aged forty-two.

17 The drawing-room at Rydal Mount, the final Wordsworth home, which the family moved into in 1813.

18 and 19 Wordsworth
and the Lake Poets
attracted a great
number of famous
visitors – though they
had known many of
them from their early
days, as young writers
struggling together – such
as Charles Lamb (1775–
1834) *above left*, and
William Hazlitt (1778–
1830) *above right*.

20 Sir Humphry Davy,
1778–1829, a young
friend from the West
Country with literary
leanings, who did proof
corrections on *Lyrical
Ballads*; later famous as
a chemist.

21 *above left* Sir Walter Scott, 1771–1832, best-selling poet of the age, but a friend to all the Lake Poets. In 1805, Scott, Davy and Wordsworth climbed Helvellyn together.

22 *above right* Sir George Beaumont, 1753–1827, artist and landowner, a founder of the National Gallery, friend and benefactor to Wordsworth for many years.

23 Lowther Castle, seat of the Earl of Lonsdale, a suitably impressive home for the most powerful friend in Wordsworth's life.

24 An early version, in Wordsworth's handwriting, from the section 'There was a boy ...' which later appeared in *The Prelude*.

25 Dorothy's Journal, 15 April 1802; the section which later helped William when he composed 'Daffodils'. 'I never saw daffodils so beautiful they grew among the mossy stones about and about them, some rested their heads upon these stones as on a pillow for weariness and the rest tossed and reeled and danced and seemed as if they verily laughed with the wind that blew upon them over the lake, they looked so gay ever glancing ever changing. This wind blew directly over the lake to them. There was here and there a little knot and a few stragglers a few yards higher up but they were so few as not to disturb ...'

26 William Wordsworth by Benjamin Haydon, painted in 1842 as if on Helvellyn – which Wordsworth climbed for the last time in 1840, aged seventy. Wordsworth died at Rydal Mount in 1850, aged eighty, and is buried in Grasmere Churchyard.

news from his publisher, Longman, that his latest book, *Madoc*, had earned him only £3 17s 1d in a year, and he was looking around, in vain, for a nice foreign posting, such as Portugal.

While in London, William managed to have the use of some rather stylish quarters, instead of sharing someone's lodgings, as he'd done in his early London days. He stayed first of all with his brother Christopher, who was still busily ascending the Church of England hierarchy, having been made domestic chaplain to the Archbishop of Canterbury and Rector of Lambeth, where he had a handsome, if not completely fashionable, residence. After that, William moved into the heart of Mayfair, staying at Sir George Beaumont's in Grosvenor Square. He also made a quick trip out to Windsor, to see his uncle, Canon Cookson – the uncle who at one time had banned him from the house, back in his disreputable, revolutionary days, though now, since William was a much more upright and respectable person, he was a welcome visitor.

William had his portrait drawn while he was in London; the artist was Henry Edridge, who had drawn Southey a year previously while up in the Lakes. He'd missed Wordsworth then, but the drawing he did now (used on the cover of this book) is probably the best and most attractive one of Wordsworth and was considered a good likeness of him in his middle years. There's a slightly amused look about the mouth, sensitive but not sour, which is not apparent in many of his portraits: the later ones, especially, make him look very dour.

Sir George, who paid for Edridge's drawing of William, was an amateur artist of note, as well as a great patron of artists of all sorts, and William dutifully went along to the Royal Academy exhibition, where he saw a painting of Peel Castle by Sir George, which moved him sufficiently to compose a poem about it.

William didn't fail to look up his old London friends, such as William Godwin, with whom he dined, though Godwin and his philosophy were now out of favour and he'd become somewhat obscure. He also saw Charles Lamb, who was, as ever, well in touch with London life and London happenings. All in all, it was a very busy eight weeks and, as he said, he hardly had more than five minutes free, certainly not enough time to do any reading. Dorothy was pining for him, trying to compose some poems of her own, and wrote what is tantamount to a love-letter to him, expressing the sort of emotions that had been common in her letters until his marriage: 'While Mary is undressing to go to bed I take my pen – The wind is howling away the rain beats. Oh my dear William that thou was humming thy own songs in time to it or resting thy hands upon thy knees as thou art used in musings between while work pauses – but thou art happy and it is better perhaps that we should sometimes be separated, even if thou didst not take so much pleasure in things as thou dost. . . .'

William had in fact indulged in lots of pleasures while away, whatever Dorothy might have felt about them being separated, and came home very refreshed, though in minor ways he would have appreciated an attentive lady in his wake. Six years of domestic bliss had made him rather absent-minded. First of all, he arrived in London with someone else's key which didn't fit his trunk, and then, for weeks after his arrival back in Grasmere, Dorothy was writing endless letters trying to sort out the mess he'd made with his belongings. He'd come back with two neckcloths belonging to Sir George, a waistcoat belonging to Canon Cookson, two pairs of socks belonging to his brother Christopher (they were now quite worn out), and a copy of *The Lay of the Last Minstrel*, which certainly wasn't his, as the Wordsworths' copy, sent by Scott himself, was at Dove Cottage. On the debit side, he'd lost a pair of shoes. Women do have their place, even in a poet's life. . . .

The Wordsworths' third child was born not long after William's return in June 1806: a second son whom at first they thought of calling William. Southey came over two days after the birth to pay his respects to the baby and the mother, who'd had a difficult time in labour, the pains being the worst she had suffered so far. Southey said, oh no, not *two* William Wordsworths!

Southey might have meant this satirically, but the family took it as a serious point. 'Southey is decided against William,' wrote Dorothy to Lady Beaumont, 'he would keep the father's name distinct and not have two William Wordsworths. It never struck us this way, but we have another objection which does not go beyond our own household and our own particular friends, i.e. that my brother is always called William amongst us and it will create great confusion.' This is an interesting observation. Coleridge, for example, was apparently always known to his friends – by all the Wordsworths and even by his own wife – as Coleridge. There's no record that I can find of him having been called Samuel by his contemporaries. It's hard to know what this indicates, if anything. Fashions in styles of address change. The use of surnames, even amongst very old friends, was normal in those days. William always wrote 'Dear Scott', not 'Dear Walter', even when he'd known Scott for years, and he addressed an old college friend like Francis Wrangham, whom he'd known most of his adult life, as 'Dear Wrangham'. William in his turn was addressed as 'Wordsworth' by such friends, but in his own house and in his immediate circle he was always William. It could be said to have been a sign of affection, and, as the years went on and he developed his own little ways, like losing his clothes, or taking up some new cause or passion, the ladies of the house became rather teasing in their references to 'Dear William', joking him along, making gentle fun of him. They were always reverential about his poems, but a nicely relaxed attitude to him as a person comes through in their letters. They didn't see him as the stern voice of God, as many outsiders did later, when reading his 'Ode to Duty'.

In the end, after all the discussions about the name William, the new son was called Tom. It came from Mary's brother Tom Hutchinson, and he and his wife were godparents.

William was very fond of all his children, and was an attentive father, though from the earliest days Dora seems to have been his favourite. Just after the birth of Tom, William and Dorothy walked across the mountains to Patterdale and Ullswater with Dora, aged two, on William's back. Whooping cough was raging in Grasmere and they thought they would at least get Dora, who was never very strong, away for a few weeks to their Hutchinson relations on Ullswater. On the highest parts of the mountains, a young man they met took turns in carrying her. 'She walked as happy as a bird,' wrote Dorothy, 'though in a stranger's arms. She noticed everything we saw and sang her pretty baby songs to the sheep and the cattle as she passed them. "Baa Baa black sheep" etc and "Cushy cow bonny let down thy milk". She never expressed one want or one wish except now and then to carry her can in her own hands out of which she drank out of streams or when Wm and I were at a distance from her she would say "Ather turn back again".'

When they got to Ullswater, Dora had done so well that – even though it was very late, and the stars were out and they'd intended to halt and find accommodation for the night – they decided to get a boat there and then and go straight down the lake to John Hutchinson's house. 'The little creature had never cried once, never given us anything but sweet smiles, except for the first half hour after we got into the Boat when she screamed and struggled dreadfully, wanting to be out on the water. . . .' Dora fell asleep at last, just as they got there, which is what so often happens to toddlers on long journeys.

From all Dorothy's letters, even when she is writing on mundane, everyday subjects, a gentle glow comes forth, a warmth and happiness. As Coleridge never tired of observing, William was most fortunate in his domestic life.

It was in Patterdale, overlooking the shores of Ullswater, that William espied a property: the picture-book setting he'd always wanted for himself. Most Lakeland connoisseurs, to this day, would probably choose Ullswater as their favourite lake. Grasmere and Rydal, though exquisite, are too small. Buttermere is very pretty, but doesn't have the grandeur of Ullswater. It was noticeable that when they were in Scotland, looking at every Scotsman's pride, Loch Lomond, they should all immediately have compared it with Ullswater.

William had a look round the nineteen acres that were on sale with the little farmhouse, realized the property could be developed one day with a little money and made big enough for their household, and made an offer of £800. He thought that was a realistic price – expensive for the amount of land, but worth it to him for the situation. The owner came back at length and demanded £1,000. A local rector had entered the bidding and although Wordsworth wrote to him, asking him to witdraw, he refused and the price remained at £1,000.

William had as good as forgotten about the property, leaving the matter in the hands of a local friend, who'd put in his bid of £800 for him, when, some time later, he was suddenly informed that the little estate had been bought for him, at the asking price of £1,000. William only had £800 available and, anyway, that was all he considered it was worth. Who was the mysterious person who had made up the difference of £200? Which figure, once a dreaded name in the Wordsworth family, had now appeared as a fairy godfather? Yes, none other than Lord Lowther, soon to be made Earl of Lonsdale by a second creation in 1807, just a few months after he arranged William's property deal.

He was the Good Earl, a distant relation of the Bad Earl. On the old Earl's death in 1802, he'd taken over the Lowther estates and paid off the family debts to the Wordsworths. Despite this, he had been a remote figure in William's life so far, since his return to the Lakes, and they'd never met – though, strangely enough, his name was on the guest list of one of the London routs William had attended the previous year.

The Earl had obviously heard of William's poetry and of his frugal life in Grasmere, and had decided to step in and help him when, through a mutual friend, he'd been told about William's frustrated desire to buy the little Ullswater property. William was most embarrassed. Dorothy, to use one of her favourite words, was mortified. William was upset on account of his own frugality – upset by the fact that £1,000 had been paid for a property he thought was worth only £800. 'I was unwilling to pay an exorbitant price out of my own money,' he wrote to his go-between friend, Wilkinson. 'I should be still more unwilling to pay it out of another's, especially a person who had shown to me so much kindness, treated me with such respectful delicacy.'

The property was bought, with William and Mary each providing £400 (Mary might not have received any wedding presents from her family, but she had inherited £400) and Lord Lonsdale paying the balance of £200.

William was overwhelmed with gratitude, once he'd got over his initial embarrassment – realizing that the great landowner himself, the most powerful man in Cumberland and Westmorland, had troubled to help a struggling poet. When William called at Lowther to offer his personal thanks, the Earl was out, but William sent him a humble, not to say grovelling, letter, all about the high honour the Earl's delicacy of mind had bestowed upon him, and ending with such a flourish that he hardly had enough space on the page to fit it all in. He usually signed himself either with his name or initials when writing to friends – or perhaps with 'your affectionate friend' if the acquaintanceship was less close – but in this, his first letter to Lord Lowther, he really let himself go:

> *My Lord,*
> *with the greatest respect and esteem,*
> *and the most lively sense of your kindness,*
> *Your Lordship's*
> *obedient Servant,*
> *William Wordsworth.*

It was the beginning of a long – and some alas might say rather nauseating, relationship – a relationship however, which eventually did blossom into a valuable friendship.

Meanwhile, Coleridge was due to return home. The Ullswater property, delighted though the Wordsworths were with it, was really part of a long-term plan, giving them a stake in the Lakes and making William a freeholder of Westmorland as well as of Cumberland; but their immediate aim was to link up with Coleridge on his return and live near wherever he might choose to live.

Coleridge had had an excellent first year abroad, getting himself a job as an acting secretary to the Governor of Malta, Sir Alexander Ball. He did the job very well, from all accounts, learning enough Italian in just a few months to settle a seamen's dispute and writing reports on Malta's political and economic strategies: all this was enough to make the governor extend his tenure of the post and keep him longer than he had planned. The sun did Coleridge's health good and he took some energetic holidays, as when he travelled across to Sicily and climbed Etna.

In the autumn of 1805, he finally left Malta and started making his way home. This was hardly the best time to start wandering round the Mediterranean. Napoleon was sweeping the sea, which he wanted to control as the last stage in his bid to master Europe, and only Nelson was holding out against him. The various blockades – with ships sinking, fighting or being captured – endangered Coleridge's own movements and clouded his friends' knowledge of them. No wonder they were all so worried about him in England, where nothing was heard of him for months, except for second-hand reports by people he'd met on his travels. Dorothy, no doubt thinking of John, dreamed one night that he had perished. 'I am too often haunted with dreadful images of Shipwrecks and the Sea when I am in bed and hear a stormy wind, and now that we are thinking so much about Coleridge it is worse than ever.' Coleridge arrived safely in Naples – which, however, wasn't safe for long, as the Napoleonic army was advancing towards it. Coleridge maintained later that he'd been on Napoleon's list of wanted men – which isn't too far-fetched a claim, as he'd written several strongly anti-French articles over the years in the *Morning Post*. He left Naples in time and made for Rome, where he stayed for almost six months, getting as usual into all the literary and artistic circles, just as he'd done in Germany.

Coleridge's voyage home, in an American ship, was equally hazardous, and the journey from Leghorn took thirty-nine days. He'd made friends with some American painters and writers, who had been attracted by his sympathy for the American war of Independence. Coleridge arrived back in Portsmouth in August 1806, two years and four months after he'd left England, his health just as bad as it had ever been, since the benefits of his first relaxed year in the Maltese sun had been dissipated by his subsequent wanderings and adventures.

The Wordsworths were horrified when they met him ten weeks later in Kendal. Tired of waiting to hear what his plans were, they had all set off south, to spend the winter at Sir George Beaumont's country home at Coleorton in Leicestershire.

Never did I feel such a shock as at first sight of him [wrote Dorothy]. We all felt exactly in the same way – as if he were different from what we have expected to see; almost as much as a person of whom we have thought much, and of whom we had formed an image in our own minds, without having any personal knowledge of him.

He is utterly changed; and yet sometimes, when he was animated in conversation concerning things removed from him, I saw something of his former self ... that he is ill I am well assured, and must sink if he does not grow more happy. His fatness has quite changed him – it is more like the flesh of a person in dropsy than one in health; his eyes are lost in it ... the divine expression of his countenance ... a shadow, a gleam there was at times, but how faint and transitory.

He has no plans for his residence, and as yet has taken no notice of anything we have said of our movements depending upon him and his. His misery has made him so weak and he has been so dismally irresolute in all things since his return to England.

The big problem was his wife. He just couldn't face going back to her and had decided that a separation was now the only solution. The Wordsworths were all in favour of him trying one more time to make a success of it, while concentrating his mind on a proper literary project and settling down to work again, though they knew that he and his wife were unsuited. Coleridge's plan was that he should be responsible for the education of his two boys, Hartley and Derwent, making a living for himself by lecturing and journalism, while his wife stayed up in Keswick with Sara, having the boys in the holidays. He hoped she could live on his Wedgwood annuity, as she'd done while he'd been abroad.

Coleridge and Hartley joined the Wordsworths at the Beaumonts' Leicestershire estate and spent the winter with them. It turned out to be quite a success. Sarah Hutchinson, now living almost full-time with the Wordsworths, was there, which was nice for Coleridge, who settled down to some work and to regular, sober habits.

'He does not take such strong stimulants as he did,' wrote Dorothy, 'but I fear he will never be able to leave them off entirely. He drinks ale at night and mid-morning and dinner time.

'He says he will write today to Mrs Coleridge his letter of final arrangements, but I shall not depend upon him till I see the letter sealed up and directed. Poor Soul! He is sadly deficient in moral courage.'

It must have been quite dispiriting for him, to have William in the same house, showing such wonderful powers of concentration, such energy and inspiration, working away at his poems. He knew only too well that, by comparison, his creative powers had almost faded and that Sarah, who'd once loved and cared for him, now appeared to love and admire William more than she'd ever loved him. William wasn't just working hard at his writing, but was busy landscaping and re-organizing Sir George's estate for him, drafting enormous detailed letters about what should be done. At Coleorton, all the Wordsworths started attending the local church twice on Sundays, something they'd never done in Grasmere. William, however, was very critical of the local village preacher. 'His sermon was, as Village sermons often are, very injudicious,' William wrote to Sir George, who was now at his Grosvenor Square house. 'A most knowing discourse about the Gnostics and other hard names of those who were Hadversaries to Christianity and Henemies of the Gospel. I don't know that I ever heard in a Country pulpit a sermon that had any special bearing on the condition of the majority of the Audience. The congregation consisted almost entirely of old persons.'

It's nice to see that his sense of humour hadn't left him – he displayed the sort of dry wit he'd used on the affected parson in *The Prelude*. It was the beginning of a more serious approach to religion, confirming him soon in his strong support of the Established Church. At Coleorton, however, it looks as if he went to church for the sake of appearances as much as anything, feeling that as he was living in the squire's house, and using the squire's servants and amenities, he should do the correct thing by the villagers.

The Wordsworths all returned to Dove Cottage in the spring of 1808, but not for long. They'd at last got a new house to move into – a much bigger, handsomer one, still in Grasmere – and it appeared to solve all their problems. It was arranged that Coleridge should have a room in it, where he could work and where Sarah Hutchinson could act as his secretary. Coleridge had decided to start his own magazine, something he'd attempted earlier in his life, which he would produce from

Grasmere and which would yield him an income; at the same time he would be near, but not too near, his wife.

Mrs Coleridge wasn't enthusiastic about this arrangement at first. Her big worry was that the disgrace of their separation would become public; Dorothy wrote about this in her letters at great length, thinking Mrs Coleridge was being very selfish, and worried only by her own image and reputation. The Wordsworths now thought that the separation should be made public, once and for all. In the end, the situation was greatly eased by Coleridge moving in with the Wordsworths at Grasmere. Hartley and Derwent went to a local school in Ambleside, spending weekends with the Wordsworths, and Mrs Coleridge was able to visit her sons fairly often at Grasmere, so that a semblance of family togetherness was kept up.

Coleridge, in his usual irresolute way, nearly ruined all the careful arrangements by not appearing. He hung around London after their winter at Coleorton, still unable to face being so near his wife; then he fell ill and said he was dying. William had to go down specially to London to find out what was wrong with him, doing some business at the same time in connection with his poems and having a passing visionary experience while walking down Fleet Street, of all places:

> I left Coleridge and walked towards the City in a very thoughtful and melancholy state of mind [he wrote to Sir George]. I had passed through Temple Bar and by St Dunstans, noting nothing, and entirely occupied with my own thoughts, when looking up, I saw before the avenue of Fleet Street, silent, empty, and pure white, with a sprinkling of new fallen snow, not a cart or carriage to obstruct the view, no noise, only a few soundless and dusky foot-passengers here and there; you remember the elegant curve of Ludgate Hill and towering above it was the huge and majestic form of St Pauls, solemnized by the thin veil of falling snow. I cannot say how much I was affected at this unthought of sight, in such a place, and what a blessing I felt there in habits of exalted imagination. My sorrow was controlled and my uneasiness of mind not quieted and relieved altogether, seemed at once to receive the gift of an anchor of security.

William's uneasiness had been caused by Coleridge's accusation that he had somehow been tampering with Sarah's letters, influencing her affections and turning her against Coleridge. It was nonsense, and part of Coleridge's growing paranoia, but the trouble was eventually settled to everyone's apparent satisfaction. Sarah was eager to help Coleridge in any way she could, and keen to work with him on his new project in the new house, so at last Coleridge arrived in Grasmere and by the autumn of 1808 they'd all settled down again. Life for the Coleridges and the Wordsworths was now once more very much as it had been before, or so it seemed....

The work which Wordsworth had been so busy on for so long was another selection of new poems, in two volumes, which were published in the summer of 1807 and are usually known simply as the *Poems in Two Volumes*. These poems represented almost seven years' work, as he'd published nothing new since the 1800 edition of *Lyrical Ballads*, and so they were eagerly awaited by his publishers, by his growing number of admirers, and also, alas, by the even more rapidly growing number of his enemies.

Looked at today, the two volumes contain some of Wordsworth's finest work, the peak of his last great creative phase, poems still enjoyed by the general public and admired by academics, such as 'Daffodils', 'To the Daisy', 'She was a Phantom of Delight', 'Among all Lovely Things', 'Ode to Duty', the sonnet on Westminster Bridge, 'The World is too much with us', 'The Solitary Reaper' and 'My Heart leaps up'. In all, there were one hundred and thirteen new poems, of different lengths, in different moods, in different forms, reflecting different but important stages in his life over the previous seven years, from the Scottish tour, and from waiting on the shore at Calais, to his new spirit of political patriotism. Some were complicated and philosophical. Others were simple verses about simple, natural objects. The second volume closed with his great 'Ode on the Intimations of Immortality'.

It was almost as if the critics had been waiting for him, sharpening their claws, having already made up their minds what they thought about him – and especially about his own views on poetry, as expressed in the Preface in every new edition of *Lyrical Ballads* which had appeared over the last five years. Even Walter Scott, while liking Wordsworth greatly as a person and admiring many of his poems, was worried slightly by what Wordsworth, and to a certain extent Southey, appeared to be doing: 'Were it not for the unfortunate idea of forming a new school of poetry, these men are calculated to give it a new impulse; but I think sometimes they lose their energy in trying to find not a better but a different path from what has been travelled by their predecessors.'

This was a very mild and affectionate way of putting it; but then,

Scott was a friend. Wordsworth's enemies also saw him as the head of a new school, but one they hated intensely. The idea of a School of Lake Poets, which had stuck in the public mind, had no strict basis in the facts. Coleridge had been away for about three years and had in any case written very little poetry about or in the Lakes. Southey, although a friend and neighbour, was never a poetic colleague, never a collaborator or even a fellow poetic spirit. It was the accident of marriage which had brought him to the Lakes. The school, such as it was, consisted of Wordsworth. It has to be admitted, however, that Wordsworth did see himself as a school on his own, someone sent to put poetry back on its feet, a self-elected arbiter of true poetic taste.

I've seen bad reviews in my lifetime, but I don't think I've ever read anywhere such vicious reviews as the ones Wordsworth received in 1807. It makes one feel protective towards him, sorry for an honest man made to suffer in such a way. It's impossible now fully to understand what the critics thought he had done to deserve such an annihilation. We know he had to expect to be taken down a peg or two because of his presumptuous Preface, but as for the vitriol, one can only mutter as excuse that it was the style of the times to be so savage.

The critical coverage of the various editions of *Lyrical Ballads* had been middling, roughly three bad and three good reviews, spread over some years. It was word of mouth which took them to four editions. Immediately, with the 1807 *Poems*, the big guns were out, and, over the next year, ten extensive reviews or articles were devoted to Wordsworth – and *each* one more or less slammed him.

The first review, in July 1807, was in the *Monthly Literary* and was by Lord Byron – the greatest Wordsworth-hater of his age, though this review was written early in his career, when he was just nineteen and still stretching his wings, or claws. Compared with the other reviews, it expresses what one might call a mild dislike.

Byron started his review by being rather kind and praising *Lyrical Ballads* – like almost all other young writers and poets of the day, he had admired, enjoyed and been greatly influenced by them – but then he quickly went on to say that this new offering was not equal to Wordsworth's former efforts. (It's strange how, even today, reviewers always seem to catch people *after* their peak, a peak which at the time was hardly noticed by anyone.) Byron found a couple of poems he quite liked for their 'native elegance, natural and unaffected, totally devoid of the tinsel embellishments and abstract hyperboles of several contemporary sonneteers'. He particularly picked out the patriotic poem, 'Another year, another deadly blow'. A couple of other reviewers, when they managed to find a kind word to say, also picked on this or another poem, 'The Happy Warrior', which contained some manly lines. After the death of Nelson, there had been a wave of fervent patriotism throughout the country, which even tough, cynical reviewers dare not mock.

After his few words of praise, Byron then got down to tearing the rest of the hundred-odd poems to shreds, calling the language puerile and the ideas commonplace. He had good sport with a poem called 'Moods of my own Mind' – 'We certainly wish these Moods had been less frequent' – and then quoted the nursery rhyme 'Hey diddle diddle, the cat and the fiddle,' saying that many of Wordsworth's poems were in the same namby-pamby style and the 'same exquisite measure'.

He managed one final nice word, noting that Wordsworth did have a genius worthy of higher pursuits, if only he wouldn't confine his muse to such trivial subjects.

The next review, in the *Critical Review*, was an absolute, non-stop attack, saying a silly book like this was a serious evil, that Wordsworth should be ashamed of himself, that even ridicule had failed to bring him to his senses, and that he was now beyond a laughing matter. He should practise self-denial and humility, wean himself from vanity and stop 'drivelling to a redbreast and pouring out nauseous and nauseating sensibilities to weeds and insects'.

Wordsworth had feared that a known enemy of his would review the book in the *Critical Review* and he'd written in advance to his friend Wrangham, who often reviewed for this magazine, asking him to use any influence to keep the book from the hostile critic. This particular enemy didn't in fact write the review, but this had obviously made no difference. 'Out of the frying pan into the fire,' William sadly remarked afterwards in a letter to Wrangham.

The worst, most extensive and most damaging review was by the dreaded Jeffrey in the *Edinburgh Review*. This magazine spared few people, and had a go at Byron the next year, savaging his first book of poems. (Byron later turned on them in a famous attack on the 'Scotch Reviewers'.) Jeffrey said that *Lyrical Ballads* had been deservedly popular, but the new poems were childish, tedious, miserable, disgusting, absurd; Wordsworth was obviously raving and many lines simply made no sense; the new school was perverse and in bad taste, and must be killed off at once before it gained any more ground. Jeffrey went so far as to hope that these new volumes would not sell – in fact, he was *convinced* they would never sell – and he finished by looking 'for a verdict against publication'. One later reviewer cynically welcomed the new poems – saying that they signified 'the suicide of the new school'.

It would be too cruel, even now, to go on any further. There were admittedly some banal lines and some flat verses in the collection. One poem addressed to 'The Spade of a Friend' had all the wits falling about in mirth, and there were numerous verses to weeds and insects, but it's remarkable that not one of the ten reviews praised the great 'Immortality' ode, or even mentioned the dozen or so other poems which appear in all the anthologies and selections to this day.

Considering the violence of the onslaught, William took it all very stoically. The London wits and witlings, he said, were too busy running around from rout to rout in the senseless hurry of their idle lives to have any time for love or reverence. The critics and the public would have to be educated. 'Trouble not yourself upon this present reception,' he wrote to Lady Beaumont. 'Of what moment is that compared with what I trust is their destiny, to console the afflicted, to add sunshine to daylight by making the happy happier, to teach the young and the gracious of every age, to see, to think and feel and therefore to become more actively and securely virtuous; this is their office which I trust they will faithfully perform long after we are mouldered in our graves.'

He had never expected the volumes to sell well, not like *The Lay of the Last Minstrel*, nor to be critically well received. While in London, he'd been told of a gentleman who'd picked up a copy of the poems, glanced through them and chanced to light on 'Daffodils', remarking 'A fine morsel this for the Reviewers'. 'When this was told me, for I was not present, I observed that there were two lines in that little Poem which if thoroughly felt, would annihilate nine tenths of the Reviews of the Kingdom; the lines I alluded to were those: "They flash upon that inward eye, which is the bliss of Solitude."'

He maintained that he hadn't seen all the reviews, having read some of them simply by chance, and that he'd only been told, for example, how malicious and spiteful the *Critical Review* had been. 'But Peace to this gentleman, and all his Brethren,' as Southey neatly says, 'they cannot blast our laurels, but they may mildew our corn.'

William put on a brave face, but there's little doubt he was deeply hurt and distressed. He had with him the finished manuscript of a new long poem, *The White Doe of Rylstone*, when he had gone to visit Coleridge in London, and Coleridge helped in the negotiations with the publishers. William was demanding a hundred guineas for a thousand copies, on condition that it was published untouched, which at first the publishers refused to do, though they later consented. But now William himself refused to proceed, as he had become disillusioned with the whole idea of publication, despite Coleridge's efforts to persuade him to agree to it. The mauling he'd received from the reviewers had obviously affected him.

Dorothy was distraught when she heard he was now opposed to publishing his new poem. They were just about to move into their new and bigger house and needed the money desperately. She took the view that to give up now would only make the reviewers the winners:

As to the Outcry against you, I would defy it – what matter if you get your 100 guineas into your pocket? Besides, it is like as if they had run you down, when it is known you have a poem ready for publishing, and keep it back.... Without money what can we do? New house! new furniture; such a large family; two servants.

We cannot go on so for another half year. We must ... dismiss one of our servants and work our fingers off our poor bones. Do, dearest William, do pluck up your disgust to publishing. It is but a little trouble and all will be over and we shall be wealthy and at our ease for one year, at least.

William stuck to his decision not to publish *The White Doe*, and he also kept back an even longer and, to him, more important poem, *The Excursion*, which he was soon near to completing. In fact, he published no new poems for another seven years. All the same, the Wordsworth tribe, closely followed by Coleridge, did move into the big new house, did get themselves some furniture, and did keep on the two servants, despite the lack of those hundred guineas in William's pocket.

THE WORLD IS TOO MUCH WITH US

One of the many new poems published in the 1807 collection. He was not aware, when writing, how viciously the outside world would react to them.

THE world is too much with us; late and soon,
Getting and spending, we lay waste our powers:
Little we see in Nature that is ours;
We have given our hearts away, a sordid boon!
This Sea that bares her bosom to the moon;
The winds that will be howling at all hours,
And are up-gathered now like sleeping flowers;
For this, for everything, we are out of tune;
It moves us not. – Great God! I'd rather be
A Pagan suckled in a creed outworn;
So might I, standing on this pleasant lea,
Have glimpses that would make me less forlorn;
Have sight of Proteus rising from the sea;
Or hear old Triton blow his wreathed horn.

13

The Great Estrangement
1808-1813

YOU may recall Wordsworth's horrid remarks about that new house being built in Grasmere, the 'abomination' which would 'ruin' his beloved vale. This was the house, Allan Bank, into which he moved in 1808.

It's a large, handsome, detached house, set in its own grounds just outside the village of Grasmere, under the slopes of Silver Howe, on the other side of the Grasmere Vale from Dove Cottage. It has subsequently been altered, but as residences go, it was and is much more desirable than the little cottage at Town End, not just in size but in its superior position, raised slightly above the village, without that rather enclosed, rather dampish, claustrophobic feeling which lingers over the houses in the valley bottom, especially on damp, rainy days – which, alas, are a feature of the Vale of Grasmere. The Wordsworths took it because nothing else was available and its size was perfect for their large household. They grew to like both it and Mr Crump, whom they'd earlier disparaged. William even came back especially from a trip to Penrith, just because Mr Crump wanted some advice on laying out the gardens, and all of them enjoyed picnics with the Crump family on Grasmere island.

They needed a large house because, as Dorothy half boasted in a letter, they regularly found themselves a family of fifteen people. It had all started with just William and Dorothy, but now they were a veritable commune. Firstly, there were William and Mary and their four children – the fourth, another girl called Catherine, was born in September 1808, a few months after they'd moved into Allan Bank.

Then there were Dorothy and William's sister-in-law Sarah Hutchinson, which makes eight so far. Coleridge was another permanent guest, plus Derwent and Hartley at weekends (which makes eleven); then Mrs Coleridge and her daughter Sara came for a week or so at a time (bringing the number to thirteen), and the two servants bring the total to fifteen. That's not taking into account the outside visitors, especially in the summer, who often stayed several weeks.

When Lady Holland, the fashionable London hostess, made her tour of the Lakes with her husband, calling on William *en route*, as part of what was becoming a statutory itinerary for rich tourists, she didn't ask to stay with the Wordsworths, but invited William out to dinner at their hotel. He went, and regaled them with his views on the latest developments in Lakeland – how he hated white houses and buildings which ruined the scenery. Lady Holland was much taken with him, but her diary contained a rather back-handed compliment: 'Much superior to his writings, and his conversation is even beyond his abilities. I should almost fear that he is disposed to apply his talents more towards making himself a vigorous conversationalist.'

Since it wasn't often that people said William was good in conversation – unlike Coleridge – and usually noted that his forte was the monologue, this doesn't say a great deal for Lady Holland's opinion of his writings.

Coleridge had his own room at Allan Bank and it was here that he worked out plans for the *Friend*, a 'Literary, Moral and Political Weekly Paper, excluding personal and party politics and the events of the Day, conducted by S.T. Coleridge of Grasmere'. William rallied in support and wrote to his new smart friends, including Walter Scott and Lord Lonsdale, asking them to take out subscriptions, which became a little embarrassing when after six months the magazine still hadn't made its first bow, despite the subscriptions having been paid. Coleridge, as ever, needed time to settle, going off to Penrith and Kendal for weeks at a time, negotiating the printing and the buying of the stamped paper which was needed to post copies to subscribers, before finally getting down with Sarah to producing the first issue, which appeared in June 1809. To everyone's surprise, particularly the Wordsworths', new issues kept on appearing – if only just – and Allan Bank became a hive of happy industry, with most of the womenfolk busy provisioning and cleaning and bringing up the assorted children, and the men working hard and soberly at their creative writing.

William turned increasingly to prose in the next few years, perhaps partly on the rebound from his reviews, but partly to help Coleridge with his magazine. He almost filled several issues with a long tract on his 'Advice to the Young', telling them how to conduct themselves, morally and spiritually, in these unsettled times, and he also wrote a long essay on epitaphs. Perhaps his most important prose work, which he threw himself into with enormous passion, was his pamphlet on the Convention of Cintra. It was based on an international political row, now long forgotten and too complicated even to begin to unravel, which concerned the British Government having allegedly let down Spain and Portugal in their fight against the French oppressors, withdrawing their troops when they could have helped them more. Even at the time, the details had almost been forgotten when William finally published his pamphlet, as he'd taken so long correcting and recorrecting the proofs. Coleridge, like Southey, was in agreement with his views, and was all ready to march and sign petitions and organize meetings of protest; but he realized that, because of the delays, Wordsworth had missed his chance with his political appeal and was probably also going to fail with his moralizing in general.

'Had I not known the author I would willingly have travelled from St Michael's Mount to Johnny Groat's house on a pilgrimage to see and reverence him,' Coleridge wrote to Stuart, editor of the *Courier*, who had published William's introductory essays on the same subject.

But from the public I am apprehensive, first, that it will be impossible to re-kindle an exhausted interest respecting the Cintra Convention and therefore that the long porch may prevent readers from entering the Temple. Lastly, I fear that readers even of judgments may complain of a want of shade and background; that it is all foreground, all in hot tints, that the first note is pitched at the height of the instrument and never suffered to sink. . . .

It was a good reflection on much of William's work, not just his prose. Coleridge was slightly wrong about the pamphlet in that it was quite well received by the handful of critics who bothered to notice it; three of them praised William's humanity, while regretting some of his verbal faults. Canning was reported to have considered it the 'most eloquent production since the days of Burke'. But Coleridge was right about the public's reaction. Most of the five hundred copies printed remained unsold. 'Many copies were disposed of by the publishers as waste paper and went to the trunk makers,' Christopher Wordsworth reported in the *Memoirs*.

It was a very impassioned appeal to humanity in general to defend the poor and unprotected, over and above its concern for a passing political event, and it was reprinted during the First World War, in 1915, by a publisher who thought it could be used to rally enthusiasm for the war against Germany. (He said it helped a lot.) It reveals a great deal about Wordsworth's political views at the time – and also about the power of his passions. He was a most emotional man, often carried away by causes and grievances, campaigns and ideologies. The Cintra campaign went on for months and for a time took up all his energies, what with writing to Lord Lonsdale, trying to get his help, sending copies of his pamphlet to the Portuguese and Spanish ambassadors, and walking along the road to Keswick at two o'clock one morning, desperate to find the carrier with the newspapers and the latest intelligence from the Iberian struggles.

From now on, William was involved in many other passionate causes, in widely differing fields – always sure that he was in the right. He took up the cause of education, for example, at about this time, convinced that an educationalist called Dr Bell, with his so-called Madras system, using pupil-monitors to teach the children, was going to be the saviour of humanity. He wrote many letters on his behalf and for a few months taught according to Dr Bell's methods at the local school in Grasmere.

Then there was the simple, straightforward humanitarian campaign he organized for a local poor family, the Greens, whose parents had perished in the snow on the fells, leaving six orphaned children. The Wordsworths took in one of them, Sally, as a sort of nanny for their own children, agreeing to house and feed her and be responsible for her well-being, and they launched an appeal for £500 to secure a future for the rest of the orphans. It was a most stirring and heartening campaign, which was a huge success. They wrote to all their well-off friends, such as Lady Holland, who organized a collection from the members of her own circle (which included the Duke of Devonshire), and she sent them £32 which she'd raised in two-guinea subscriptions. Walter Scott sent an unsolicited donation.

Dorothy wrote a little pamphlet about the Greens – graphic, heart-breaking and going into the whole family saga – which was sent round to likely subscribers. Several people said she should publish it, but she declined, saying that would only bring the six orphans too much personal publicity, which might affect their future lives. They closed the appeal at £500, when more could possibly have been raised, not wanting to overdo it.

William's passions (and several of them ran concurrently) were either ideological or humanitarian. There were no signs any more of animal passions, no fleshly sins or vices, not even any luxuries or self-indulgence.

When he was down in London that time, trying to rescue Coleridge from his sick bed, they all attended a little party at the *Courier* offices, given by the editor. Coleridge was there, and Southey, plus Charles Lamb and a few others. As they were leaving, Lamb, in his jocular way, remarked that everyone would now be going out into the streets to 'make up to the first pretty girl he sees'. Only William questioned this light-hearted speculation. 'Sad Josephs are some of us in this very room,' replied Lamb.

Some chinks slowly began to appear in the image of the one big happy family, all working away together at Allan Bank. Firstly, their original criticism of the workmanship of the house itself was proving to be correct. Despite endless modifications, the fireplaces were found to be badly built and, once winter came, the whole house was constantly full of dirt and dust. 'Smoky house, wet cellars, workmen by the half dozen make attempts, hitherto unsuccessful, to remedy these evils,' Dorothy wrote.

There was one stormy day in which we could have no fire but in my brother's study and that chimney smoked so much that we were obliged to go to bed with the Baby in the middle of the day to keep it warm and I, with a candle in my hand, stumbled over a chair, unable to see. We cooked in the study, and even heated water there to wash dishes. The Servants, you may be sure, have been miserable, and *we* have had far too much labour, and too little quiet. At the height of the storm, Mrs Coleridge and her little Girl were here, and Mr Coleridge is with us constantly, so you will make out that we were a pretty large Family to provide for in such a manner. Dishes are washed, and no sooner set in the pantry than they are covered with smoke. Chairs, carpets, painted ledges of the room, all are ready for the reception of soot and smoke, and are never clean.

Mr Coleridge was also beginning to prove troublesome. He was soon up to his old habits, taking to the bottle and other stimulants, falling ill, staying in bed all day, accusing everyone of being against him. Dorothy, for long his champion, was betraying signs of growing irritation in her letters to friends, though, having severely criticized Coleridge, she usually gave them instructions to keep it all private. Even William, writing to Coleridge's old friend Thomas Poole, was becoming rather harsh in his attitude:

You will consider me as speaking to you now in the most sacred confidence and as under a strong sense of duty. I give it to you as my deliberate opinion, formed upon proofs which have been strengthened for years, that he neither will nor can execute anything of important benefit to himself, his family or mankind. Neither his talents nor his genius, mighty as they are, nor his vast information will avail him anything; they are all frustrated by a derangement in his intellectual and moral constitution ... nor is he capable of acting under any constraint of duty or moral obligation.... The *Friend* cannot go on for any length of time. I am *sure* it cannot.... The disease of his mind is that he perpetually looks out of himself for those obstacles to his utility which exist only in himself. I am sure that if any friend whom he values were in consequence of such a conviction as I have expressed, to advise him to drop his work, he would immediately ascribe the failure to the damp thrown upon his spirits by this interference. Therefore in this way nothing can be done.... Pray burn this letter when you have read it.

In February 1810, Sarah decided to leave, having had enough. 'We shall find a great loss in her as she has been with us more than four years,' wrote Dorothy, 'but Coleridge most of all will miss her as she has transcribed almost every Paper of the *Friend* for the press. The fact is that he either does a great deal or nothing at all. He has written a whole *Friend* more than once in two days ... and he generally has dictated to Miss Hutchinson who takes the words down from his mouth.'

Sarah went off to stay with her brother Tom, who was now farming in Wales, and Coleridge managed somehow to produce one more issue of the *Friend*, the 28th number, in March 1810. It was the last to appear.

We have no hope of him – none that he will ever do more than he had already done [wrote Dorothy]. If he were not under our Roof, he would be just as much the slave of stimulants as ever; and his whole time and thoughts are employed in deceiving himself and seeking to deceive others. He will tell me that he has written half a *Friend*, when I know that he has not written a single line. I am loathe to say it, but it is the truth. He lies in bed till after 12 o'clock and never walks out ... he goes [to his room] the moment his food is swallowed ... sometimes he does not speak a word. The Boys come every week and he talks to them especially to Hartley but he never examines them in their books. He speaks of the *Friend* always as if it were going on ... do not think it is his love for Sarah which has stopped him in his work – do not believe it; his love for her is no more than a fanciful dream, otherwise he would prove it by a desire to make her happy. No! he likes to have her about him as his own, as one devoted to him, but when she stood in the way of his gratifications it was all over. I speak this very unwillingly and again I beg, burn this letter.

What a sad household. Ten years previously, romantically roughing it in the West Country, William might have put up with the responsibility of having a drug addict in the house, but now, with his many commitments and his new sense of propriety and moral duty, it became unbearable. Coleridge was poisoning the whole family. He wasn't just letting William and Dorothy down, but all the friends and contacts whom they had persuaded to help him set up the *Friend*. You can so clearly see the poison seeping through all their letters from Allan Bank. They'd grown quite fond of Mrs Coleridge over the last year or so, feeling sorry for her, and they quite enjoyed her regular visits, when she came to see the boys; but they were beginning to feel slightly resentful, as they realized that they, not Coleridge's wife and family, were having all the trouble looking after him. Dorothy wrote:

Sara [Coleridge] is to stay with us till next Monday when her Mother will come and spend three or four days here.... Mrs C. is desirous to put off the evil day, for she dreads the contamination which her lady-like manners must receive from our rustic brood worse than she would dread illness. As to poor little Sara, she has behaved very sweetly ever since her Mother left her, but there is nothing about her of the natural wildness of a child.... Mrs C. does not look as if any of her cares have kept her awake, but she says she sleeps badly; however this may be, she is very fat and looks uncommonly healthy.

The problem was at last solved when Coleridge, after a spell back in Keswick at Greta Hall, as a guest in his own home, was offered a room by Basil Montagu, William's old friend, in his London house. Montagu had been to stay at Allan Bank and had taken pity on

Coleridge's pathetic physical and mental condition. Montagu was now married to his third wife – the previous two having died – and was at last prospering as a lawyer. William and Dorothy had taken in his child, all those years before, when he himself had been having a hard time. Now he and his wife had a large London house and felt they could provide a room in it for Coleridge, and, with the aid of their family doctor, perhaps manage to rehabilitate him, though it seemed obvious to most people that he was almost beyond recovery. In October 1810, Coleridge climbed into Montagu's carriage and headed for London ...

The Wordsworths breathed many sighs of relief and returned to their normal life, at last being able to give proper attention to some new friends who had come into their lives in the last couple of years, especially a young gentleman called Thomas De Quincey.

Just as Coleridge moved off stage, at least for the moment, De Quincey had moved on – a young, very healthy, very eager young man, almost as well read as Coleridge, and, as far as they could see, with none of Coleridge's unsavoury propensities for stimulants such as opium.

It was through a fan letter that De Quincey became known to William. The first known fan letter to him had been from that Glasgow university student, John Wilson, who had recently followed up his correspondence by moving into the Lake District, taking a house on Lake Windermere with his mother. He was a very wealthy young man, literate and talented, yet at the same time a great athlete, a lover of all Lakeland sports, very fond of outings and expeditions, and the Wordsworths went on several of his picnics and boating trips. Wilson also interested himself in the *Friend*, and William's rather pompous and long-winded articles, 'Advice to the Young', were written in reply to a letter in the *Friend* from Wilson, asking Wordsworth, the sage, to offer the fruits of his wisdom.

De Quincey sent a similar fan letter. He was a mere stripling of seventeen at the time, about to go up to Oxford. This was in 1803, after he'd read the two-volume edition of *Lyrical Ballads*, and he wrote to William, via Longmans (William's publishers), to say how he'd been enslaved by William's poetry for two years. 'The whole aggregate of pleasure I have received from some eight or nine other poets that I have been able to find since the world began falls infinitely short of what these two enchanting volumes have singly afforded me.' The mere thought of meeting Wordsworth had rescued him from despair during the last two years, but what chance had he to meet him? 'What claim can I urge to a fellowship with such society as yours, with genius so wild and magnificent?' He added that he was just a boy, 'but that my life had been passed chiefly in the contemplation and worship of nature'.

De Quincey was indeed only a boy, but the use of the word 'nature' was a little misleading: he had been living for many months with the down-and-outs in London, consorting with drug addicts and prostitutes, until his money had run out. He was born in Manchester, the son of a wealthy merchant who had died when De Quincey was seven. He went to Manchester Grammar School, where he'd been brilliant at Latin, but had run away. William was so impressed by De Quincey's sensitivity and language that he wrote a letter in reply, adding an invitation to visit him at Grasmere.

Nearly three years later, during which time De Quincey had continued to idolize from afar Wordsworth and Coleridge, he made an attempt to take up the standing invitation. He got as far as Coniston, where he spent the night at an inn, but gave up out of shyness and returned to Oxford.

In 1807, however, he managed to get himself introduced to Coleridge, who was staying with friends in Somerset, before his arrival at Allan Bank. De Quincey knew all Coleridge's work by heart, and they had three hours of philosophical and intellectual dicussion. De Quincey arranged to make an anonymous gift of £300 to Coleridge, doing it through a third party and saying it was 'from a young man of fortune who admired his talents'. Coleridge had to go to London, to do some lecturing, so De Quincey offered to squire Mrs Coleridge and the children by coach back up to the Lake District. And so, in November 1807, De Quincey at last met Wordsworth – almost five years after being first invited.

Their first stop in the Lakes had been at Dove Cottage. The three Coleridge children – Hartley (nine), Derwent (seven) and Sara (five) – were all very excited, and Hartley ran ahead as they approached the gate. De Quincey could hardly contain himself. 'This little cottage was tenanted by the man whom, of all men from the beginning of time, I most fervently desired to meet – that in less than a minute I should meet Wordsworth face to face. I did tremble.'

De Quincey's account of the great meeting, in his *Recollections of the*

Lake Poets, is perhaps the most readable description ever written of Wordsworth, if rather waspish:

> He was, upon the whole, not a well made man. His legs were pointedly condemned by all female connoisseurs in legs; not that they were bad in any way which would force itself upon your notice – there was no absolute deformity about them; and undoubtedly they had been serviceable legs beyond the average standard of human requisition; for I calculate, upon good data, that with these identical legs Wordsworth must have traversed a distance of 175,000 to 180,000 English miles – a mode of exercise which, to him, stood in the stead of alcohol and other stimulants; to which indeed he was indebted for a life of unclouded happiness, and we for much of what is excellent in his writings. But, useful as they have proved themselves, Wordsworth's legs were certainly not ornamental; and it was really a pity, as I agreed with a lady in thinking, that he had not another pair for evening dress parties – when no boots lend their friendly aid to mask our imperfections from the eyes of female rigorists.

De Quincey was excellent with the Wordsworth children, inventing games and amusements for them. He was also very good with the womenfolk – chatting to them, accompanying them on little trips, squiring them on social occasions when William wouldn't go. On his first visit he stayed for a week.

Eventually, when the Wordsworths moved out of Dove Cottage, De Quincey took it over and held the tenancy for the next twenty-eight years. Dorothy made him curtains, and his moving-in was remembered for the never-ending books that continued to arrive in packing cases for several months in succession. He was very proud to be a resident of Grasmere – one of the literary Lakers at last – and thrilled by the beauty of Dove Cottage and by life in Grasmere.

When the lake froze over in winter, he watched the Wordsworths skating. De Quincey, ever observant of William's physical appearance, wasn't as enchanted by William's skating as he himself was: 'He sprawled upon the ice like a cow dancing a cotillion.' De Quincey was fascinated by William's marriage and by his whole attitude to women. He just couldn't imagine William ever being head over heels in love with a woman:

> I could not conceive of Wordsworth as submitting his faculties to the humilities and devotion of courtship. That self surrender seemed a mere impossibility. Wordsworth, I take it upon myself to say, had not the feelings within him which makes this total devotion to a woman possible. There never lived a

woman whom he would not have lectured and admonished under circumstances that should have seemed to require it; nor would he have conversed with her in any mood whatever without wearing an air of mild condescension. Wordsworth, being so, never could in any emphatic sense, have been a lover.

If only De Quincey had known about Annette, what a surprise he would have had! He surely didn't know, because in his *Recollections* he mentions William's stay in Orleans, but gives no hint of the affair. And De Quincey, who repeated and enlarged on every piece of gossip, would certainly have used it in his book, as he spared nobody's feelings. But this was how he now found William – a prematurely aged and rather stiff, self-centred man, surrounded by doting women.

Whatever De Quincey may have thought of William's personality, he always had a very high estimation of his work and rejoiced in all his success and good strokes of fortune: 'A more fortunate man, I believe, does not exist than Wordsworth.'

Dorothy was particularly fond of De Quincey, though William tended to treat him rather more formally. In letters to him, for example, he would refer to his wife as 'Mrs Wordsworth', whereas he called her Mary in writing to his old friends, like Coleridge. He used De Quincey very much as an extra secretary, finding him very helpful, for example, in seeing his Cintra pamphlet through the press in London.

De Quincey often stayed at Allan Bank, while Coleridge was there, for weeks at a time, either because work was being done on Dove Cottage, or because it was too crowded with his latest purchase of books, or because they all wanted him to stay in the family, playing with the children and helping with the latest literary project.

'We feel often as if he were one of the Family,' wrote Dorothy. 'He is loving, gentle, and happy – a very good scholar and an acute Logician – so much for his mind and manners. His person is unfortunately diminutive, but there is a sweetness in his looks, especially about the eyes which soon overcomes the oddness of your first feeling at the sight of so very little a man. John sleeps with him and is passionately fond of him ...'

De Quincey was devoted to all four Wordsworth children – even to Catherine, the baby of the family. Dorothy wrote: 'Mr De Quincey has made us promise that he is to be her sole Tutor; so we shall not dare to show her a letter in a book when she is old enough; and you may expect that she will be a very learned lady, for Mr De Q is an excellent scholar. If however he fails in inspiring her with a love of learning, I am sure he cannot fail in one thing. His gentle sweet manners must lead her to sweetness and gentle thoughts.'

The fifth and final Wordsworth child was born in May 1810. He was another son, and they decided they would after all use the name William, despite their previous hesitations, though he was always known as Willy, which stopped any possible confusion with his father. The depth of love and affection for their young learned friend Mr De Quincey is shown by the fact that he was made one of the godfathers, the other being John Wilson, the fellow fan. It must have been great comfort to the Wordsworths, in their problems with Coleridge, to have had the charming Mr De Quincey so constantly in attendance.

During that coach trip to London in October 1810, Montagu started to tell Coleridge a few of the personal words of wisdom and warnings that William had imparted to him before they'd left Grasmere. Perhaps on their overnight stops Coleridge had already displayed some of his more annoying personal habits and Montagu was just trying to warn him, to make him sober up and mend his ways, and it was out of temporary exasperation that he repeated what William had told him in confidence. Montagu had always been a rather idle gossip, thoughtlessly repeating things – not really out of malice, more out of amusement. Whatever the provocation, it was on this journey, so Coleridge maintained, that Montagu told him some of the awful things William had said: Coleridge had become an 'absolute nuisance in the family'; he was now a 'rotted drunkard' who had 'rotted his entrails out by intemperance'.

This was the beginning of one of the best-known literary rows of the nineteenth century. There were many to come – Dickens and Thackeray were embroiled in equally juicy rows – but the London wits and witlings got particular pleasure out of this one, watching the two leaders of the new school, whom they didn't like anyway, coming to verbal blows.

William, alas for him, didn't know anything at all about Coleridge's grievance for months. All winter, he dined out in London on the terrible indignities he'd been forced to suffer, telling everyone about his utter mortification that the friend whom he'd dearly loved – had, in fact, given his whole life and being to for so many years – had secretly hated him and had wanted him out of his house, after he, Coleridge, had given William years of 'consummate friendship' and had been ever 'enthusiastically watchful' over his literary fame. 'Yet the events of the last year have now forced me to perceive – no one on earth has ever LOVED ME ... So deep and rankling is the wound which Wordsworth has wantonly and without the slightest provocation inflicted in return for 15 years self injuring Friendship ... that I cannot return to Grasmere or its vicinity. ...'

The Wordsworths didn't hear any of this from Coleridge – which wasn't unusual, as Coleridge in the past had often not written or replied to them for months. It wasn't until the following spring that they heard some of the allegations from the Charles Lambs, but they didn't take much notice at first, Dorothy assuring Lamb that there was certainly no coolness towards Coleridge on William's part. But in May, Mrs Coleridge let them see a letter she'd received from her husband, in which he inferred that William had caused the disarrangement of his mind. 'Coleridge has been driven to madness by Wordsworth's cruel or unjust conduct towards him,' Dorothy said, reporting the allegations.

William wrote to Mrs Coleridge, explaining that all he'd done was warn Montagu that Coleridge had one or two habits which might spoil his tranquillity. He asked her to pass the message on to Coleridge. He didn't want to write directly to Coleridge, who hadn't conveyed his displeasure directly to him. Mrs Coleridge said she was too frightened to do what he asked, and she shouldn't have shown her letter to the Wordsworths in the first place. ... And so it went on, with the row building up through third persons, Coleridge becoming more manic and William gradually realizing the whole matter had got out of hand and was doing serious damage to his reputation.

In February 1812, Coleridge came up to the Lakes on a brief visit, to clear up the business side of the closure of the *Friend*. He picked up the boys from their school at Ambleside, and then drove right past the Wordsworths' house in Grasmere on his way to Keswick, with little Hartley pointing and shouting and wanting to go and see his friends; but Coleridge refused to stop or even look. News of that incident was soon all over London.

Dorothy felt very sorry for William, the butt of all Coleridge's slanders, after all the things William had had to put up with throughout the years, such as going down to London that time when Coleridge was supposed to be very ill. 'Poor William went off, in consequence of his having solemnly assured Mrs Coleridge that he could not live three months more, and when William arrived, he had to wait daily for admittance to him, till 4 o'clock in the afternoon, and saw no appearance of disease which could not have been cured.'

In the end, William went down to London once again, in April 1812, 'with a determination to confront Coleridge and Montagu upon this vile business'. At first, Coleridge refused to see him. There were yet more letters, and much to-ing and fro-ing, as Lamb and others tried to act as mediators. Finally, it was Henry Crabb Robinson, a new friend of Wordsworth's, a minor literary figure trusted by both sides, who brought about a reconciliation of a sort.

William had, indeed, said some pretty tough things about Coleridge, but he denied having said the exact words which Montagu was supposed to have relayed and, anyway, what he did say had been said in confidence, not to be repeated. It was really all Montagu's fault. Wordsworth and Coleridge shook hands and went for a long walk to Hampstead in May 1812, talking peacefully and amicably, two rather worn-looking gentlemen, now more worldly-wise and a little more cynical than in those first heady days of their passionate friendship. William was now forty-two and looked it, having for a long time appeared much older than his years; while Coleridge was just a few months away from his fortieth birthday, but looked at least fifty, sickness and intemperance having prematurely aged him.

In many senses, they had failed each other. Coleridge's genuine love and admiration for William's genius had turned to bitterness as he abused his own genius and his own body, becoming jealous of his friend's success, energy and, most of all, domestic happiness. Coleridge failed William because he'd failed himself. William had loved his friend equally and those years of separation had been agony for him, wishing desperately that Coleridge would return, convinced that all would be well again, that Coleridge would once again stimulate and inspire him, and that their life together, wherever it might be, would blossom and flourish as it had done in the past. Whether he also *admired* Coleridge is more in doubt. There's no record of any lavish praise by William of Coleridge's talent – nothing like the praise Coleridge poured forth on William. And as for Coleridge's character, William had doubts and worries about his friend's moral fibre from the earliest days, and was aware of his weaknesses and his vices.

Coleridge also saw clearly, from the earliest days, that there were differences between them. In 1803, a rather bitter and malicious literary friend from London had spent a depressing evening with them at Dove Cottage, and Coleridge wrote afterwards about how the evening affected him: 'This had produced a very unpleasant effect on my Spirits. Wordsworth's mind and body are both of a stronger texture than mine; and he was amused with the envy, the jealousy, and the other miserable passions that had made their Pandaemonium in the crazy Hovel of that poor Man's heart – but I was downright melancholy at the sight.' One of the most remarkable features of Wordsworth, throughout his life, was his soundness of mind and body. His stability was an enormous strength.

When Coleridge could no longer give anything to William, because of his own mental and physical state, it was then, even though he had brought a great deal of his troubles on himself, that he needed William most. But William couldn't help. He did try, and, for nearly four years after Coleridge's return from Malta, did his best to restore him to health, helping with his magazine, creating a working environment for him, organizing the household around him; but it didn't work. Even today, with our superior knowledge of drug addiction and our increased medical facilities, rehabilitation is not an easy task.

Wordsworth was essentially moral and moralistic, strong and determined in mind and body. Coleridge was sinful and suffering, weak in almost every way. De Quincey considered that Coleridge probably had the greater mind and the more abundant talents, but that he squandered them. Wordsworth had the 'profounder and more ascetic solemnity', while Coleridge had 'prodigal and magnificent eccentricities'.

As poets, no-one can really evaluate what they gave each other. Coleridge's greatest poetic work was done quickly and magnificently, during that first incredible year when they met, when he produced 'The Ancient Mariner' and 'Kubla Khan'. After about 1802, he became inhibited as a poet, giving up very quickly, declaring that he was leaving the creative work to Wordsworth. Wordsworth too had enjoyed an inspired burst of activity, and though *Lyrical Ballads* was originally a joint creation, most of the content was Wordsworth's. His genius continued to grow for the next ten years, despite long absences from Coleridge's company and supposed inspiration. Might they have done just as well without each other? The consensus of critical opinion over the last hundred and fifty years is that their early work was a joint explosion. They needed each other.

After reading the relevant letters and the reviews carefully, I think that it could be argued that in fact they *harmed* each other, just as much as they helped each other. Coleridge very quickly disintegrated as a poet, and Wordsworth never really gave him much critical advice or inspiration.

Coleridge did give Wordsworth much help, seeing in him what others had missed, drawing attention to his greatness, explaining him to his friends and then to a confused public – especially in *Biographia Literaria*, which Coleridge published in 1817. But perhaps Coleridge overdid it. He embarrassed Wordsworth by his praise, which rebounded somewhat. Calling him a genius at every opportunity, and saying he was so ahead of everyone else that he was out of sight, naturally caused resentment, creating expectations which couldn't be met, especially as Coleridge was well aware that in Wordsworth's greatness there was always the possibility of banality, the possibility that he could be ridiculous instead of revelatory.

Many of those savage critics talked in their reviews about Wordsworth's 'injudicious friends and flatterers'. Who could they have had in mind but Coleridge, the social butterfly, who went round the London salons, gave public lectures, wrote in the public prints, and took every opportunity, always for the best of motives, to praise his friend?

Like so many partnerships in history, it ended in a silly squabble, a sad spectacle which did credit to neither side. Coleridge never came back to the Lakes and was never part of the Wordsworth household again.

The year of the so-called reconciliation, 1812, turned out to be a sad one for the Wordsworths in several ways. They'd moved to another house in Grasmere, the Parsonage, in the summer of 1811, and this was the home which Coleridge passed that time, without stopping. They hoped they would be free at last from smoking fires, but their short stay at the Parsonage proved just as uncomfortable as life at Allan Bank.

'Now I must tell you that we like our new house very much,' wrote Dorothy. 'There are only three important objects to it. First, that it fronts the East and has no sitting rooms looking westward therefore we lose the sun very soon; secondly that it is too public; and thirdly that the field in which the house stands is very wet and cannot be drained. It is no playing place for the children and leads them into continual temptation to dirty and wet themselves.'

They got used to the lack of direct sun and planted a few shrubs to hide themselves from the road, though, being right in the centre of Grasmere village, right beside the church, they were always in public view; but it was the damp in the end which got them down. They hadn't realized till they'd been in residence for some time that when the field flooded, their house became waterlogged. Ever afterwards, they thought the dampness in the Parsonage was one of the reasons for the ill health of their children.

Little Catherine, aged three, had been weak for some time, ever since a convulsion a year earlier after she'd eaten some raw carrots. De Quincey, in his *Recollections*, unfairly put the blame for this on Sally Green, the orphan girl, then only eleven, who was supposedly looking after little Catherine at the time; but there's no reason to think Sally had been negligent. However, Catherine was left with a limp and, despite various treatments, never regained good health. William and Mary took her, and Thomas who was two years older but also a sickly child, to the seaside, down the Cumbrian coast, which was a great success, and for a while her health did seem to improve.

But in June 1812, Catherine had another convulsion while both William and Mary were away from home. William was just about to leave London, after his reconciliation walk with Coleridge in Hampstead, and join Mary in Wales, where she was having a short holiday with her brother Tom. While they'd been away, Dorothy and Sarah, who had now returned to the household, were in charge of the five children. Dorothy wrote:

On the Sunday afternoon and the Monday I had been for several hours with Willy and her [Catherine] in the Churchyard and they had run races. I then particularly noticed how little was to be seen of her lameness and several persons who came up to speak to us observed how trifling the lameness was. That very night on which she was seized she ran up to bed in such glee striving to get before Willy, and proud that she was going to sleep in her Mother's bed, an unusual treat. We returned from our walk at a little after nine and John called me to her about a quarter to ten. He was going to bed, found that she had been sick. She was lying with her eyes fixed – and I knew what was going to happen and in a fright called Sarah. She would have persuaded me that the child was only overpowered with sickness but I had seen her before and knew only too well. We lost no time in sending for Mr Scrambler [the doctor] and the meantime applied the remedies used before. Mr Scrambler gave us no hope....

She died on Wednesday the 4th and was buried on the 8th. We all three, Sarah, John and I followed to her grave. She lies at the South West corner of the church yard, under a tall and beautiful hawthorn which stands in the wall.

Dorothy immediately wrote to William in London, the letter just catching him as he left, asking him to tell Mary the dreadful news when he reached her in Wales; but she also wrote a little note to Tom, Mary's brother, warning him that William would be arriving with bad news. Tom unwittingly read the letter in Mary's presence, and when she saw his face, she realized something must have happened and he was forced to tell her. She was distraught and was still ill when William arrived – hardly able to move or speak, except to say that she feared that another child would soon die.

Dorothy also wrote at once to De Quincey, knowing that Catherine had always been his special favourite. 'It is a great addition to our affliction that her Father and Mother were not here to witness her last struggles and to see her in the last happy weeks of her short life – she never forgot Quincey. Dear innocent. She now lies upon her Mother's bed, a perfect image of peace.'

De Quincey was more than distraught. For a while, he became mentally deranged by little Catherine's death, stretching himself every night for two months on her grave in Grasmere churchyard, where she had run races only just before her death, convinced that he could still see her, running happily around. Coleridge, whom they thought might be equally grief-stricken, took little notice of Catherine's death, neither coming to Grasmere to console the family (as they half expected), nor writing, which hurt them deeply.

Mary's awful premonition came true. Just six months later, in December 1812, Thomas died, catching pneumonia after a serious bout of measles. William and Mary were both at home. On this occasion, it was Dorothy who was away. William did the letter-writing this time, as Mary was too ill with grief. 'Pray come to us as soon as you can,' he wrote to De Quincey, who was in Liverpool at the time. 'My sister is not at home. Mrs W bears her loss with striking fortitude, and Miss Hutchinson is as well as can be expected.'

William also wrote to Southey, letting them all know at Greta Hall,

I dare not say in what state I am. I loved the Boy with the utmost love of which my soul is capable and he is taken from me – yet in the agony of my spirit in surrendering such a treasure I feel a thousand times richer than if I had never possessed it. God comfort and save you and all our friends and us all from a repetition of such trials. O Southey feel for me. You will impart this sad news to your wife, Mrs Coleridge and Mrs Lovel and Mrs Wilson. Poor woman. She was good to him. Heaven reward her.

Catherine was not quite four and Thomas six and a half. Their deaths clouded the family for many years, much in the same way as the death of John had done seven years previously. William's grief-stricken sonnet, 'Surprised by joy – impatient as the wind', was written in memory of little Catherine. Coleridge at last wrote in sympathy at this second death, when he heard about Thomas, expressing his pain and saying he would come when he'd finished work on a play; but he never did.

The final days at Grasmere ended, therefore, in great sorrow. They were desperate to get out of the Parsonage, the scene of each death, and shake off all the bad memories which Grasmere now had for them, both at Allan Bank (with the Coleridge troubles) and the Parsonage. The next year, 1813, they finally moved out of Grasmere and into a new house and a new life: a change of scene which coincided with a change in their fortunes.

SURPRISED BY JOY

'This was suggested by my daughter Catherine long after her death,'
so Wordsworth said. Catherine died in June 1812, aged three years
and nine months.

SURPRISED by joy – impatient as the Wind
I turned to share the transport – Oh! with whom
But Thee, deep buried in the silent tomb,
That spot which no vicissitude can find?
Love, faithful love, recalled thee to my mind –
But how could I forget thee? Through what power,
Even for the least division of an hour,
Have I been so beguiled as to be blind
To my most grievous loss! – That thought's return
Was the worst pang that sorrow ever bore,
Save one, one only, when I stood forlorn,
Knowing my heart's best treasure was no more;
That neither present time nor years unborn
Could to my sight that heavenly face restore.

14

Fine Folks
1813-1817

THE Wordsworths moved into Rydal Mount on May day, 1813, without ever having been inside before. The previous owners, a family called North from Liverpool, had left the house empty for several weeks, but refused to let the Wordsworths go inside until they had removed their wine from the cellar. The Wordsworths already knew, just from the outside, that they would be happy there. It's still a fine, handsome house today, up a steep lane from the roadside, with tremendous south-facing views across to Rydal Water and the northern edges of Lake Windermere. It was high and dry and nicely secluded, compared with the damp and exposed Parsonage in Grasmere, and was very much a house of style and taste – far smarter than anything they'd ever had before – with over four acres of gardens and a splendid drawing-room.

They never owned Rydal Mount, nor any other house they ever lived in, though they owned property they didn't inhabit. Their landlady, called Lady Fleming, was their nearest neighbour; she lived at Rydal Hall with her mother, Diana, also a Lady Fleming. The elder Lady Fleming was very fond of William and his poetry and encouraged him and his family to call. 'Lady D. has bought a little present for Willy,' wrote Wordsworth, 'what it is she has not told us, but he is very anxious to call there, expecting gratification from her little Dogs, her Peacocks or perhaps from the sight of her perenially blooming and brilliant cheeks!' They were never as friendly with the younger Lady Fleming and when Lady Diana died in 1816, relations were occasionally strained.

Rydal was only two miles away from Grasmere, along the road to Ambleside, but it was in many ways part of a different world. Grasmere was very much a working village (though one or two merchants from Lancashire were already buying up plots and building their holiday homes), but Ambleside had always had definite pretensions, with a sprinkling of old county families, ladies and gentlemen of quality who led an active social life. At Rydal Mount, the Wordsworths were now well within calling distance for the Ambleside gentry.

'The place is a paradise,' wrote Dorothy, 'but my inner thoughts will go back to Grasmere. I was the last person who left the House yesterday morning. It seemed as quiet as the grave ... the house only reminded me of desolation, gloom and emptiness and cheerless silence – but why do I now turn to these thoughts? The morning is bright and I am more cheerful today.'

They all settled down to furnish and equip the new house, knowing that, with the weather improving, they would soon have lots of visitors, coming to see their fine house as much as the fine new occupants. Even William went to the sales with the whole family to buy tables and chairs and ornaments, returning home with goods by the cart-load. These Lakeland country sales, to this day, are great social occasions, with the whole neighbourhood congregating in the house whose goods are for sale, bringing their children and sandwiches and making a day of it. 'We stayed the sale out to the very last and the beds were sold by candle light,' wrote Dorothy. 'All walked home in the bright moonshine, I with a water decanter and glass in my hand and William and Mary with a large looking glass, oval with a gilt mirror, to be hung in the best lodging room, very cheap, £1 13s.' Dorothy was writing this letter to Sarah and she described how all the time William had wished Sarah had been there, knowing how much she enjoyed a good sale: 'William bitterly regretted you were not here to talk over the humours of the Sales.'

Almost all their furniture was second-hand. But, though at first they thought they would buy cheap Scottish-made carpets, they then decided that only the best would do for the Wordsworths of Rydal Mount and bought the finest new carpets.

Now I must tell you of our grandure [wrote Dorothy]. We are going to have a Turkey!!! carpet – in the dining room and a Brussels in William's study. You stare, and the simplicity of the dear Town End cottage comes before your eyes and you are tempted to say 'are they changed, are they setting up for fine folks? for making parties, giving dinners, etc? No, no, you do not make such a guess, but you want an explanation and I must give it to you. The Turkey carpet (it is a large room) will cost 22 guineas and a Scotch carpet would cost 9 or ten. The Turkey will last four Scotch therefore will be the cheapest, and will never be shabby, and from this consideration we were all of one mind that the dining room carpet should be a Turkey one.

Mary and I were rather ashamed of the thought of a Brussels (for William's room) and inclined to the Scotch as looking less ambitious and less like setting up ourselves upon the model of our neighbours – the Ambleside gentry, who all intend calling upon us, though happily most of them considered it would be inconvenient at present, and I assure you we take their apologies very quietly and say as few civil things in return as possible. Our Master was all for the Brussels and to him we yielded. A humour took him to make his Room smart and we did not oppose him.

William was equally anxious to smarten up their life style, personally hanging up some water-colours that had been painted by his landed friend, Sir George Beaumont, and working out plans for landscaping the large gardens. But then he wasn't just the new occupant of a desirable residence. He had a new position in society, one of some responsibility and standing, one which needed some dignity and the keeping-up of appearance. Just as he moved into Rydal Mount, he got himself a job, the first one in his whole life.

During the whole of the previous year William had been very worried about his financial situation. He had three children to educate, a large household to support and very little money coming in. The Lowther debts had been paid long before, and Montagu at last paid his in 1813; most of these monies had been carefully invested by Richard, who still looked after the family's financial affairs, but William's total investment income was relatively slight, possibly not much more than £200 a year. He had long since realized that he could never count on his poems bringing him in much money. He reckoned in 1812 that his total returns so far from his poetry – and by now almost twenty years had elapsed since his first book was published – came to only seven score pounds. Not even Wordsworth, who always travelled on the outside of coaches, rarely ate meat, often wore second-hand clothes, never took strong drink and never wasted candles, could exist on an average income from his writing of £7 a year. If he was going to be a best-selling poet, like Scott, it would have happened by now. A future as a poet who could support his family appeared impossible.

He wrote to Lord Lonsdale in early 1812, asking him if he had any situations available for which he could recommend him. It was an ever-so-humble, bending-over-backwards-to-please sort of letter, and it is hard to tell if any of the sentiments expressed were in the slightest way cynical – if perhaps he was half revolted by having to beg – or whether he was totally unaware of any humiliation.

In the letter he said that literature had been the pursuit of his life, but for many reasons it had turned out unprofitable: his writings didn't suit the taste of the times and he was unwilling to associate with the more fashionable literary men of the day. He felt emboldened to beg a favour because of his family connection with Lord Lonsdale. 'My father and grandfather did conscientously, I believe, discharge such trusts as were reposed to them through that connection. But *my* situation is a peculiar one and I have been chiefly encouraged by a knowledge of your Lordship's attachment to Literature and by particular marks of kindness with which you have distinguished me.'

One might have thought that William would have wanted to keep out of the grips of the Lowther family, of all people, having suffered so much from them in the past, but presumably it appeared to him to offer his only hope. He was indeed a genuine admirer of the new Earl of Lonsdale, who was a civilized man, and their families had had long connections. It was the custom of the times for the landed gentry, especially the truly wealthy and landed such as the Lowthers, to spread around their largesse, though there were not many like Sir George Beaumont, who had a real interest in all the creative arts. Young artists, of all sorts, depended on such patronage. You might get a government pension, if you were old enough or had distinguished yourself in some way which usually meant having made friends with some important politicians or lords. But the best solution of all was to find a patron.

Twenty years before William had hated the very idea of the Lowthers and all their inherited wealth. He wanted the aristocracy destroyed. Now he neither hated them nor even felt disapproving of their money.

It seemed to him the natural and ideal scheme of things, that there *should* be vast landowners; as long as they treated their subjects with wisdom and kindness, he approved of their power. Lord Lonsdale was touched, and said he would look out for an opening, but there was nothing at the moment.

By October 1812, William was becoming rather desperate and wrote to Daniel Stuart, his London friend, editor of the *Courier*, saying that his 'powerful neighbour Lord Lonsdale' had promised to help, but that some time might elapse before anything might happen.

Now you know I live chiefly in a retired corner of the world and therefore there is no chance that I should hear of anything suitable likely to be vacant. Will you then be so kind as point out to me anything which is likely to answer my purpose that may come to your knowledge. Of course this is *between ourselves*. I have no objection, I must add, to quit this part of the country, provided the salary be adequate, and the duty what I am equal to, without being under the necessity of withdrawing myself wholly from Literature.

It's interesting to note that William was still prepared, at this late stage, to leave the Lakes.

Lord Lonsdale eventually approached the Prime Minister, Lord Liverpool, hoping to get William a pension, but though the Prime Minister was favourable, so William was told, the pension fund was limited. Instead, Lord Lonsdale personally offered William a pension of £100 a year from his own pocket, till such time as a situation presented itself. This put William in a difficult position, since he did not want to accept such blatant charity, despite his blatant begging (in another letter to Lonsdale he'd mentioned the tragic deaths of his two children in half a year, and how the remaining three were all down with measles), but, at the same time, he needed the money. Sir George Beaumont, asked for his advice, urged William to accept, otherwise the good Lord might be upset, but William decided to wait a while.

In early 1813, there was at last a job in the offing, and Lord Lonsdale offered William £100 in advance – which William readily took – till the appointment was confirmed. In March 1813, the new job became official, and William was unveiled as the new Distributor of Stamps for Westmorland.

It was a government job, and so, technically, William had become a civil servant, occupying one of the many provincial positions which a local feudal lord usually managed to control, putting forward the nomination in the right quarters when the position became vacant. It was by no means a sinecure, involving much more work than William expected, and less money than he'd been led to believe. He'd hoped to earn himself £400 a year, not realizing that the retiring Distributor had to be paid a pension of £100 from William's earnings and that he also needed to take on a clerk, John Carter (who doubled as gardener), to help with the paper work. But it was a secure income of about £200 a year. In the first year or so, while he was settling in to the post, it was taking up two-thirds of his time, so Dorothy said.

In those days, all legal documents, wills, insurance policies, pamphlets and books required government stamps, which could be bought from sub-distributors, usually local tradesmen or shopkeepers. The Distributor appointed his sub-distributors, handed out the stamps and collected the money, and so the job involved a lot of travelling round his area, a lot of paperwork, and a certain amount of worry – the ladies, in particular, worried when William was away from home and they were in charge of the stamps. Some skill was also needed to choose the right sub-distributors. One, in Kirkby Lonsdale, went bankrupt, owing £300 in stamp money. William, fearing that he would personally be held responsible for the debt, rushed across to Kirkby Lonsdale, took legal proceedings and was able to sell off the poor man's belongings and effects, managing in the end to recoup the losses.

It sounds rather a demeaning job for a poet, to become in effect a local collector of government taxes, but William was only the latest in a long line of English poets who'd become servants of the government. Chaucer had been clerk of works to Edward III; Spenser was secretary to Lord Grey in Ireland; Milton was Latin secretary to the Council of State under Oliver Cromwell. There are worse ways to earn a living.

Naturally, the whole Wordsworth family was very pleased. They could move in and furnish their fine new house, getting the Turkey carpet instead of the Scotch, without too many worries. The financial security would give William an easier mind and, when he'd organized the new job, some clear time to devote himself properly to his poetry. The London wits, however, didn't quite see it in the same light. They considered William had sold himself to the government and had become a Lowther lackey – a social crime for which some of them never forgave him.

In the same year that Wordsworth became Distributor of Stamps, Robert Southey became Poet Laureate – a much more distinguished position, though one that didn't pay much money (only £90 a year, plus a butt of sack). Then, as now, there were those who ridiculed the Laureate, pointing to the great poets who had never been so ennobled; but, on the whole, it was looked upon as a high honour, despite the fact that Walter Scott, the best-selling poet of the day, had just turned it down. Scott didn't feel up to writing the required odes on royal occasions, which often brought abuse down on the writer's head, and, anyway, he already held two public appointments. Instead, he put in a good word for Southey, as being a very deserving poet, with no other means of income and no government job, one who would dignify the profession of poet. It was a safe and popular choice. Southey consented on condition that he would write odes only when the spirit moved him, and not when the occasion demanded, which has remained the system to this day. Southey looked upon the Laureateship as something of a literary duty. For the previous hundred years – at least since Dryden, in the late seventeenth century – the position had been held by some very undistinguished poets. The Laureate who had just died was Henry James Pye, and you don't find him in many anthologies.

It was, in a way, an honour for the Lake Poets, as Southey was linked in popular minds with Wordsworth while, in critical minds, he had been spared most of the viciousness. At the same time, the honour was regarded as a stigma in some quarters. 'Mr Southey and even Mr Wordsworth have both accepted offices under the Government,' wrote Leigh Hunt, 'of such a nature as absolutely ties up their independence.' Wordsworth later refused another government job, again put in his way by Lord Lonsdale: that of a Customs Collector at Whitehaven. If he had accepted it he would have had to move, which by now he didn't want to do, being settled at Rydal Mount. As Sarah Hutchinson ruefully remarked, the London newspapers were not so ready to publish his refusal of this public post as they had been to publish his acceptance of the Stamp Office appointment.

One of William's little duties as a local Stamp official was to look up his superior, the Comptroller of Stamps, when he was in London. This particular official was a very self-important gentleman called Mr Kingston, who was looking forward to his first meeting with his well-known subordinate. In fact, he could hardly wait. He was a post-dinner guest at a dinner party, held in 1817, at which Wordsworth was a guest of the painter Benjamin Haydon, who had arranged the dinner so that young Keats and others could meet Mr Wordsworth for the first time.

It was a very jolly, very distinguished literary gathering and the guests included Charles Lamb. Everyone was extremely embarrassed when the awful Kingston duly arrived – except Lamb, who, being rather tipsy, made fun of him to his face.

Lamb had already been teasing Wordsworth, calling him a 'rascally Lake Poet', which William had taken in good part, laughing as Lamb had gone on to abuse Voltaire and Newton (not present, but there in spirit). When Kingston arrived, Lamb turned on him, calling for a candle to examine his phrenology, and pronouncing him a 'silly fellow' for calling Milton a great poet.

Keats afterwards felt rather sorry for William having to put up with such a man, and refused Kingston's invitation to his house. However, on the morning of Kingston's dinner, Keats chanced to call on William and found him dressed up in knee-breeches and silk stockings, all ready to go off and dine with his superior. Keats's romantic image of Wordsworth as a radical spirit diminished from that moment on.

A week later, William invited Keats for dinner, where he met Mary. He also thought he met Dorothy, according to his own accounts, but it was Sarah he met, as Dorothy had stayed at home at Rydal with the children. Keats had for long admired William's poems, and his private letters contain many quotations from 'Tintern Abbey', the 'Immortality' ode and others, but at dinner, he found William at his pontifical worst, laying down his own rules on poetry, and running down almost everyone and everything else. The scales dropped from Keats's eyes, as far as Wordsworth the man was concerned: 'For the sake of a few fine imaginative or domestic passages are we to be bullied into a certain Philosophy engendered in the whims of an Egotist. . . . I am afraid Wordsworth went rather huffed out of town – I am sorry for it. He cannot expect his fireside Divan to be infallible, he cannot expect but that every man of worth is as proud as himself.'

William didn't feel at all huffed out of town, and he had many new and distinguished admirers to huff him up, not down. Benjamin Haydon, for example, a painter of great note and reputation in his day, who knew and had painted most of the eminent writers and statesmen, was a close friend of his. Another new friend to visit was Henry Crabb Robinson, the gentleman who had helped with the so-called reconciliation between William and Coleridge. He was a wealthy bachelor, a lawyer by profession, who had met most of the great writers of Europe, including Goethe and Schiller. He later spent many holidays with the

Wordsworths and became perhaps William's closest non-Lakeland, non-family friend.

But it was a shame that William had disappointed the new young writers such as Keats. Today, we tend to classify this new young generation of poets along with Wordsworth – like Keats, Shelley and Byron – as the Romantics. You can see all their handsome images today, headed 'The Romantic Poets', grouped together in one room at the National Portrait Gallery in London. The new generation had been genuinely inspired by Wordsworth and Coleridge; they had thrilled to *Lyrical Ballads* and realized that the old order had gone, that a new spirit was in the air. It was a spirit that was simultaneously rushing through continental Europe, as poets, writers, artists and musicians generally were overthrowing the eighteenth-century classical framework and developing a more romantic, spiritual, lyrical inspiration, based on feeling rather than on form. The Romantic movement changed the culture of the civilized world, and in the English-speaking countries, Wordsworth is looked upon as its poetic leader.

At the time, however, the new poets didn't quite see Wordsworth in this light. They were becoming increasingly biased against him, upset by reports and gossipings of his growing reactionary attitudes, and, in the flesh, his rather pompous, didactic manner hadn't helped. He thought he was helping them, giving young people the benefit of his collected wisdom; but that wasn't how they saw it. William, alas, once a rebel, once a violent and opinionated young radical writer and activist, seems almost to have forgotten that he was ever young himself.

Remember how our hero, as a young blood at Cambridge in 1790, had ignored the system, refused to take honours and generally rebelled against most of the disciplines? In 1816, writing to his friend Thomas Clarkson, we find him heavily advising a young man at all costs to *conform* at Cambridge, and not to refuse to sit for an honour. The letter is full of weighty calls to duty and responsibility, with not a hint of tolerance or understanding, nor any reference, even as a warning, to how he himself had acted while in the same situation.

Remember that Bishop of Llandaff, the one against whom William had written his fierce, radical pamphlet in 1794? Not long after they had moved into Rydal Mount in 1813, William actually went to dine with him at his home on the shores of Lake Windermere. The bishop was one of the gentry who lived within calling distance of Ambleside, still an absentee Professor of Divinity at Cambridge, amongst other things, who had arranged for others to do his duties for over thirty years.

Remember William's own peccadilloes as a young man in France? These didn't stop him getting on his high horse whenever anyone else started what he thought was an inappropriate relationship, however respectably it might end. In 1814, his elder brother Richard, then aged forty-six, married a girl of twenty-two. 'He has done a foolish thing in marrying one so young; not to speak of the disgrace of forming such a connection with a servant, and that, one of his own,' wrote William to their other brother Christopher, the cleric.

William had never been particularly close to Richard, who had sometimes annoyed them by his slowness in answering their endless letters and queries about their finances, and had rather hurt them by only once coming to visit them in the Lakes, despite endless invitations and despite having his own property near Penrith. But, as he was their brother, they felt personally slighted by his unseemly marriage.

Dorothy proved more forgiving. A year later, when she'd at last met the girl, she was pleased to find she wasn't such a disgrace as they feared. 'You will be glad to hear that I like my Brother R's wife very well – the circumstances of her education, her rank in Society, her youth, etc, being got over. She is a very respectable woman and kind and attentive to her husband. She is not vulgar, though she has nothing of the natural gentlewoman about her. Her face is very comely and her countenance excellent.'

When young Thomas De Quincey, their devoted young friend and neighbour, committed what they considered an even more shameful act, they couldn't quite bring themselves to forgive him, though their row with him had a more basic cause than merely an unsuitable liaison.

Firstly, there appears to have been disagreement over changes De Quincey started making at Dove Cottage, such as cutting down some hedges to give more light to the apple-trees, which upset Dorothy. He was excellent with the children, and loved them all, but the Wordsworths began to be rather critical when he didn't always do what he said he would do. 'John now goes to Mr de Quincey for a *nominal* hour every day to learn Latin,' wrote Dorothy in 1813, when John, their eldest, was ten. 'This said nominal hour now generally is included in the space of twenty minutes; either the scholar learns with such uncommon rapidity that more time is unnecessary, or the Master tires.'

De Quincey, when in London, often took on the job of seeing some work by Wordsworth through the press, which was a thankless task, as William was always making corrections. One book went on for months, mainly because of William's changes, but they all blamed De Quincey each time things went wrong at the printers and he got little thanks in the end for all his pains.

Dorothy had begun to take quite a delight in passing on gossip about him, once relaying to a friend that his housekeeper was thinking of leaving him: 'What a prize she would be to your brother as a housekeeper. She is tired of Mr De Q's meanness and greediness.' Dorothy had been the one who'd absolutely adored De Quincey, whereas William, though liking him, had been more restrained and had kept his distance. When ill feeling arose, William tended to ignore it, not stooping to malicious remarks. 'Mr De Quincey has taken a fit of solitude,' he wrote in 1816, giving nothing away. 'I have scarcely seen him since Mr Wilson left us.'

What had happened in 1816 was that De Quincey had taken up with a servant girl, Margaret Simpson, the daughter of a small farmer at Nab Cottage, just half a mile from Rydal Mount.

She had a child by him, much to the disgust of the Wordsworth household. He married her the following year, and she made him a perfectly respectable and loving wife, but the ladies of the Wordsworth household refused to call on the pair. Crabb Robinson visited both households in late 1816 and found that De Quincey had broken with the Wordsworths, which he thought was rather sad, though he tried not to take sides, managing to remain friendly with both of them.

There was also the matter of opium. They'd had enough of that with Coleridge, and when they discovered that De Quincey was becoming addicted, they now began to discourage his visits, not wishing to be involved.

The specific cause of the break in 1816 was De Quincey's relationship with the servant girl, but perhaps the real reason for it was that the friendship had been built on a dangerous premise in the first place. De Quincey had arrived into their lives as an admirer, a slavish follower of Wordsworth, and they expected him to remain so, devoting himself completely to the Wordsworth cause but expecting very little in return. Coleridge had always been an equal, whatever else he became, but De Quincey had been consigned from the very beginning to play a secondary role – though, alas for him, he didn't realize this for many years.

De Quincey's *Recollections of the Lake Poets*, written many years later, shows how often, even in the early days, he had been hurt by little things. He was out walking with William and Southey one day when Southey asked William a question about Charles Lloyd, their friend and neighbour, who was ill. De Quincey didn't quite catch William's reply and asked him to repeat it. 'To my surprise, he replied that in fact what he had said was a matter of some delicacy and not quite proper to be communicated except to *near friends* of the family. This to me – ye gods! – to me, who knew by many a hundred conversations how disagreeable Wordsworth was to both Charles Lloyd and his wife. The arrogance of Wordsworth was well illustrated in this case of the Lloyds.'

De Quincey was a great book-man and in the early days was perfectly willing to let William or anyone else borrow his books. At one time, he reckoned that between them, Coleridge and William had borrowed five hundred of his books and had taken them to Allan Bank. But he soon grew to resent William borrowing his books. Unlike Southey, De Quincey said, William didn't know how to care for books; his own wretched collection, no more than two or three hundred, were 'ill bound and in tatters' and he hardly ever read them, unless the weather was really bad and he was stuck indoors. One day, De Quincey let him borrow a book by Edmund Burke: a virgin copy, unopened and straight from the publisher.

Wordsworth took down the volume and . . . unfortunately it was uncut; fortunately, and by a special Providence as to him, it seemed, tea was proceeding at the time. Dry toast required butter; butter required knives and knives then lay on the table; but sad it was for the virgin purity of Mr Burke's as yet unsunned pages that every knife bore upon its blade testimonies of the service it had rendered. Did that stop Mr Wordsworth? Not at all. He tore his way into the heart of the volume with this knife that left its greasy honours behind it upon every page; and are they not there to this day?

Most of De Quincey's stories are very amusing, though probably not necessarily always quite accurate, and his physical descriptions of William, especially (as we have seen) his legs, have a vividness and immediacy which the more reverential and probably more truthful accounts sadly lack.

De Quincey always numbered William amongst the luckiest people he had ever met – lucky in his love of simple pleasures, lucky in his health, lucky in his windfalls, like the Calvert money and Lord Lonsdale's help with the Stamp job, and perhaps most fortunate of all, lucky in the women of his household – especially Dorothy. He never lowered his estimation of William as a poet, considering that of the three Lake Poets, William was the original, the true genius, even if he preferred the others as people. Nonetheless, he had to admit that, as a person, William was still interesting. Southey might be pleasanter to meet, but he was rather boring. William, despite what De Quincey considered his arrogant ways, was worth meeting, though in the end he confessed that he, personally, had had enough of him. He couldn't put up with the strain of keeping in with him, having to hold himself in check, always feeling himself to be in the wrong. 'Having observed this human arrogance, I took care never to lay myself under the possibility of an insult. Systematically I avoided saying anything, however suddenly tempted into any expression of my feelings, upon the natural appearance whether in the sky or upon the earth. Thus I evaded one cause of quarrel. Wordsworth was not aware of the irritation and disgust which he had founded in the minds of his friends.'

De Quincey doesn't mention his own conduct, either his drugs or his love life, as being a possible cause of the parting. But he was certainly not alone amongst the younger generation in finding the middle-aged Wordsworth difficult to put up with. John Wilson, the other young student admirer who'd arrived in the Lakes especially to be near Wordsworth, left the area at about the same time. He went to Edinburgh, where he became a contributor to *Blackwood's Magazine* and wrote several critical articles about Wordsworth. No row is known to have occurred between them, but Wilson's relationship with William was much the same as De Quincey's, with William accepting the adoration, but giving little in return.

In later years, William's friendship with De Quincey was somewhat renewed. De Quincey didn't finally leave the Lakes till about 1830 – by which time he'd taken another local house, keeping Dove Cottage for his books – and he also moved eventually to Edinburgh. But the friendship was never again of the same intensity, after what the Wordsworths considered had been his most ungentlemanly behaviour.

It does look, despite Dorothy's half-joking remarks, as if the Wordsworths of Rydal Mount had begun to consider themselves as rather fine folks.

ODE TO DUTY

This heavy moralizing ode, published in the 1807 collection, was an indication of the new stern Wordsworth, warning of weaknesses in himself and in his friends. It was written like a hymn and proved very popular with later Victorians.

STERN Daughter of the Voice of God!
O Duty! If that name thou love
Who art a light to guide, a rod
To check the erring, and reprove;
Thou, who are victory and law
When empty terrors overawe;
From vain temptations dost set free;
And calm'st the weary strife of frail humanity!

Serene will be our days and bright,
And happy will our nature be,
When love is an unerring light,
And joy its own security.
And they a blissful course may hold
Even now, who, not unwisely bold,
Live in the spirit of this creed;
Yet seek thy firm support, according to their need.

To humbler functions, awful Power!
I call thee: I myself commend
Unto thy guidance from this hour;
Oh, let my weakness have an end!

Give unto me, made lowly wise,
The spirit of self-sacrifice;
The confidence of reason give;
And in the light of truth thy Bondman let me live!

15

Politics and Poems
1815-1818

THE finest folks of all were of course the Lowthers, lords of all they surveyed. William developed an almost lemming-like longing to serve them, going out of his way to cultivate their friendship, as if a recessive gene from his father and grandfather, long dormant and despised, was eating into his soul. Without being asked, and without any formal agreement, he started to do what his father had done before him. In effect, he became their spy. This might seem rather a melodramatic description, but, as he was never their employee, and he should not officially have been doing what he did for them, it is fair to call him one of their under-cover agents. Strangely enough, the present Earl of Lonsdale maintains that both Wordsworth and his father were *employed* by the Lowthers. It is presumably a family belief, handed down through the generations, though in Wordsworth's case it certainly was not true. If he *had* been employed as some sort of official agent, then his behaviour would have been easier to explain.

Over a period of twenty years, Wordsworth came round to honestly and genuinely believing that his patriotic duty was to support the Tories, the Established Church and the Landed Gentry. The Lowthers personified the values he approved of. At the same time, he considered himself a lover of liberty and national independence, and when friends and strangers wrote to him, accusing him of being a turncoat, for example in his attitude to France, then he replied by saying that he had always been consistent in his hatred of tyranny. He had stayed the same – it was the tyrants who had changed their coats. He had approved of the early days of the French Revolution, when the tyranny of the *ancien régime* had been overthrown, but when he saw at first hand the Reign of Terror, when the mob themselves became tyrants, followed by a third form of tyranny, Napoleon's, then naturally he opposed them all. He had been against English intervention in the early days, but he stoutly supported England in her war against Napoleon. He'd always loved liberty and would oppose tyranny, whatever its form.

On some minor matters, he did have the grace to admit that he'd changed his mind slightly. He had believed that the press must be free, as a vital element in democracy, but his early romantic notions, believing it should be *completely* free, had gone. By the 1820s he favoured restraints: the press should be independent, but subversive elements had to be checked. One couldn't allow the fabric of society to be endangered by these new radical elements. He knew only too well where it could all lead. At the root of Wordsworth's new political belief was fear. He did not like many things that were happening in the world at large and he feared the consequences if they were allowed to get worse. The only hope, as he saw it, was a return to the status quo. For the good of everyone, for the individual and for the community, society should not be torn apart.

It has to be remembered that Wordsworth, as he approached fifty, had lived through some stirring times – perhaps the most dramatic period in British history since the Civil War. Previous upheavals had often been localized, limited to one class or one region, but the changes in the first half of the nineteenth century affected every single person. It is one of the many fascinations of Wordsworth's life, to see how, in his thoughts and in his writings, he responds to all the changes taking place. From the French Revolution to railways, Wordsworth was a front-line observer, an eye-witness with some very strong opinions.

Three revolutions were happening at once, all of them related – industrial, political and social. Wordsworth, in his letters to the Earl of Lonsdale and to his other friends, diagnosed the changes with great accuracy. He could see quite clearly the ravages created in family life by the Industrial Revolution and the new factories: the all-night shifts, the abuses of child and female labour, the dangers to health and morals, and the breakdown in rural life as people fled from the country to the towns.

He saw the new political agitators, pressing for reforms and freedoms, encouraging insurrection in the towns and amongst the agricultural labourers. In his letters he constantly drew comparisons with the agitators he had seen at work in France. Even reading expressions of relatively harmless liberal opinions in the local paper, the *Kendal Chronicle*, led him to the gloomiest of thoughts. 'Never was the press more atrociously abused than in that journal at present,' he wrote to Lord Lowther in 1818. 'Every sentence almost in it reminds me of what I used to read in France in the year 1792 when the Revolution was advancing towards its zenith.'

He also saw the breakdown in class divisions – which, again, he bitterly regretted. He looked back to his boyhood days, that wonderful halcyon period in Hawkshead at the end of the eighteenth century, when men served their masters happily, when each had his own job and his own respect, when landowners and tenants pulled together, when enlightened property-owners helped the poor and the poor were grateful and not resentful. One recurring theme in his letters is how, in the good old days, the gentry mixed freely with tradesmen, personally using their shops, treating them, if not as equals, then as people with their proper place in society. Here he was obviously thinking of his Penrith days, which had not been at all happy for him at the time. Now, in middle age, he saw all the good points. His own shopkeeping relations had indeed been socially mobile – marrying into the gentry, securing social and educational advancement for their children, all without having to storm the battlements or overthrow the established order. Wordsworth *saw* what was happening, as he went round, carrying out his duties as Distributor of Stamps – his province soon grew to include parts of north Lancashire and the west Cumbrian industrial coast – and he heard the radicals fomenting disruption. His diagnoses were correct, and well in advance of events, even if they were slightly exaggerated (he had the grace to admit in one letter that he was possibly an alarmist), but his remedy was the wrong one. He tended to favour political repression, even though he also wanted more education and better conditions for the working classes. In his view, all these reforms could be brought about under the auspices of the old order. He had seen the extremes at first hand and didn't want them to happen in England. It was a very English viewpoint, and still is to this day: moderation in all things. Let the Tory Party, the Church of England and the landed squires continue to run the country in their decent, moderate way, and in the long run everyone will be better off. At all costs, the 'mob' must not be allowed to dictate events.

Together with the 'mob', a vague term at the best of times, though he often used it, he feared the new grasping manufacturers. He despised their methods and their values, their lack of culture and their vulgarity. Though there was no lack of contemporary reports, Wordsworth's own prejudice was mostly based on ignorance, since, to judge from his letters, it would appear that he personally never met such people. He compared what he had picked up about them to the Lakeland statesmen, whom he did know, and naturally preferred.

He seemed unaware of the growing, if still small, number of enlightened manufacturers, especially Quakers, who were doing more for their work-force, in the way of social benefits and improved conditions, than the Tories, such as himself, who were trying to turn the clock back. Robert Owen, the great Scottish social reformer, tried to interest both Southey and Wordsworth in his schemes, and Southey went to look at his model factory in New Lanark. The Wordsworth household thought him a good man, but a 'little cranky'.

It was the rise to power of the manufacturers generally which Wordsworth dreaded, especially if the Reform Bill should ever be passed, giving them political importance and making them a direct threat to the traditional landowners. Manufacturers, he believed, were motivated by self-interest. Owning property, on the other hand, made you care.

Wordsworth admitted that in his early days he hadn't quite appreciated the worth of the property classes. It was something the London radicals and wits and new poets still didn't understand; he himself now knew from his own experience that the landowners, on the whole, were a power for good. They kept the country together. Cynics might say, and did say, that Wordsworth was motivated by self-interest, since he was now one of the property-owners himself, on the fringes of the landed classes, living in his smart house and with smart neighbours. He had a public post, which had been obtained for him by the local lord; so naturally he was in favour of the status quo. When someone has climbed to the top of the ladder – or at least, to the lower rungs – he doesn't want the rules changed, the ladder taken down, and everyone having to start again – not when it has taken him so long to get there. This would be one nasty interpretation of Wordsworth's new political beliefs. His own life style would belie it: he wasn't trying to amass luxuries and wealth for himself or his family, though he was thankful for his new financial security.

Wordsworth apologists – most of whom are lovers of his poetry who suspect any criticism of his life and politics as being an attack on his art – always point to the worthy sentiments expressed in his poetry, and to his concern for the working man, and they dismiss as unimportant his agitation for the reactionary Tories and his underground political letters. Another defence is to say that he was never *really* a violent radical. His French Revolution phase was basically romance, and in any case, he supported the Girondists (the moderate radicals), not the more extreme Jacobins. In his mind, he probably hoped that the Revolution would make France into a nice, fairly liberal place like England. When it all went wrong, he retreated to his love for good old England, which had always been there. It is an attractive argument.

My view is that he was a definite radical but that, over a twenty-year span, a turnabout took place, a *volte-face*, in his political and social beliefs, and his letters prove it. This is not necessarily reprehensible. It is a change which is there to be studied, not denied.

The big event which brought it all out into the open, revealing William's new loyalties, was the general election of 1818. Westmorland had two MPs, Lord Lowther and Colonel Henry Lowther, both the sons of the Earl of Lonsdale. For forty-four years, the Lowthers had held their two seats unopposed; they'd controlled the two constituencies, just as they'd controlled another seven or so seats in the north-west, filling them with their own placemen (either members of their own family or trusted supporters).

William, while in London in December 1817, heard rumours that Westmorland was going to be opposed and wrote a letter to Lord Lonsdale, thanking him for a present ('Your Lordship's boots were of infinite service to me, as owing to the Mail being full I was obliged to venture on the outside'), tipping him off about the rumours and promising to investigate and report further. The opponent turned out to be Henry Brougham, a member of a distinguished landed family who had an estate near Penrith. He had been born and educated in Edinburgh and was one of the founders of the *Edinburgh Review*. That should have been a warning to William, though they had met some eight years or so earlier and had been quite friendly. Brougham was later to become one of the leading Whig politicians of his day, a cabinet minister, Lord Chancellor and eventually a baron. (His name went into Victorian household usage with his invention of the Brougham coach.) However, in 1818, aged forty, Brougham was still something of a wild radical – not trusted by the mainstream Whig politicians, but admired for his oratory and his skill in handling mobs.

William was determined that Brougham, whom he called a dangerous demagogue, shouldn't succeed in Westmorland, and he started organizing support for the Lowthers. He sent them detailed reports from every place he visited, listing the personal politics and beliefs of the leading citizens, marking down the religious Dissenters (who in the main were anti-Tory) or reformers, and naming those who could be trusted to do the right thing and those who could not. He named all the leading lawyers in Kendal, for example, telling Lord Lonsdale which ones should be retained (bribed, in other words) to support the Tories. He reported on people's relations and friends, and on how much property they owned. Years before, William had himself been spied upon by a government agent, when it was thought he was a radical. Now, he was informing on people behind their backs, and basing much of his testimony on local hearsay.

Just before the election started, William had been privately negotiating, with Lord Lonsdale's help, to take over the stamp distribution for north Cumberland, a much more lucrative domain than the other areas for which he was responsible. He had arranged with the present incumbent to pay him off with an annuity of £350 – which shows just how valuable a job it was – but he dropped negotiations during the election. It would have looked very bad if, at such a time, he had been procured another government job. Also, he was not supposed to engage in any electioneering or in any other political activity, being a government servant.

Most people in local politics knew he was canvassing for the Tories, who had now been in power for over three decades, and were to remain in power for a further twelve years. Brougham, who seems to have been amused rather than terrified by William's intriguing, often made veiled criticisms of his poetry in his public speeches, knowing William was skulking at the edge of the crowd. People warned William to keep out of all political activity, and at one stage, so William reported in a letter to Lord Lonsdale, he had been told he could be fined £100 'for having intermeddled'; but he still continued, sending back his confidential dossiers.

One of the murkier areas of William's electioneering concerned the buying of land with Lowther money, then dividing it up into lots and letting Tory supporters buy it on reasonable terms, on condition that they voted the right way, now that they'd been made freeholders. Several of William's relations did well out of these sales of land. Another area in which political pressure could be brought to bear was the law of enfranchisement. Technically, you had to own property to have a vote, but there was a rule that a substantial tenant, having farmed someone else's land for a long time, could be enfranchised, *if* the landlord agreed. Naturally, a Tory landowner was not going to enfrancise his radical tenants.

William was also instrumental in writing anonymous letters and articles for the *Kendal Chronicle*, which, when the election began, proclaimed that it was politically independent, but soon moved to support the Broughamites. William then printed two pamphlets, presumably using Lowther money, in which he addressed the Freeholders of Westmorland. One pamphlet was written in high, flowing phrases for the gentry; the other, for the less educated merchant class. At the same time, William helped the Lowthers to try and buy up shares in the *Kendal Chronicle*, determined by any means to make the paper toe the right line; but this failed, and the Lowthers were then forced to start their own paper, the *Westmorland Gazette*. William wrote to his London newspaper friends, such as Stuart, asking if they knew any likely editors.

There was great excitement when at length the two Lowther candicates made their official entry into Kendal; but it ended in violence, with riots in the street, stones being thrown and many people getting hurt. The Lowthers blamed it on the Broughamites, alleging that they had hired hooligans to disrupt the proceedings. The Broughamites denied this accusation, saying the riot showed how strong the anti-Lowther feeling was.

The Broughamites wore blue and the Lowthers yellow – the traditional Lowther family colour and one which Tories in Cumbria still sport at election time, even though, in the rest of the country, Tories are always true blue. Dorothy got caught up in all the election fever – unlike Mary and Sarah, who stayed at home, thinking William should direct his energies into more useful channels. She went out canvassing in Kendal with William, who was taking care to avoid being seen near Lord Lonsdale or his sons, and using different hotels to avoid public contact. 'The misguided mob, including almost all the lower classes who have no votes, cry aloud for Brougham,' Dorothy wrote. 'No lady would venture to appear in a yellow ribband in Kendal streets, though you cannot walk thirty yards without meeting a dirty lad or lass with a blue one and the *ladies* of that party also have no fear of displaying their colour.'

There were some real ladies, and gentlemen, on the Brougham side, including some other titled landowners and even some of the Wordsworths' own relations, such as their cousin William Crackenthorpe. They met him on one occasion and discussed their political differences amicably. Even sadder for William, one of their dearest friends, one whom they greatly admired, Thomas Clarkson, the anti-slavery campaigner, was a supporter of Brougham.

William took it all very seriously, but he could still on occasions see the lighter side. 'My youngest Son is a complete Yellow,' he wrote to Lord Lowther in March 1818, 'having got the jaundice, poor lad, so that he has no occasion for Ribbons, though he wears them. The Daffodils are anxiously looked for that the young ladies in Rydal may adorn their bonnets with them.'

He also had to admit that Brougham was a good speaker, even passing on one of his jokes to Lord Lowther. He'd heard Brougham speak in Grasmere, where he'd fallen upon the local rector and the local butcher, mocking them in public, knowing they were both strong Lowther supporters. 'He concluded his lampoon,' William reported, 'with this elegant witticism – that the Spirit and the Flesh were both against him. . . .' It says much for Brougham's oratory that he could appeal to the rabble, make jokes about the tradesmen and also include clever insults to amuse the educated.

The highlight of the election was Brougham's own triumphal entry into Kendal. William and Dorothy had got themselves a good vantage point, in the window of a house overlooking the place chosen for him to give his speech, and even Dorothy had to admit it was a stirring display, despite a snow-storm which greeted the great arrival:

Music, banners, horsemen, all joining in one huzza, fearless of the storm . . . one condensed line in motion wedging in the horsemen and Carriages . . . the spectacle was grand. If the cause had been better, my feelings as a Spectator would have been really sublime. Of course when he appeared at the window, he was hailed by a tremendous shout – or when anything fell from his lips that particularly took their fancies, the cry of applause was repeated with more or less vehemence. I could have fancied him one of the French Demagogues of the Tribunal of Terror at certain times, when he gathered a particular fierceness into his face. He is very like a Frenchman.

Dorothy took detailed notes of Brougham's speech, like a good private secretary, and William sent a copy of her notes to Lord Lonsdale, like a good informer, including even the personal attacks on the Lowther family. Brougham made great play with Lowther *Castle*, pointing out sarcastically that it had formerly been Lowther Hall, till they'd recently spent a fortune rebuilding it on a vast scale, turning it into a Gothic masterpiece. 'They have great riches,' declaimed Brougham. 'How did they get their riches? It comes out of *your* pockets!' Loud cheers all round.

Brougham attacked William personally (though not by name) knowing he must be watching somewhere, calling him 'the most active of the secret agents, a man with a sinecure in the country, with nothing else or very little to live upon'. He then warmed to his theme, referring to William firstly as an anonymous writer, and then, more specifically, as a poet. This particular poet, he said, worked hard at being a secret agent, though 'it was much harder work to read his writings'. All Brougham's immediate entourage laughed exceedingly heartily at this, though presumably most of the rabble didn't understand the joke.

As one might expect, the Lowthers, having controlled Westmorland for so long, won the day, and Lonsdale's two sons got over 1,000 votes each and took both seats; but Brougham did surprisingly well, obtaining 889 votes. William and the Lowthers didn't cease their activities once the election was over, knowing they had to keep vigilant from then on and fight future elections in the same yellow spirit, which they did.

The new paper, the *Westmorland Gazette*, first appeared in the early summer of 1818, just as the election was reaching its climax, so it didn't play such a vital part in the campaign, but it remained a Lowther platform for many years. William was successful in his search for a suitable person to be its editor, finding a friend to take it over after it had been going for just a few weeks. It was young Thomas De Quincey.

De Quincey's misdemeanours were forgotten – or, at least, partly forgotten – when William recommended him for the job: 'The editorship of the new Kendal paper has passed into the hands of a most able man, one of my particular Friends, but whether he is fit (I mean on the score of punctuality) for such a service, remains to be seen.' William still blamed De Quincey for the delays in getting his Cintra pamphlet through the press nine years previously, but De Quincey assured him that his punctuality had 'altered since I last had the happiness to associate with you'. It was a generous gesture on William's part, to help someone who had now fallen on rather hard times – stuck with a wife and young child, deserted by many of his old friends and with no regular income – but, at the same time, William felt he could use De Quincey to his own advantage, believing that he could be trusted politically, even if his personal habits might not be altogether desirable.

Judging by the look of the early issues, De Quincey tried very hard, filling the pages with juicy court cases to raise the circulation and writing many of his own leaders, attacking the enemies of the Tories in good rabble-rousing fashion. At times, he rather overdid the invective, so that Lord Lonsdale himself began to be slightly worried. 'I think our own Kendal paper is now getting too libellous. Last week's specimen is certainly a blackguard production.'

De Quincey's initial burst of enthusiasm and activity didn't last long and very soon he was writing the whole paper from home in Dove Cottage, over in Grasmere, hardly ever appearing at the office in Kendal. He was reprimanded by the proprietors in June 1819 for missing the London news, for not contacting the printer and for residing at such a great distance from the office, failings which would be hard to excuse in even the most gifted writer. He announced in the columns of the paper in July that he had received a letter from one of the proprietors which he proposed to 'notice fully next week'. Alas, they got him first, extracted his resignation before he could reply publicly. He was eased out, after fourteen months in the job, leaving the paper established as a Tory rag, but with a loss of £42 in its first year of trading. It is a pity he never got his reply published. It would have been interesting to see if he had turned against the Fine Folks who had hired him. As it was, the fine folks went on to flourish and find fresh fortune.

The first volume of new poetry which William published after his move to Rydal Mount was dedicated to the Earl of Lonsdale: 'Illustrious peer, a token of high respect and gratitude sincere.' This was *The Excursion* which came out in 1814, followed the next year by a new edition of William's *Collected Poems* and by *The White Doe of Rylstone*, the poem he had written some years before but had kept back. He had published no poetry for seven years, after that mauling he'd had over his 1807 *Poems*, but his friends were full of hope this time.

The Excursion was treated as a major literary event, which indeed it was. It was William's first long poem (some four hundred and twenty pages) to be published, and had taken him almost twenty years to complete. It was meant, as he explained in a rather confusing preface, to come after his long proposed 'The Recluse' – a work which he never completed, apart from a section called 'Home at Grasmere'. Coleridge had always wanted William to produce a major poem, instead of so many short pieces. Crabb Robinson was full of excitement and so was Southey. The critics were equally excited and they cleared the pages in readiness. The big names among them were commissioned and they were given an enormous amount of space for their reviews, between two and three thousand words each. Imagine any poem today being given such attention.

Beforehand, William himself was rather cynically jocular about the critics' possible reaction. 'I am about to print (do not start!) eight thousand lines, which is but a small portion of what I shall oppress the world with, if strength and life do not fail me. I shall be content if the Publication pays its expenses, for Mr Scott and your friend Lord B. flourishing at the rate they do, how can an honest *Poet* hope to thrive?' These remarks were made in a private letter to a London literary friend, Samuel Rogers. If only William could occasionally have been as light and self-deprecating in his public pronouncements. Once again, his new preface – like the one to his collected poems – put many people off, partly by its arrogance and self-importance, and partly by the sheer difficulty in understanding it.

The comment about Scott and Lord Byron wasn't meant entirely as a joke. William came to hate Byron, as a poet and as a person, considering him both evil and immoral. Scott he greatly liked as a person, and they were always good friends, but he never considered him a *real* poet – by which of course he meant a poet like Wordsworth. Scott simply told stirring tales, with lots of colour and emotion, but had no philosophy of poetry. He was the kindest and most genuinely loved of all the literary giants of the time – a time noted for its venomous literary back-biting – and he was quite without self-importance or arrogance. He agreed with Wordsworth: he didn't think his own poetry was very good and always rated Wordsworth and Southey higher than himself.

William was in a way slightly envious of Scott's and Byron's huge commercial success. Even with his friend Scott, he could be a little spiteful behind his back, though William's family were at least aware of his lingering jealousy. In another letter to Samuel Rogers, William adds a nice PS about Scott's poetry:

What you say of W. Scott reminds me of an Epigram something like the following –

> Tom writes his Verses with huge speed,
> Faster than Printer's boy can set 'em,
> Faster than we can read,
> And only not so fast as we forget 'em.

Mrs W, poor Woman! who sits by me, says, with a kind of sorrowful smile – this is spite, for you know that Mr Scott's verses are the delight of the Times and that thousands can repeat scores of pages.

Scott himself hoped William would do well with his new volumes of poetry – he'd personally provided some of the background material for *The White Doe* and had discussed the work in many letters to William.

The great critical brains of the time thought they knew best. Jeffrey, of the *Edinburgh Review*, made his opinion of *The Excursion* clear in the very first sentence of his extensive review: 'This will never do.' It doesn't exactly make you want to read on. Jeffrey did admit there were some good single lines, 'that sparkle like gems in a desert and startle us with an intimation of the great poetic powers that lie buried in the rubbish that has been heaped around them'.

Hazlitt wrote a long review for *The Examiner*, which wasn't as savage but was also a condemnation; he regretted that the skill with which William had chosen his material wasn't equal to his skill in writing about it. He likened *The Excursion* to a stupendous structure, which had been left half-finished and suffered to moulder into decay. In passing, Hazlitt, who had long since ceased to be a friend of William or of his politics, had a swipe at the inhabitants of the 'boasted mountain districts' William persisted in writing about, calling them stupid, selfish and insensitive. He was presumably thinking of those natives who had hounded him out for his misdemeanours.

Charles Lamb, in private letters, had been flattering about *The Excursion*, and Wordsworth prevailed on him to write a review, which he did at last; but it was hacked about and cut and didn't help the sales. Coleridge kept quiet for months, making no comments to his friends, and when he eventually told Wordsworth what he thought, it was obvious he was disappointed. He knew the poem was nothing like as good as the unpublished work, *The Prelude*. On the whole, this view is still held today, though there are sections of *The Excursion* which are still studied and admired by scholars, such as that about the ruined cottage. It was the longest poem Wordsworth ever wrote – *The Prelude*, when it was finally published, was slightly shorter – and is very rambling and didactic. The poet-hero wanders into the Lake District, where he meets several characters, such as a Parson and a Pedlar, who all sit and tell long tales, with Wordsworth using them as mouthpieces to elaborate his views on life, covering everything from the French Revolution and the Industrial Revolution to the Church of England and blindness.

The *Collected Poems* of 1815 were interesting in that Wordsworth re-arranged his *Lyrical Ballads*, plus all the other poems included in the volume, into different sections, according to their mood, such as 'Poems of Childhood' and 'Poems of the Imagination'. There were some new poems, such as 'Yarrow Visited', and three poems written by Dorothy (though he said they were by a 'female friend'). It was the Preface, however, that got most attention; it either annoyed or stimulated people, since, in effect, Wordsworth tried in it to defend himself and his poetry from previous attacks. He wrote it in a very magisterial style, expounding at great length on his own definitions of 'fancy' and 'imagination'.

The White Doe of Rylstone, which William personally always thought was one of his finest poems, didn't get as much attention as *The Excursion*, but was treated in a similar manner. The *Edinburgh Review* began in its usual uncompromising style: 'This, we think, has the merit of being the very worst poem we ever saw imprinted in a quarto volume. ...' The reviewer went on to consider whether it was all a joke – a satire by someone pretending to write in the style of Mr Wordsworth – but no, they decided it must be genuine: 'Nothing in the nature of a joke could be so insupportably dull.' The *Monthly Review* said it was now tired of pointing out Mr Wordsworth's errors, and the *Eclectic Review* dismissed the poem as 'arrogant egotism'.

One of the many obstacles to the success of the new publications, apart from those damning reviews, was their price. *The Excursion* cost two guineas, an enormous sum for those days. (It was only in the early 1970s that virtually all book prices jumped above the £2 level.) William tried his hardest to promote sales, writing letters to his well-off friends, hoping they would buy; when he did give a free copy to friends, such as Charles Lloyd, it was on the understanding that it should not be loaned to anyone. He personally refused a copy to a lady whom he knew could well afford it: 'a widow with £1,500 per annum … a blue stocking Dame who considered two guineas an outrageous price'.

Signing sessions were unknown in those days, as were publicity appearances, but William, in his modest way, mounted a public relations campaign on his own behalf. One day, he decided to take *The Excursion* to a rich old lady to whom he read out choice passages, in the hope that she would be tempted, or persuaded, into buying her own copy. Dorothy has a description of their foray in a letter to Sarah:

> William and Mary and little Willy paid a visit to old Mrs Knott yesterday with the Exn. in hand, William intending to read the old Lady the history of the Grasmere Knight. She could not hear his loud voice, but understood the story very well when her Niece read it. Today they have returned the Book and poor Miss K. has written a complimentary but alas! unintelligible note. She must have been in a strange ruffled state of mind. She concludes however by saying in plain words that she had written to Kendal to order the Book. I tell William that the family made a trading voyage of it. Certainly the Book would never have been bought by Miss K. if Willy and his Father and Mother had stayed quietly at home.

Despite such personal efforts, the sales were poor. After a year, only three hundred copies of the first edition of five hundred had been sold. The publishers, Longmans, doubtless had to price it highly, because of its great length and because they knew, or feared, it wouldn't be a best-seller. William kept on working hard at promoting sales, hoping desperately for a second and cheaper edition, which would bring the poem to the attention of the less well off. He comforted himself by telling everyone about the famous people who had told him they had personally loved the book, and by dismissing the reviewers as idiots:

> Jeff. has already printed off a Review beginning with these elegant and decisive words 'This will not do', the sage critic then proceeding to show cause why. This precious piece is what the Coxcomb's Idolators call a *crushing* review.

I much doubt whether he has read three pages of the poem.... The Bishop of London is in raptures, the Duke of Devonshire made it his companion in a late jaunt to Ireland, a Lady of Liverpool, a Quaker, breaks through all forms of ceremony to express her gratitude by letter.

William affected to be above the attacks and, with his eye steadily aimed at posterity, to be immune from the critics' puny arrows, maintaining he never stooped to reading their pathetic reviews – it was always other people who told him about them, or brought them to his attention: 'I am astonished that you can find no better use for your money than spending it on those silly Reviews,' he wrote to Sarah, finishing with an affectionate farewell, to show he was in good humour. 'I send you love and a kiss, two or three if you like, that prove the better for being liberal.'

But the family worried on his behalf, especially as they needed the money. 'I have no anxiety about the fate of either *The Excursion* or *The White Doe*,' wrote Dorothy, 'beyond the sale of the first edition – and *that* I do earnestly wish for. There are few persons who can afford to buy a two guinea book, merely for admiration of the Book. The edition has no chance of being sold except to the wealthy; and they buy books for fashion's sake than anything else and alas we are not yet in the fashion.' What Dorothy hoped for was that 'somebody would but puff the Book amongst the fashionable and wealthy' – which is a nice early use of a hackneyed phrase. She wanted a puff of wind to blow it to success.

William was greatly saddened by the attacks, despite his lofty dismissals and his bitter jokes at his own expense. 'Why don't you hire somebody to abuse you?' he wrote to a literary friend in 1817. 'For myself, I begin to fear that I should soon be forgotten if it were not for my enemies.'

At other times, he seriously thought of retiring, or said he was seriously thinking of it: 'As to publishing I shall give it up, as nobody will buy what I send forth; nor can I expect it seeing what stuff the public appetite is set upon.'

His old friends were equally hurt by the attacks on him, especially the *Edinburgh Review*'s, which was the talk of all the literary circles of the day. 'Jeffrey, I hear, has written what his admirers call a *crushing* review of *The Excursion*,' Southey wrote to Walter Scott. 'He might as well seat himself upon Skiddaw and fancy that he could crush the mountain. I heartily wish Wordsworth may one day meet with him and lay him alongside, yard arm and yard arm in argument.'

Southey, who suffered by being associated with William and was attacked just as lustily by the *Edinburgh Review*, was the friend who had previously observed to William that though Jeffrey could not spoil their laurels, he might mildew their corn. The bad reviews undoubtedly did have an effect on William's sales. The books would probably not have been great popular sellers, but over twenty years his income would have been greatly improved, if it had not been for the *Edinburgh Review*.

They are altogether incompetent judges [wrote William]. These people in the senseless hurry of their idle lives do not *read* books, they merely snatch a glance at them, that they may talk about them. Never forget what, I believe, was observed to you by Coleridge, that every great and original writer, in proportion as he is great or original, must himself create the taste by which he is to be seen. For those who dip into books in order to give an opinion – for this multitude of unhappy and misguided and misguiding beings, an entire regeneration must be produced, and if this be possible it must be a work of time.

William could be philosophical because, at heart, he was convinced of his own genius. 'All men of *first* rate genius have been as distinguished for dignity, beauty and propriety of moral conduct,' he wrote on one occasion – an arguable generalization, which excludes Byron but includes Wordsworth. At the time, he was actually thinking of Burns, whom he thought had been cruelly used after his death, when all his sexual behaviour was brought into the open; in a published letter about Burns he maintained the charges were mainly untrue and certainly unfair.

But the Wordsworth family would have liked some financial rewards there and then. Living with a genius didn't pay the rent. 'We shall never grow rich,' wrote Dorothy after all the reviews had come out.

For I now perceive clearly that till my dear Brother is laid in his grave his writings will not produce any profit. This I now care no more about and shall never more trouble my head concerning the sale of them. I once thought *The White Doe* might have helped off the other, but I now perceive it can hardly help itself. It is a pity it was published in so expensive a form (one guinea for a slim volume) because some are thereby deprived of the pleasure of reading it; but however cheap his poems might be, I am sure it will be very long before they have an extensive sale – nay it will not be while he is alive to know it. His writings will live – will comfort the afflicted and animate the happy to purer happiness when we and our cares are all forgotten.

The White Doe

The first six lines of this introduction to The White Doe of Rylstone, *published in 1815, were originally used in his unperformed
play,* The Borderers.

ACTION is transitory – a step, a blow,
The motion of a muscle – this way or that –
'Tis done; and in the after-vacancy
We wonder at ourselves like men betrayed:
Suffering is permanent, obscure and dark,
And has the nature of infirmity.
Yet through that darkness (infinite though it seem
And irremoveable) gracious openings lie,
By which the soul – with patient steps of thought
Now toiling, wafted now on wings of prayer
May pass in hope, and, though from mortal bonds
Yet undelivered, rise with sure ascent
Even to the fountain-head of peace divine.

16

Mary, Dorothy and the Children
1813-1820

WHILE much has been written about the possibility of an incestuous relationship between William and Dorothy, no-one appears to have given much thought to what happened *after* his marriage. Did it go on for ever, whatever it was that went on? Did William's marriage to Mary make no difference? It has usually been assumed that poor Mary was assigned the role of mother and joint housekeeper, with Dorothy still continuing to be the most important person in William's life.

For the first ten years of the marriage, outwardly nothing much appeared to change. Mary was too busy with childbirth and children to have the time or the physical energy to attend to some of William's other needs or interests. They married in 1802 and had five children in eight years, finishing with Willy in 1810, the year she was forty; then she lost two children in six months in 1812. For most of these ten years, when she wasn't pregnant, she was ill and tired out, and the family letters are full of her ill health. Meanwhile, William was caught up in the excitement of his early published poems, with Dorothy beside him to take all his work down, or to go off on jaunts with him to Scotland or round the Lakes when he wanted a break, usually after the birth of another child.

By 1813, when Mary was beginning to recover from the emotional shock of the two deaths, and the other children were beginning to grow up reasonably healthy and safe, she had more time and energy to share William's very active life.

It looks as if she might have had at least one miscarriage, possibly in 1813, when she was forty-three. Some members of the family had welcomed another birth, the idea being that a new baby might compensate for the loss; but in the end they were all glad when she was no longer pregnant. 'Our domestic occupations are now comparatively few,' wrote Dorothy in October 1813. 'Willy goes to school – and there is no likelihood of more children to nurse; and though, if we could nurse them with the same cheerful confidence as before I should be glad that Mary were likely to have another child, I do not now wish it ... there is no prospect of it.'

She doesn't say how they knew Mary would have no more children. Forty-three is late, but not necessarily too late, unless she'd been told by the doctor or attended to by him. William was greatly upset by the depression which Mary had gone into after the deaths of the two younger children, and did everything he could to help. In July 1814, he took Mary and Sarah to Scotland for six weeks, hoping it would improve Mary's health, leaving Dorothy at home with the children. It would appear, from the family letters, to be the first time he'd gone on such a holiday without Dorothy for almost fifteen years.

In 1814, Dorothy started being actively encouraged to help out people with their problems – nursing the children of friends, or being a companion to old people – a pattern that continued for many years. She was away for over three months in early 1814, nursing young Basil Montagu in Keswick; then, for three months at the end of the year, she was in Wales with Sarah. Throughout 1814, Dorothy and William spent hardly more than three months in each other's company, a dramatic change from the previous twenty years.

At the end of the year, William wrote to her in Wales, asking her to come home as Willy was ill. 'Dearest Mary has been a good deal exhausted with waiting upon him, and I cannot but wish that you would come home. Mary will not consent that I should write, till we can say that the Child is quite well. It is solely to relieve Mary from fatigue – who at the best you know is not very strong.'

William added a strange PS to this letter, which has either a hint of guilt in it or of some sort of apology which only Dorothy would understand: 'I repeat that I have no motive for writing but an earnest wish you were at home on Dear Mary's account, and that when I have had any anxiety I always wish for you. . . .' Had Dorothy begun to feel or sense that she wasn't needed in the household any more?

In 1815, William and Mary went off to London, leaving Dorothy again with the children; on their return, she went off to nurse the children of Charles Lloyd. In 1816, William and Mary went to Stockton for a holiday, and then Dorothy herself went off alone to Halifax for five months.

These long separations wouldn't be remarkable, if they had been happening regularly in the past, or if the letters between them had still been full of the usual 'beloved', 'dearest', 'how I miss you passionately', 'how long till we meet', which had characterized all their letters in the past, when by chance fate had separated them. The letters dating from 1813 to about 1818 show very little emotion: they are about ordinary matters, with no passionate expressions of love. In fact, Dorothy is quite surprised by herself not *wanting* to rush back to William. She'd only intended to stay for a month with her old friends in Halifax, but the weeks had gone by and she kept on missing dates on which she'd promised to return. There was obviously nothing vital or urgent to drag her back to Rydal, not as in the old days.

William, in his letters of this period, starts boasting about what a wonderful marriage he has: a theme he continued to dwell on for the rest of his life. 'My marriage has been as happy as man's could be,' he wrote to his old West Country friend Thomas Poole in April 1814.

As Dorothy was not present to share the discovery of so many new friends, references to her start to decrease in his letters. Instead of passing on Dorothy's activities and kind regards to a friend, it is more often Mary's that he sends. Mary was coming into his public life more and more, while Dorothy was becoming the housekeeper. He tended to take Mary when he visited the Lowthers in their stately home, not Dorothy. Perhaps Dorothy was a little too wild and unkempt-looking for such smart company, or perhaps, when one mixes with fine folks, one's wife is the proper companion.

The White Doe, the poem William was personally so proud of, was fulsomely dedicated to Mary. At the beginning of this little dedication he mentions her by name:

> And, Mary! oft beside our blazing fire,
> When years of wedded life were as a day ...
> Beloved Wife, such solace to impart,
> As it hath yielded to thy tender heart.

This poem appeared in 1815, thirteen years after they had been married – quite a long time to wait before giving such a puff of wind to one's beloved. It might or might not be significant, this pretty dedication to his wife, but it is certainly noticeable that from about 1813 Dorothy appears to have slightly faded from the mainstream of William's life.

It was only when reading the letters about the 1818 election, when Dorothy was suddenly right at his side again, sharing the excitements, that I realized that for the previous five years she had been banished to the wings, rarely sharing the big events in her brother's life, not even living at Rydal for much of each year. What had happened? Had there been a change in the relationship?

There is no sign of any row, or of any difference of opinion. It's more a feeling in the letters of these years, rather than any facts – but a feeling which is markedly different from that in the letters of the previous years. On only one occasion is there a hint of criticism of Mary by Dorothy; even then, she is overtly praising her goodness, and it's only by reading between the lines that one can detect that perhaps she was becoming irritated by some aspects of Mary's character:

We happen for the last ½ year to have had the worst cook in England but Mary Dawson is coming to live with us and Sarah and I intend to give her unlimited commission to cook all sorts of nice things for Mary, to which Mary will not object; for, strange it is, Mary in these little things would be far more easily ruled by a servant than by us. Thus extremes meet. The more she loves people the less attentive she is to their happiness in trifles which makes up so much of human life – but her own health is not a trifle yet that same disposition of self-sacrifice which has characterized her through her life prevents her from taking care of herself, though she sees and knows how uneasy it makes us....

It has to be admitted that there's not much to go on, in building up a theory that William's and Dorothy's relationship had begun to cool after ten years or so of his marriage. I can't pinpoint the date, or list any disagreements. All I can suggest is that, after being married to her for ten years, William suddenly fell passionately in love with his wife.

Until now, there has been little hard evidence to prove that William ever loved his wife, either before or after his marriage. Very few letters between them have ever been seen. There has been nothing to suggest William *didn't* love her, and, in normal circumstances, the lack of written protestations between husband and wife might not have been worth remarking on, but, with such an enormous wealth of passionate writing between William and his sister, it has always seemed strange that, by comparison, William wrote so seldom to his wife, or she to him. Coleridge, for example, wrote very affectionate letters home to his wife during the Scottish tour in 1803, despite his loss of love for her, while William apparently wrote nothing home to his wife, even though they'd been married under a year and she'd just borne their first child. It's not surprising therefore that Mary should have been considered so far a minor figure, though it is always dangerous to build arguments on negative evidence. As with the Annette discovery, there may be vital facts yet to be unearthed, turning old theories upside down, giving the characters new roles.

In July 1977 a collection of Wordsworth and Coleridge manuscripts and letters suddenly turned up for sale at Sotheby's in London. They were bought by Cornell University for £38,500, but were then sold, for the same amount, to the Dove Cottage Trustees in Grasmere, who now own them. They'd been bought in a bundle of old letters for £5 by a young stamp-dealer in Carlisle. He was about to burn them, since they were useless to him, when he noticed the names 'Wordsworth' and 'Rydal Mount'.

At the time of writing, the manuscripts and letters are still being analysed and edited by the Wordsworth scholar Beth Darlington and have not yet been published – though she says that their publication will lead scholars to wrangle over how the references should be interpreted, especially those concerning the 1800–1802 period – but from my brief look at them, first at Sotheby's and then when they were on exhibition at Dove Cottage, the most fascinating items in an enormously rich treasure trove are thirty-five letters between William and Mary.

'Husband loves wife' isn't exactly shattering news – not like the discovery of mistress Annette in the 1920s – but it is this revelation in the letters which completely alters the traditional view of Mary. Firstly, she will now be seen to have been highly literate and intelligent. The scholars will no doubt start wondering if she, and not Dorothy, could have provided the inspiration for the Lucy poems and other love poems. William always gave Mary credit for having thought of the best two lines in 'Daffodils' ('They flash upon that inward eye / Which is the bliss of solitude'), and boasted about it on several occasions, but this always seemed an isolated example of her influence on his poetry, as if he was just mentioning it to humour her, or to give her some sense of status and importance.

Secondly, the letters show William to have been very passionate, in itself a rare enough phenomenon. There are no love-letters from him to Annette, although there is internal evidence of his love in her letters, and even in the relationship with Dorothy, most of the passionate sentiments were from Dorothy's pen. William has gone down to posterity as a rather stern, unbending figure – an image which he himself did little to alter in his middle and later years. De Quincey's remark about his face revealing 'animal passions' has always been rather puzzling. De Quincey never knew about Annette, and was sure that William could never subjugate himself to any woman. De Quincey knew William best in the early years of his marriage, when Mary was chiefly concerned with child-bearing.

William is certainly swept along by passion in the newly discovered letters, such as in the following one, written to Mary in May 1812, when they were both forty-two. He was in London at the time, having gone to see Coleridge. He'd travelled down as far as Chester with Mary, leaving her to go on to Wales to stay with her brother.

How I long (again I must say) to be with thee; every hour of absence now is a grievous loss, because we have been parted sufficiently to feel how profoundly in soul and body we love each other; and to be taught what a sublime treasure we possess in each other's love – the fever of thought and longing and affection and desire is strengthening in me, and I am sure will ... make me wakeful ... and consume me. I think of you by the waters, and under the shades of the Wye; I felt for thee ... as an expecting bride ... what thou hast been, from the hour of our first walks near Penrith till our last parting at Chester, and till this very moment when I am writing, and Thou most probably out thinking of me and losing all sense of the motion of the horse that bears thee. Oh my beloved, but I ought not to trust myself to this senseless and visible sheet of paper; speak for me to thyself; find the evidence of what is passing within me in thy heart, in thy mind, in thy steps as they touch the green grass, in thy limbs as they are stretched upon the soft earth; and in such kisses as I often give to the empty air, and in the aching of thy bosom, and let a voice speak for me in everything within thee and without thee ... oh what an age seems it till we shall be again together, under the shades of the green trees, by the rippling of the waters, and in that hour which thou lovest the most, the silence the vacancy and the impenetrable gloom of night. Ah, Mary, I must turn my pen from this course....

Mary, in her letters, is equally passionate. The date of this next letter from her to William, is not clear (not to me, anyway), but it could have been written sometime in 1812 or 1813, when William was away on business. 'Dorothy', in the first sentence, is doubtless their daughter Dora, and the 'D' later on is sister Dorothy.

Dorothy has asked me more than once, when she has found me this morning with thy letter in my hand, what I was crying about. I told her that I was so *happy* – but she could not comprehend this. Indeed, my love, it has made me supremely blessed – it has given me a new feeling, for it is the first letter of love that has been exclusively my own – Wonder not then that I have been so affected by it, Dearest William! ... that you cannot fully enjoy your absence from me, indeed, William, I feel; I have felt that you cannot, but it overpowers me to be told it by your own pen. I was much moved by the lines written with your hand in one of D's letters, where you spoke of coming home thinking you 'would be of great use' to me – indeed, my love, then you would, but I did not want thee so much then, as I do now that our uncomfortableness is passed away – if you had been here, no doubt there would have existed in me that inner consciousness that I had my all-in-all about me; that feeling which I have never wanted since the solitary night did not separate us, except in absence; but I had not then that leisure which I ought to have and which is necessary to be actively alive to so rich a possession and to the full enjoyment of it – I do, William, and shall to the end of my life consider the sacrifice as a dear offering of thy love; I feel it to be such, and I am grateful to thee for it, but trust that it will be the last of the kind that we shall need to make....

They might of course have been sending such tender letters to each other all their lives, but it is unlikely, considering that these newly discovered ones, written in their forties, are the only ones which exist. Mary's remark about it being 'the first letter of love' is an indication of their rarity. Their early teenage love in Penrith which, we have to assume (despite the lack of much evidence), certainly faded for many years during all William's wanderings – perhaps it was caused by some sort of disagreement. Their renewed courtship and subsequent marriage appear sudden and mysterious with no letters like these to indicate any passion. Altogether, Mary's letter is most intriguing. What is the 'uncomfortableness' that has passed away? Could it have been her fear of pregnancy which came between them, causing him to make 'the sacrifice' for which she is now so grateful? Or was it connected with the deaths of their children?

There are no similarly passionate letters from later in their life – or earlier – but one of these days more might turn up. In the meantime, from the evidence so far, the passion first appears in letters written after ten years or so of marriage. It is obvious that they have settled down to a very happy middle age, joined in domestic bliss, enjoying a marriage of deep spiritual, imaginative and physical intimacy, with moments approaching ecstasy – experiencing a love which may even have grown stronger, if anything, as the years went on, judging by William's continuing references to his happy marriage and his delight in his wife's company.

A great deal of the domestic bliss revolved around the children – not only for William and Mary, but for Dorothy too – though there were moments of alarm and several periods of constant worry. As they'd lost two children so quickly and so suddenly, it was to be expected that the parents should grow nervous at every loss of appetite, every sign of paleness.

It was William, particularly, who fretted and clucked whenever one of them was ill. By comparison, he himself was healthier and stronger than any of his children. He was rarely ill – apart from trouble with his eyes, which started in his late thirties and became more serious as he grew older (it appears to have been trachoma, a disease which spread in England with the return of the soldiers from the Napoleonic wars). His healthy, spartan diet and his long walks obviously helped to keep him fit. You don't hear so much about that poetic pain in his side, as he grew older and more successful.

John, their eldest child, was ten when they moved to Rydal, and he went to a local school in Ambleside, along with the Coleridge boys. (William would have liked his sons to have gone to his old school in Hawkshead instead, but he didn't approve of the new headmaster or of their new system.) His education was always a source of concern and they were all impatient at his academic slowness. They had such high hopes, probably too high, and he in turn tried hard for their sake, but with little success. They kept telling friends and relations how *nice* a boy he was, so popular and happy, but their disappointment is obvious.

John goes to Ambleside school with Hartley and Derwent [wrote Dorothy in 1812]. He walks every morning and returns at night with a bottle over his shoulder and a basket in his hand. He always meets us with smiles, enjoys school, his play with his school fellows, and is never tired in Body, a proof that he is so strong. The thought of his strength strikes now suddenly upon me many and many a time, and my heart is humbled and I fear the more because he is so strong. As to his lessons, he is the backwardest Boy I ever knew, yet I am convinced he is not a dunce in soul.

Two years later, she decided he *was* a dunce: '... certainly the greatest dunce in England, yet I am confident that if the difficulty of learning were once got over he would have great pleasure in Books. He has an excellent memory and his attention never sleeps when anyone is reading to him.'

William himself was equally critical, using much the same language: 'John is for book attainment the slowest child almost I ever knew. He has an excellent judgement and well regulated affections, but I am disappointed in my expectations of retracing Latin and Greek classics with him. Incredible pain has been taken with him, but he is to this day a deplorably bad reader of English even.' They decided to make him a boarder at Ambleside, which his father thought would help to make him a better scholar, but it failed to get him into the public school of their choice, Charterhouse.

William had rather enlightened views on education, for those days. He was against learning by rote and against cramming, and disapproved of those who made a virtue out of encyclopaedic knowledge. He preferred the imagination to be inspired and encouraged and the whole person developed; and he uses many of his poems to give us the benefit of his views on education. But he was nonetheless a product of his times and, when it came to his own children, he knew that the Classics and mathematics were vital for entry into Oxford or Cambridge and that the children would therefore have to get down to serious book learning. He'd long forgotten about his own revolt against such disciplines, as he constantly lectured John on the need to improve his grasp of the Classics. He spent a great deal of time teaching John at home, but John's shyness and slowness made William impatient and irrritated, which didn't help either of them. In 1820, however, he got John into the grammar school at Sedbergh. (It was in a part of Yorkshire which is now in Cumbria, and is still a well-known school.)

William was soon writing to his old friends and contacts at Cambridge, hoping he could ease John's path to university, though the Sedbergh staff pointed out that John's slowness at mathematics gave him little chance of getting into Cambridge.

There's an air of sadness about John. You don't hear so much about his smiling face as he approaches his late teens. A large number of family letters are devoted to his lack of academic ability, and though his parents would surely never have called him a dunce to his face, he must have known their thoughts. William saw around him the brilliant Coleridge boys, especially Hartley – children from a broken home, with no devoted father taking such pains – and no doubt he drew unfair comparisons. John's shyness forced him somewhat into William's shadow: ever eager to do his best as the eldest, carrying the family name, but unable to please his father. Even worse, a sense of fear on John's part entered their relationship.

Dora was very different. If anything, she was too clever and too quick, easily bored and distracted, but she was witty and lively and a great source of pleasure to the whole family. Catherine, the one who died at four, was equally lively and amusing, and even at two years old, she enchanted her parents with her sense of humour. Dorothy, when she was sending out strands of her hair to relations after her death, was still remembering her laughter.

They were fortunate therefore with Dora, their only surviving daughter; in her personality and in her talents. It is obvious why she was, from the beginning, William's favourite, though she too caused them many worries. Even when she was only six, they recognized her good and her bad points. 'Dorothy is a delightful girl,' wrote Dorothy, in 1810. 'Clever, entertaining and lively, indeed so very lively that it is impossible for her to satisfy the activity of her spirit without a little naughtiness at times – a waywardness of fancy rather than of temper.' Two years later, Dorothy was complaining that Dora was turning out rather bossy and self-willed: 'I am sorry to tell you that we still have much trouble with Dorothy. She *can* do anything but she is extremely wayward and is desirous to master everybody. She has been with me two hours and a half this morning and has been very good and industrious – but sometimes we have terrible Battles – and long confinements. I hope that perseverance may conquer her, and that the sense will in time come that it is wiser not to make herself miserable.'

Dora did go for a while to day-school at Ambleside, but for long periods she was taught at home by Dorothy. William's attempts to teach John at home rather broke his son's spirit; but, though Dorothy had many little battles with Dora, her spirit was never cowed. She was always going on about Dora's need for firm discipline, convinced that a good school would knock her into shape. William, knowing how quick and clever she was, wished she would give her mind more to her lessons: 'She is very careless and inattentive, but capable of learning rapidly would she give her mind to it.'

Dorothy also helped with Dora's physical well-being, and had a little more success with that. It was decided by the local doctor, Mr Scrambler, that what was needed to buck you up for a Cumbrian winter was an all-over cold-water wash every morning. Dorothy describes how Dora, never being a healthy-looking child, was therefore forced to conform and received the cold-water treatment every morning.

We had one terrible struggle with her, but she now likes it and I hope we shall have no more difficulty about the matter. Dorothy's temper is very obstinate by fits and at such times nothing but rigorous confinement can subdue her. She is not to be moved by the feelings and the misfortune is that the more indulgence or pleasure she has, the more unmanageable she is. Yet she is affectionate in the extreme and patient and docile whenever she is called upon to perform the duty of attending upon the sick or helping to nurse.

When Dora was fourteen, the ladies of the house at last persuaded William to let her board at the school in Ambleside, where she stayed happily for three years, coming home for weekends. When she left, in 1821, they gave a little coming-out ball for her, which the 'beauty and the fashion' of the neighbourhood attended. Dora wasn't a beauty – though, in the painting of her which survives, done when she was twenty-five, she looks attractive, with enormous blue eyes. 'She is a fine looking girl,' Dorothy had written when Dora was twelve. 'At times her face is very plain, at other times it is even beautiful. She is rather stout and tall – but neither in the extreme – holds her head up well, has a broad chest and good shoulders, but walks and runs most awkwardly. Vanity she has little or none, and is utterly free from envy.'

All in all, Dora's was a most engaging personality, with signs of

William's own youthful obstinacy and wilfulness, but without his reck-lessness. As she was a girl, her opportunities for wildness were limited. There was no chance of her being allowed to go walking across Europe. Her chances of a career were even more restricted. So she did what most girls did: being a dutiful daughter, she returned home after her school-days were over and waited for something to happen. William of course was delighted. He loved Dora dearly, dreamed about her and wrote poems about her. She loved him in turn, though without any of that cloying sentimentality that her aunt had once shown towards William, nor with a blind reverence of her Father the Poet. She could tease and jolly him along, poke fun at him and his foibles, and was a lively and interesting companion in almost every circumstance. Lucky William: he now had four ladies at home, looking after his needs.

Then there was little Willy. Like big brother John, he inherited the Wordsworth nose, which was commented on in all the letters imme-diately after his birth. He was also like John in having little natural apti-tude for his lessons – though John did at least try hard, and his parents always had hopes that he would turn out a scholar in the end, as he seemed interested in books. Willy, alas, was neither interested nor capable.

Little Willy – am I glad to give him that title for it makes me sad sometimes when I think how we are losing the others as children – is a very sweet and interesting child [wrote Dorothy in 1816, when Willy was six]. He is backward at his books, for he has only just begun to learn at all, but he is now under a new Master, his Father's clerk [John Carter, who helped William with the Stamps], and his progress is rapid. All at once under him he became steady, whereas his mother, his aunt Sarah and I, have all by turns undertaken him and we could make nothing out. The lesson was the signal for yawning and for perpetual motion in one part of the body or another.

Willy too went eventually to the school in Ambleside, walking there daily, but without showing much promise in his lessons. As the baby of the family, the one they were sad to see growing up, as Dorothy com-mented, he was made a great fuss of by everybody and was particularly spoiled by William. He was still only a toddler when the two others had died, so naturally they had feared for him most. Mary at the time was very morbid, feeling sure they might lose yet another baby: a feel-ing that comes through in Dorothy's letters as well.

But soon the ladies of the household thought William overdid his fuss-ing, making Willy worse and more spoiled than ever. 'It would distress you to see how a pale look of that child has the power to disturb his father,' wrote Sarah in 1815, when Willy was five. 'He will scarcely suffer the wind of heaven to come near him and watches him the day through.' At the age of seven, according to Dorothy, William was still treating him like a baby:

Really, his Father fondles over him and talks to him just as if he were but a year old. I am astonished with his babyishness; He has however so fine a temper from nature that I think it is utterly impossible to undo it and by degrees he will be recovered from all leanings towards being treated as the little pet, 'the little darling'; for when he is amongst his school fellows none are more active, independent and manly than he and he disdains all notice from Father.

The ladies got him away from William's clutches in the end, getting him into Charterhouse in 1821, when he was eleven; but he stayed there for only a year, thanks to idleness and ill health. He came back to Rydal and spent the next six years at home. Hartley Coleridge, after leaving Oxford, gave him lessons at the Ambleside school for a time; this wasn't very satisfactory, for, as Dorothy remarked, Hartley wasn't exactly a disciplinarian. Hartley in turn didn't think much of Willy. 'Little Will', he said, 'is a bore.'

By 1822, the Wordsworth children had each in their different ways finished their main schooling. John was nineteen and about to leave Sedbergh – shy and slow, but hoping for some sort of university place, though his chances were not high. Dorothy, aged eighteen, was settled at home, her school-days over – a lively young lady, though none too strong and becoming increasingly liable to illness. (It looks as if, from this time, she was in the early stages of tuberculosis.) Little Willy, aged twelve, was back at home – still supposedly being schooled, but having proved the worst predictions about his being spoiled and lazy to be true. Dora wrote a joke advertisement about Willy in a home-made newspaper which she produced with a friend on holiday at Morecambe Bay in 1825: 'Wants a Situation: A youth of about 15 years of age. He is able to do any kind of work, but prefers sitting to standing, riding to walking and lying in bed to anything in the world.'

The general air of domestic bliss, which had continued untrammelled now for ten years, was helped by the fact that the Wordsworths had been spared any more illnesses as the children grew up. But, though

their immediate family as a whole suffered no tragedies, their near relations and friends had several misfortunes.

William's younger brother Christopher, the clever one, lost his wife
Priscilla in 1815. She'd just given birth to her sixth child, a still-born
girl who was born after twenty-four hours of 'tremendous sufferings',
so Dorothy wrote. The five children so far had all been boys, though
two of them had died in infancy after convulsions. Priscilla was the
sister of Charles Lloyd, William's near neighbour and old friend. At
about the same time Lloyd himself became insane and was taken into
a mental home in Birmingham, accompanied for most of the journey by
William. This was when Dorothy went to stay with Mrs Lloyd and
her eight children, to help out. William similarly offered Dorothy's services to Christopher on his bereavement, but Christopher said he would
try to manage on his own.

Christopher was left in his large Lambeth rectory, with three young
boys to bring up on his own. He never remarried, but it didn't affect
his career. In 1820 he was made Master of Trinity College, Cambridge,
a great honour, which impressed the whole Wordsworth family. His
three boys turned out to be equally clever, unlike William's two sons,
and they all went on to have distinguished academic careers. William
had never been particularly close to his brother Christopher, but after
Priscilla's death their relationship became much closer and warmer.

William had always been even less close to Richard, the eldest
Wordsworth brother. He and Dorothy were still upset that Richard
never came to visit them, especially now that he had a young baby
they would liked to have seen. He continued to handle all the family
affairs, was their banker and investor and looked after their Lowther
monies, and so, when he fell ill in 1816, William was greatly alarmed.
They had forgiven him for marrying the young, supposedly vulgar
servant girl two years previously, but were furious to discover that a man
with his responsibilities had not yet made a will or any provisions for
his and the family's financial affairs. William became obsessed by all the
awful things that could happen through lack of proper documents –
just as he had fretted all those years previously when his benefactor
Raisley Calvert was ill: 'There is much reason to regret that he has
not made a will and appointed Guardians for his child, especially considering the situation of life from which his wife was taken and the great
probability of her returning by a second marriage into that class.'
William was mainly worrying about the mess he and Dorothy might

be landed in, and his letters show him in a rather unattractive light, worrying chiefly about his own finances while his brother lay desperately ill. In the event, Richard did die, at the age of forty-seven, at Christopher's house in London in May 1816. William had intended to come and visit him several times, getting as far as Kendal on one occasion; but, for various reasons, he never actually managed to see Richard, and was consumed with remorse after his brother's death.

His worries were proved correct. Though Richard did manage to make a will in time, and William and Christopher were appointed guardians of his only child, a son, the family's finances were in a terrible mess. It took William almost the whole of the next year to sort them out. What with that, and all his political activities in connection with the Westmorland election, he didn't write a line of poetry for almost two years.

Richard was the second Wordsworth brother to die, but there was nothing like the intensity of grief that had been caused by the dreadful tragedy of John, the sailor brother, eleven years previously. For it was then that the original 'set' had been broken. Now, William and Mary had their own little set, each with a devoted sister in tow, all looking after their own brood, who were growing up healthy and happy – even if there were a few qualms, a few disappointments and a few possible worries for the future.

She was a Phantom of Delight

One of Wordsworth's love poems, published in the 1807 collection.
It is not known if he had Mary or Dorothy or anyone else in mind.
He describes it as a Poem of Imagination.

She was a Phantom of delight
When first she gleamed upon my sight;
A lovely Apparition, sent
To be a moment's ornament;
Her eyes as stars of Twilight fair;
Like Twilight's, too, her dusky hair;
But all things else about her drawn
From May-time and the cheerful Dawn;
A dancing Shape, in Image gay,
To haunt, to startle, and way-lay.

And now I see with eye serene
The very pulse of the machine;
A Being breathing thoughtful breath,
A Traveller between life and death;
The reason firm, the temperate will,
Endurance, foresight, strength, and skill;
A perfect Woman, nobly planned,
To warn, to comfort and command;
And yet a Spirit still and bright
With something of angelic light.

17

Friends and Relations
1813-1820

AFTER a shaky start, the other literary establishment across at Greta Hall in Keswick was flourishing greatly, and Robert Southey, sole male head of the Southey–Coleridge clan, achieved popularity and eminence before Wordsworth when he'd become Poet Laureate in 1813. They hadn't been close friends in the early days; perhaps they had even been unspoken rivals, though that bad review by Southey of *Lyrical Ballads* had been inspired in part by spite against his brother-in-law Coleridge, as they'd recently fallen out over pantisocracy.

Over the years, Wordsworth and Southey had grown much closer, in their lives and in their characters, each becoming more Tory and reactionary, their republican days long behind them. As people, they grew to become genuine friends. They comforted each other in family grief; but, most of all, they were brought together by their respective offspring. The Coleridge children were constantly with the Wordsworths, for weeks on end, the Southey children usually joined them, and they all paid each other return visits. The daughters of the three poets turned out to be each other's best friends.

Southey hadn't really wanted to come to the Lakes. He'd put off

Coleridge's entreaties for a couple of years, hoping something else would turn up – going to Dublin for a spell as a minor civil servant, then ending up back at home in Bristol, though still looking for some sort of paid job to keep him going. It was the death of his first child, Margaret, in 1803 that suddenly made him take up Coleridge's offer: he couldn't face the Bristol house any more and he thought his wife and Mrs Coleridge would provide sisterly comfort for each other. Even so, for the first few years in Keswick he was still hoping for a nice overseas appointment, particularly one in Portugal, his first love.

It turned out to be a watershed in his life – arriving in the Lakes after eight years of wandering, with different jobs and different homes. He suddenly revealed the most enormous willpower and single-minded concentration, qualities hidden until that moment, and for the next forty years lived in the Lakes, devoting himself to his pen and to being a parent. You often find hints in his letters that he might have been subjugating some deep passion, some yearning to wander off again; but the clues are slight and he did become the model Victorian patriarch.

His reputation as a poet was based on five epic poems, all now unread, starting with *Joan of Arc* back in 1796, which Charles Lamb said marked him as the greatest living poet. His most admired epic was *The Curse of Kehama* (1810), loved by all the new young poets, such as Keats, Shelley and Byron.

Unlike Wordsworth, who saw himself only as a poet, pure and simple, Southey had two other literary occupations which increasingly took over his working life. He'd been a hack reviewer since his early days, along with Coleridge, accepting every little book review commission that came his way; but now he grew into a journalist of great importance, writing long essays and articles on the subjects of the day. In 1809 he began writing regularly for the *Quarterly Review*; at the height of his fame he was being paid £100 an article, an enormous sum for those days. (Most of today's literary magazines still don't pay as highly.) The *Edinburgh Review* tried to tempt him away – which he knew would be good for his own books, as the magazine's reviewers would be bound to be kinder to him – but naturally, being a man of honour, he couldn't go over to the enemy and turned the offer down. In 1817 he was offered the equally large sum of £2,000 a year to write for *The Times*. Crabb Robinson, friend to all the Lake Poets, was the intermediary, and it seems possible that they might even have been going to offer him the editorship, as the owner of *The Times*, John Walter, had just sacked his editor, and Southey was much respected by the ruling Tory government. But Southey turned them down too, not wishing to leave the Lakes. By this time, his earnings from his own writings, which he worked at almost round the clock, were probably about £2,000 anyway. Wordsworth, by comparison, was at this time lucky to average £20 a year from his poetry.

Southey's other source of income was non-fiction. His passion for Portugal turned into a three-volume history of Brazil, the first one of that country; but he never got his history of Portugal itself finished. He wrote other historical books, including one on the Peninsular War, but his speciality was biography; his *Life of Nelson* did much to confirm Nelson as a public hero.

In his day, it was Southey's prose style that was chiefly admired. Even Wordsworth, who never publicly praised Southey's poetry, even when he became an intimate friend, enormously enjoyed Southey's prose, as everyone did. Byron called it perfect and Hazlitt said it could 'scarcely be too much praised'. It is forgotten now that while Wordsworth was setting out to free English poetry from gaudiness and inane phraseology, English prose was also suffering from the convoluted but empty elegance of the eighteenth-century manner.

Southey worked like a demon at each of his writing activities, turning himself into a positive industry. Over at Rydal, when William was in one of his fallow periods, preoccupied with politics, travelling or family affairs, they often wished he was as creative as Southey.

William is quite well [wrote Dorothy to Mrs Clarkson in 1821], though he has not looked at *The Recluse* or the poem of his own life, and this disturbs us. After fifty years of age, there is no time to spare, and unfinished works should not, if it be possible, be left behind. This he feels, but the will never governs *his* labours. How different from Southey, who can go as regularly as clockwork, from history to poetry, from poetry to criticism, and so on to biography, or anything else. If their minds could each spare a little to the other, how much better for both!

Southey had to work so hard because he had so many people to support by his writings alone. There were, firstly, the three Coleridge children he inherited: Hartley, Derwent and Sara; he then went on to produce eight children of his own, though two died in infancy. After a run of six girls, he had a longed-for son, Herbert, who turned out to be another child prodigy in the house, almost as clever as Hartley, knowing Greek,

French, German and Latin by the time he was nine. He died, aged ten, in 1815, a shock which greatly upset Southey and his wife, and all in the Wordsworth household, who offered to do anything they could to help. Sarah Hutchinson was the universal aunt for both households. In turn, she ministered to the needs of the three poets. After Coleridge had left, she went on to act for long spells as a secretary or just a living-in friend for the Southeys, when she wasn't doing the same for the Wordsworths. At Rydal Mount, as at Greta Hall, whenever there was a domestic upset, the cry was the same: 'Send for Sarah.'

The Southeys had a final child – a son, Cuthbert – in 1819, when Mrs Southey was forty-seven, which brought the total number of children in the house back to eight. Then there were the adults. A third Fricker sister, Mrs Lovell (widow of Robert Lovell, the young writer who was also in the pantisocracy scheme), came to the Lakes with the Southeys, though Coleridge had advised them to pension her off. She not only stayed, but outlived them all. That meant twelve permanent mouths to feed, plus many regular and impecunious visitors. There were two more Fricker sisters, maiden aunts called Martha and Eliza, who were regular guests. Southey's joke was that Greta Hall was an ant-hill – not just because of his ferocious activity, but because every lady was somebody's aunt.

Southey, in effect, had three wives – just like Wordsworth. His wife, Mrs Coleridge and Mrs Lovell all supported him as best they could and looked to him as master of the house.

A mutual friend, a Miss Barker, who lived in Keswick, said that both Wordsworth and Southey were spoiled by their three wives, 'but that Wordsworth's were much preferable to Southey's'. The Fricker sisters, on the whole, do seem to have been rather dreary, depressing ladies, and nobody, in all the memoirs, has a good word to say for them, compared with Dorothy and the Hutchinson sisters, who are constantly being praised. Both households had friends in common, such as Crabb Robinson, Humphry Davy and Walter Scott, and most people new to the Lakes tried to visit both establishments on their tour, if they wanted to boast, as everyone did, that they'd seen the Lake Poets.

Coleridge has left the worst testimony against his wife Sara; but then he would, blaming her for many of his own failings. 'If anyone wanted an exact and copious recipe, "How to make a Husband completely miserable" I could furnish her with one,' wrote Coleridge. 'Ill tempered Speeches sent after me when I went out of the House, ill tempered speeches on my return, my friends received with freezing looks, the least opposition or contradiction received with screams of passion – all this added to the utter negation of all of which a Husband expects from a wife.' Dorothy had been equally against Sara in the early days, but they all came to like her more, as she blossomed after Coleridge had left.

Southey joined the chorus which agreed that Wordsworth was a lucky man, adding a rather personal but mysterious comment on his own circumstances. 'No man was ever more fortunate in wife, sister or sister in law than he has been,' Southey wrote to a lady friend about Wordsworth. 'There is no woman out of my own house (except one whom I shall not name to you) with whom I am so intimate as Miss Hutchinson, or whom I love altogether so well.' What could that possibly mean? He could have meant Sara Coleridge, except she had married and left home; or perhaps her mother. Did he prefer Mrs Coleridge to his own wife? There was always a slight suggestion that he and Coleridge had originally married the wrong sisters.

De Quincey, in his *Recollections of the Lake Poets*, has left rather a dour picture of Southey, locked away in his library, with his fourteen thousand books, always charming and courteous to meet, but his mind always half on his work, perhaps a nicer man than Wordsworth, but far less inspiring. He was five feet eleven inches tall, an inch taller than Wordsworth, according to De Quincey, as well as being better dressed and more presentable. From his portraits, Southey does appear much the handsomer, finer figure. Byron, at his early meeting with Southey, was impressed both by his poetry and his appearance: 'The best looking bard I have seen for some time. To have that poet's head and shoulders, I would almost have written his Sapphics. His appearance is *epic* and he is the only existing entire man of letters.'

One of the best Southey–Wordsworth gatherings – and they had many picnics, expeditions and tours together – was held in 1815, to celebrate Waterloo. Each was now a confirmed French-hater, having lost all republican zeal. Southey organized a triumphant ascent of Skiddaw, with a great party on top and a massive bonfire. Most of Southey's own family were there, plus William, Mary and Dorothy from Rydal; several local lords and lordlings; friends and children, and three maids to serve the feast, all of whom were followed up the mountain by 'Messrs. Rag, Tag and Bobtail'.

At the top, they had roast beef, plum pudding and punch, and sang

'God Save the King' round a bonfire made of tar barrels. Blazing balls of tow and turpentine were rolled down the mountain side for extra effects. 'We formed a huge circle round the intense light,' wrote one guest later, 'and behind us was an immeasurable arch of the most intense darkness, for our bonfire fairly put out the moon.' They didn't get back to Keswick till after midnight, by which time some of the Messrs Rag, Tag and Bobtail were happily drunk. Mrs Coleridge hadn't gone with them, but had stayed at home with some of the younger children: 'I had a very anxious time during the nine hours of their absence for I feared lest the mists should come on and so keep them on the heights all night. Not a cloud came to distress them and not one of the party were any worse for the expedition.'

Southey welcomed all visitors, despite his crowded writing schedule, and answered all letters, giving help to every unknown who wrote. He had a long correspondence with a lady called Caroline Bowles, who sent him some poems which he not only helped to edit but for which he found her a publisher. (It was to Miss Bowles he wrote the letter about the ladies of his household.) Another letter from an unknown was one signed C. Brontë – a name he mistook for a pseudonym, as it looked so odd – enclosing some verse for his comments. In his rather discouraging reply he told her that marriage was a woman's proper career: 'The day dreams in which you habitually indulge are likely to induce a distempered state of mind, and in proportion as all the ordinary uses of the world seem to you flat and unprofitable, you will be unfitted for them without becoming fitted for anything else. Literature cannot be the business of a woman's life and it ought not to be.' However, he ended on a kinder note. 'Farewell madam. It is not because I have forgotten that I was once young myself that I write to you in this strain, but because I remember it. . . . Though I may be an ungracious adviser, you will allow me, therefore, to subscribe myself, with the best wishes for your happiness here and hereafter, your true friend, Robert Southey.'

When this letter turned up at a saleroom about seventy years later, Charlotte Brontë was found to have endorsed the letter with the following words: 'Southey's advice to be kept for ever. My twenty-first birthday. Roe Head, April 21, 1837.'

The better established young writers had introductions and were entertained at Greta Hall. One such was Shelley, who in 1811 had run away to Keswick with his child bride, and lived there for six months.

He'd hoped to see Wordsworth as well, but didn't manage it. He was an admirer of both of them, describing Southey's *Kehama* as his 'most favourite poem'. He was received by Southey, taken round the house, and shown all his books, but not allowed to handle them himself. Southey didn't approve of that. Afterwards, Shelley decided Southey was a reactionary old bore, and they later carried on a violent quarrel in letters, after Shelley had wrongly thought Southey had given him a bad review.

Southey did rather go in for acrimonious correspondence with other writers, often for the sport, and to exercise his journalistic muscles, though the issue was sometimes very serious. Like Wordsworth, who was branded with Southey as a turncoat, lost to politics and poetry, he particularly hated Byron and christened his writing the 'Satanic School of Poetry'. Byron and he had a typically convoluted literary row, in private and in published articles and verse, with accusations flying around. It ended with Byron challenging Southey to a duel, but his second never delivered the challenge.

Byron scored the most points in this public argument with Southey and Wordsworth – much to the amusement of all the young wits, who enjoyed his satirical verses in *Don Juan*, where he names the guilty men of his generation (and, incidentally, in passing, makes clear the correct pronunciation of Southey):

> Thou shall believe in Milton, Dryden, Pope,
>> Thou shalt not set up Wordsworth, Coleridge, Southey,
> Because the first is crazed beyond all hope,
>> The second drunk, the third so quaint and mouthy.

In another stanza of *Don Juan*, which started to appear in the 1820s, Byron did a very clever parody of one of Southey's own poems, copying the metre exactly:

> For pantisocracy he once had cried
> Aloud, a scheme less moral than 't was clever
> Then grew a hearty anti-jacobin
> Had turned his coat – and would have turned his skin.

By the 1820s, both Lakeland poets were long-confirmed Tories, so you can imagine Southey's outrage when, in 1817, a republican, Jacobin play he'd written twenty years earlier, which had never been performed, was suddenly on sale in the London streets. It was about Wat Tyler, the leader of the Peasants' Revolt, and very soon had sold sixty

[267]

thousand copies at threepence a time. Southey tried to obtain a court injunction to stop the sale, but failed; he took this rather stoically, despite attacks on him in the House of Commons. One MP accused the Poet Laureate of being a secret renegade and purveyor of sedition. The Whigs made great capital by pointing out, as they always did with Wordsworth, how he had changed sides: at first welcoming the Revolution, then turning against it. Southey's reply to his critics was a good example of his polished prose: 'They had turned their faces towards the east in the morning to worship the rising sun, and in the evening they were looking eastwards still, obstinately affirming that still the sun was there. I, on the contrary, altered my position as the world went round.'

Wordsworth thought Southey was now 'completely triumphant ... for a more disinterested and honourable man than Robert Southey does not breathe'. Many years later, Southey included the drama in a collection of his works, this time without apologies, saying that he was no more 'ashamed of having been a republican than of having been a boy.'

If the Wat Tyler incident was a nasty trick, his enthusiasm for the Tories was to lead him unwittingly into another embarrassing situation in 1826. An admirer of his, the Earl of Radnor, a Tory feudal lord with Lonsdale-style power in the West Country, put him forward as an MP for Wiltshire, for a seat he controlled. Unfortunately, the letter in which the earl told Southey what he'd done arrived when Southey was abroad on an extensive tour of the Low Countries. Southey arrived back in Keswick, to find the town band out in the street, waiting to greet the new MP. 'The whole posse of the place had assembled to see what alteration dignity had produced in my stature and appearance.'

The town was full of rumours, Southey said. According to one, he was now wealthy and worth £6,000 a year; according to another, he'd predicted the end of the world on Thursday last. He turned down the honour of being an MP, which he couldn't have accepted anyway, as he was the recipient of a Crown pension.

Although Wordsworth and Southey had both become high Tories, Southey never went round begging the favours of the Tory lords. Southey, as much as Wordsworth, was indebted to Lord Lonsdale, who was one of the influential people who supported his name for the Laureateship and helped with his pension; but Southey did no spying or genuflecting in return. He would appear to have been uncorrupted by his rising success and his contact with the powerful. Both writers had by now certainly risen. The two Lake Poets were confirmed in their political and social attitudes and were united as dear friends and neighbours for the rest of their lives.

In 1817, William asked Southey to do him a favour. He knew that his friend was going on a trip to Europe and would be in Paris. He would be extremely grateful if Southey, while in Paris, could just somehow manage to look up a certain young lady, a girl called Caroline, as a personal service. William, so Southey related, had told him that 'it would not be necessary nor pleasant to myself to be acquainted with the story of Caroline's birth'.

Southey duly met Caroline in Paris. As soon as she realized that Mr Southey was such a close friend and dear neighbour of Mr Wordsworth, she blurted out the full story, telling him how William came to be her father. They had a *tête-à-tête* for about an hour, with Caroline having a good weep. Next day, Southey had breakfast with her and her mother Annette. He was very impressed by their love for William and by their lack of any resentment.

William must have known the full story would come out, which shows how he trusted and respected Southey. After all, not many friends knew about William's French relations (although Crabb Robinson had been told). It is not known whether any of William's legitimate children were ever told, though they may have found out.

Contact with Annette had of course been lost during the war against Napoleon, but letters had started coming through again in 1814, when Napoleon resigned his throne. They'd also made personal contact when a young French officer, named Eustace Baudouin, a friend of Annette's family, visited the Wordsworths at Rydal Mount. He'd been a prisoner of war, captured by the English, and he brought first-hand news of how Annette and her daughter had fared during the long war. Like the Wordsworths, they were delighted by the end of Napoleon, as they were still staunch royalists and hoped for the return of the Bourbons – and perhaps also for some recognition, such as a pension, for all their dangerous work in helping royalist supporters.

In 1814, Caroline, now twenty-one, became engaged to Baudouin's brother, Jean Baptiste, who was thirty-three and a minor civil servant. The letters were flowing freely between Rydal and Paris, where Annette and her daughter now lived. William was apparently a little worried by Baudouin's financial position, and was concerned whether he would have enough money to support Caroline, but he gave his consent to the wedding. It's interesting to note that the proprieties were kept, despite their lack of contact for well over ten years. William hadn't written any letters, as far as is known, and even now, with his daughter about to get married, it was Dorothy who did all the corresponding. Annette would appear to have been the one most determined to keep up the contact – proud of her one-time English lover, and not ashamed of being called Madame William, nor of Caroline having an absentee father, now married to someone else.

Dorothy and Sarah made plans to attend the wedding – there was no sign of William wanting to go – but Sarah worried about travelling with no male companions and Dorothy wondered if it might not be better to save the travel money and spend it on a better wedding present for Caroline. There were many delays while they made up their minds, though Annette kindly put back the wedding date to suit their plans.

'Both Caroline and her Mother urge my going in October,' wrote Dorothy. 'On this account, that, after a young woman is once engaged to be married, it is desirable that the delay afterwards should be as short as possible, as she is subject to perpetual scrutiny and unpleasant remarks, and one of the reasons they urge for marriage in general is that a single woman in France unless she have a fortune, is not treated with any *consideration*.'

World events overtook their domestic arrangements, as world events often do. Napoleon escaped from his exile on Elba in early 1815 and by March was advancing on Paris, becoming master of France once again. 'For the sake of our Friends I am truly distressed,' wrote Dorothy to Mrs Clarkson, referring, as she often did, to Annette's family as 'our *Friends*', presumably to keep their identity as secret as possible. 'The lady whom I mentioned to you from the first was a zealous Royalist, has often risked her life in defence of adherents to the cause and she despised and detested Buonapart. Poor Creature! The letter was concluded at midnight. My Friend says: "I hear troops entering the City. Good God! What is to become of us."'

As we know, world events came to the rescue. Napoleon was finally defeated at Waterloo, though, as ten-year-old Dora said, when they were discussing Napoleon's escape from Elba, as no doubt it was discussed in every British home, 'Why did they not kill him when they *had* him?'

In February 1816, after endless delays and when it had become clear that William was not going to come, his daughter Caroline got married. She was described on the marriage certificate as the daughter of 'William Wordsworth, demeurant à Grasner Kendan duche de Westmorland, Angleterre'. None of the Wordsworths was present at the ceremony. Annette, despite her slim resources, did her best to make a big show of the wedding, turning it almost into a royalist celebration: she laid on a grand dinner party and invited all her notable royalist friends.

'The mother's details of the wedding festivities would have amused you,' wrote Dorothy to Mrs Clarkson. 'She perhaps for half a year to come will feel the effects at every dinner she cooks! Thirty persons were present to dinner, ball and supper. The deputies of the department and many other respectable people were there. The bride was dressed in white sarsnet with a white veil, was the admiration of all who beheld her, but her modesty was her best ornament. She kept her veil on the whole of the day. How truly French this is!'

Over a hundred years later, this rather light-hearted account by Dorothy of Annette's big day upset the distinguished French scholar Emile Legouis. He was the gentleman who did most to reveal the Annette connection in his book published in 1922 (*William Wordsworth and Annette Vallon*). As a Frenchman, he obviously felt rather protective towards Annette: 'The mother had done her utmost, thrown away the last of her gold to attain, as it were, this exaltation of their daughter. What matter if she did it according to her ideas, which were those of a humble French bourgeoise and in the manner of her country. The absent father, the kind aunt herself who had not been able to come, would have done better to check their sense of humour.'

Professor Legouis also suggested that William, with his '£400 a year stamp sinecure', could have helped them more financially. But, as we know, not only did William have to deduct from this figure a sum for payment of staff and expenses, he also had his own large household to provide for. No details exist of any dowry or wedding presents, but from this date, William did start sending an annual payment to his daughter of £30, which was generous enough, considering his circumstances. It was sent from London, through Daniel Stuart, of the *Courier*. This looks like a device to keep the arrangement private, or a way of preventing William from being directly bothered by the Baudouins. William faithfully sent the money every year, and in 1835 settled a lump sum of £400 on Caroline, bringing the financial arrangements to a close.

Caroline had a daughter just ten months after the wedding, in December 1816; the child was called Louise Marie Caroline Dorothée – the last name out of affection for Dorothy, who had always addressed Caroline in loving terms. There were two other daughters, but one died aged six. Some time later, Annette did finally get a small government pension from the returned royalists.

In 1820, William at last visited France again. On the way back from a European tour, he, Mary, Dorothy and Crabb Robinson took lodgings in the Rue Chalot, the street where Annette and the Baudouins were living. The first meeting between Mary Wordsworth and Annette, her husband's former lover, took place in the Louvre and the encounter was as civilized as the surroundings. No outbursts of emotion were noted, no tears or recriminations. It was all utterly placid and pleasant. Annette and her family didn't speak English and William's French must have been rather rusty by now, since he had not been to France for eighteen years. It was at this time that William apparently gave his French family a pencil portrait of himself and a copy of the two-volume *Collected Poems* of 1815. One of the volumes is said still to be in the hands of the French branch of the Wordsworth family today.

Crabb Robinson thought the great meeting was perhaps a trifle too civilized. Caroline called Wordsworth 'Father', which he thought rather 'indelicate'. But then, by 1820, William was a very civilized gentleman. Not all passion was spent, by any means, but a lot of his fervour – whether animal, political or emotional – was gradually subsiding.

IT IS A BEAUTEOUS EVENING

The 'Dear Child' is Caroline, his daughter by Annette Vallon. He wrote the poem in August 1802, when Caroline was nine, walking along the Calais sands.

It is a beauteous evening, calm and free,
The holy time is quiet as a Nun
Breathless with adoration; the broad sun
Is sinking down in its tranquillity;
The gentleness of heaven broods o'er the Sea;
Listen! the mighty Being is awake,
And doth with his eternal motion make
A sound like thunder – everlastingly.
Dear Child! dear Girl! that walkest with me here,
If thou appear untouched by solemn thought,
Thy nature is not therefore less divine:
Thou liest in Abraham's bosom all the year;
And worshipp'st at the Temple's inner shrine,
God being with thee when we know it not.

18

Fame
1820-1830

A FRIEND of Keats played a literary trick on William in 1819. He saw advertised a forthcoming poem by Wordsworth, 'Peter Bell, A Tale in Verse', and before it was published, and before he had read it, he decided to write his own version. To be parodied before publication might not be very amusing for an author, but it is certainly a sign of some kind of success.

'Peter Bell' had been written twenty years previously, but for various reasons William had never published it. He had contemplated doing so in 1815, but the bad reviews of *The Excursion* and *The White Doe of Rylstone* probably put him off.

Since then, there had been a perceptible change in attitude in the literary magazines: formerly critical publications, like the *Eclectic Review*, referred to Wordsworth and Southey in 1816 as the 'two greatest living poets' and gave a serious consideration of their respective merits and weaknesses. 'There are passages in all his poems,' they wrote of Wordsworth, 'that are fitted with exquisite skill to find their way to the heart. But ... when he aims to teach, he fails to please.'

There was therefore a reasonable glow of anticipation from the critics when the appearance of 'Peter Bell' was imminent, though not amongst the younger wits and witlings.

'Wordsworth is going to publish a poem called "Peter Bell",' wrote Keats to his brother. 'What a perverse fellow it is! Why wilt he talk about Peter Bells? – I was told not to tell – but to you it will not be tellings – Reynolds hearing that said "Peter Bell" was coming out, took it into his head to write a skit upon it call'd Peter Bell. He did it as soon as thought on. It is to be published this morning.'

The very name 'Peter Bell' struck them as highly ridiculous, but typical of Wordsworth, and they advertised their version in *The Times*, with the motto, 'I am the real Simon Pure.' The parody was published by Keats's own publisher. Coleridge wrote to them, saying it was rather bad form and a breach of trust, but they replied that, as the author hadn't seen a word of the original poem, they saw nothing wrong. The parody was complete with a Wordsworthian Preface and heavy notes, which even amused Coleridge. It was in the metre of 'The Idiot Boy' and contained what were now considered the characteristic Wordsworthian rustic characters.

Keats reviewed it anonymously for Leigh Hunt's *Examiner* and the review was reprinted in the *Kendal Chronicle*, the local Whig paper which was against Wordsworth and the Tory Yellows. Keats did a clever double bluff, calling the skit false and 'hurried from the press, obtruded into public notice while for ought we know the real one may be still wandering round the woods and mountains'.

Shelley wrote a much more serious skit on 'Peter Bell'. He had the reviews of the joke one and the real one sent out to him in Italy. He called his 'Peter Bell III', using it as a vehicle to attack all the high Tories like Wordsworth, whom he blamed for the poverty and deprivation in the new industrial towns; but he was persuaded not to publish it, as it would harm his reputation – just as one imagines Wordsworth had been persuaded not to publish his radical pamphlet some thirty years previously.

Byron's satire was much more gentle this time. He pretended he was writing a letter to a friend from Germany:

You are not aware of the works of William Wordsworth, who has a baronet in London who draws him frontispieces and leads him about to dinners and to the play; and a Lord in the country who gave him a place in the Excise and a cover at his table. You do not know perhaps that this gentleman is the greatest of all poets past, present and to come. His principal publication is entitled 'Peter Bell' which he has withheld from the public for one and twenty years – to the irreparable loss of all those who died in the interim and will have no opportunity of reading it before the resurrection....

William had the last laugh. The real 'Peter Bell' was published in April 1819, with a drawing of Peter Bell done by Sir George Beaumont and a dedication to Southey, the Poet Laureate. The first edition of five hundred copies sold out in two weeks. Bad publicity can sometimes be better than none at all. No poetry by Wordsworth had ever sold so quickly. A reprint was immediately ordered.

All the same, the reviewers were obviously disappointed. Crabb Robinson and William himself feared they wouldn't like the poem, but, on the whole, the reviewers were gentle in their criticisms, referring to William as a great poet, with some works of genius behind him, but sad that on this occasion he had failed. The *Eclectic Review* said he was 'a poet that, after all, cannot be laughed down'. The *British Critic*, in a very long review, said that Wordsworth would always have enthusiastic admirers, in every age, and that people would always derive from Wordsworth 'as high gratification as any poet is capable of bestowing'. At the same time, they said that, in every long poem of Wordsworth which was longer than a mere sonnet, a reader had to expect something not to his taste. Other reviewers, making the same point, put it more brutally. One suggested that all his best pieces should be collected in one volume, 'while his idiots and waggoners were collected into a bonfire on the top of Skiddaw'.

Even today, the most passionate devotees of Wordsworth would admit that he has lapses, even in his finest poems. You are always tempting fate when you aim for simplicity, and for almost all of the thirty years that Wordsworth had so far been displaying his works before the public, the bad parts had blinded the critics to the good parts. In their reviews, they tended to reproduce, out of context, the more ridiculous lines, which naturally didn't help sales. People then quoted the more awful parts at dinner parties, without ever having read the whole.

This time, with the publication of 'Peter Bell', there was only one really abusive review. It was in the *Monthly Review* (the *Edinburgh Review* doesn't appear to have noticed the poem), which called it daudling drivel and infantine. 'If a nurse were to talk to any of her children in this manner, a sensible father and mother would be strongly disposed to dismiss her without a character.' Apart from that, every critic considered it a major work from a major poet.

It is hard to explain, or even date precisely, the change in feeling of the critical public. It seems to have started in about 1817-18, years in which Wordsworth did *not* publish any poetry. It could be said that after all these years before the public, resolutely going his own way, sticking to his poetic last and not being deflected, he had taught readers the taste by which his poetry should be appreciated, as Coleridge always said must happen. Looking back, people realized that there had been a lot that they had enjoyed and benefited from, despite all the easily parodiable material.

Coleridge himself helped immensely by the publication in 1817 of his masterly literary-philosophical *Biographia Literaria*. In this he wrote that it was Wordsworth's prefaces that had caused all the abuse, but that now he stood 'nearest of all modern writers to Shakespeare and Milton'.

Despite twenty-five years of generally abusive reviews, many of them by minor writers, now long forgotten, almost all the best minds of the day did basically rate Wordsworth highly as a poet, whatever they might have thought of some poems or whatever they might have thought of him as a man. Keats, notwithstanding all the jokes, considered him a genius: 'He is superior to us, in so far as he can, more than we, make discoveries and shed a light on them.' Shelley acknowledged he was a 'great' poet, and even Byron was guilty of what was considered plagiarism of the Wordsworthian style in *Childe Harold*. Few writers of the day were not influenced by him in some way, whatever they may have asserted about him as a person.

Leigh Hunt, another of the London wits who scorned Wordsworth personally, put him amongst the three living poets who had characters of their own – the other two were Byron and Moore: 'Wordsworth ... is generally felt among his own profession to be at the head of it.'

Hazlitt, perhaps the keenest critical mind of his day, always admitted Wordsworth's genius, though he had attacked Wordsworth for publishing that letter defending the character of Robert Burns, and had accused Wordsworth of being pompous and full of cant, and his poetry for lacking joy: 'It is because so few things give him pleasure that he gives pleasure to few people.' Crabb Robinson, Wordsworth's devoted friend, was in the audience one day when Hazlitt expressed these opinions and was absolutely furious. 'I lost my temper and hissed ...'

But in 1818, in his *Lectures on the English Poets* (which were both delivered and published that year), Hazlitt described Wordsworth as 'the most original poet now living ... he has produced a deeper impression, and on a smaller circle, than any of his contemporaries'. Hazlitt still considered that Wordsworth was deficient in the mechanics of poetry, and unable to construct the perfect whole poem, but that as the leader of the Lake School of poetry, inspired by the sentiments of the French Revolution, he had been most responsible for rescuing English poetry: 'Poetical literature had, towards the close of the last century, degenerated into the most trite, insipid and mechanical of all things in the hands of the followers of Pope. It wanted something to stir it up. The Deucalions who were to perform this feat of regeneration were the present Poet-Laureate and the two authors of *Lyrical Ballads*.' This observation by Hazlitt in 1818, just twenty years after *Lyrical Ballads* was published, is still the accepted wisdom in literary circles today, though Poet Laureate Southey would not now receive such a kindly mention.

Wordsworth's next publication was his own personal break-through. The year after 'Peter Bell' – 1820 – saw the appearance of his series of sonnets on the River Duddon – and this finally established his literary fame and general acceptance. At the age of fifty, he at last received almost universal acclaim for a volume of his poems. Apart from all the praise for the beautiful sonnets, the generously long reviews hit back at his detractors. *Blackwood's Magazine*, published in Edinburgh, and with half an eye on its deadly local rival, quoted extensively from the sonnets, saying they would 'suffice to make our readers loath for ever all the cant about "Lakish Ditties" and "Pond Poets" and acknowledge at once that this author is a genuine English classic'. They considered that the Duddon poems showed there had been 'total failure of all attempts which have been made to check the fame of Wordsworth'.

The Duddon sonnets are delightful to read – and display the joy Wordsworth had always felt in that beautiful stream, which rises near Wrynose Pass and flows south to the sea in Furness, through the prettiest valley in the whole of the Lakes. He'd gone there first as a young school-boy at Hawkshead; that was the route of his fishing expedition, when he'd had to be carried back, tired out, on the back of the adult fisher-man. He'd gone there many times since, though perhaps his nicest memory, one which had helped to inspire the poems, was of an incident which took place when he was alone on the banks of the river with Mary in 1811, returning from the seaside. 'I have many affecting remembrances connected with this stream,' he recalled. 'These I forbear to mention, especially things that occurred on its banks during the later part of that visit. . . .' They had been married almost ten years at that time, but it was one of the few occasions they had been alone on a journey together.

More poems followed in 1822, particularly his *Ecclesiastical Sonnets*, a history in verse of the Church of England which concided with the appearance of a book by Southey on the same subject. They were delighted by the accident, hoping they would help each other; but Wordsworth's poems didn't sell very well, though they were kindly received by the critics – apart from the *Edinburgh Review*, which was on the attack, as ever, abusing his new work as prosy, feeble, obscure, egotistical, puerile and worthless (all the things, in other words, that they'd been saying for twenty years without respite), and bringing in his Stamp job for good measure, saying he was now 'blinded by the possession of a sinecure place'.

The strange thing about Jeffrey (later Lord Jeffrey), the editor of the *Edinburgh Review* and Wordsworth's chief scourge, was that, in private, he maintained that he liked Wordsworth's work and kept a copy of *Lyrical Ballads* on his desk. The magazine was of course a Whig publication, of which Brougham, the Westmorland election candidate, was cofounder, and they all genuinely hated and despised Wordsworth's politics; but Jeffrey denied that his criticism had been inspired by politics and personalities. He just wanted to keep Wordsworth in his place, to counter the worship of his admirers and help him to rid himself of his faults and excesses. 'I was always among Wordsworth's admirers,' Jeffrey told Crabb Robinson years later. 'You had an odd way of showing it,' replied Robinson.

William had, at long last, found fame on his own terms. 'Up to 1820 the name of Wordsworth was trampled underfoot,' said De Quincey. 'From 1820 to 1830 it was militant.' This didn't necessarily mean that overnight the sales had boomed and the money was flooding in, but William was suddenly doing much better. Even his new admirers knew he could never have a mass following, like Scott. His poetry was always going to be hard for light readers. He didn't, however, immediately exploit his newly acquired reputation; perhaps, indeed, he was hardly aware of the change in the atmosphere. No volumes of new poetry were published for the next ten years, from 1822 until the early 1830s. Instead, he was busy revising and publishing new editions of his old work.

The 1820s turned out to be, creatively, rather a fallow decade, as if, at fifty, he was beginning to be deserted by his muse.

But in every other way it was an extremely active decade. After all, famous poets can be quite busy, just being famous, especially ones like Wordsworth, who enjoyed pronouncing on all subjects. With the increased income that his fame was bringing him, by helping to sell the new editions of his work, he was able to travel again and devote more time to his many family and domestic affairs, some of which were beginning to prove rather worrying.

One of the penalties of fame – or perhaps some might call it one of the pleasures – is that people go out of their way just to gape at you. As early as 1816, there were trippers coming to the Lakes, who hoped for a sight of Mr Wordsworth, as part of their itinerary. In that year, 'fourteen Cantabs' were spotted, doing a reading and walking tour of the Lake District. 'Some have been introduced,' said Sarah Hutchinson, 'and I suppose most of them will find means to get a sight of the Poet before the summer is past.' It became a normal feature of Rydal Mount from then on, with little huddles of visitors arriving at the gates during the summer months. Hazlitt, in his lectures in 1818, could mention Rydal Mount in passing, and everyone in the audience would know whose house he was referring to.

Undergraduates in debating clubs argued who was the better poet, Wordsworth or Byron, and after serious consideration of their respective merits, votes would solemnly be taken. Byron usually won in about 1816 or 1817; but after that, it was often a close-run thing. William was particularly liked in Cambridge, and when he went to stay with his brother Christopher, the Master of Trinity, he was always fêted and dined and listened to with great attention. The first recorded letter simply asking for his autograph was sent in 1825 – and William sent it off, with great pleasure. Letters were soon coming in from all over the world, especially from America. Little biographical memoirs of William began to appear in the magazines from 1819, usually with a portrait. A couple of people did approach him with a proposal to write a biography, but he dissuaded them. He wasn't at all keen when a publisher – not his own – first wanted to issue an edition of his poems for school-children. A pirated edition of his collected works appeared in France in 1828, much to his annoyance. This was before the international copyright agreements. The Paris publisher produced his edition at little over a quarter the price of the equivalent English edition, thereby ruining the English sales, though he did send William a special vellum-covered presentation copy. William later went on to fight a long battle to get the British copyright laws changed and extended.

William generally refused to write for the magazines, sticking to his vow to try to live and work only as a poet, even when all the magazine editors wanted was to print his poems. 'I have had applications, I believe from nearly every Editor but complied with none.' However, in 1828 he gave in when a friend who was editing the *Keepsake*, a publication which included excerpts from all the best-known writers of the day, made him an offer he could hardly refuse, especially as he needed the money at the time for family affairs. They offered a hundred guineas for twelve pages of poems. He hadn't written anything for a long time and during the 1820s he often observed in his letters that his poetic days were over. 'My vein I fear is run out. . . . The Muses and I have parted company.' But he managed to produce six sonnets, the only poems he produced to order, though, when the *Keepsake* appeared, he found they'd only used two. 'I am properly served for having had any connection with such things.'

He had his bust sculpted in 1820. Copies were on sale to the general public for £5; for personal friends he could order copies at £3. He arranged for many members of his family to have one of his busts, including his three nephews – sons of his brother Christopher – when they each in turn distinguished themselves with university prizes and fellowships. It was the fashion of the day to have a bust of one's famous friends or relations, or just one's heroes, on the mantelpiece. William himself proudly displayed the busts of two of his poetical friends, Scott and Southey. 'Your bust is nearly twice the size of the Laureate's,' he wrote to Scott in January 1826. 'On Christmas Day my daughter decked the Laureate with the appropriate wreath and stuck a sprig of Holly in your Mantle and there it is, "with its polished leaves and berries" among the other indoor decorations.'

Famous people have of course to put up with nasty gossip in the magazines and newspapers, and tittle-tattle was soon appearing about the Wordsworth household: poking fun at all the ladies attending on him, or at his pride in his friendship with the Lowthers. The piece of gossip which hurt him most was a story written by Hazlitt in a series called 'Table Talk', still a popular name for a gossip column, which appeared in the *London Magazine* in 1821. Though Hazlitt admired

William as a poet, he still kept up his personal attacks on him for praising the common people in his poetry, while 'with one stroke of his prose
pen, he disenfranchises the whole rustic population of Westmorland
and Cumberland from voting at elections'.

The story which Hazlitt passed on had come from Charles Lloyd,
William's old friend and neighbour, who had now recovered from his
bout of mental illness. According to the story, William, when he first
lived in the Lakes, used to snuff out one candle when there were two
on the table. 'It was a shame to indulge in such extravagance,' he was
alleged to have said, 'while many a poor cottager has not even a rush
light to see to their evening's work.' This incident was said to have taken
place in 1802, wrote Hazlitt. 'In 1816 (Oh! fearful lapse of time, pregnant with strange mutability) the same enthusiastic lover of economy
and hater of luxury, asked his thoughtless friend to dine with him in
company with a certain lord and to lend him his man servant to wait
at table; and just before they were sitting down to dinner, he heard
him say to the servant in a sonorous whisper – "and be sure you don't
forget to have six candles on the table!"'

The story highly amused the literary world, as tales had already gone
round about Wordsworth's meanness and about his relationship with
the Lowthers, and here was a tale incorporating both rumours. William
wasn't mean – though he was certainly normally very frugal – but when
he was entertaining 'the quality', the local beaux and belles could sometimes be seen enjoying themselves in his drawing-room, eating venison
and pheasant which was often personally supplied by Lord Lonsdale.

Lloyd appeared unaware of the fury Hazlitt's candle story had
caused in the Wordsworth household and long afterwards sent William
a volume of his poetical essays which had just come out. When he received no acknowledgement, he wrote again, asking if perhaps William
didn't like his little volume. William wrote back in a tone of high moral
disgust, reprimanding Lloyd for his ungentlemanly conduct in passing
on stories, misrepresenting him through knowledge he had acquired
'as a guest invited to my table'. The truth of the story, Mary said in
one of her letters, was that, in the first instance, William had 'walked
to see the reptile [Lloyd] thro' the darkness and the glare hurt his eyes'.
And as for the second anecdote, the servant had been borrowed to re-
strain Lloyd himself because of his insanity, and only two extra candles
had been called for, not six.

William eventually forgave Lloyd, as he did most people who had caused him some offence. He was certainly never vindictive nor harboured grudges. John Wilson, the young admirer who had moved to the Lakes especially to be near him, then wrote some rather unpleasant things in a magazine, asked him for a reference when he was being considered for the post of Professor of Moral Philosophy at Edinburgh. William kindly agreed and Wilson got the job. Wilson later had breakfast with William at Rydal Mount in August 1825, along with Sir Walter Scott and his son-in-law, John Gibson Lockhart. Canning, the Foreign Secretary, was also a visitor at the same time and became very friendly with William.

One of the grandest parties they ever had to entertain at Rydal Mount was when the Wilberforces were their guests in 1818. It was twenty-eight years since Dorothy had first met William Wilberforce – at the house of her clerical uncle in Norfolk – and had been teased by her friend that perhaps Wilberforce might have his eye on her. Wilberforce was now married, with six children, and arrived with a party of nineteen, including servants. They took two houses at the bottom of the hill, beside Rydal Mount, plus five beds in different houses in the village. An advance party arrived first, with the chief servants, to supervise the quarters and inspect the arrangements Dorothy had made for them – which didn't please Dorothy.

First of all I had to receive 7 servants (William and Mary were at Keswick at the time) and on their arrival I was a little out of heart. Add to this the old Cook's observation upon my answering one of her questions 'such and such things must be sent for to Ambleside' 'Our men don't like going errands, they are not used to it' and her exclamation 'what an inconvenient place' when she found they could not get a drop of beer nearer than Ambleside – besides objections of the housemaid and kitchen maid to sleep upon a Matress.

All was satisfactory when the Wilberforce family did arrive, though Dorothy was not completely convinced about Mrs Wilberforce. 'Mrs W. looked very interesting ... when the family came ... for she was full of delight and talked as fast as any of the young ones, but I must say that she has never since appeared to me to such advantage. Yet I like her very well, admire her goodness and patience and meekness – but that slowness and whininess of manner tending to self righteousness, I do not like.'

Many people, taken with Wordsworth and the local scenery, bought themselves homes nearby, just to be near him, such as Dr Arnold, the headmaster of Rugby, who built himself a holiday home, with Words-worth's guidance, at Fox How. Arnold was a great radical, and they disagreed on education, religion and politics, but they became firm friends and both families enjoyed many social occasions together.

Other new friends of the Wordsworths were Edward Quillinan and his family, who arrived at a cottage near Rydal in 1821. Quillinan was an Irish cavalry officer, who'd met the Wordsworths in 1820–21, when he was quartered with his regiment in Penrith, and had subsequently left the army on half-pay, to settle in the Vale of Rydal. He and his wife named their second daughter Rotha, after the river near their cot-tage. Quillinan had published some verses, and his wife was the daughter of Sir Egerton Brydges, a noted literary figure of the day. Quillinan had an introduction to Wordsworth, but their first meeting wasn't very successful. He'd several times been to the gate, once observ-ing 'Mr Wordsworth come out of his Cottage with a party of visitors among whom were some lovely young ladies', but had lost heart and turned away. He eventually introduced himself and was shown in to the library at Rydal.

He received me very stiffly, but asked me for the letter. I told him that I had not brought it with me but that it was an open letter of introduction, but that it spoke of me in a manner so extravagantly laudatory that I had not the face to present it. He seemed quite angry; whirled a chair about and made short and stiff remarks. I was getting indignant and thought him most disagreeable. Suddenly the door opened and a young lady, rather tall of good features perhaps, not handsome, but of most engaging innocence and in-genuousness of aspect, stood at the door. Then it was that I saw the Poet's countenance to advantage. All the father's heart was thrown into his eyes and voice as he encouraged her to come in.

After that, thanks to the influence of Dora, William softened in his approach to Quillinan – and they all became firm friends, visiting each other's houses. Dorothy, particularly, found Quillinan most engaging, a lively conversationalist and a trusted friend, and when Mrs Quillinan fell ill, Dorothy moved in with the family to nurse her. It turned out to be a fatal illness. She had had a mental breakdown and, while still recovering, accidentally burned herself and subsequently died. Dorothy was with her at the end, Quillinan being away in London at the time. Not long afterwards, Quillinan moved to London with his two young daughters, but the letters between the families were regular and very friendly, with love and kisses flowing from both sides. The Wordsworths usually stayed with him when in London.

It often surprises people to learn how sociable William was, with their London friends flowing through their drawing-room from May till September – the 'Season', as the Wordsworth ladies called it, rather wearily – and they in turn made constant visits to other friends, new and old. New friends discovered he wasn't the recluse some still believed him to be, retired to the wilds to escape the world. The world came to him.

His brother Christopher, Master of Trinity, a position which, in theory, put him at the centre of the academic and theological world, was much more of a recluse. William's personality was outgoing: he loved travel and tours and meeting people, and was a success at most social engagements, charming people by his rustic manners and dress – he looked more like a shepherd than a poet – and by his lack of affectation. On his home ground, he was often less interesting, going in too much for monologues. Away from home, he could be the life and soul of the party.

Wordsworth in town was very different from Wordsworth in the country [wrote William Jerdan, an editor who tried to get him to contribute to his journal]. In the former case he was often very lively and entertaining. I recollected meeting him at breakfast after his being at the Italian Opera the preceding night and his remarks on the singing and his limning of the limbs of the dancers were as replete with shrewdness and pleasantry as anything I ever heard from the most witty and graphic lips. I was so charmed both with the matter and manner, that I wrote immediately to offer carte blanche for his correspondence from the Continent.... Had he complied with my wish, and written letters in the tone and spirit of the criticisms of the opera, I am sure the public would have had a variation in the style of Wordsworth which would have surprised it.

During the 1820s, William made regular trips to London and the Continent. Almost every second year, he was off on one long journey of some sort, and so it is no wonder that his output of poetry suffered. He was often away from home for up to six months at a time.

The 1820 foreign tour – the one that ended in Paris, with the visit to Annette – started off in June in London, and the Wordsworths didn't finally get back to Rydal until just before Christmas, having been through Belgium and up the Rhine by boat to Switzerland, then into Italy, retracing much of William's old pedestrian route, that he took with his friend Jones almost thirty years previously. This time, they took carriages, having more money, though this didn't stop William fretting endlessly when he felt he was being overcharged. 'William at the inn door looked as fierce as Bonaparte,' wrote Dorothy. 'When he came bustling up to us after his conflict, M. and I said to each other "they will think that B. himself is come back again to threaten this poor town."' On another occasion, William refused to take rooms at an inn because of the prices, and the whole party spent the night sitting in their coach. A thunderstorm roared and fleas crawled, and they had the most dreadfully uncomfortable night.

While they were in Switzerland, an English traveller came across them in a hotel in Lausanne, and has left a description of their little encounter which shows William at his most typically North-country-mannish:

The husband of one of them soon followed. I saw by their utilitarian garb, as well as by the blisters and blotches on their cheeks, lips and noses, that they were pedestrian tourists. The man was evidently a denizen of the North, his accent harsh, skin white, of an angular and bony build, self confident and dogmatic in his opinions. The precision and quaintness of his language as well as his eccentric remarks on common things, stimulated my mind....

On their leaving the room to get ready for their journey, my friend told me the strangers were the poet Wordsworth, his wife and sister. Who could have divined this? I could see no trace in the hard features and weather-stained brow of the outer man, of the divinity within him. In a few minutes, the travellers reappeared. Now that I knew that I was talking to one of the veterans of the gentle craft, as there was no time to waste, I asked him abruptly what he thought of Shelley as a poet. 'Nothing,' he replied as abruptly.

In 1823, William was off again, this time just with Mary, on a much more modest Continental tour, visiting only Belgium and Holland. It lasted a month and was slightly marred by problems with William's eyes. As usual, though, having left Rydal, he saw several other places and friends *en route*, and was away for five months in all. The next year, 1824, William didn't go abroad, but he visited London, with Mary and Dora, and made a long tour of Wales, revisiting yet more old haunts. They watched the Menai Bridge being erected and visited Robert Jones. William composed several poems, trying them out aloud, while Dora sat beside him, sketching.

In 1828, William spent several weeks in London with Mary and Dora, staying at the Quillinans'. Sir Walter Scott was also in town, and the two parties jointly went round Hampton Court, along with several other literary people of the day, though, according to the poet Thomas Moore, who was in the party, the public had eyes for only one famous face: 'Walked about in the gay walk where the band plays, to the infinite delight of the Hampton blues who were all *eyes* after Scott, the other scribblers not coming in for a glance.' Well, when it came to best-sellers, not many people could compete with Sir Walter.

During this London trip, William established cordial relations with Coleridge, now settled and leading a much healthier life since he'd been taken in by Dr Gillman, a Highgate doctor. On what seems to have been a spur-of-the-moment decision, William, Coleridge and Dora decided to leave London for a quick tour of Belgium and the Rhineland, without even telling Mary they were going. William left in such a hurry that he only took a carpet-bag, borrowed from Crabb Robinson.

'They get on famously,' wrote Dora in her journal, following the family tradition for Wordsworth females to record all journeys. 'But Mr C sometimes detains us with his fiddle faddling and he likes prosing to the folks better than exerting himself to see the face of the country. Father with his few half dozen words of German makes himself much better understood than Mr C with all his weight of German literature.'

In Brussels, they met another writer, the Irishman Thomas Grattan, who accompanied them on part of their journey. Grattan recorded:

Wordsworth was, if possible, more unlike what he must appear in the fancy of those who have read his poetry and have never seen the author. He was a perfect antithesis to Coleridge – tall, wiry, harsh in features, coarse in figure, inelegant in looks. He was roughly dressed in a long brown *surtout*, striped duck trousers, fustian gaiters and thick shoes. He more resembled a mountain farmer than a 'lake poet'. His whole air was unrefined and unprepossessing. ... But, on observation and a little reflection, I could not help considering that much that seemed unfavourable in Wordsworth might be really placed to his advantage. There was a total absence of affectation or egotism; not the least effort at display or assumption of superiority over any of those who were quite prepared to concede it to him. ... I remarked Wordsworth's very imperfect knowledge of French and it was then that he accounted for it by telling me that five and twenty years previously he understood and spoke it well but that his abhorrence of the Revolutionary excesses made him resolve if possible to forget the language altogether and that for a long time he had not read or spoken a word of it.

As William grew older and better known to the general public, the number of such first-hand descriptions of him, by people who met him on his travels or at London social engagements, or visited him at home in the Lakes, steadily increased. Almost everyone was struck by his lack of poetic manners and looks – which presumably means they expected a long-haired aesthete, a fragile and delicate flower like the young Keats, or someone who struck mannered poses like Byron. In the Lakes, William was often taken for a rather hard-up curate, in his unfashionable, worn-out clothes. Away from home, he appeared more the shepherd figure.

As he got older, he grew into his face. He'd never been handsome, with his knobbly features, prominent nose and receding hair, and his was a face that aged quickly. Not that he minded. He once reported a conversation he had on a coach, going back to Rydal, when his fellow-travellers tried to guess his age – one of them putting him at sixty. He was only thirty-six at the time.

'Wordsworth's was a face which did not assign itself to any class,' wrote a friend, Henry Taylor. 'It was a hardy weather-beaten face which might have belonged to a nobleman, a yeoman, a mariner, or a philosopher. For my own part, I should not, judging by his face, have guessed him to be a poet. Perhaps what was wanting was only *physical* refinement. It was a rough grey face, full of rifts and clefts and fissures, out of which ... you might expect lichens to grow.'

There are fewer references, with his advancing years, to his alleged egotism, the trait which had once upset several people on first meeting him, such as Keats. Wordsworth had always denied that he was egotistical as a person. It was in his poetry that he was an egotist, as he was proud to admit. Perhaps, as time went on and he became better known, people encouraged his monologues, wanting to hear his wisdom, and never for one moment considered them a sign of egotism. He appears to have grown into his personality as well as into his physical appearance. Dogmatism does better suit the older man, especially one with so much hard-won experience of life and travel.

He went for five weeks to Ireland in 1829, his first visit, but moved round at such a rate – rising at five in the morning, in order to gallop to the next place or engagement – that he had hardly time to pause to think or even give his muse a chance. Almost every journey throughout his life spawned verses – even if they were written long afterwards – including all his Continental tours, and his journeys in Wales and, especially, in Scotland; but nothing at all came out of his Irish visit. He didn't have any members of his family with him this time –

just some friends. Dora might have slowed him down, if she'd been there.

But he was well observed on his whirlwind Irish tour, with people remarking, as usual, on his rustic appearance and naturalness.

Everything he said and did had an unaffected simplicity and dignity and peacefulness of thought that were very striking [wrote one lady]. There was such an indescribable superiority, both intellectual and moral, stamped upon him in his very silence, that everything of his I had thought silly took the beautiful colouring of a wondrous benevolence, that could descend through love to the least and most insignificant things. . . . I think it would be quite impossible for anyone who had once been in Wordsworth's company ever again to think anything he has written silly.

In the autumn of 1831, he made a long Scottish tour with Dora (now his favourite travelling companion), starting at Abbotsford, where they visited Sir Walter, then going to Edinburgh, the Trossachs and the Highlands, once again going over old haunts, the ones he had originally seen with Dorothy and Coleridge. He was now over sixty, but usually managed to walk twenty miles a day, often walking behind the carriage. His eyes were once again bothering him and he set off wearing a special shade which intrigued the children in Carlisle as they drove through. 'There's a man wi' a veil and lass drivin'.'

They managed to reach Mull in the Western Isles, taking the new steamboat from Glasgow. 'Father is hammering at a horrid sonnet and he cannot give me his ear for the moment,' wrote Dora to her mother. 'His eyes are wonderfully well considering he will work.' There's a nice parenthesis in this letter, giving an insight into their domestic relationships. 'Mother you did not name his eyes in your last letter which he did not like!'

Wordsworth published no prose about his foreign tours, but a travel book he wrote about the Lakes, which originated very much by chance, sold better than any of his poems and made him famous amongst those who had never heard of his poetry.

Wordsworth's *Guide to the Lakes*, as it eventually became known, first appeared under his own name as a separate volume in 1822, but it began life in 1810, when William was asked to contribute, anonymously, some descriptions of Lakeland scenery to a collection of drawings made by a Norfolk vicar, the Rev. Joseph Wilkinson. He wasn't particularly proud of the book and criticized Wilkinson's etchings in a letter to Lady Beaumont, saying that Sir George would no doubt view them with disgust. One can only presume that in 1810 he had needed the money, though no record of the payment exists. He was always genuinely interested in guiding people to the Lakes and many of his letters give detailed descriptions of the best approaches and best routes.

As far back as 1807, after they'd been touring west Cumberland, Mary had suggested that he should write some sort of guide-book, and Dorothy was always well aware of the possibilities of a proper book, if he could expand his introduction to the vicar's sketch-book. 'It would sell better and bring him more money than any of his higher labours.'

It is surprising, in a way, that William took so long to write his own guide-book, considering that works of this kind were amongst his favourite reading. The book he eventually produced is a little didactic for modern tastes, though writers of contemporary guide-books were obsessed by the picturesque and by the desire to lay down the law on what was or was not a beautiful view; but the book is of great interest to anyone interested in the Lakes, or in Wordsworth. It finally sealed them together in the public's mind. Indeed, it will be a central theme in the new Wordsworth Museum now being built at Grasmere.

As in his poetry, the moral teachings were not far away. In fact, only the first twenty pages are devoted to straightforward tourist information, after which he moves on to discussing such topics as 'Causes of False Taste in Grounds and Buildings' and 'Effects of Light and Shadow upon the Vales'. He used the book as a vehicle for his personal hates, such as the current fashion for larch plantations or for whitewashing cottages. He said both ruined the natural beauty of the scenery. He considered himself an expert on such things and maintained that he had a calling for three professions: poet, art critic and landscape gardener. A lot of the new settlers did come to him for advice, on everything from their gardens to their chimneys, and he did much to create an awareness of the natural landscape. His great love for the Lakes shines through the book and he was amongst the earliest of the preservationists, forming guide-lines which were later followed by the National Trust, National Park and other bodies.

The book was in constant demand after it first appeared in 1822 and William regularly revised and expanded it. The fifth edition, which appeared in 1835, is looked upon as the definitive one, and a facsimile of it still sells well today.

It was Matthew Arnold who first told the story of the clergyman who asked Wordsworth if he'd written anything else – apart from his guide to the Lakes. . . .

During the 1820s, family affairs also took up a great deal of William's time and thoughts. He would probably have gone on further Continental tours, if he hadn't been worried so much about the education of his three children. He needed money for their schooling and he needed to be there in person to push them along. His two sons, particularly, needed all the help they could get. William, in his own teenage years, had been offered endless help and advice and contacts, as friends and relations rallied round to launch him into life, but he had spurned them all. Now he was the heavy father, refusing to even consider John's wish, for example, to go into the army, an ambition William once had. He said the cost of a commission was impossible. 'The Army is out of the question,' wrote his mother. 'He knows that; and strong as his bias towards the profession seems to be, at his age and in times of peace he would not give way to it.'

John was accepted at St John's College, Cambridge, William's old college, but his mathematics had been so bad at Sedbergh that he talked his father into letting him try to get into Oxford instead. So William then wrote to one of his influential Oxford contacts, John Keble, the great Oxford theologian, later Professor of Poetry.

'I shall be greatly disappointed if we cannot get your son into Oxford,' Keble replied. 'It will be a real kindness to point out any little service that I can render to him, or anyone connected with you, there or anywhere else. For I feel deeply your debtor for the real advantage as well as for the great pleasure which I find in reading your publications.'

In 1823, John went up to New College, Oxford, aged twenty, where his tutor was another devoted admirer of Wordsworth's works. John studied away quietly at Oxford, but without any distinction, failing to get an honours degree; William said it was because of ill health at the time of the examinations.

'It would be most satisfactory to us if John's thoughts should rest upon the Church,' wrote Mary, 'but this is a delicate subject, and unless his own mind – in conjunction with our own wishes, which are not unknown to him – led him thither, we should think it wrong to press him into the sacred profession merely to gain a worldly maintenance.' It was history repeating itself; but this time, unlike William, John acted the dutiful son and agreed. The next stage, which was what his uncles had hoped for, for William, was to get John a fellowship somewhere, till it was time to take holy orders.

One has to admit William's pushing was masterly. He left no contact untapped. Not only did he write off about an imminent fellowship to his well-connected friends, such as Lord Lonsdale and Canning; he sent off duplicated lists of the Electors – 'to spare you the trouble of consulting the Oxford Callendar' – so that his powerful friends could cast their eyes at once over the list of people who would choose the Merton College fellows, and identify any they could influence. Lord Lonsdale turned up trumps, and named one such person. 'I see two names on the list of voters which you have enclosed,' replied Canning, 'with whom it is possible that, if not pre-engaged, the expression of my wishes on your Son's behalf may have some weight.'

Alas, after all that valiant string-pulling, John was disqualified for the Merton Fellowship on a technicality. It turned out that his birth-place in the Lakes put him in the diocese of Chester (today, it's the see of Carlisle), and they already had a fellow. Poor William had to write and apologize to Lord Lonsdale, and his other friends, for all their work. He now had to support John himself till it was time for him to take orders, which John did in 1828, when he took up a curacy in Leicestershire, in an area full of impoverished stocking-weavers, which wasn't quite the sort of clerical position William had in mind for his elder son. However, it was near Coleorton, the Beaumonts' family home, and the vicar in charge was, again, a personal friend of William's.

Dorothy, who was now established as the family's travelling housekeeper and nurse, when she wasn't looking after the home while they were all away, went down to Leicestershire for the winter of 1828, to join John in his lonely and draughty parsonage and help him set up a home, though William, having done so much for him, realized that he was now on his own. 'He will be thrown for advancement and maintenance upon his own exertions.'

Dora, as we have seen, had by now become William's regular travelling friend and companion, another lady in his household. In a way, she took over from Dorothy: a fresh source of female comfort and pleasure at William's side, an eager sightseer, a keen observer of the world and an excellent letter-writer, though slightly sharper than Dorothy in her gentle teasing of her father. 'This letter with the usual Wordsworthian coolness is to give note that the two Poets and their amiable Daughter hope to steam it from Ostend Tuesday,' she wrote to Quillinan from her Low Countries tour with William and Coleridge. 'Yesterday a pouring rain at Rotterdam gave Father time to half persuade himself into an Ague – but the symptoms have disappeared – I am a saucy Child as you know full well. He had a little cold from damp feet, was a little doleful and I was wicked enough to say it was ague.'

In one of her Rydal letters, to a girl friend, she passed on a tit-bit of local conversation, having overheard what a neighbour had said about her father's impending return from a long absence: 'Why then we shal hae 'im booing again in that wood; he boos like a bull enough to freighten a body.'

Dora's health was a constant worry for her father and mother. 'She is a complete air gage,' wrote her mother in August 1827, 'As soon as damp is felt the trouble in her throat returns – something connected with the trachea, that causes a cough and other inconveniences.' To protect her from the Lakeland winter, they sent her south, from September to May, to stay with a friend, with William soon joining her, and she was away for a year in all. It seemed to help her quite considerably.

She was devoted to her father, and he to her, though some family friends thought that it was a little unhealthy for such a lively girl, now approaching her late twenties, to be devoting her life to her father. 'I have my suspicions,' wrote Hartley Coleridge in 1830, 'that she would be a healthier matron than a virgin, but strong indeed must be the love that could induce her to leave her father, whom she almost adores, and who quite doats upon her.'

Willy turned out to be the biggest problem of all. After leaving Charterhouse in 1822 when he was twelve, he spent the next six years at home, supposedly being educated locally at Ambleside, but, in practice, doing and learning very little. William tried to put a brave face on it, telling Walter Scott in a letter in 1825 that Willy had left Charterhouse as his health had failed, 'and is now with me preparing for Oxford'. In the winter of 1827, when his parents were in the south with Dora, hoping for an improvement in her health, Willy began thinking of the army. Dorothy, who was left at home looking after him, wrote to Quillinan, hoping he might put Willy off, having been in the army himself. 'His thoughts turn (I fear constantly) on the Army. What have you to say for and against the profession? Not I expect much for it. And he seems little inclined to listen to the contra-side.' Without telling his parents, Willy did apply for a commission – but was turned down.

William tried to get him a position in business, looking for openings in a counting house when he was in London, contacting manufacturing concerns and, as always, applying to Lord Lonsdale for help, hoping he might procure some minor government position. Lonsdale replied that he'd been trying for two years to get a similar position for another friend's son, and offered little hope. 'He must go somewhere,' moaned William, yet knowing he was so slow at learning of any sort, with a mind not disposed to the notion of books, that there were few openings. Willy had grown out of his early years of ill health, when the whole family had fussed over him, so that was one blessing. 'He is in excellent health,' wrote William, 'nearly six feet high and for the exercise of walking equal perhaps to any man in Westmorland. Notwithstanding, I am afraid, that severe confinement, with hard *head*-labour, would revive his old complaint.'

Even with his outdoor activities, which he appeared to love best of all, Willy wasn't all that successful. 'We are yet in a painful sort of uncertainty what is best to be done for Willy,' wrote his mother to Quillinan in November 1828. 'You shall hear when a decision is made, which ought to be shortly. Meanwhile, he does not make much havoc among the Snipes and Woodcocks – but he has caught a bad cold in search after them, wading up to the knees does not suit him.'

William, in the same letter – it was often their custom to share letters to family friends – regretted the fact that Canning had recently died (in 1827). 'Had Mr Canning now been living, I would have stated his situation, and given briefly Wm's history to him, and I am simple enough to believe, for Canning had a respect for literature, and was a good natured man, that such a step would not have been without effect. As things are, his Mother and I are very anxious about him.'

William wrote round to several places about possible tutors or crammers, at home and in Europe, where Willy might be sent to learn a language, or learn something. At length, in 1829, they packed him off to Bremen, hoping a knowledge of German might help him find some sort of an occupation.

Domestically, life was very settled at Rydal, though there was one slight shock in 1826 when Lady Fleming, their landlady, said she wanted the house for her heir and the Wordsworths would have to leave. William bought the field adjoining the garden for £300 and threatened to build his own house in it, getting plans and designs ready, but Lady Fleming and the heir eventually let them remain. William later gave the field to Dora, and it's still known as Dora's field, a mass of daffodils every spring and much admired by visitors to Rydal.

Sarah Hutchinson, Mary's sister, was still part of the family, living most of the time with them, and a very jolly household it was. Dorothy often talked in her letters about Sarah and William having jokes together, on one occasion making up a skit on a well-known poem. 'The first stanza of Ben Jonson's poem slipped from W's lips in a parody – and together they finished it with much loving fun. Oh! they laughed. I heard them in my room upstairs and wondered what they were about.'

Mary had blossomed as the years went on, judging by her increasing part in the Rydal Mount correspondence. As she accompanied William on most of his travels, she wrote many of the letters afterwards, keeping up with their new friends. 'From Idle Mount, which just now well supports that title,' she wrote in 1827, 'I have nothing but good to communicate. . . .' That Idle Mount joke appears to have been hers, and she repeats it in other letters. The joke was true, as well, when one considers the Southey industry at Greta Hall. Old William had produced no new volumes for years and young Willy was still hanging around the house.

Dorothy and William were still a devoted sister and brother, despite Dorothy's now secondary role. She continued to go off on her lone little travels, most of them mercy visits, though she did have one good holiday in 1822, when she went to Scotland with Joanna Hutchinson, Mary's sister. They did a lot of walking, proving she was still as strong as ever, but, like William, she was visually ageing quickly. As early as 1819, when just forty-eight, she was telling her old girlhood friend Catherine Clarkson that the years had caught up with her. 'You will be surprised when you see me, in face a perfect old woman. I have only eight teeth remaining – two in the upper jaw, the rest below and those two or three are on the point of coming out. William preserves his teeth and does not look older for his years than formerly.'

Just a few months later – in 1820, when she was in London with William and Mary – Dorothy realized her teeth had had their day. William wrote round to the leading dentists, comparing prices and references, as if he was dealing with innkeepers, and was somewhat alarmed that the best dentist was going to charge fifty guineas to make Dorothy some dentures. However, it was decided that she had to have them made, regardless of expense. She was delighted to get rid of her old teeth, and felt much more comfortable, but knew it didn't improve her looks: 'For now my mouth is drawn up to nothing and my chin projects as far as my nose; but I look healthy enough, though I have lost 8 lbs since I was last weighed, being now only 6 stones 12 lbs.'

Nonetheless, she was always ready and willing to go off on any long walk with William when required, and in 1828, aged fifty-six, she was boasting in a letter that she could still walk fifteen miles as briskly as ever.

William's own health was remarkable. In 1830, when sixty, Dorothy, with sisterly pride, wrote that he was still the crack skater on Rydal Water. 'And as to climbing of mountains, the hardiest and the youngest are yet hardly a match for him.' There's no record of him ever having a day in bed because of any illness, even having colds and coughs, though he did have one nasty accident when he fell off his horse. It bolted as he was trying to mount it, and he was thrown against a stone wall and badly cut his head. He was never much of a rider, and usually preferred to walk, though he did one marathon ride, on his own, from Lancaster to Cambridge on Dora's pony, encountering tremendous thunderstorms and other adventures. He contented himself, and forgot his discomfort, by composing verses for Sir George Beaumont as he sat in the saddle, soaked to the skin.

His eyes were his only physical problem, and even his temperate habits, to which his family ascribed his normally perfect health, did nothing to alleviate them. He often found that he was unable to read for more than fifteen minutes without a hot and prickling sensation at the back of his eyes. In a letter to Charles Lamb in 1830, he told him he had the books he'd sent but was waiting for better light – he was writing in January – as he could no longer read at all in candlelight. 'But alas, when the days lengthened my eyesight departed, and for many months, I could not read three minutes at a time.' He did have good spells and he was always surrounded by enough helping eyes and hands, who could read to him and write his letters for him.

Although he was still very careful with his money, he was in a much better financial state by the 1820s than he'd ever been, despite the cost of his children's education. The new editions of his poems sold well and he expanded his stamp duties to embrace further areas. In 1821, he reported to Lord Lowther that he was collecting £18,000 a year in stamp revenues – you can see why the ladies were so worried when he was absent – but that only £200 in cash ended up in his pocket. In the same letter he bemoaned the fact that he was unable to take much advantage of a perquisite which usually came the way of a Distributor: 'I might gain something by leaving it in my Banker's hands till the end of the quarter were it not that the Currency in my district consists mainly of provincial notes, principally Scotch, on which the Bankers allow no interest till they have had them six weeks.'

In 1825, he decided he wasn't making enough money from the sale of his books and told Longmans, his publishers, that he was going to look elsewhere. William had been particularly upset when he'd discovered that so much of his profits were taken up by paying for *their* advertising costs, which appears to have been a custom of the time. He was also worried that some of his books were out of print. In reply, Longmans said they were sorry, but Wordsworth was a slow seller and they couldn't improve their terms.

Wordsworth got his friends to do the pushing for him, as he so often did, asking Samuel Rogers to contact the eminent publisher John Murray. William had decided in his head that he wanted a new edition of all his works, in some six volumes, for which he wouldn't take less than £300, and without any advertising expenses being charged.

Murray appeared very keen, so Rogers reported, but nothing happened. Rogers then went to see Murray in person several times, and Murray said how much he admired Wordsworth and his poems, but still no contract was forthcoming, nor even a letter. Finally, after many months of silence, William, greatly upset, told Rogers not to bother with Murray any more. 'I am persuaded that he is too great a Personage for anyone but a Court, an Aristocratic or most fashionable Author to deal with.'

Negotiations then began with another publisher, but they fell through – the publisher turned out to be going bankrupt – and William was forced in the end to go back to Longmans, where he lowered his terms, though he got a slightly better deal than he'd had in the past. In 1827, a new edition of his poems at last appeared on the book-stalls.

William was always careful in all his financial affairs, writing endless letters to ask for advice when he had money to invest – and he often had quite a lot. In 1820, he was thinking of investing £2,000 in French stocks. In 1825, he had £500 available for railway shares. He was as temperate and sensible, careful and calculating with his money as he was with most things in his life. It was typical of his luck and prudence to escape from joining the publisher who was going bankrupt, just before the catastrophe happened, when he might well have suffered with him.

They were all terribly upset at Rydal when the news of Sir Walter Scott's financial disaster came through in 1826. His complicated publishing investments had collapsed and Scott became responsible for huge debts – and was himself declared bankrupt.

Poor Sir Walter Scott! [wrote Dorothy]. I was indeed sorry to hear of his name in the *Gazette* – I did not see it myself and was in hopes there might be a mistake on the part of my informer. But the Sale of furniture, Books etc etc too clearly confirms the truth. How *could* it happen that he should so enter into trade as to be involved in this way. He a Baronet! A literary man! A lawyer. I wish very much for particulars. How does he bear the Change? I hope well, but am fearful that Lady Scott may not be fortified to the needful point having heard that she was a person fond of distinction and expense.

They were very fond of William's own distinction at Rydal Mount, now that he was famous, and were proud of his poems and his newly acquired favour with the critics; but they, like William, didn't go in for any expensive show. They were all too sensible.

DUDDON

The last of his Duddon sonnets, which were based on his memories of journeys down the Duddon valley in the Lake District, especially with his wife Mary. They were published in 1820 to general acclaim.

I THOUGHT of Thee, my partner and my guide,
As being past away. – Vain sympathies!
For, backward, Duddon! as I cast my eyes,
I see what was, and is, and will abide;
Still glides the Stream, and shall for ever glide;
The Form remains, the Function never dies;
While we, the brave, the mighty, and the wise,
We Men, who in our morn of youth defied
The elements, must vanish; – be it so!
Enough, if something from our hands have power
To live, and act, and serve the future hour;
And if, as toward the silent tomb we go,
Through love, through hope, and faith's transcendent dower,
We feel that we are greater than we know.

19

Troubles and Triumphs
1830-1843

AS we have seen, Dorothy left Rydal in the autumn of 1828 to spend the winter with John, acting as his housekeeper and helping him out generally in his first position as curate at Whitwick Church in Leicester-shire. It appeared to be just a routine trip. Dorothy had been a universal aunt for several years now. She'd just finished almost a year in charge of Rydal Mount, while William, Mary and Dora had been away. She saw it as a pleasure, comforting her nephew in a strange new area, but there was something a bit plaintive in her letters written on arrival, describing John in his loneliness, suffering the dullness of long, empty evenings, stuck in a strange village, full of 'poverty and all the bad habits attendant upon petty manufactures in a crowded village ... barren of society'. She planned to stay six months. After all, what else had she to do. 'I am more useful than I could be anywhere else.'

She faithfully reported John's progress and how he was drawing larger congregations than the church had had before: 'I cannot say that he yet *preaches* with boldness and full effect, but really he reads the prayers, to my ear, very pleasingly, having a fine voice and a serious manner of delivery.'

She didn't complain that she herself was lonely, though she was rather wistful in a letter to Crabb Robinson, who had mentioned a trip to Rome. William had already seen every sight and city in Europe which he'd wanted to see, except for Rome. It had been a topic in family letters for years.

'Alas for Rome. I never expect to set foot upon that sacred ground,' wrote Dorothy. 'Nor do I ever visit it even in a day dream. Indeed, when my Brother talks of Rome it always rather damps my hopes of even crossing the Channel again. So many circumstances must occur to make so large a scheme practical, and years slip away. On Xmas Day, I, the youngest of the three elders of the house, shall have completed my 56th year....'

In April 1829, by which time John had heard that a living of his own had been secured for him in Cumberland by Lord Lonsdale, Dorothy suffered a serious illness. For forty hours, it looked as though she would die. She'd apparently been for a long walk on a cold day and had been struck down by 'internal inflammation', suffered 'excruciating torture' and, even when the pain began to abate, was unable to speak for some time. It is now thought the illness was an attack of cholicystitis, with gall-stones. Willy happened to be there at the time, staying with his brother on the way to Bremen in Germany, and both nephews devotedly nursed her, till their mother came rushing down from Rydal.

'What a shock that was to our poor hearts,' wrote William, after Dorothy at last began to regain her strength. 'Were she to depart, the Phases of my Moon would be robbed of light to a degree that I have not the courage to think of.' Back at Rydal, she recovered enough to walk round the house, but over the next four years came a series of relapses, confining her to bed, though her mind was still active and her thoughts were harmonious. She was fit enough in the autumn of 1834 to start her *Journals* again, and on 4 October there's an interesting insertion, showing she'd never forgotten what happened between William and Mary, on that day thirty-two years ago: 'The wedding day, and if Dora recollected it she did not tell me and we let it pass unnoticed. I have again had the resolution not to go out, beautiful as the weather was, yet so beautiful at home I could not but be pleased with walking from room to room and feeling and seeing the lovely sunshine.'

In the spring of 1835, William and Mary felt sufficiently confident of Dorothy's condition to go to London. One of their main objects was to try to secure some sort of government job for Willy. Since he had come back from Germany, the only employment they had been able to find for him was as his father's sub-distributor of stamps in Carlisle. William, through Lord Lowther, sought the help of Sir Robert Peel, the Prime Minister, who was an admirer of Wordsworth's poetry; but this came to nothing, as Peel's government was about to fall.

When William returned to Rydal, full of gloom at the Whigs coming to power, he found the house almost like a hospital. Everyone was struck down, or about to be struck down, with influenza. Dora, Dorothy and Sarah Hutchinson were all seriously ill, and so was the cook. Naturally, they feared most for Dorothy, who had been an invalid for the last five years, and were convinced that she was about to die, a release at last from her physical misery. But it was Sarah who died. Quickly, quietly and unexpectedly, just as they were sure she was recovering, Sarah passed away on 23 June 1835. 'She had no acute suffering whatever,' William wrote to Southey, 'and within a very short time of her departure ... she opened her eyes in strength and with a strong and sweet voice, said "I am quite, I am perfectly comfortable."'

Sarah Hutchinson was sixty years old and had made her home with the Wordsworths for thirty years, sharing their pleasures and their pains. She'd been a vital part of those exciting early years in Grasmere. Her name was in all their hearts, carved in their memories and carved in stone on that rock where they'd all placed their names, a rock which William still stopped and stared at when he passed, often taking a knife with him to keep the letters fresh. She'd shared the excitement of Coleridge, helping him in his creative urges, perhaps even sharing his romantic urges. Was she ever in love with him, as he was with her? We will never know.

But she had also loved John, the brother who died at sea, and, according to Coleridge, it was he who had been expected to marry her. She was equally loved by Southey and his whole household; she was a friend in time of need, called in to nurse the sick, transcribe for the literary, or just cheer up the family. Perhaps they missed her laughter as much as anything. She was the one who enjoyed best the fun of the country sales, or could jest William out of his mental gloom or pain in his side. Coleridge perhaps left the best one-word description of her. She had a quality, he once said, which he called 'entertainingness'.

Dorothy recovered from her bout of 'flu, but that was about all. As her physical strength returned, so her mental power went. The family put it down to the shock of Sarah's death, allied with the amounts of opium which had been prescribed to relieve her pain, and hoped that, with careful nursing, her mind would return, but it never did.

Dorothy had always been a highly emotional lady, and it would seem from many of her early letters and journal entries that at times she had not been completely stable. De Quincey, and others, always commented on her wild, staring eyes. Her struggles to control her emotions, alternately subduing them or letting them burn with fire, made strangers become distressed, even frightened. 'At times,' said De Quincey, 'the self counteraction and self baffling of her feelings caused her even to stammer.'

From now until the end of her life, she lived in her own twilight world, eventually confined to a wheel-chair, taken out round the garden on days of sunshine, though she often protested, determined to sit roasting by the fire, even on the hottest days. William and Mary proved absolutely devoted nurses, despite Dorothy's frequent outbursts of anger, shouts and screams. They did it with no sense of embarrassment, still looking on her as a normal member of the household, never for a moment considering hiding her away from public or private gaze, far less putting her in a home. Strangely enough, her few lucid spells were usually poetical. Whenever a line of poetry was quoted, she could carry on the passage, reciting whole sections by William and by other poets. She had given William ears and eyes as a boy. Now, he gave her love.

Sarah's was the first death to occur in the family household since the two children had died all those years previously, but William's own contemporaries, both personal friends and poets, had already begun to fall. The first old friend to go was Sir George Beaumont in 1827, aged seventy-four. 'Nearly twenty five years have I known him intimately,' wrote William, 'and neither myself nor my family ever received a cold or unkind look from him.' He had been comfortably, rather than enormously, wealthy, and his presents to William had been truly generous, such as the little estate near Skiddaw, which was meant to provide a home for William near Coleridge. He had done several paintings of William's poems, such as 'The Thorn', which is still in the Wordsworth family today. The foundation of the National Gallery in 1823, for which he worked, is perhaps his best-known single achievement. He left sixteen of the best paintings from his collection to the nation, including works by Rembrandt, Rubens, Poussin, Canaletto, Reynolds and Claude. In his will, he left Wordsworth a legacy of £100 a year for life.

William's last meeting with Sir Walter Scott was in 1831, when he and Dora visited him at Abbotsford. Scott was then about to make his final trip abroad, to Italy, in the hope of improving his health, but he was already in a frail state, hardly able to write in Dora's album. Dora took this album on most journeys with her father, collecting something from almost all his famous friends. Scott managed a few stanzas, though in signing the verses he omitted the S from his own name. 'I should not have done anything of this kind, but for your father's sake,' he told Dora. 'They are probably the last verses I shall ever write.'

William was terribly upset by Scott's appearance. 'How sadly changed did I find the man I had seen so healthy, gay and hopeful a few years before when he said at the inn in Patterdale, in my presence, his daughter Anne also being there, with my own wife and daughter and Mr Quillinan, "I mean to live till I am eighty, and shall write as long as I live."'

It had been a typical Walter Scott statement, full of cheerfulness and gaiety, but one that William knew he himself could never make. Even at the time, it struck him as tempting fate. 'I was startled, and almost shocked at that bold saying which could scarcely be uttered by such a man, sanguine as he was, without a momentary forgetfulness of the instability of life.' Scott died the next year, 1832, aged sixty-one, worn out by his herculean literary labours to clear his debts.

Coleridge died in 1834. Although they had taken that surprise foreign tour, with Dora, in 1828, they had not become real friends again and William never saw him during the last four years of his life. After all his wanderings and drug addiction, he'd remained for the last eighteen years of his life in reasonable stability and happiness with James Gillman, his physician, in Highgate. He'd even managed to get his play put on in the West End, and it ran for twenty nights.

Charles Lamb, another life-long literary friend, died a few months later. The next year, 1835, the Ettrick Shepherd, James Hogg, died, and though Wordsworth hadn't been a particular friend of his, or an admirer of his poetry, the event inspired him to write a poem in memory of all his literary friends who had so recently died. It all took place in a sudden upsurge of inspiration, the sort he hadn't had for many years, and it produced what is generally considered as the best of his late poems.

A niece who was staying with them at Rydal Mount happened to bring in a copy of the *Newcastle Journal*, which contained the news of Hogg's death. William left the room, but returned in half an hour, asking his niece to write down some lines which he had just composed – lines now known as 'Extempore Effusion upon the Death of James Hogg'. It was similar to 'Tintern Abbey', written some thirty-seven years previously, in that it was produced without Wordsworth's usual alterations and corrections. In commemorating the dead poets, such as Coleridge, Scott, Lamb, Crabbe and Hogg, it was almost as if he felt his own death was imminent.

William became active poetically again in the 1830s, after a fairly barren decade, but he produced little of note – at least, little of what the scholars consider notable. He was also busy revising and re-editing various collections of his poems, as well as putting the final, final touches to *The Prelude*, which he at last completed in 1839, then put away, probably in the iron chest which he used for the stamp money, with instructions that it should not be opened until after his death.

Mary, and all his family and close friends, hoped that he might get back to 'The Recluse', his master work, of which *The Prelude* was to be the first part; but he never did, contenting himself with sonnets and little verses, produced as the mood took him, and written on a multitude of likely and unlikely subjects. 'Has Wordsworth written no sonnet on the Income Tax,' asked a friend in 1842.

Off and on, over the previous twenty years, William had often remarked that he thought the muse had gone, but there's no sign that he *really* believed it. He worked as hard as ever, whenever he felt a poem taking shape, and was as proud of the result.

Mrs Wudsworth would say 'ring the bell' but he wouldn't stir [a former servant at Rydal Mount later recalled]. 'Goa and see what he's doing,' she'd say, and we wad goa up to study door and hear him mumbling and bumming through it. 'Dinner's ready, sir,' I'd ca' out. He'd goa mumbling on like a deaf man, ya see. And sometimes Mrs Wudsworth 'ud say, 'Goa and brek a bottle, or let a dish fall just outside door in passage.' Eh dear, that maistly would bring him out, wad that. For ye kna that he was a verra careful man, and he couldn't do with brekking t'china.

William was by now well into his late sixties, and not many great poets have been creative at that late stage. The Great Decade, as far as Wordsworth's poetry is concerned, is usually said to have been 1796–1806, but little-known works, written in later years, are constantly being reanalysed and revalued. After the James Hogg effusion in 1835, however, there is very little that people trouble to read today.

The 1830s were altogether a fairly depressing time for William. Apart from Dorothy's decline, and then the deaths of his friends and contemporaries, there was the state of the nation in general. He was upset by the movement for reform, which culminated in the 1832 Reform Bill, when the Whigs had at last achieved office, and prophesied that nothing but doom would result from the enlargement of the franchise. 'I was so depressed with the aspect of public affairs,' he wrote to his brother Christopher in 1832, 'that were it not for our dear sister's illness, I should think of nothing else. They are to be envied, I think who from age or infirmity, are likely to be removed from the afflictions which God is preparing for this sinful nation.' He also prophesied economic ruin, political chaos and social disintegration. On all sides, he saw threats to the Church of England, which he stoutly defended from all attacks – either from the Dissenters or from the Roman Catholic Church. He was against Catholic Emancipation and felt the monarchy would be in danger should it ever happen: 'These two islands are likely to reap the fruit of their own folly and madness in becoming, for the present generation, the two most unquiet and miserable spots upon the earth.'

He grieved for what he considered the depressed state of poetry and of the English language – 'the disgusting frequency with which the word *artistical*, imported with other impertinencies from the Germans, is employed by writers of the present day' – and for the poverty of the publishing business. He even managed to chastise the scientists of the day, condemning them for their airs and graces, and for being more concerned for titles than for caring for humanity. This could have been a dig at his old friend Sir Humphry Davy, who was now a man of high fashion.

It was a time of general social unrest, and William himself did have many personal reasons for gloom and despondency, but, throughout the 1830s, an air of melancholy seems to have pervaded even his happiest moments. One day in 1836, walking up Easedale, his favourite walk near Grasmere, on a perfect autumn day, he came with some friends upon a beautiful tumbling stream.

I have often thought what a solemn thing it would be [he said, turning to his friends] if we could have brought to our mind, at once, all the scenes of distress and misery, which any spot, however beautiful and calm before us, has been witness to since the beginning. That water break, with the glassy, quiet pool beneath it, that looks so lovely, and presents no images to the mind but of peace – there, I remember, the only son of his father, a poor man, who lived yonder, was drowned. He missed him, came to search, and saw his body dead in the pool.

In 1837, William undertook a trip to Italy with Crabb Robinson. They managed to pay a quick visit to Caroline on their way through Paris (this was the last time father and daughter ever met). The tour as a whole ended earlier than they'd planned. William found that he and Crabb Robinson, for all their years of friendship and intimacy, had different habits. William loved to be up and on his way at the crack of dawn, while Robinson was still asleep. William went to his bedroom when the sun went down, unable to read by candlelight, while Robinson was just getting ready for the town, to visit the reading rooms and parties. 'One night I heard him in bed composing verses,' wrote Robinson, 'and on the following day I offered to be his amanuensis; but I was not patient enough, I fear, and he did not employ me a second time.'

William missed having any of his regular female companions with him, and vowed never to travel without one again. He was very homesick, writing home quite pathetic letters to Mary, promising never to be irritable or cross with any of them again and saying how much he loved them all.

In 1838, William learned some news which, on the face of it, should have made him extremely happy, but which drove him to the depths of misery and worry. Dora wanted to get married.

John, his eldest child, was already married, to everyone's satisfaction and relief. Not long after he had moved to his living at Moresby, near Whitehaven, John had married Isabella Curwen, in October 1830. She was the daughter of Mr Curwen, of Workington Hall and of Belle Isle in Windermere. The Curwens were a noted Cumbrian family, well known by William since his school-days at Hawkshead. (He mentions Mr Curwen twice in his *Guide to the Lakes*, both times favourably, complimenting him on his plantations, little knowing that his son would one day marry into the family.)

The person Dora wanted to marry didn't have quite such a solid or favourable background. She was in love, so she told her father, with Edward Quillinan.

Dora had been just seventeen when she first met Quillinan, and he was then a family man of thirty, married with two children, a man of the world, an army officer who had served in various parts of Europe during the Napoleonic Wars. As we have seen, he had become very much a family friend of William's and Dorothy's, part of *their* generation rather than of the youthful Dora's. They had visited him as a family, when they stayed with him in London, but gradually, when he came to Rydal on visits, it was Dora he most wanted to see. By 1825, she was confiding to a girl friend that she liked 'the heavy dragoon, better than any other man'.

In their family letters to Quillinan, Dorothy and William always passed on Dora's best wishes. Even when she was sending him 'a thousand loves', William seems to have been completely unaware of their courtship, looking upon Quillinan as one of his own dearest personal friends. Quillinan once sent them some of his poems, which Dora read to her father. William was much impressed by them, writing to tell Quillinan that, if he could correct a few faults, it was in his power 'to attain a permanent place amongst the poets of England'. It was a terrible shock when Dora finally told her father that she and Quillinan wanted to become engaged. William's immediate reaction was to refuse his permission.

It is easy to say that William was being possessive, that he selfishly didn't want to lose his only daughter. She had certainly been his favourite travelling companion for the last ten years. She was so good for him – cheekier, as she said herself, than any of his other household ladies. There was a joke amongst their friends that some men were henpecked, but that Wordsworth was chicken-pecked.

Although she now travelled a lot, thanks to her father, she had spent a very sheltered girlhood. Her best friends were over in the Southey household, where there were no boys of her age. John, her elder brother, doesn't appear to have brought any of his own male friends to the house – none, at least, that she took a fancy to. Mr Quillinan, then, although her father's friend, must have appeared a very dashing figure, charming and amusing, experienced and worldly, but at the same time a cultivated figure, a poet like her father – or a would-be poet.

William was patently horrified when he was told what had been going on under his nose, but he denied that he was reacting selfishly. Nor was Quillinan's age ever mentioned in all the arguments that ensued, nor even that he was a Roman Catholic. It was his lack of prospects which worried William. He had no income, apart from his army pension, and no fixed abode. He wandered around, between London and Portugal, where his family had lived, or in rented cottages in Rydal. He already had two young girls to support. How could he take on a new wife, especially one who had always been delicate, one who needed the best attention and care?

Family friends eventually persuaded William to agree to the engagement, but it was on the understanding that Quillinan would now be looking for a secure job and steady home. Having for years been so enthusiastic in his letters about Quillinan, so solicitous and friendly, William now changed completely. He almost refused to discuss the topic of the marriage; in fact, he virtually refused to admit Quillinan's existence.

Quillinan, naturally, became impatient, unwilling to postpone the marriage indefinitely, which appeared to be William's hope. Dora told her father one day that Quillinan had written to her, suggesting that they should take a chance on marriage, not waiting for financial security. 'I must direct your attention,' wrote Wordsworth in reply, the heavy-handed father, 'to the fact that you must have overlooked the state in which Dora has long been, or you could not have called upon her Parents to give their Daughter up to a "rough chance".'

Quillinan took great exception to William's letter, and for several months the two men were not on speaking or corresponding terms. Eventually, after pressure from family friends, the marriage was at last arranged – a good two years after Dora had hoped it would take place. William had finally agreed on negative grounds: he would not oppose the marriage, but he was still not *for* it. He said he loved Dora too much and cared too much for her future happiness to bless such a marriage. 'But I must submit and do submit, and God Almighty bless you my dear child, and him who is the object of your long and long-tried preference and choice.'

The marriage took place in Bath in 1841, at the home of a family friend who had taken Dora's side in the long and bitter family row. John, her brother, came down from his west Cumberland vicarage to marry her, and her younger brother Willy gave her away. William and Mary came down for the wedding and William intended to go to the church, but at the last moment he did what Dorothy had done at his own wedding thirty-nine years previously. He couldn't face it. He talked to Dora alone before the ceremony and then told Quillinan that 'this interview with my child has already so upset me that I think I can hardly bear it'.

It is difficult not to feel some sympathy for everyone concerned. William's anguish for his delicate daughter was more than just fatherly emotion. Quillinan could not, on the face of it, give her the sort of stability she needed.

Dora, for her part, was now nearly thirty-seven. So far, she had given absolute devotion to her father, but she wanted to marry the man she loved, a man whom she'd known for twenty years, all her adult life. He was a dear family friend, someone they'd all loved and whose company they'd always all enjoyed. She wasn't running away with a stranger. She couldn't understand why her father had turned against him. William put a brave face on it. He invited them to have their honeymoon up at Rydal Mount, while he and Mary continued on a little tour of the West Country.

Over at Greta Hall, the 1830s brought some similarly sad events, plus a few very happy ones. A great bond of friendship had grown up between the members of the next generation at Greta Hall and Rydal, with Dora being the best friend of Sara Coleridge and Edith Southey. When Sara got married in 1829, to her first cousin Henry Nelson Coleridge, the bridesmaids included the three Southey girls (the youngest, Isabel, had died in 1826) and Dora, and the ceremony was performed by John Wordsworth.

But as the older children grew up, married and moved away, Greta Hall became a much quieter house, though still a hive of literary industry, with Southey as busy as ever. In 1835, Peel asked him to accept a baronetcy – an honour Wordsworth was never offered – but Southey declined. He didn't think he had the wealth to support such an honour. 'I could afford to die,' he wrote to a friend, 'but not to be disabled.' By this, he meant he had good insurance policies, and some property which could be sold, but that he was still completely dependent on turning out books every year to support his family. In place of the baronetcy, Peel increased his small government pension, which he'd had since 1807, to £300 a year.

The first domestic tragedy at Greta Hall occurred in 1834. A visitor chanced to arrive at the house at the moment it happened and later a friend described what he'd witnessed.

On passing the drawing room he noticed several ladies apparently in a cheerful mood. On giving his name, after waiting five minutes, Southey came to him, the very image of distraction, took his hand and led him into his study. For a long time he remained silent – at length he told him he believed he must dismiss him; in time he disclosed to him that within the last five minutes, Mrs Southey had, without previous indication or symptom, gone raving mad, and to that hopeless degree that within an hour, he must take her to an asylum.

Edith Southey had been in a fairly depressed state since the death of her daughter Isabel, but appeared to have recovered, though she had never been a particularly lively lady – prone to fears about money, susceptible to religious mania. Southey did send her for a few months to a Retreat for Lunatics at York, then brought her home; but she never recovered her sanity.

Within a matter of months of each other, Rydal Mount and Greta Hall had been stricken with mental illness, each with what appeared to be incurable cases. But whereas Dorothy Wordsworth at least managed to gain some physical strength – enough to walk round the house on occasions – Edith Southey quickly deteriorated. She died two years later, in 1837.

In 1839, Southey surprised almost everyone by marrying Caroline Bowles, one of those literary ladies with whom he'd corresponded and whom he'd helped. She was twelve years younger than Southey and most of his children were greatly upset by the union. The family was split down the middle, with the Wordsworths taking the side of Kate, Southey's last unmarried daughter, who for a while took refuge at Rydal Mount. Southey's brother, and another daughter, approved of the marriage and tried to support the new Mrs Southey. Southey had pleaded with Caroline to marry him, feeling old and lonely and very miserable, but she quickly realized that she had become more of a nurse than a wife. His own mental and physical powers began to fade very quickly.

Within a year, Southey's mind had gone. When William came to visit him in July 1840, he found him still trying to read. 'Past taking pleasure in the presence of any of his old friends, he did not recognize me till he was told. Then his eyes flashed for a moment with their former brightness, but he sank into the state in which I had found him, patting with both hands his books affectionately, like a child.'

Southey died in March 1843, aged sixty-eight, and internal family hostilities broke out once again, with Kate Southey's dislike of her stepmother splitting their relations and friends. The Wordsworths, still taking Kate's side, were not invited to the funeral by Mrs Southey, but William went all the same, unasked, and later wrote the words for one of the memorials.

So ended the literary life of Greta Hall, for forty-three years one of the power-houses in the history of English literature. Together, Wordsworth, Coleridge and Southey had managed to move the centre of English poetry up to the Lake District and keep it there for well-nigh fifty years. Southey's poems and books gave pleasure to thousands, but sadly, out of the forty-five books he published, very few are read today. Perhaps his best-known work, apart from his *Life of Nelson*, is his children's story, 'The Three Bears'. (In his original version it's an old lady who eats their porridge.) He wrote prose with enormous fluency and great style, and, arguably, had more of either than Wordsworth, but in his poetry he lacked that vital ingredient: content. Whatever the faults in Wordsworth, and there are many, he did offer the world a philosophy, moral substance and deep feeling.

Within ten days of Southey's death, Wordsworth was asked to be Poet Laureate, but at first he refused. He felt too old to write any commemorative verse. Southey, during his thirty years as Laureate, had not been officially obliged to write commemorative verse, but he usually had done so, all the same, though, when he had failed to think of anything suitable for Queen Victoria's coronation, he had been greatly upset.

William had not gone unhonoured in the preceding years. In 1838, he received his first honorary degree, from the new University of Durham, which had pleased him. He even made a joke about it, telling Crabb Robinson in a letter that now he had a DCL, 'you will not scruple when a difficult point of law occurs to consult me'.

The following year, the University of Oxford gave him a similar honour, and he received a tremendous ovation from all the undergraduates. He was told it had only been exceeded by the welcome for the Duke of Wellington. His own college at Cambridge, St John's, gave him a lot of pleasure by commissioning his portrait by Pickergsill, to be hung in the college.

In 1842, William had given up his Distributorship of Stamps, having at last, after lengthy and devious negotiations, arranged that his son Willy could take it over. His numerous collections of poems were now selling much better than they'd ever sold before, bringing him in an income, by the late 1830s, of £500 a year; but, even so, the loss of his annual £400 Stamp income was quite a substantial one. Poor Willy had failed to get any job all these years, but now, at least, he had an income and a position for life. However, William's loss had been made good a few months later when, thanks to Peel, he was made a pensioner on the Civil List, with a sum of £300 a year.

William was therefore rather obliged to Peel, and when Peel wrote personally to him, asking him again to take on the Laureateship, he felt forced to reconsider his decision. 'I will undertake,' wrote Peel, 'that you will have nothing required from you. As the Queen can select for this honourable appointment no one whose claims for respect and honour, on account of eminence as a poet, can be placed in comparison with yours, I trust you will no longer hesitate to accept.'

In April 1843, Wordsworth therefore graciously agreed to be Poet Laureate. As his nephew Christopher observed, his grey hairs had long since deserved to be wreathed with laurels. 'By his earlier poetical effusions, he had earned the bays before he wore them. He wrote laureate odes before he was the laureate. Those lyrical poems are more valuable because they were not official but the spontaneous effusions of inspiration.'

The muse fell silent after the acceptance of the Laureateship, but, at seventy-three, William was still fit and healthy and physically remarkably active. There were more triumphs, and troubles, to come.

JAMES HOGG

*Wordsworth's 'Extempore Effusion Upon the Death of James Hogg'
was written in a sudden burst of sad inspiration in 1835, almost thirty
years after his supposedly greatest writing years were over. He was
mourning the recent deaths of Coleridge, Lamb and others, wondering
who would be next.*

THE mighty Minstrel breathes no longer,
'Mid mouldering ruins low he lies;
And death upon the braes of Yarrow,
Has closed the Shepherd-poet's eyes:

Nor has the rolling year twice measured,
From sign to sign, its steadfast course,
Since every mortal power of Coleridge
Was frozen at its marvellous source:

The rapt One, of the godlike forehead,
The heaven-eyed creature sleeps in earth:
And Lamb, the frolic and the gentle,
Has vanished from his lonely hearth.

Like clouds that rake the mountain-summits,
Or waves that own no curbing hand,
How fast has brother followed brother,
From sunshine to the sunless land!

Yet I, whose lids from infant slumber
Were earlier raised, remain to hear
A timid voice, that asks in whispers,
'Who next will drop and disappear?'

20

Mellow Moods
1840-1847

TWO new ladies moved into the Wordsworth circle in the last dozen or so years of his life, the more important of whom was Isabella Fenwick. It was almost as if, with Dorothy an invalid, Sarah Hutchinson dead, and Dora about to be married, he needed another female companion to share his moods and his memories. Mary was part of this new friendship, and all three of them were close friends, but it was William and Miss Fenwick who had a special intimacy.

They first met in the early 1830s, when Wordsworth was sixty-five and Miss Fenwick was about fifty. She came across from Greta Hall for dinner one night, with Southey and his daughter Kate. She was a lady of independent means, with a house in Bath, but had originally come from Northumberland, as her border name might indicate. ('The Forsters, the Fenwicks, they rode and they ran,' wrote Sir Walter Scott in 'Young Lochinvar'.) Miss Fenwick was well read, something of an intellectual (though she had no literary pretensions herself), generous, warm-hearted and of a liberal inclination. She was devoted to William and to his poetry, but was well aware of all his faults, which, as their friendship grew, she became well acquainted with. She made frequent and long visits to Rydal, staying and helping for many weeks at a time to nurse Dorothy, and then eventually took her own cottage at Ambleside.

After she arrived, William went regularly to visit her, sometimes reciting passages from *The Prelude* to her. 'Or as his little grandson says,' so Miss Fenwick related, ' "Grandpa reading without a book." '

William's liking for his new lady friend apparently became the talk of the neighbourhood. 'Wordsworth goes every day to Miss Fenwick,' wrote Harriet Martineau, the other of William's new lady friends, 'gives her a smacking kiss and sits down before the fire to open his mind. Think what she could tell, if she survives him!'

William himself realized what people might think, although the friendship was doubtless completely innocent. He and Mary moved into Miss Fenwick's cottage for a while. 'For the sake of her society and change of air,' William wrote to Crabb Robinson, 'and above all, because it may not be prudent for me to walk to see her so often as I could wish.'

He did go off on journeys with her: to Cambridge, where he took her to St John's and showed her his old room; and to Durham, to take his honorary degree. They went on the new railway from Carlisle to Newcastle and did some sightseeing in Northumberland, near her family home. It was a time of great stress for William, with Dorothy's illness and then Dora's infatuation for Quillinan, so Miss Fenwick saw him in many moods. 'What strange workings are there in his great mind, and how fearfully strong are his feelings and affections! If his intellect had been less powerful they must have destroyed him long ago.... I witness many a sad scene, yet my affection and admiration, even my respect, goes on increasing with my knowledge of him.' She wrote this in 1839, at the height of William's row with Quillinan. It was thanks to Miss Fenwick that Dora eventually got William's permission, albeit grudging permission, to get married. She took Dora's side during the long arguments and talked William into changing his mind, and it was from her house at Bath that the couple got married.

William admired Miss Fenwick for her resolution, listened to her good common sense, and very often acted on her advice. 'I feel quite sure I know all his faults, all that they have done, are doing and may do. I think I never love a person thoroughly till I know how far they are liable to take the wrong way. I always want to have as little room for my imagination to work as possible.'

Sara Coleridge, herself a young woman of great intelligence and talent, spoke very highly of Miss Fenwick: 'I take great delight in her conversation ... her mind is such a noble compound of spiritual feeling and moral strength, and the most perfect feminism. She is intellectual, but ... never talks for effect, never keeps possession of the floor, as clever women are so apt to do. . . .'

Perhaps Miss Fenwick's greatest triumph lay in persuading William to dictate to her his memories of his poems and of the circumstances in which they were written. These notes, known to scholars as the I F notes, were written down by Miss Fenwick in 1843 and have been the basis for countless biographical and literary studies of Wordsworth. She entered William's life at the stage in which he was beginning to look back on his past, to delight in telling stories of his famous contemporaries (most of them dead by then) and of his own early struggles. 'He recognized his own greatness in the midst of the neglect, contempt and ridicule of his fellow creatures which strikes one as what is most extraordinary in his character.' He was against anyone writing a full biography of him, believing that his life was in his poetry, but, at Miss Fenwick's promptings, he agreed that it would be useful for posterity to know the background of his better-known poems.

The other lady who came close to William in his final years was herself a professional writer. Harriet Martineau was an eccentric lady who had published many books and had travelled extensively round the world, from the United States to the Middle East. She wrote and gave lectures on economics, religion, tax laws and history. Just before she settled in the Lakes, she had been very seriously ill, confined to her bed, expecting to die, though, at the same time, she somehow managed to publish yet another book, *Life in a Sick Room*. Then suddenly she got out of bed, left her room and came back to normal life once more, announcing she had had a miracle cure, thanks to mesmerism. In the Lakes, she took a daily bath in her outdoor swimming-pool and lectured the local people on hygiene, anatomy and mesmerism.

She arrived in the Lake District in 1845, aged forty-three, and bought herself a plot of land near Ambleside. She was one of that new breed of immigrants who had been attracted by the literary life associated with Wordsworth. As a young girl, she had been a devoted admirer of his poetry and had pinned up his portrait in her room. She could quote his verse by the hour. On first meeting him, she was rather disappointed, thinking he was now cut off from reality. She was shocked by what she considered the loose living of the peasantry, which William appeared not to notice: 'Here is dear old Wordsworth for ever talking of rural innocence and deprecating any intercourse with towns lest the purity of his neighbours should be corrupted.'

Everyone was surprised when she and William became friendly. The rest of the Wordsworth household considered her rather potty and strange, and didn't care for her Dissenting views, her politics or her general free-thinking attitude to life. She gave Quillinan a hundred cabbage plants for his cow, as part of her campaign for agricultural reform in the Lakes.

At their first meeting, William told her that she'd taken the wisest step in her life by buying her plot of land. She expected him to go on and say that it was the perfect retreat for an elderly woman recovering from an illness, but he explained that he was thinking in financial terms: 'The value of your property will be doubled in ten years.' She was confused by William's own little economies, which she saw as a strange mixture of meanness and generosity. When she drank tea with him, there was not a drop of cream available, yet she'd seen him earlier giving away milk with a lavish hand to the surrounding cottagers. 'They were perfectly well able to buy it, and would have been all the better for being allowed to do so.'

William ignored most of her political opinions, and was totally sceptical about her mesmerism and vegetarianism, but found her a warm and vital character. He went on many an outing with her, charmed by her liveliness and her capacity for enormously long walks. 'She is the briskest and most active person in the vale,' said Mary Wordsworth. 'Miss Martineau's intellectual activity shames all idlers,' said Quillinan. Long after William's time, she went on to become an institution in the Ambleside district.

The local farm workers found her just as amusing as the gentry who dined with her.

I met her the other day walking along the muddy road [recalled a peasant woman]. Is it a woman, or a man, or what sort of animal is it. There she came, stride, stride, great heavy shoes, stout leather leggins on and a knapsack on her back! Ha, ha, that's a political comicalist, they say. But I said to my husband, goodness, that would have been a wife for you. She'd ha' ploughed, and they say she mows her own grass and digs her own cabbages and potatoes. Well we have some queer uns here. Wordsworth should write a poem on her. What was Peter Bell to a comicalist?

One of the gentry who met Miss Martineau was the Rev. Sydney Smith, a founder of the *Edinburgh Review* and later a Canon of St Paul's. Perhaps the wittiest cleric of the century, he is remembered today for his definition of heaven as 'eating pâtés de foie gras to the sound of trumpets'. He was an acquaintance of Miss Martineau, but not exactly an admirer. His definition of hell is not quite as well known today as his remark about heaven. Hell, so he realized in a dream one night, was being in a madhouse, shut up with Harriet Martineau....

William himself was looked upon as something of an eccentric by the local people, with his shepherd's style of clothing – his rough plaid trousers, loose brown frock-coat and black handkerchief round his neck. He had allowed his hair to grow longer at the back, which gave him a very distinctive appearance, and he often wore a straw hat, with a veil to shade the sun. When his eyes were really bad, he wore green shades, though, in his last decade, his eyes don't seem to have bothered him as much as they did in earlier years. Thomas Carlyle met him several times in London, at breakfast parties, and described a device Wordsworth had taken to using: 'He carried in his pocket something like a skeleton brass candlestick in which, setting it on the dinner table, between the most afflictive or nearest of the chief lights, he touched a little spring and there flirted out, at the top of his brass implement, a small green circle which prettily enough threw his eyes into shade and screened him from that sorrow.'

Wordsworth's teeth, which he'd been so proud of keeping, eventually started to go and he had to have some false teeth fitted. 'This little box contains my artificial teeth which want repairs,' he wrote to his publisher, Edward Moxon (who'd worked at Longmans and then set up his own firm, which William joined). 'Be so good as to take them if you can find time or let them be sent if you cannot to the Dentist.' London publishers do have their uses. At Rydal, William usually took his teeth out in the evening, when he and Mary were alone together, which annoyed Harriet Martineau. After she got to know him, and began calling in to see him on her evening walk, he refused to put them in, and she couldn't understand half the things he was saying; so she changed her habits and made her social calls during the day. He usually talked at great length about his poetry, she recalled, complaining that it was the reviewers who had prevented him from earning more than £100 a year for a very long period.

Wordsworth never had any sense of smell, so this was one faculty which wasn't affected by age. It appears to have been a congenital deficiency, which must have been rather a handicap, for a poet of nature, and if you read his words carefully, you'll notice an absence of reference to smells. When he writes about flowers, for example, he tends to glorify scentless flowers, like daisies and lesser celandines, rather than roses. It has often been said that the lack of real passion of the sensual or sexual variety in Wordsworth's poetry is the outcome of his northernness, which sets him apart from such hot-blooded southerners as Keats, Byron and Shelley. But perhaps the explanation lies in his lack of a sense of smell. You miss a lot of lush sensations when your olfactory organs are not working.

According to Southey, there was only one occasion in William's life in which his dormant sense of smell was suddenly awakened. It happened back in 1797 at Racedown, when Mary Hutchinson came to visit him and they walked past a bed of stocks in full bloom. 'The fact is remarkable in itself,' Southey recalled in a letter, 'and would be worthy of notice, even if it did not relate to a man of whom posterity will desire to know all that can be remembered.' But this story is completely denied by William's nephew Christopher, who, in his *Memoirs* of his uncle, dismisses it as purely imaginary: 'Miss H. expressed her pleasure at their fragrance, a pleasure which he caught from her lips, and then fancied to be his own.' William himself never appears to have remarked on this handicap, either in his letters or in his poetry.

Wordsworth was also unmusical; though, when abroad, he might go to the opera, as part of a sight-seeing trip. This again fits in with his rather chaste, frugal, unsensual outward image, which shows in his poetry – if not always, as we now know, in his life. He did get very worried once that he thought his hearing was going. He was in Italy in 1837 with Crabb Robinson (the long-planned trip, one which Dorothy now could no longer manage) when they heard a cuckoo – or rather, Crabb Robinson heard it, and William didn't. 'I recollect perfectly well that I heard the cuckoo at Laverna *twice* before he heard it,' wrote Crabb Robinson, 'and that it absolutely fretted him that my ear was first favoured; and that he exclaimed with delight, "I hear it! I hear it!"' The cuckoo, which William often wrote about, is, as birds go, unmusical.

Apart from his eyes, William remained in perfect health well into his seventies, going on long walks and, even at seventy-five, so he said in one letter, helping with the hay in his field (Dora's field) from half past eight in the morning till one o'clock.

On his seventy-fourth birthday (on 7 April 1844), a huge party was given in the garden of Rydal Mount, to which all the children of the neighbourhood were invited – some three hundred of them – plus one hundred and fifty adults of all ages, both sexes and all classes. 'We had music of our preparing,' wrote William to an American friend, Professor Reed, 'and two sets of casual itinerants, Italians and Germans, came in successively and enlivened the festivities.' Each child got an orange, a piece of gingerbread and a hard-boiled pace egg. William did his bit by romping with the children and playing games. One of his neighbours remembered the scene years later, as if it had all been a dream: 'It is perhaps the only part of the island where such a reunion of all classes could have taken place without any connection of landlord and tenant, or any clerical relation or school direction.' The party was the inspiration of Miss Fenwick, who paid for it and organized it – another example of her understanding of William, her knowledge of what would delight him. Another of her inspired birthday gifts, presented when he was seventy, was a German-made cuckoo-clock (she was aware of his great love of cuckoos), which hung at the top of the stairs at Rydal Mount and delighted the family, especially Dorothy. Dorothy watched it from her wheel-chair and rocked with laughter, so Mary said, at the 'sudden exit of the little Mimic'. William wrote a poem about the cuckoo-clock, saying how its voice soothed him during sleepless nights. (It now hangs on the stairs at Dove Cottage.) 'It has been a work of real pleasure,' wrote Mary to Miss Fenwick, 'for no children were ever more delighted with a toy.'

William's delight in children was well known and never diminished; on his walks, at home or away, he was always stopping and talking to them – often asking them to repeat the Lord's Prayer, and then going through the words with them and giving them pennies. 'In winter time,' wrote Harriet Martineau when he was in his late seventies, 'he was to be seen in his cloak, his Scotch bonnet and green goggles attended by a score of cottagers' children – the youngest pulling at his cloak or holding by his trousers while he cut ash switches out of the hedge for them.' But was William still in touch with the ordinary country folk, as opposed to their children? Miss Martineau hinted that he had grown away from them, and a strange little book, produced after his death by Canon Rawnsley, of Keswick, entitled *Reminiscences of Wordsworth among the Peasantry of Westmorland*, indicates that in later life he hadn't much contact with the peasants. 'He'd pass you, same as if yan was nobbut a stean,' recalled a butcher who'd delivered meat to the Words-worths four times a week as a lad. 'He wozn't a man as said a deal to common fwoak,' said one old waller, 'but he talked a deal to hiseen. I often seead his lips a ganin.'

According to their memories, it was the two women of the household who had appeared to the local people to be the clever ones. They found Mrs Wordsworth plain and stiff, but very good at accountancy, while Dorothy, until she became ill, impressed the most of all. 'Miss Dorothy, she was ter'ble clever woman. She did as much of his poetry as he did and went completely off it at the latter end, wi' studying it, I suppose.'

None of them ever read his poetry, or knew anything about it; but, there again, the local Cumbrian gentry didn't exactly rush to buy it either. In 1833, William was complaining to Moxon that there 'was no genuine relish for poetical publications in Cumberland, not a copy of my poems having been sold by one of the leading booksellers, though Cumberland is my native county'. But of course the quality *knew* all about him and invited him to their tables, and he invited them back. 'There's nea doot but what he was fond of a quality, and quality was fond of him, but he niver exed fowk aboot their wark, nor noticed t'flocks or nowt; not but what he was a kind man if fwoaks was sick or taen badly.'

Random memories, even taken down by someone as assiduous as Canon Rawnsley, aren't completely reliable, but there are enough of them, plus the diaries of local ladies like Miss Martineau, to suggest that Wordsworth had rather lost contact with the rustic characters on whom his poetic reputation had been founded. It wasn't surprising of course. His Tory views, his landed friends, his honorary degrees and government recognition had obviously distanced him from them.

One of his last campaigns was to stop the railway coming into the Lake District. He feared all the common people from Lancashire would come into his vale and ruin it. Being uneducated, they therefore couldn't appreciate mountains and lakes and would therefore spoil the scenery for those of taste and discrimination, such as himself. It was an extremely élitist view, and one which brought William many enemies as he argued his cause in letters to the newspapers and in appeals to Gladstone – all to stop the proposed Kendal and Winder-mere railway getting as far as Grasmere and Rydal. Even Crabb Robinson thought he was harming his reputation. In his poetry, he'd exalted the poor and glorified the beauties of nature, and he'd made a lot of money from his *Guide to the Lakes*, but now that *they* were going to descend on him, he was horrified. He wasn't against railways as such: he had written a poem about them and used them with pleasure. He just didn't want ten thousand Lancashire folk coming on day trips, or, even worse, the new merchant class building even more holiday homes. In the end, when the railway opened in 1847, it stopped at Windermere, thanks to his and other people's protests, and never reached Ambleside.

Apart from his outburst against the local railway, William had mellowed considerably by the 1840s. All the family tragedies of the 1830s, and the general state of the country, had conspired to make him an alarmist and a reactionary, forever prophesying doom and the end of civilization, as he knew it. But, by his seventies, he had in a sense outgrown the fears and worries of his middle age. As he looked around at the world in general, he realized that the 1832 Reform Bill had not brought about all the disasters he had predicted. His heart was nearly always in the right place – though his younger radical critics would never have put it so generously – but during his long middle age he had backed the conservative factions in almost every public debate, as the only way, he thought, of bringing about the freedom and happiness of all classes.

By living so long, he outlived his own and the country's latent reactionariness. By the 1840s, his letters are suddenly full of sentiments and attitudes which it would have been impossible to find in his letters of the 1830s. In that letter about his seventy-fourth birthday party, for example, he holds out hope for the future, albeit with a backward look:

One would wish to see the rich mingle with the poor as much as may be upon the footing of fraternal equality. The old feudal dependencies and relations are almost gone from England, and nothing has yet come adequately to supply their place. There are tendencies of the right kind here and there, but they are rather accidental than aught that is established in general manners. We are, however, improving, and I trust that the example set by some mill owners will not fail to influence others.

In 1845, he had a long discussion on education with his neighbour Miss Fletcher, during which he told her that he felt indulgent towards young men who could not decide on a profession. He himself had been in the same position, he said, and had incurred the strictures of his friends and relations. He had been unable to decide between the Church, the law and the army. 'He always felt he had talents for command, but he felt if he were ordered to the West Indies, his talents would not save him from the yellow fever.' A few years earlier, he had been telling friends that sons should be *made* to learn a profession, and should be pushed into habits of discipline and perseverance, which was how he tried to bring his own sons up (though he had singularly failed in the case of Willy). But now, in his seventies, William was expanding on the theme that young men should be allowed to enter the profession 'of their own choice'.

When one of the Chartists, Thomas Cooper, called on him at Rydal in 1846, he said that the Chartists were right in their campaign to extend the franchise, and they would surely achieve their aim in the end. He had only ever been against their *methods*, especially the use of physical force. Back in 1832, however, at the time of the first Reform Bill, his recurrent fear in all his letters had been rather different, terrified that the lower classes would one day attain power. In old age, he fulfilled his own prediction, made in London in 1794 when he was a poor wanderer, but one he had forgotten for many years: 'I am of that odious class of men called democrats, and of that class I shall ever continue.'

William was walking on a private estate one day with Coleridge's nephew, when the lord who owned the ground came up and told them they were trespassing. Much to his companion's embarrassment, William argued that the public had always walked this way and that it was wrong of the lord to close it off. 'Wordsworth made his point with somewhat more warmth than I either liked or could well account for. He had evidently a pleasure in vindicating these rights, and seemed to think it a duty.'

On the subject of moral freedom, he also became less doctrinaire as he grew older. One day in 1844, in the market-place in Ambleside, he met a friend who was seeing off on the mail-coach a young man who was going up to Balliol. 'He entered at once on a full flow of discourse ... on the subject of college habits and of his utter distrust of all attempts to nurse virtue by an avoidance of temptation. He expressed also his entire want of confidence (from experience he said) of highly wrought religious expression in youth.'

He realized, as an old man, that the characters of youth and age were very similar. He explained to a friend how the inherent variety and originality of youth merged into dull uniformity in middle age, but then reappeared afresh in old age. He likened the process to the growth of trees. In the summer, they all appeared the same. It was only in the spring and autumn that you saw their *real* characteristics. This certainly applied to Wordsworth's life, though his middle years did seem to go on for an unconscionably long time, as he trotted out his uniformly conservative reactions on almost every issue. Which was the *real* Wordsworth – the radical youth, the solid reactionary middle-aged citizen or the liberal and mellow old man? What a fortunate life, anyway, to have three selves to look back on.

By the 1840s, not only William's contemporaries, like Coleridge and Scott, had gone, but so many writers of the next generation, who had been coming up so hard on his heels, had died young – one of the tragic coincidences of English literature. Keats died in 1821, aged only twenty-six; Shelley in 1822, aged thirty; and Byron in 1824, aged thirty-six. In a matter of only three years, the three brightest flames of their generation had perished. For over twenty years, Wordsworth had been virtually on his own, the first and also the last of the Romantic poets.

If Wordsworth *had* died young, he might have been spared much of that abuse which dogged him in his late thirties and forties. An early death would have lent enchantment to his image. The young poets could not have accused him of selling out in his middle age, if he'd never reached middle age, as they sadly didn't. Now, he had outlived all his critics. He had come back into favour and seen the tide completely turn; the public had now been educated to his tastes.

By the 1840s, the poet who once wrote verse which 'would never do' was being asked by all and sundry for locks of his hair. In 1844, he gave some to Basil Montagu, one of his few old friends who had survived: 'I send you the lock of hair which you desired, white as snow, and taken from a residence which is thinning rapidly.' One of his faithful servants, James Dixon, who acted as gardener, groom and manservant, was also responsible for cutting William's hair. 'But the locks were never thrown away from that venerable head,' wrote Edwin Paxton Hood, 'but found their way into hundreds of hands in every part of the Empire. He kept also a quantity of cards with the poet's autograph and with this he sometimes comforted those who failed to see him, by either a lock of his hair or a dash of his pen.' The famous today are not nearly so considerate, though doubtless Dixon managed to be suitably recompensed for his troubles by William's admirers.

During the 1840s, the crowds came so frequently to Rydal that during the summer season there were often long queues at the gate. Harriet Martineau estimated that he received about five hundred strangers a year into his garden, and, if they were lucky or had brought an introduction, they got a tour of the house as well and a peep at Dorothy.

Wordsworth lectured them on nature and on what it was like to be Wordsworth, hardly listening to their own views and opinions. One day, Miss Martineau sent round two eminent educationalists, knowing William loved discussing education, but he didn't hear their introductions and addressed them as part of his ever-changing audience. Later, on learning that two eminent educationalists were in the district, he sent for them, unaware that he'd already met them.

On another occasion, a visitor who had travelled in the East managed to break into Wordsworth's usual flow about Lakeland, and had the daring to say that he personally preferred the solitude of the Arabian deserts. 'My blood was up,' Wordsworth related to a nephew of Coleridge's who was visiting him. 'I said "I'm sorry you don't like this, perhaps I can show you what will please you more." I strode away and led him from crag to crag, hill to vale, for about six hours, till I thought I should have to bring him home, he was so tired.'

William received many lords and ladies, bishops and knights, but his only royal visitor to Rydal was Queen Adelaide in 1840, the Dowager Queen, widow of William IV. William described how she was much taken by the beauty of the scenery and told him how she would like a little cottage in the Lakes. 'I led the Queen to the principal points in our little domain ... she took her leave, cordially shaking Mrs Wordsworth by the hand as a friend of her own rank might have done. She had also inquired for Dora who was introduced to her.'

It wasn't until 1845, by which time he was Poet Laureate, that he met Queen Victoria herself. He made a special trip to London for the Queen's Fancy Dress Ball, where he was presented to the Queen. He was wearing the full court dress, with sword and cocked hat, borrowed from his old friend, the writer Samuel Rogers. (It was the same outfit which Tennyson later borrowed to wear when meeting the Queen, after he in turn had become Poet Laureate.) William told his American friend, Henry Reed, that the wife of the American ambassador witnessed his meeting with the Queen and he described how she was moved to tears. 'To see a grey haired man of seventy five years of age kneeling down in a large assembly to kiss the hand of a young woman is a sight for which institutions essentially democratic do not prepare a spectator of either sex.... How must these words shock your republican ears!'

When in London, on his regular trips, he still rushed through the social round, often having three breakfasts in one morning, just to cram in all the people who wanted to meet him. 'He complains of being worn out,' wrote Mary in 1843, 'yet we cannot get him to spare himself. He complains of a pain in his chest, but I doubt the cause is his talking often against London noises, and in London society.' He met Mr Gladstone and dined with the Archbishop of Canterbury. Tennyson was introduced to him and signed Dora's album, writing for it his poem, then unpublished, 'The Eagle'. William afterwards spoke most generously of Tennyson, who was just making his name, calling him 'the first of our living poets'. In earlier years, he'd usually been highly critical about almost all the younger poets. Now he felt the grand old man, the sage of Lakeland, come down to pass on his wisdom and dispense his kindness.

One of William's oldest London friends was Benjamin Haydon, for a time the most successful portrait-painter of the day, who had introduced him to Keats at his 'immortal dinner party', as Haydon called it, in 1817. Haydon had included William in his massive painting, *Christ's Entry into Jerusalem*, along with Voltaire and Newton. He painted William again in 1842, showing him against a background of Helvellyn; the picture is now in the National Portrait Gallery. In 1840, aged seventy, William had climbed Helvellyn, but Haydon hadn't been there at the time. As in the Jerusalem painting, Haydon was using artistic licence. These paintings were well known and well exhibited in their day, and reproductions appeared in many books. The Helvellyn portrait even inspired Elizabeth Barrett Browning to write a sonnet about it, 'Wordsworth upon Helvellyn', which she sent to William in a copy of her poems. Haydon also made a life mask of William's face in plaster. He had taken all William's measurements, which amused William, who proudly copied them out to show Mary. He was 5 feet 9⅝ inches high, he said, and of very fine proportions.

Haydon eventually fell from fashion and his paintings ceased to be popular, though William remained faithful to his old friend. Haydon was something of a megalomaniac and couldn't accept rejection. The most humiliating incident occurred in 1846, when an exhibition of his paintings was mounted in the same building in which Tom Thumb, the midget, was being displayed. Haydon went to see how his exhibition was faring and was very pleased by the hurrying crowds. It turned out that they were all going to see Tom Thumb. Only two spectators were in the room where his paintings were hung. Not long afterwards, he shot himself. As Elizabeth Barrett Browning remarked, 'His love of reputation was a disease. The dwarf slew the giant.'

The giant Wordsworth, however, strode on, though a little less energetically. He was planning a further European trip in 1849, at the age of seventy-nine, but it never took place. His trip to Italy with Crabb Robinson in 1837 proved to be his last journey to the Continent.

William's last Lakeland tour of any duration was in 1844, when he went with Mary, his son-in-law Edward Quillinan and some others up the Duddon valley, retracing one of the happiest and most frequent expeditions of his boyhood and manhood alike. The trip was a slightly melancholy one. Early one morning, Miss Fletcher, one of his companions, found him wandering slowly down the road on his own, while the party slept, and she went with him into a churchyard. He told her he had not slept well. The recollection of former days and people had crowded in upon him, especially the memory of his dear sister. 'When I thought of her state, and of those who had passed away, Coleridge and Southey, and many others, while I am left with all my many infirmities, if not sins, in full consciousness, how could I sleep?'

Travelling was always one of William's pleasures, and he had long been fortunate that after Dorothy, his old travelling companion, had begun to suffer failing health, Dora had for many years been able to take her place. He was also fortunate that he saw in his lifetime the most dramatic changes in transport that the world had ever seen. In his youth, the world moved at the speed of the fastest horse. By his middle age, steamboats and steam trains were commonplace, and travelling has never been the same again. He had a new pair of eyes beside him when he went back to places like Loch Lomond, and took pleasure in Dora's fresh observations on the same sights he'd seen with Dorothy some thirty years or so before; but this time he saw them from a steamboat, chugging up the Loch, as opposed to being rowed across on a ferry.

Railway

His sonnet 'On the Projected Kendal and·Windermere Railway' was composed in 1844, when he was seventy-four. The opening lines are still very popular with preservationists.

Is then no nook of English ground secure
From rash assault? Schemes of retirement sown
In youth, and 'mid the busy world kept pure
As when their earliest flowers of hope were blown,
Must perish; – how can they this blight endure?
And must he too the ruthless change bemoan
Who scorns a false utilitarian lure
'Mid his paternal fields at random thrown?
Battle the threat, bright Scene, from Orrest-head
Given to the pausing traveller's rapturous glance:
Plead for thy peace, thou beautiful romance
Of nature; and, if human hearts be dead,
Speak, passing winds; ye torrents, with your strong
And constant voice, protest against the wrong.

21

Last Days
1847-1850

WILLIAM'S worst prediction about Quillinan appeared to come true almost immediately after his marriage to Dora. He'd always worried about Quillinan's lack of financial security, but he'd discounted several rumours alleging his involvement in suspicious deals. In 1842, Quillinan was arrested on a charge of fraud in connection with the property of his first wife's family, and, though he was cleared at the trial of any criminal charges, his weakness of character was publicly revealed. William stood by him completely, aware of his lack of discretion but convinced of his basic honour. Quillinan was left facing large debts, and it was obvious that on an annual income of £70, with which he had to support a wife and two children, he would never clear them. For the next four years he took Dora and his two children on endless wanderings – to London, to lodgings in Ambleside, and to the Cumberland coast. He was supposedly working on a translation of the Portuguese writer Camoens, although everyone knew that, even if finished, it would bring him very little money.

'You say he could not procure employment,' wrote William to Miss Fenwick, who was still defending Quillinan. 'I say he does not *try*.' The

Wordsworths stayed with Quillinan and Dora at the seaside once, and William was perturbed by his apparent lack of interest in his wife and children, preferring his books and newspapers. 'Yet, poor Creature, she is very fond of him.'

At Rydal Mount, they had rigged up a special shower bath, which Dora could use when she was in lodgings nearby; she came three times a week, and they hoped the showers would improve her health. Quillinan thought they did, though the shower frightened a young gardener's boy, who'd never seen such a thing before: 'Blowed if I didn't watch butler fill it and then goa and pull string, and down came watter and I was 'maazed as owt and I screamed and Mr John come and fun' me and saaved my life.'

Dora's health hardly improved, despite the showers, and she spent much of every day lying on a couch, trying to conserve her feeble strength. The latent tuberculosis, which she had showed signs of from the age of eighteen, was made worse by the slightest mist and rain, and she was always susceptible to colds and coughs. In 1845, Quillinan decided to take her off to Portugal, hoping the sun would finally cure her. Quillinan had been born in Portugal and his brother, who worked in the family wine firm, offered them a villa near Oporto. The Wordsworths weren't very keen on the plan, fearing perhaps they'd never see Dora again. William is usually portrayed as the one who fussed most over Dora, but Mary was equally concerned. 'Mrs W's anxiety is natural,' wrote Quillinan, 'and Dora's unwillingness to pain her, and to leave her at 75 is all right – but it is a pity that Mrs W does not take more cheerfully to the only plan to restore her daughter's health.'

After a poor start, for May can be as unreliable in Portugal as in England, Dora's health did improve dramatically, and she was writing ecstatic letters to her friends, saying how 'Old Daddy, Mammy and Dearest Miss F would be amazed by her recovery. She climbed mountains, rode Andalusian ponies and 'slept like a top and ate like a ploughboy'. They were away for a year, and out of the experience came a book which Dora published soon after their return: *A Journal of a Few Months Residence in Portugal and Glimpses of the South of Spain*. The inscription read, 'These notes are dedicated in all reverence and love to my Father and Mother for whom they were written.'

Dora came back glowing, and Sara Coleridge, who met her in Hampstead in June 1846, said she had not seen her look so well since her 'teenish girlhood'. Even nicer for the Wordsworths, Dora, her husband

and her two step-daughters decided to come back to the Lakes for good, taking a house at Loughrigg Holme. William had for a while his three children and grandchildren all settled at the same time near him in the Lakes. John, who had been abroad with his family for the sake of his wife's health, was now back at his vicarage with his five children. Willy, the proud Distributor of Stamps, at last got married in January 1847, aged thirty-six. He'd been engaged once, four years previously, to a distant cousin; but the engagement was broken off, since the girl turned out to be mentally unstable. The girl he did marry, Fanny Graham, was from the Carlisle area, though her parents had moved to Brighton.

Dora went to Carlisle at Christmas, to help Willy, to whom she was devoted, furnish a home for his bride. She caught a cold in Carlisle (which, for all its many attractions, is not quite as warm as Portugal) and, despite resting and taking things easy, was quite unable to throw it off. By April 1847, she was in such a weakened state that her husband realized she was dying.

William and Mary were in London at the time, staying with friends in Hampstead, but they left London on 1 May when they heard the news, never to return. They moved Dora into Rydal Mount, which in reality had always been her home, and together they nursed her for eleven weeks, knowing all the time that she was dying. The end came on 9 July 1847, just a year since she'd returned from the sun, convincing everyone that her health was now better than it had ever been. William was totally shattered.

There had been much mourning in the Wordsworth family all those years ago, when brother John had died at sea. There had been deep distress only the previous year, when William's only surviving brother Christopher, now retired as Master of Trinity, had died. But the death of Dora was a truly emotional shock from which William never recovered.

Two other distressful deaths occurred almost immediately after Dora's. The first was of Isabella, the wife of John, who had gone off once more to Italy for the sake of her health, but had died while abroad. The second was of Hartley Coleridge – not a blood relation, but someone who had, from birth, been part of the Wordsworth family circle.

Hartley Coleridge had always been a strange figure. As a child, he had amazed everyone with his brilliance, but, even when Hartley was only six, Wordsworth had worried about his future, as he showed in his prophetic lines, written in 1802: 'To HC, Six Years Old'.

> O blessed vision! happy child!
> Thou are so exquisitely wild,
> I think of thee with many fears
> For what may be thy lot in future years.

The childhood visions which Hartley clearly experienced, and others saw radiating in him, were in a way reflected in William's great 'Immortality' ode. Hartley did seem to arrive trailing clouds of glory; but then everything went wrong. He succeeded in winning his fellowship at Oxford, but lost it after a year, through intemperance. He tried schoolmastering and journalism with little success; then returned to the Lakes, where he lived in a series of rented rooms, drinking too much and borrowing from the Wordsworths. William always stood by him and loved him like a son, despite his vagrancy and dissolute life. Everyone, indeed, loved Li'le Hartley, as he was called. Those peasants whom Canon Rawnsley interviewed preferred reminiscing about Little Hartley to reminiscing about Wordsworth, remembering him for his endless cheerfulness and willingness to talk amusingly all day long to anyone who cared to listen. In 1849, he died in an upstairs rented room at Nab Cottage, Rydal Water, just a few hundred yards down the road from Rydal Mount.

William went to Grasmere Church with Derwent Coleridge, Hartley's brother, to choose a site for Hartley's grave; they picked a spot beside the grave of Sarah Hutchinson and near to Dora's. 'Let him lie by us,' said William. 'He would have wished it.' Then William instructed the sexton to measure out the ground for his own and for Mary's grave. As William looked up once more from Dora's grave, he told Derwent that he could see Hartley standing there, on the spot where he'd stood at Dora's funeral. Finally, turning to the sexton, he said, 'Keep the ground for us – we are old people, and it cannot be long.'

Though William was distraught by Dora's death, and for months was inconsolable, so that friends feared for his mental state, his final days were not unhappy. At first, he refused to go and visit Quillinan, who himself needed comforting, and this in turn led to Quillinan being indignant and upset. But this sad family rift was at length healed, thanks mainly to the good offices of Crabb Robinson. He came to stay with the Wordsworths every Christmas at Rydal in the latter years; it delighted him, as a bachelor, to join in their family festivities, playing games and giving out presents. The Crabb, as he was known in the family, was a great talker: Miss Fenwick's joke was that when he wasn't talking he was asleep.

He was a funny-looking old man, who mocked his own unattractiveness, not being at all upset when Wordsworth's grandchildren asked about his strange face and where he'd got it from. He wasn't as ugly as little Hartley, who'd made a profession of his own ugliness, boasting that he was going to start an Ugly Club, with himself as first chairman. The Crabb loved playing whist, which was their usual winter evening occupation, though, during that first Christmas after Dora's death, William at first refused to play, as he was reminded of all the hands of whist he'd played with Dora. He would start weeping uncontrollably at the mention of her name and go from room to room, avoiding Crabb; but by the time Crabb had left to go back to London, William had much improved.

William took comfort in his five grandchildren – the children of his son John, and, when visiting them, used the opportunity to revisit his childhood haunts nearby in Cockermouth, an area which held no memories of Dora. William took in his stride a mild escapade involving Jane, the eldest of John's children. In 1848, aged fifteen, she ran away from her rather dull boarding-school at Brighton and spent the night on the railway station. Mary was terribly upset, but William appeared hardly disturbed. 'He you know takes things easily,' Mary told Miss Fenwick.

William was more upset when a niece took up with a religious sect and embarked at Liverpool, bound for America. 'Do you know anything of a wretched set of religionists in your country, Superstitionists I ought to say, called Mormonites or latter day saints?' he wrote to his American friend Henry Reed. 'If you should by chance hear anything about her, pray let us know.'

By the following summer, William appeared to have recovered from the worst of his grief, and Miss Martineau reported that he was 'very cheerful and amiable', showing visitors round the grounds once more. The accounts which had appeared in some newspapers about his failing mental powers, she said, were 'utter nonsense'.

Mary recovered the quickest from the bereavement. She had the main burden of the invalid Dorothy to contend with and struggled on bravely, while William was still giving way to his emotions over Dora. 'I have no help from my beloved Mourner,' she wrote to Miss Fenwick. 'He is bowed to the dust.' But soon they were both making the best of it together, going on little jaunts in their coach to see friends and relations in the Lake District. 'I have met with very few faultless people in my journey through life,' Mrs Basil Montagu remarked, 'but Mrs Wordsworth seemed to me faultless.'

Since Dorothy had become an invalid, Mary had taken a greater part in William's creative work. In 1835, when he'd finished some poem and Mary had told him he was cleverer than she'd thought he was, there were tears in his eyes: 'It is not often I have had such praise; she had always been sparing of it.' Mary kept urging him to work on 'The Recluse' in his final years, and not to concern himself with slight sonnets. Before he and Crabb Robinson had left for Italy in 1837, she told Crabb not to encourage him to pursue vagrant subjects: 'Jingling rhyme does not become a certain age.' One of the people who has left a poor account of Mrs Wordsworth was Thomas Carlyle: 'A small, withered, puckered winking lady who never spoke and was visibly and sometimes ridiculously assiduous to secure her proper place of precedence at table.' Carlyle only knew her late in life, at London dining-tables, away from her home ground. Mr Carlyle could be fairly nasty in his descriptions of most people.

Keats, many years earlier, told a story which also suggested that, when in London, Mary was very aware of her position. At dinner one evening, Mary Wordsworth prevented Keats from disagreeing with her husband by putting her hand on his arm: 'Mr Wordsworth is never interrupted.' As for her 'winking' eye, it was De Quincey who first noticed this, saying she had a 'considerable obliquity of vision'.

Dr Arnold, who got to know Mary at Rydal, agreed that she was no beauty when he met her, but 'the kindness of her looks, tones and actions was rightly valued by all who knew her'. De Quincey, who did know her at a much earlier stage, also spoke of her kindness: 'The sweetness of temper which shed so sunny a radiance over Mrs Wordsworth's manners sustained by the happy life she led, the purity of her conscience, made it impossible for anybody to have quarrelled with *her*; and whatever fits of ill temper Wordsworth might have – for, with all his philosophy he had such fits – met no fuel to support them, except in the more irritable temperament of his sister.'

It was a happy marriage, full of love and understanding, as the newly discovered letters show. Mary was quiet, and, according to De Quincey, Thomas Clarkson used to say that all she ever said was 'God bless you!' But there's little reason to think she was subservient. She let William have the open arguments with Dora and Quillinan, but in the background she was equally strong, if not stronger than William. According to Sara Coleridge, Mary wished all her life that Dora, because of her delicate nature, should avoid two things – marriage and authorship. When both happened, she found it hard 'to submit to these vulgarities'.

William and Mary shared their little jokes, as any couple would after nearly fifty years of marriage – and after over seventy years of friendship, if you consider that they first met at school, when they were each three years old. One day, as they were waiting for their little carriage to take them on a drive up Easedale, William was ready and she was not. 'My dear, the carriage is waiting,' he said. 'Well, don't be cross,' she answered. 'Ah, I wish we could; it would make a little ripple in our lives.' You could take that remark as pure pathos, but it seems more likely to have been gentle Wordsworthian irony.

Similarly, when the young Algernon Swinburne, aged eleven, was presented to William by his parents in 1848 on a visit to Rydal Mount, William told him, as they were leaving, 'I do not think, Algernon, that you will forget me.' At this, young Algernon is reported to have wept. Was William being ironic, displaying North Country dead-pan humour, or was this simply the conceit of an old man?

In August 1849, when William was in his eightieth year, an American called Ellis Yarnall came to see him – one of that steady stream of Americans who had begun to treat Rydal as a pilgrimage centre. In America, there were even little celebrations each year on the Laureate's birthday and stories about him were printed in the American press. Yarnall was a friend of Professor Reed, who had recently published a collection of Wordsworth's poems in America. (*Lyrical Ballads* first appeared in the United States in 1802.) On Yarnall's return, he sent Reed a blow-by-blow account of his day with the Wordsworths: 'Wordsworth came in, it could be no other – a tall figure, a little bent with age, his hair thin and grey and his face deeply wrinkled. The expression of his countenance was sad, mournful I might say; he seemed one on whom sorrow pressed heavily.' Being a good American scholar, he then went on to repeat every little detail of the day: the furniture observed, the busts and paintings which Wordsworth showed him, how many times the cuckoo-clock chimed and all about a little walk down the lane, where they met a beggar 'of the better class'. William put his hand in his pocket at once, muttering' that he'd given to four or five already that day, but found his pocket was empty.

The conversation, as a whole, is completely unremarkable, but there's one interesting exchange which, in passing, the American reports in his letter. Only an American bent on recording everything would even have bothered to note it. William was talking about his experiences of the French Revolution, and of how he'd missed the wildest excesses by being in Orleans: 'Addressing Mrs W. he said "I wonder how I came to stay there so long and at a period so exciting."'

The remark obviously meant nothing at that time to the American, and perhaps it meant nothing anyway. Perhaps William was just rambling on. But the fact that he addressed the remark personally to Mary indicates, to me at least, that he was exchanging private looks with her behind the American's back, enjoying a little piece of teasing. By now, the Annette episode must have seemed centuries away, at another time and another place; but so also were his long middle years, when he was in his stern, voice-of-God, reactionary period, and when it seemed as if he was trying to forget that such an incident had ever happened. Now – an old man, relaxed, indulging his memories and himself, tolerant of the world and its failings – he could afford to be amused by life. Few people have witnessed such dramas, such tragedies, such changes, as the world thundered its revolutionary way past his front door, sucking him in, at several stages, into its raging torrents.

In his own personal world, he had so much to look back upon, both good and bad. Deaths in the family had rarely been far away, from the early loss of his own parents to the death of his children. He'd outlived almost everyone and everything. He knew the time was very near when he would go to meet Dora.

William made his last trip outside the Lake District in June 1849, when he and Mary went to visit relations in Great Malvern. Crabb Robinson, who joined them there, noticed for the first time a decline in William's mental vigour, though he was in good physical health. They came back to Oxenholme on the express train from Birmingham, but at Oxenholme they had a two-hour delay, while waiting for the Windermere train. When it came, it was full of holiday-makers – the sort William had always dreaded – heading for the Lakes which William had made famous, and perhaps hoping for a glimpse of the poet himself. He was by now seventy-nine, and the journey proved very tiring.

The following March, when the better weather came, William was out taking little walks round Grasmere, visiting old friends. One of them asked him how Mrs Wordsworth was. 'Pretty well, but indeed she must be very unwell indeed for anyone to discover it; she never complains.' It was William they really worried about. He now looked very weak, walking with stick in hand, lightly clad, as usual. A few days later, he walked across White Moss Common to visit another friend, with Mary this time. The friend was out, and, while Mary walked round the garden, William sat down on the stone seat of the porch to watch the setting sun. Two days later, he was taken ill with pleurisy.

He was still in bed on his eightieth birthday, on 7 April, while, in nearby Rydal Chapel, they prayed for his life in the morning and afternoon services. Two weeks later, the doctors told Mary that he was dying. She went into his room and told him very gently, 'William, you are going to Dora.' He made no reply, and she felt perhaps that he had not heard her. Next day, when her niece came into his room and was drawing the curtain, William awoke and said, 'Is that Dora?'

William died on Tuesday, 23 April 1850, Shakespeare's and England's day, at twelve o'clock exactly, while Miss Fenwick's cuckoo clock was striking the hour.

To the Cuckoo

Dorothy in her Journals *describes William working on this poem in 1802, around the same time as he was writing 'To a Butterfly'. Both poems go back to childhood and his earliest memories, simple, child-like poems written during his greatest creative years.*

O BLITHE New-comer! I have heard,
I hear thee and rejoice.
O Cuckoo! shall I call thee Bird,
Or but a wandering Voice?

While I am lying on the grass
Thy two fold shout I hear;
From hill to hill it seems to pass
At once far off, and near.

Though babbling only to the Vale,
Of sunshine and of flowers,
Thou bringest unto me a tale
Of visionary hours.

Thrice welcome, darling of the Spring!
Even yet thou art to me
No bird, but an invisible thing,
A voice, a mystery;

The same when in my schoolboy days
I listened to; that Cry
Which made me look a thousand ways
In bush, and tree, and sky.

To seek thee did I often rove
Through woods and on the green;
And thou wert still a hope, a love;
Still longed for, never seen.

And I can listen to thee yet;
Can lie upon the plain
And listen, till I do beget
That golden time again.

O blessed Bird! the earth we pace
Again appears to be
An unsubstantial, faery place;
That is fit home for Thee!

22

Postscript

DOROTHY, who had been an invalid for the last twenty years of William's life, outlived him by five years, dying in 1855, aged eighty-three. Mary lived longest, dying of old age at eighty-eight, in 1859. It says much for their policy of plain living and high thinking that all three lived to be octogenarians.

Mary's first task, on William's death, had been to take out from its resting place the 'poem of his own life', as it had always been called, and send it to Moxon, the publisher. The dedication was still to S.T. Coleridge, as it had been when William had begun it, some fifty years previously. It was Mary who named it *The Prelude*.

Almost immediately after William's death, there were approaches from Baudouin, the husband of William's French daughter Caroline, who maintained he and his wife should have a share of William's estate, despite the fact that in 1835, when William had finally settled £400 on Caroline, Baudouin had signed a document agreeing that William's financial obligation was at an end. Annette had died in 1841, aged seventy-five; from what is known of her character, it is unlikely that she would have allowed such grasping behaviour, had she still been alive. Caroline herself was now fifty-eight, and her two daughters were grown up and married. Baudouin, however, threatened to come to England, 'to look after his *interests* if necessary', so Crabb Robinson recorded in his memoirs. He and Quillinan conferred on the best way to deal with him, fearing that money would be the price of his silence, as there were hints that he would publish certain revelations. They took legal advice and sent a long letter in French but nothing more, apparently, was ever heard of the matter.

Caroline herself died in 1862. She was survived by her two daughters, the elder of whom (the one who included Dorothée among her names) married twice, bearing two daughters, who in turn produced seven children. Today there are several direct descendants of Wordsworth, living in France. On the legitimate side, there are many direct descendants of the poet living in England today, including five great-great-grandchildren.

Mary's next problem, after the publication of *The Prelude*, was a biography of William. She knew that he had been against any formal work of this kind, believing that his best biography was his collected poems and that an additional brief memoir would be sufficient for posterity. It had been thought by many friends and relations that Edward Quillinan might write the official biography, and he himself hoped that he would; but in 1847, the year of Dora's death, William and Mary had quietly drawn up an agreement with William's nephew Christopher by which he was to be given permission to write a biography and was to be offered all the help he would need. This happened at a time when Quillinan and William were temporarily estranged. Quillinan knew nothing of the agreement until a week after William's death. Nonetheless, he gave Christopher all the help he could, making available the invaluable notes which Miss Fenwick had made and had given to Dora.

When the two-volume biography was published in 1851 – it appeared in the same year in the United States, edited by Henry Reed – many friends thought it dwelt too much on the conservative and religious side of William's life, glossing over his revolutionary and anti-clerical youth. It was also thought a shame that someone who hardly knew him should have been entrusted with the task. Today, the book is still not considered by some scholars to be very valuable, but it does contain many first-hand explanations of the background to his works mainly based on Miss Fenwick's notes, which are still primary sources. It probably helped to reinforce the general Victorian view of Wordsworth as a stern, god-fearing, humourless figure. It contains almost nothing about Mary. There is indeed a chapter entitled 'Marriage', but it is one of the shortest chapters in the book, only five pages long, and consists almost entirely of quotations from William's poems. Did Mary refuse to provide any details about herself? She was known to be against such a publication, as being contrary to William's wishes, but had allowed it to go ahead, not wanting further family disagreements.

Strangely enough, Dr Christopher Wordsworth, then a Canon of Westminster and later Bishop of Lincoln, wanted to include something of the Annette relationship. He maintained that it was a commonplace rumour and that someone had even mentioned it to him in the street. He did, apparently, include some information about it in his first draft, but Crabb Robinson and Mary, who wished to 'prohibit it absolutely', Crabb Robinson said, persuaded Christopher to omit everything. The only reference, in the published version, was to Wordsworth being 'encompassed with strong temptations' while in France, which Crabb Robinson still worried might give a hint of some sort of immorality. But, as we know, nothing about Annette became public till the 1920s.

The publication of *The Prelude* in 1850 did not turn out to be as important an occasion as Wordsworth might have hoped. The 1830s had been William's greatest decade for sales, critical acceptance and general popularity, but, in the 1840s, Tennyson was quietly coming to the forefront. The publication in 1850 of *In Memoriam* coincided with Wordsworth's death, and was Tennyson's most successful publication so far – and it helped to secure him the Laureateship. For the next three decades, Wordsworth suffered something of a decline, as Tennyson became the great Victorian poet. It wasn't until 1897, when the French scholar, Emile Legouis, produced his study of *The Prelude*, that the importance of the poem was fully realized, though by then, many of Wordsworth's poems were back in critical favour again, thanks mainly to the works of Matthew Arnold. Arnold's careful selection in 1879 of the best of Wordsworth in the 'Golden Treasury' series was a best-seller. At a time of falling creeds and religious doubts, Arnold pointed the way back to Wordsworth – though, at the same time, he was very aware of his faults.

Wordsworth's faults have always been well recognized, from the *Edinburgh Review* onwards. It was Coleridge who observed that a work of art should never be judged by its defects, which is a good basic rule for all critics; but, in a way, Wordsworth's defects are part of his fascination. They have caused him to be more parodied than any other English poet. In his lifetime, Byron, Shelley and Keats all had sport at Wordsworth's expense, and this continued throughout the nineteenth century, with wits and witlings sharpening their baby teeth on him, from Thackeray (whose first published work was a Wordsworth skit) to Lewis Carroll ('I saw an aged, aged man,/A-sitting on a gate').

The best-known satirical poem about Wordsworth, by J. K. Stephen, appeared in *Granta* in 1891 and includes the lines

> There are two Voices; one is of the deep,
> And one is an old half witted sheep
> And Wordsworth, both are thine....

The Two Voices of Wordsworth have been an endless source of study to this day, although it was Hartley Coleridge who first put his finger on the two-sided Wordsworth: 'What a mighty genius is the Poet Wordsworth! What a dull proser is W.W. Esqre of Rydal Mount, Distributor of Stamps.' Tennyson referred rather neatly to Wordsworth's sheep-like verse as his 'thick-ankled' element.

Between the World Wars, with the emergence of T.S. Eliot and a starker, urban, intellectual poetry, most of the Romantic poets suffered a slight eclipse, but today the Romantic movement generally is in favour, as we perhaps try to escape back to nature and the senses, to basic truths and simple pleasures. Wordsworth is probably more studied today in universities round the world than he has ever been, but he has never really been away. In his poetry and in his life, the giant Wordsworth has left more than enough for each of us.

'Wordsworth was nearly the price of me once,' so Philip Larkin, the poet, said in an interview in the *Observer* in December 1979. 'I was driving down the M1 on a Saturday morning; they had this poetry slot on the radio, "Time for Verse". It was a lovely summer morning and someone suddenly started reading the Immortality ode, and I couldn't see for tears. And when you're driving down the middle lane at seventy miles an hour ... I don't suppose I'd read that poem for twenty years. It's amazing how effective it was when I was totally unprepared for it ...'

THE FAMILY TREE OF WILLIAM WORDSWORTH

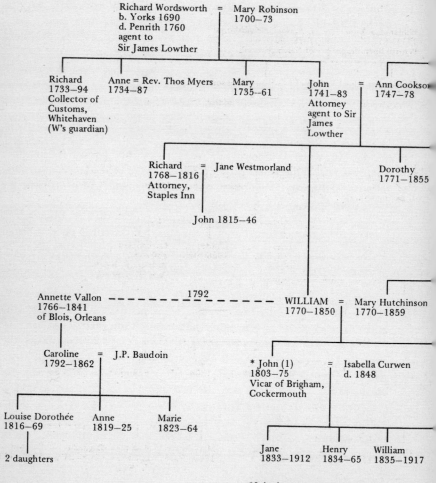

Richard Wordsworth = Mary Robinson
b. Yorks 1690   1700—73
d. Penrith 1760
agent to
Sir James Lowther

Richard   Anne = Rev. Thos Myers   Mary   John = Ann Cookson
1733—94   1734—87   1735—61   1741—83   1747—78
Collector of   Attorney
Customs,   agent to Sir
Whitehaven   James
(W's guardian)   Lowther

Richard = Jane Westmorland   Dorothy
1768—1816   1771—1855
Attorney,
Staples Inn

John 1815—46

Annette Vallon — — — — — — 1792 — — — — — — — WILLIAM = Mary Hutchinson
1766—1841   1770—1850   1770—1859
of Blois, Orleans

Caroline = J.P. Baudoin   * John (1) = Isabella Curwen
1792—1862   1803—75   d. 1848
                                 Vicar of Brigham,
                                 Cockermouth

Louise Dorothée   Anne   Marie
1816—69   1819—25   1823—64

2 daughters   Jane   Henry   William
                                 1833—1912   1834—65   1835—1917

*John later remarried three times:
(2) Helen Ross — d. 1854
(3) Mary Ann Dolan — d. 1866
     daughter Dora 1858—1934
(4) Mary Gamble — d. 1903

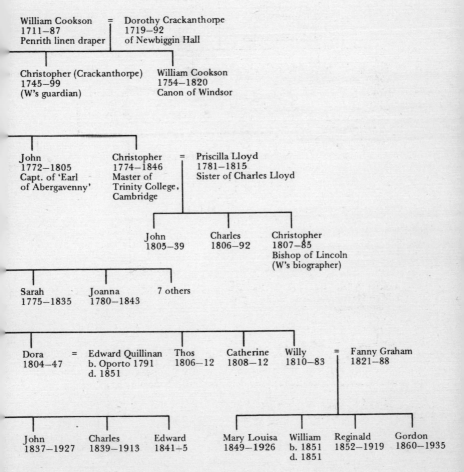

William Cookson
1711—87
Penrith linen draper
=
Dorothy Crackanthorpe
1719—92
of Newbiggin Hall

Christopher (Crackanthorpe)
1745—99
(W's guardian)

William Cookson
1754—1820
Canon of Windsor

John
1772—1805
Capt. of 'Earl
of Abergavenny'

Christopher
1774—1846
Master of
Trinity College,
Cambridge
=
Priscilla Lloyd
1781—1815
Sister of Charles Lloyd

John
1805—39

Charles
1806—92

Christopher
1807—85
Bishop of Lincoln
(W's biographer)

Sarah
1775—1835

Joanna
1780—1843

7 others

Dora
1804—47
=
Edward Quillinan
b. Oporto 1791
d. 1851

Thos
1806—12

Catherine
1808—12

Willy
1810—83
=
Fanny Graham
1821—88

John
1837—1927

Charles
1839—1913

Edward
1841—5

Mary Louisa
1849—1926

William
b. 1851
d. 1851

Reginald
1852—1919

Gordon
1860—1935

APPENDIX

A list of places, associated with William Wordsworth,
which readers might wish to visit

COCKERMOUTH

The house where Wordsworth was born in 1770 is in the main street. It is owned by the National Trust and is open to the public from March to the end of October (telephone: 01900 824805). The house has been recently refurbished and contains some good furniture of the period. Dressing up clothes available for children. Real food gets cooked in a real kitchen. Excellent garden.

PENRITH, 1775–8

The draper's shop in the market square, where Wordsworth lived with his grandparents, is still a shop (Arnison's), but has been substantially rebuilt.

Penrith Beacon, which Wordsworth climbed as a young boy, and wrote about in *The Prelude*, is a hill just outside the town, to the north, and still offers a popular local walk, with excellent views over the Lake District. St Michael's Church, Baron, Pooley Bridge, contains his grandfather's grave.

HAWKSHEAD, 1779–89

Hawkshead Grammar School is closed as a school but open as a museum from Easter to October (telephone: 015394 36675). The desks and books are all laid out, as if the boys had just gone out to play. A good new booklet was published in 2008.

St Michael's Church, described in *The Prelude* as snow-white, has now been unwhitewashed, but still stands graciously on a little hill.

Ann Tyson's cottage, where Wordsworth lodged for some time, is a private dwelling but can be admired from outside. Mrs Tyson's other home, half a mile away at Colthouse, has still not been satisfactorily identified, but is one of two cottages, both owned by the National Trust and privately occupied.

CAMBRIDGE, 1789–91

St John's College contains the Pickersgill portrait of Wordsworth in the Hall.

WEST COUNTRY, 1795–8

Wordsworth rented two homes in this region: Racedown Lodge, near Birdsmoorgate, Crewkerne, Dorset, is now a private home and not open to the public; Alfoxden House, Nether Stowey, Somerset, is now a hotel. Coleridge Cottage, at Nether Stowey, is owned by the National Trust and is open to the public in the summer months, 2 pm–5 pm, closed Mondays, Tuesdays and Wednesdays (telephone: 01278 732662).

DOVE COTTAGE, GRASMERE, 1799–1808

The main pilgrimage centre for tourists and scholars.

The Cottage, closed early January to early February, is preserved as it was in Wordsworth's day, with furniture and relics (telephone: 015394 35544). It is best to go early, in order to avoid the crowds.

The Museum contains the major paintings and personal belongings. It is open to the public and has special exhibitions.

The Jerwood Centre, open by appointment, contains the library and manuscripts, and can be used for research on application to the Curator. Dove Cottage also has a bookshop, tea rooms and a small guest house nearby, How Foot Lodge.

ALLAN BANK, GRASMERE, 1808–11

Once a Wordsworth home, this house is now owned by the National Trust and rented privately.

THE PARSONAGE, GRASMERE, 1811–13

Another Wordsworth home, the Parsonage is now once more inhabited by the Vicar of Grasmere. It is opposite St Oswald's Paris Church, whose wooden rafters, as described in *The Excursion*, are still exposed.

RYDAL MOUNT, NEAR AMBLESIDE, 1813–50

Opened to the public since 1970, this house is still owned by a member of the family (telephone: 015394 33022). Closed in January. Paintings, mementoes, teas, gardens.

KESWICK

Old Windy Browe (telephone: 017687 72254), the house owned by the Calverts and lived in for several months by William and Dorothy Wordsworth in 1794, is under the slopes of Latrigg Fell, just outside Keswick. Now used by the Calvert Trust for the disabled and can only be seen by appointment.

Fitz Park Museum, Keswick (telephone: 017687 73263), contains a collection of Southey, Coleridge and Wordsworth material, plus many other odd delights. Open March–October.

Greta Hall was for forty-three years the home first of Coleridge (1800–3) and then of Southey (1803–43). It was part of Keswick School and is now a family home which offers self-catering accommodation (telephone: 017687 75980).

In the churchyard of Crosthwaite Church, Keswick, is Southey's grave.

NAB COTTAGE, RYDAL WATER

This was the home of De Quincey's wife and the final home of Hartley Coleridge, who died in an upstairs room in 1849. It is now a guest house (telephone: 015394 35311).

BIBLIOGRAPHY

THE following is a list of the main biographical sources which I used. Collections of Wordsworth's poetry and purely critical works devoted to him, of which there are hundreds, are not included. Mention, however, must be made of John O. Hayden's edition of the *Poems* (2 vols, Penguin, 1977), which I found most useful.

By far the most important biographical material on Wordsworth is to be found in the Wordsworth letters. They were first edited by Ernest de Selincourt (6 vols, Oxford University Press, 1935–9).
From 1969, the Clarendon Press have issued new revised editions, as below:

The Letters of William and Dorothy Wordsworth
 I   *The Early Years, 1787–1805*, rev. Chester L. Shaver, 1967
 II *The Middle Years: Part 1, 1806–1811*, rev. Mary Moorman, 1969
 III *The Middle Years: Part 2, 1812–1820*, rev. Mary Moorman and Alan G. Hill, 1970
 IV *The Later Years: Part 1, 1821–1828*, rev. Alan G. Hill, 1978
 V   *The Later Years: Part 2, 1829–1834*, rev. Alan G. Hill, 1980
 VI *The Later Years: Part 3, 1835–1840*, rev. Alan G. Hill, 1981
 VII *The Later Years: Part 4, 1841–1850*, rev. Alan G. Hill, 1983
 VIII *A Supplement of New Letters*, ed. by Alan G. Hill, 1993

The official biography of Wordsworth (by the poet's nephew) is Christopher Wordsworth *Memoirs of William Wordsworth*, 2 vols, London, 1851. The standard modern biography is by Stephen Gill, *William Wordsworth, A Life*, Clarendon Press, 1989. Also of interest is Mary Moorman, *William Wordsworth: A Biography*: vol. 1, *The Early Years, 1770–1803*; vol. 2, *The Later Years, 1803–1850*; Oxford University Press, 1957, 1965.

Wordsworth's own prose: Wordsworth's *Prose Works* are available in the edition by W.J.B. Owen and J.W. Smyser (3 vols, Oxford University Press, 1974), and his *Guide to the Lakes* (1835) in the facsimile of the 1906 edition edited by Ernest de Selincourt (Oxford University Press, 1977). Dorothy Wordsworth's *Journals* have been edited by Mary Moorman (with a reprinted Introduction by Helen Darbishire, Oxford University Press, 1971).

Other Publications

Bateson, F.W., *Wordsworth, A Reinterpretation*, London, Longman, 1954

Beatty, Frederika, *William Wordsworth at Rydal Mount*, London, Dent, 1939

Blanchard, F.M., *Portraits of Wordsworth*, Cornell University Press, 1959

Clutterbuck, Nesta, ed., *William Wordsworth, 1770–1970*, Dove Cottage Trustees, Grasmere, 1970

Coburn, Kathleen, *In Pursuit of Coleridge*, London, Bodley Head, 1977

Coleridge, Samuel Taylor, *Biographica Literaria* (1817), ed. G. Watson, London, Dent, 1975

———, *Notebooks*, ed. Kathleen Coburn, 6 vols, London, Routledge and Kegan Paul, 1957–62

Curtis, Jared, ed., *The Fenwick Notes of William Wordsworth*, Bristol 1993

Darbishire, Helen, *Wordsworth*, London, Longman, 1953

De Quincey, Thomas, *Recollections of the Lake Poets*, ed. David Wright, Penguin, 1970

Fink, Z.S., *The Early Wordsworthian Milieu*, Oxford University Press, 1958

Harper, G.M., *William Wordsworth, his Life, Work and Influence*, 2 vols, 1916

Hood, Edwin Paxton, *William Wordsworth*, London, Cash, 1856

Howe, H.W., rev. Robert Woof, *Greta Hall*, Keswick, 1977

Johnstone, Kenneth R. and Ruoff, Gene W., eds, *The Age of William Wordsworth: Critical Essays on the Romantic Tradition*, Rutgers University Press, 1987

Legouis, Emile, *The Early Life of William Wordsworth*, London, Dent, 1897
William Wordsworth and Annette Vallon, London, Dent, 1922

Maclean, C.M., *Dorothy and William Wordsworth*, Cambridge University Press, 1927

Margoliouth, H.M., *Wordsworth and Coleridge, 1795–1934*, Oxford University Press, 1953

Purkis, John, *A Preface to Wordsworth*, London, Longman, 1970

Raine, Kathleen, *Coleridge*, London, Longman, 1953

Rawnsley, Canon H.D., *Recollections of Wordsworth among the Peasantry of Westmorland* (1882), London, Dillons University Bookshop, 1968

———, *A Reminiscence of Wordsworth's Day*, Cockermouth, 1896

Read, Herbert, *Wordsworth*, London, Cape, 1930

Reed, Mark, *Wordsworth, Chronology of the Early Years, 1770–1799*, Cambridge, Mass., Harvard University Press, 1967

———, *Chronology of the Middle Years, 1800–1815*, Cambridge, Mass., Harvard University Press, 1975

Robertson, Eric, *Wordsworthshire*, London, Chatto and Windus, 1911

Robinson, Henry Crabb, ed. Edith J. Morley, *Correspondence with the Wordsworth Circle*, 2 vols, Edinburgh, 1889

Roe, Nicholas, *Wordsworth and Coleridge: The Radical Years*, Oxford, Clarendon Press, 1988

Schneider, Ben Ross, *Wordsworth's Cambridge Education*, Cambridge University Press, 1957

Simmons, Jack, *Southey*, London, Collins, 1945

Smith, Elsie, *An Estimate of Wordsworth by his Contemporaries*, Oxford University Press, 1932

Thompson, T.W., ed. Robert Woof, *Wordsworth's Hawkshead*, Oxford University Press, 1970

Wheatley, Vera, *The Life and Work of Harriet Martineau*, London, Secker and Warburg, 1957

Woof, Pamela, *Dorothy Wordsworth, Writer*, The Wordsworth Trust, 1994

Woof, Robert, *The Wordsworth Circle*, Dove Cottage Trustees, Grasmere, 1979

Wordsworth, Dorothy, *The Grasmere Journals*, ed. Pamela Woof, Oxford, Clarendon Press, 1991

Wordsworth, Jonathan, Abrams, M.H., Gill, Stephen, *The Cornell Series*, Ithaca, Cornell University Press, 1975

Wordsworth, Jonathan, Jaye, Michael C. and Woof, Robert, *William Wordsworth and the Age of English Romanticism*, Rutgers University Press and the Wordsworth Trust, 1987

Wordsworth, William, *The Prelude* (1799, 1805, 1850), eds Jonathan Wordsworth, M.H. Abrams and Stephen Gill, New York, W.W. Norton & Co., 1979

Wu, Duncan, *Wordsworth's Reading, 1770–1799*, Cambridge University Press, 1996

———, *Wordsworth's Reading, 1800–1815*, Cambridge University Press, 1996

MORE RECENT BOOKS

Barker, Juliet, *William Wordsworth: A Life*, New York, Viking, 2000

Wordsworth: A Life in Letters, New York, Viking, 2002

Gill, Stephen, *William Wordsworth: A Life*, Oxford University Press, 1989

Johnston, Kenneth R., *The Hidden Wordsworth: Poet, Lover, Rebel, Spy*, London, W.W. Norton & Co., 1998

———, *The Hidden Wordsworth*, London, Pimlico, 2000

Jones, Kathleen, *A Passionate Sisterhood: The Sisters, Wives and Daughters of the Lake Poets*, London, Constable, 1997

Sisman, Adam, *The Friendship: Wordsworth and Coleridge*: London, Harper, 2006

Speck, W.A., *Robert Southey: Entire Man of Letters*, London, Yale University Press, 2006

Wilson, Frances, *The Ballad of Dorothy Wordsworth*, London, Faber, 2008

Woof, Robert, *Treasures of the Wordsworth Trust*, The Wordsworth Trust, 2005

INDEX

Note: Wordsworth's writings are indexed under the entry for Wordsworth himself

Abbotsford, 289, 304
Adelaide, Queen, 326
Alfoxden House (Somerset), 113, 348; move to, 89; Hazlitt's first meeting with William at, 91, 106, 163; local suspicions of life at, 94–5, 110, 115; lease not renewed, 95, 110; Dorothy's daily journal begun at, 100, 133; poems written at, 105
Allan Bank (Grasmere), 348; move to, 186, 192, 194–5; Coleridge at, 195, 199–200, 204; deficiencies of, 198, 209; visitors, 200, 204; De Quincey at, 204–5
Ambleside, 136, 324; Coleridge boys at school in, 187, 206, 252, 253; gentry of, 215, 222, 316, 317–18; Wordsworth children at school in, 252–3, 255, 256, 257, 293
'Ancient Mariner, The Rime of the' (Coleridge), 93, 102, 106–7, 123
Applethwaite (near Skiddaw), property at, presented to William by Beaumont, 152, 303
Arabian Nights, The, 9, 58
Arch, John, 102
Arnold, Matthew, 290; restores William to critical favour, 342
Arnold, Dr Thomas, 283–4, 335

Ball, Sir Alexander, 184
Bateson, F. W., and theory of incest between William and Dorothy, 138
Bath, Dora's marriage in, 309, 316
Baudouin, Caroline – *see* Vallon, Caroline
Baudouin, Eustace, 269
Baudouin, Jean Baptiste: marriage to Caroline Vallon, 269–72; claim to share of William's estate, 340–1
Baudouin, Louise Marie Caroline Dorothée, 272, 341
Beaumont, Sir George, 173, 180, 185, 217, 218, 290, 296; as amateur artist, 152, 179, 216, 276, 303; founder of National Gallery, 152, 303; patronage of William, 152, 165, 171,

179, 303, 304; William's letters to, 171, 174–5, 186, 187; death, 303
Beaumont, Lady: Dorothy's letters to, 166, 167, 168, 180; godmother to Dora, 166; William's letters to, 191, 290
Beaupuy, Captain, and Revolutionary influence on William, 52–3
Beethoven, Ludwig van, 164
Belgium, 47, 285, 286, 287
Bell, Dr Andrew, 197
Biographia Literaria (Coleridge), 209, 277
Birkett, Ann, 12, 142
Blackwood's Magazine, 278
Blois, Annette's home in, 53–4, 140, 142
Boswell, James, 75
Bowles, Caroline, 266; as Southey's second wife, 311
Bremen, Willy in, 294, 301
Brighton, 51
Bristol, 86; Pantisocratic group in, 77–8, 81, 82–4
British Critic: on *Lyrical Ballads*, 123, 124; on 'Peter Bell', 276
Brompton (Yorks), William and Mary married at, 145–6
Brontë, Charlotte, Southey's advice to, 266
Brougham, Henry, 125, 279; and 1818 election, 232–6
Browning, Elizabeth Barrett, 327, 328
Brussels, 287
Brydges, Sir Egerton, 284
Burke, Edmund, 225
Burns, Robert, 25, 156, 157; William's defence of, 243, 277
Bute, John Stuart, third Earl of, 7
Buttermere, 182
Byron, Lord, 243, 262; on Preface to *Lyrical Ballads*, 126; attack on 1807 *Poems*, 189–90; William's hatred of, 238; praises Southey's prose, 263; literary row with Southey, 267; satire on 'Peter Bell', 275; influenced by William, 277; compared with William, 280; death, 325

Calais, meeting of William and Dorothy with Annette in, 140, 141–2

Calvert, Raisley, 68, 69, 91; William as companion to, 71–3; death, 73, 258; legacy to William, 73, 75, 95, 171

Calvert, William, West Country tour with, 68–9

Cambridge: William at St John's, 26, 28–35, 38–40, 42–4, 48, 50–51, 316; his disillusion with, 31–5, 43, 45, 51; academic life, 31–3; social life, 33–5, 36; William's portrait commissioned by St John's, 312, 348

Canning, George, 197, 283, 292, 294

Carlisle, 289; Hatfield trial at, 155–6; Willy at, 302, 332

Carlyle, Thomas, 63; on William's eyeshade, 319; poor account of Mary, 338

Carroll, Lewis, 343

Carter, John, 219, 256

Cartmel, 30

Castlerigg Stone Circles, 112

Charlotte, Queen, 66; buys copy of *Lyrical Ballads*, 127

Charterhouse, Willy at, 257, 293

Chester, John, 98, 159

Childe Harold (Byron), 277

'Christabel' (Coleridge), 93, 123, 161

Christian, Edward, 30, 49, 86

Christian, Fletcher, 10, 30; William's letter in defence of, 86

Christ's Entry into Jerusalem (Haydon), 327

Cintra, Convention of (1808), 196–7

Clarkson, Catherine, 112; Dorothy's letters to, 153, 165, 167, 270, 271, 295

Clarkson, Thomas, 112, 222, 235, 336

Cocker, River, 5–6

Cockermouth, 5–6; birthplace, 5, 6, 7, 71, 347; childhood in, 9–11, 14, 21; grammar school, 10; William revisits, 334

Coleorton (Leics), 185–6, 292

Coleridge, Berkeley, 107

Coleridge, Derwent, 120, 202, 333; and parents' separation, 185, 187; at school in Ambleside, 187, 206, 253; at Allan Bank, 195; Southey's support of, 263

Coleridge, Hartley, 88, 89, 117, 135, 202; precocity, 154, 254, 263, 332–3; and parents' separation, 185, 187; at school in Ambleside, 187, 206, 253; at Allan Bank, 195, 200; teaches Willy, 257; Southey's support of, 263; on Dora's devotion to William, 293; death, 332, 333, 349; on two-sided William, 343

Coleridge, Henry Nelson, 310

Coleridge, Samuel Taylor, 33, 34, 125, 133, 151, 192, 238, 243, 342; and Pantisocracy, 78, 79, 80–82, 84, 261; early life, 78–9; meets Southey, 79, 80; differences with him, 82, 84; lectures, 82–3; meets William, 83; ends friendship with Southey, 84, 261; marriage to Sara Fricker, 84; begins correspondence with William, 85, 87–8; first meeting with Dorothy and William, 88; importance to William, 88, 91, 94, 122, 131–2, 208–9; contacts with Southey as brother-in-law, 88; increasing intimacy with Dorothy and William, 89–96, 110; worship of William's genius, 90, 91, 92, 106, 122, 128, 277; character, 90–91, 92, 131, 208; rejection of play, 92; concentration on poetry, 93–4, 96; drug-addiction, 93, 119, 159, 185, 199, 200, 201; obtains annuity, 95–6, 185; publication of *Lyrical Ballads*, 96, 101–2, 106–7; in Germany, 96, 98–9, 100, 107; *Prelude* addressed to, 101, 165, 340; and 'Idiot Boy', 105; tour of Lakes with William, 108, 111–12, 116; rents Greta Hall, 117–18; shared life with William and Dorothy, 118–22; passion for Sarah Hutchinson, 119, 120, 149, 158, 187, 200, 302; health problems, 119–20, 150, 154, 158; fell-walking, 120; collapse of marriage, 120–1; journalism, 121–2; renewed friendship with Southey, 122, 262; helps William with new edition of *Lyrical Ballads*, 122, 123, 125–6, 127; grouped with William and Southey as Lake Poets, 129, 189; William's light-hearted letter to, 135; affection for Dorothy, 137; and William's marriage, 149–50; strange dream, 149–50; jealousy of William's domestic happiness, 150, 166, 173, 182, 207; godfather to John Wordsworth, 152; methods of child care, 153–4; Scottish tour with William and Dorothy, 154, 249; depression and self-pity, 156, 158, 171, 199–201; continues tour alone, 158–60; tensions between William and, 159, 161; portrait painted by Hazlitt, 163; leaves Lakes for Malta, 165; lack of news from, 166, 167, 171, 184; uncertainty over future plans, 167, 171, 173; on death of William's brother John, 170; usually addressed by surname, 180; in Malta, 184; return to England, 184–5; poor health and changed looks, 185, 207; separation from wife, 185, 186, 187; winter on Beaumont estate, 185–6; move to Allan Bank, 186–8, 192, 195, 198, 204; illness in London, 187, 198; produces *Friend* magazine, 195–6, 199; on William's Cintra pamphlet, 196; causes unhappy atmosphere, 199–200; given home by Montagu, 201, 205; gift from De Quincey, 202; grievances and slanders against William, 205–7; so-called reconciliation, 207, 209; contrasted with

William, 207–9; and deaths of Wordsworth children, 211, 212; disappointed in *Excursion*, 240; affectionate letters to wife, 249; castigation of her, 264–5; and Keats's skit on 'Peter Bell', 275; his part in changing public attitude to William, 277; Hazlitt's praise of, 278; tour of Belgium and Rhineland with William, 287, 293, 304; on Sarah Hutchinson, 302; death, 304

Coleridge, Sara (wife) (formerly Fricker), 81, 82, 83, 88, 96, 152, 195, 202, 262, 266; marriage, 84; at Nether Stowey, 88, 89; Coleridge's neglect of, 89, 92, 98, 119, 121; at Greta Hall, 117, 120; Dorothy's antipathy to, 120, 150, 154, 200, 265; collapse of marriage, 121–2; separation, 185, 186, 187; at Allan Bank, 195, 198, 200; and Coleridge's grievance against William, 206; Coleridge's castigation of, 264–5; blossoming after separation, 265

Coleridge, Sara (daughter), 120, 153, 195, 198, 202, 265, 331, 336; and parents' separation, 185; at Allan Bank, 200; Southey's support of, 263; marriage to cousin Henry, 310; on Miss Fenwick, 316–17

Colthouse, Ann Tyson's house in, 21, 24

Como, Lake, 138

Cookson, Ann – *see* Wordsworth, Ann

Cookson, Christopher – *see* Crackenthorpe, Christopher

Cookson, Dorothy (grandmother), 9, 12, 13–14, 17, 26, 70

Cookson, Mary (cousin), 66

Cookson, William (grandfather), 9, 12, 13–14, 26

Cookson, Rev. William (uncle), 9, 31, 32, 68, 180; help and advice to William, 28–9, 40; disappointed in William, 39, 40, 66, 75; marriage, 40; gives Dorothy a home, 40, 66, 70, 75; reaction to news of Annette, 63; as Dean of Windsor, 66, 179; changed attitude to William, 179

Cooper, Thomas, 324

Cottle, Joseph, 86, 87, 91, 108; arranges lectures by Coleridge and Southey, 82–3; publishes *Lyrical Ballads*, 96, 101–2, 107; ceases publishing, 102, 122, 298

Courier, 196, 198

Cowper, William, 33

Crackenthorpe family, 9

Crackenthorpe (formerly Cookson), Christopher (uncle), 9, 13; dislike of William, 13, 23, 26, 28; as guardian, 22, 25, 39, 62–3, 68, 70; death, 145

Crackenthorpe, Mrs Christopher (aunt), Dorothy's letter to, 70–71

Crackenthorpe, William (cousin), 235

Critical Review, attack on *Poems in Two Volumes*, 190, 191

Crosthwaite Church, Southey's grave at, 349

Crump, Mr (Liverpool attorney), builder of Allan Bank, 172, 194

Cumberland Pacquet, 22

Curse of Kehama, The (Southey), 262, 267

Curwen family, 37, 38, 307

Dalton, John, 11

Danton, George Jacques, 54

Darlington, Beth, 249

Davy, Sir Humphry, 92, 173, 264, 306; sees new *Lyrical Ballads* through press, 123, 133; visits Lakes, 167

Dawson, Mary, 248

De Quincey, Margaret, 224, 349

De Quincey, Thomas, 210, 336; impressed by Dorothy, 137, 303; fan letter to William after reading *Lyrical Ballads*, 201–2; introduction and aid to Coleridge, 202; momentous meeting with William, 202–3; takes over Dove Cottage, 203; on William's attitude to women, 203–4; devotion to Wordsworth children, 203, 204–5, 211, 223; his comparison of William and Coleridge, 208; ill-feeling between Wordsworths and, 223–4; break in friendship, 224–6; liaison and marriage, 224; renewed friendship with William, 226, 236; edits *Westmorland Gazette*, 236–7; on William's 'animal passions', 250; description of Southey, 265; on William's achievement of fame, 279; on Dorothy's strong emotions, 303; on Mary's kindness, 335

'Dejection: an Ode' (Coleridge), 149

Derwent, River, 5, 6

Derwentwater, 111, 117

Devonshire, fifth Duke of, 197

Devonshire, Georgiana, Duchess of, 127

Dixon, James, 325, 326

Don Juan (Byron), 267

Dove Cottage (Grasmere), 321, 348; first seen by William, 108; move to, 112–13; life at, 113–22, 128, 135; garden hut, 114, 174; neighbours, 115; visitors, 116–20, 135, 145, 149, 150, 163–4, 167, 202–3, 208; William and Mary's return to, with Dorothy, after marriage, 146, 148, 150; domestic routine, 150–1; overcrowding, 166, 167, 177; move from, 186, 192; taken over by De Quincey, 203, 204, 223, 226, 237

Duddon valley, 166, 278, 299, 328

Dumfries, 156

Durham, University of, honorary degree for William, 312, 316

'Eagle, The' (Tennyson), 327
Earl of Abergavenny (ship), 41; John Wordsworth as captain of, 116, 168–9; sinking of, 169, 170
Easedale, 114, 306, 336
Eclectic Review, 240, 274, 276
Edinburgh, 160, 289
Edinburgh Review, 232, 243, 262, 276; ignores *Lyrical Ballads*, 125, 128; originates 'Lake Poets' term, 129; attack on *Poems in Two Volumes*, 190–1; attack on *Excursion*, 239, 241, 242; on *White Doe of Rylstone*, 240; on *Ecclesiastical Sonnets*, 279
Edridge, Henry, his portrait of William, 179
Ennerdale, 108
'Eroica' Symphony (Beethoven), 164
Esthwaite Water, 19, 20, 35
Evans, Mary, 78, 82
Examiner, 275; Hazlitt's review of *Excursion* in, 239

Fenwick, Isabella, 334, 335; joins Wordsworth circle, 315–17; defends Quillinan, 316, 330; her notes on William's memories of background to poems, 317, 341; and birthday festivities, 321
Fisher, Molly, 115, 135, 151
Flagellant, 79
Fleming, Lady Diana, 214–15
Fleming, Lady Diana the younger, 214, 215, 294–5
Fletcher, Miss (Rydal neighbour), 323, 328
Fox, Charles James, 141; William's obsequious letter to, 127; William's meeting with, 178
Fox, Mrs Charles James, 178
France: 1790 trip to, 40, 42, 45–8; 1791–2 stay in, 51–5, 100, 111; possible trip in 1793, 67, 69; 1802 visit, 139–42; 1820 visit, 272, 285–6
French Revolution, 43, 45, 48, 50, 52–5, 79, 140–1, 164, 173–4, 229–30, 232, 287
Fricker, Edith – *see* Southey, Edith
Fricker, Eliza, 264
Fricker, Martha, 264
Fricker, Sara – *see* Coleridge, Sara
Friend, The, Coleridge's weekly paper, 195, 199–200, 201, 206
'Frost at Midnight' (Coleridge), 93

George III, 66
Germany, 1798–9 trip to, 96, 98–101, 107, 110, 159
Gillbanks, Rev. Joseph, 10, 11
Gillman, Dr James, 287, 304
Gilpin, William, 37, 98, 112
Gladstone, William Ewart, 322, 327

Glasgow, 156
Godwin, Mary Wollstonecraft, 74
Godwin, William, 92, 103, 179; influence on William, 74
Goslar, 99–101
Grantham, 'abandoned women' in, 29
Grasmere, 41, 70, 114, 151; move to Dove Cottage in, 108, 110, 112,–13; local life, 115, 215; changes in, 172, 194; plans to leave, 172, 177; move to new house (Allan Bank) in, 186, 192, 194–5; move to Parsonage, 209–10, 349; deaths of Catherine and Thomas at, 210–12; final move from, 212, 214, 215; Wordsworth Museum, 290, 348; Coleridge and Wordsworth graves at, 333. *See also* Allan Bank; Dove Cottage
Grasmere Lake, 114, 182, 203
Grattan, Thomas, on William's 'unrefined' appearance, 287
Gray, Thomas, 32, 33, 38, 47
Great Malvern, 337
Green family, appeal for, 197–8
Green, Sally, 197, 210
Greta Hall (Keswick), 349; Coleridge at, 117, 120, 122, 148, 149, 150, 161, 167–8, 200; Southey at, 122, 161, 167–8, 261, 263–6, 310–12, 315; Hazlitt hidden at, 163
Gretna Green, 156
Guide to the Lake District (Gilpin), 98, 112

Halifax: Dorothy's childhood in, 14, 23, 24; her secret meeting with William in, 68, 69–70
Hamburg, 99, 159
Hampton Court, 286
Hanway, Joseph, 36
Harper, G. M., 55
Hatfield, John, 155–6, 172
Hawkshead, 16–17, 111; Tyson house and shop in, 16, 17, 21, 35, 348; schooldays in, 17–21, 22, 23–4, 26, 27, 30, 230; grammar school, 18–19, 29, 252, 348; summer vacations in, 35–8, 43; social life, 36–8
Haydon, Benjamin, 220; close friendship with William, 221, 327–8; paintings of William, 327; suicide, 328
Hazlitt, William, 91, 97, 125, 280; first impression of William, 92, 105–6; on *Lyrical Ballads*, 106; enchanted by Dorothy, 137; at Dove Cottage after Keswick escapade, 163–4; condemns *Excursion*, 239; admits William's genius, 277–8; his 'candle' story about William, 281–2
Helvellyn, 108, 114, 118, 167, 327
Hogg, James, William's poem written on death of, 304–5, 314

Holland, Elizabeth Vassall Fox, Lady, 178; back-handed compliment to William, 195; donation to Green appeal, 197

Hood, Edwin Paxton, 325

'Hope, Hon. Augustus' (John Hatfield), 155-6

Howley, William, Archbishop of Canterbury, 327

Hunt, Leigh, 220; on William's poetic genius, 277

Hutchinson family, 143-4

Hutchinson, George, 144, 168

Hutchinson, Henry, 144

Hutchinson, Joanna, 120, 144, 154, 295

Hutchinson, John, 144, 181

Hutchinson, Margaret, 101, 144

Hutchinson, Mary – *see* Wordsworth, Mary

Hutchinson, Sarah, 117, 118, 132, 141, 144, 146, 185, 215, 220, 221, 241, 242; Coleridge's passion for, 119, 120, 149, 158, 185, 186, 187, 200; devotion to William, 149, 186; at Dove Cottage, 150, 151, 154, 166, 173, 195; possibility of marriage to John Wordsworth, 170, 302; helps Coleridge on his magazine, 186, 187, 196, 199; at Allan Bank, 196; leaves Allan Bank, 199; and Catherine's death, 210-11; in Scotland and Wales, 246; on William's spoiling of Willy, 257; as universal aunt to Wordsworths and Southeys, 264, 265, 295, 302; on 'tourist attraction' of William, 280; death, 302, 303; grave, 333

Hutchinson, Tom, 144, 199, 210, 211; godfather to Tom Wordsworth, 181

In Memoriam (Tennyson), 342

Industrial Revolution, 230

Ireland, 1829 visit to, 288-9

Isola (Italian teacher), 38

Italy, 1837 trip to, 307, 320, 328

James (family servant), 12, 17

Jeffrey, Francis (later Lord), 125; attack on 1807 *Poems*, 190; review of *Excursion* ('This will never do'), 239, 241, 242; claim to be admirer of William, 279

Jerdan, William, 285

Joan of Arc (Southey), 80, 83, 87, 102, 262

Johnson, Joseph, 61, 65

Johnson, Samuel, 121

Jones, John Paul, 11

Jones, Robert, 69, 286; accompanies William on first trip to France, 46-7, 51, 159, 285; in North Wales with William, 49

Journal of a Few Months Residence in Portugal and Glimpses of the South of Spain (Dora Wordsworth), 331

Keats, John, 262, 327, 335; first meeting with William, 220, 221; disappointed in him, 221, 222, 288; parodies 'Peter Bell', 274, 275; considers William a genius, 277; death, 325

Keble, John, 291

Keepsake, 281

Kendal, 185; 1818 election, 234-6

Kendal Chronicle, 230, 234, 275

Kendal and Windermere railway, projected, 322-3, 329

Keswick, 70, 114, 128, 152, 266, 268, 349; William's nursing of R, Calvert at, 72-4; Southey's grave, 349. *See also* Greta Hall

Kingston, Mr (Comptroller of Stamps), 220, 221

Kirkby Lonsdale, 219

'Kubla Khan' (Coleridge), 93

Lamb, Charles, 82, 89, 117, 179, 262, 296; ridicules William's shoes, 91; on *Lyrical Ballads*, 124-5, 132; possible author of teasing paragraph on William's wedding. 149; clears up doubts over John Wordsworth's death, 170; on 'sad Josephs', 198; and Coleridge's grievance against William, 206, 207; tipsy teasing of William, 221; on *Excursion*, 240; death, 304

Landor, Walter Savage, 80

Lausanne, 286

Lay of the Last Minstrel (Scott), 160, 161, 178, 180, 191

Lectures on the English Poets (Hazlitt), 277-8

Legouis, Emile, 55, 271, 342

Liverpool, Robert Banks Jenkinson, second Earl of, 218

Lloyd, Charles, 91, 117, 225, 241, 247, 258; 'candle' story about William, 282

Lloyd, Priscilla, 112; engaged to Christopher Wordsworth, 117; marriage and death, 258

Lockhart, John Gibson, 283

Lomond, Loch, 157, 158, 182, 328

London: 1791 stay in, 48-9; ambivalent attitude to, 60-61; as 1793-5 base, 63, 64-5, 74; brief 1802 visit *en route* to France, 139, 140, 147, 171; 1806 visit, 177-80; frequent later visits, 178, 187, 192, 198, 220-1, 250, 285, 286-7, 301, 326-7, 332; visionary experience in, 187

London Magazine, 281

Longmans, 102, 179, 201, 319; publish new *Lyrical Ballads*, 123, 128; publish *Excursion*, 241; William's dissatisfaction with, 297

Lonsdale, James Lowther, first Earl of, 6, 7, 8, 71; debts owed to Wordsworth family, 22, 26, 49-50, 145; death, 140

Lonsdale, James Hugh William Lowther, seventh Earl of, 228

Lonsdale, William Lowther, first Earl of second creation, 195, 237; pays off family debts, 140, 182, 216; as benefactor to William, 182–3, 197, 217–18, 220, 233, 282, 292, 294; William's obsequious letters to, 183, 217; and 1818 election, 232, 233, 235, 236; *Excursion* dedicated to, 237; helps Southey, 268; helps William's son John, 292, 301

Losh, James, 96

Loughrigg Holme, 332

Louis XVI, 54, 64

Lovell, Robert, 81

Lovell, Mrs Lovell, 264

Lowther family, 7–8, 37; legal action against, 22, 30, 48, 49–50, 51, 145; William's hatred of, 50, 217; settlement of action, 151, 182, 216; William's changed attitude to, and anxiety to serve, 217, 228, 232–6, 281, 282; and 1818 election, 232–6

Lowther, Colonel Henry, in 1818 election, 233, 234–6

Lowther, Sir James – *see* Lonsdale, James Lowther, first Earl of

Lowther, Sir John, 7

Lowther, William, Lord (later second Earl of Lonsdale), in 1818 election, 233, 234–6

Malta, Coleridge in, 165, 170, 184

Marat, Jean Paul, 54

Marie Antoinette, 64

Marshall (formerly Pollard, q.v.), Jane, Dorothy's letters to, 114, 133, 145

Martineau, Harriet, 334; on William's friendship with Miss Fenwick, 316; her own move to Lakes and friendship with William, 317–19, 326; on William's delight in children, 321

Matthews, William, 83, 87

Melrose, 160

Menai Bridge, 286

Mingay, Mr (Hawkshead dancing master), 23

Mont Blanc, 47

Montagu, Basil, 74–5, 154; promise to pay William annuity, 75; defaults, 87, 95, 152; provides London home for Coleridge, 200–201; repeats William's criticisms to Coleridge, 205, 206, 207; pays off debt to William, 216; given lock of his hair, 325

Montagu, Mrs Basil, 335

Montagu, Basil jr, 75, 86, 87, 246

Monthly Literary, Byron's attack on 1807 *Poems*, 189–90

Monthly Review, 124; on first published verse, 62; on *White Doe*, 240; on 'Peter Bell', 276

Moore, Thomas, 277, 287

Moorman, Mary, 21

Moresby (Cumberland), John Wordsworth's living at, 307

Morning Post, 107, 178; Coleridge's work for, 121, 184; teasing notice of William's wedding, 148–9

Moxon, Edward, 319, 322, 340

Mull, Isle of, 289

Murray, John, 297

Myers, John (cousin), 28

Nab Cottage (Rydal Water), 224, 333, 349

Nab Scar, 114

Napoleon, 141, 164, 184, 269, 270

Nelson, Horatio, Southey's *Life* of, 263, 312

Nether Stowey, 88, 89, 95, 348

Newbiggen Hall (Cumberland), 9

Newcastle Journal, 305

Newton, Sir Isaac, 32

Orleans, 140; 1791–2 visit to, 51–4; liaison with Annette in, 53–4

Owen, Robert, 231

Oxenholme, 337

Oxford: son John at New College, 291–2; honorary degree for William, 312

Paine, Tom, 64

Pantisocracy, 77–8, 81–2, 84, 89

Paris, 52, 54–5, 56; supposed secret 1793 visit to, 63; Southey meets Annette and Caroline in, 269; Caroline's wedding in, 271; meeting between William, Mary and Annette in, 272; last meeting with Caroline in, 307

Patterdale, 167, 181, 182, 304

Peel, Sir Robert, 302, 310, 313

Peel Castle, 179

Penrith, 7, 11–12, 26, 39, 41, 72; Cookson home in, 9, 11, 12, 13, 347; William's life with grandparents in, 11, 12–14, 21; dame school, 12, 142; Dorothy's return to, 24–5, 28, 40; Hutchinson home in, 143

Penrith Beacon, 12, 347

Pickersgill, Henry William, portrait of William, 312, 348

Pinney brothers, 75, 86

Pitt, William, 7, 31, 80

Pocklington, Colonel, 111

Pollard (later Marshall, q.v.), Jane, Dorothy's letters to, 41, 49, 66, 67–8

Poole, Thomas, 89, 95, 141; on Coleridge and Southey, 81; help for Coleridge, 91; disapproves of his journalism, 122; William's letters to, 199, 247

Potter, Beatrix, 21

Pye, Henry James, 220

Quarterly Review, 262

Quillinan, Edward, 304, 318, 328, 336, 341; unfavourable first meeting with William, 284; later friendship, 284, 286, 308; correspondence with family, 293, 294; marriage to Dora, 308–10, 316; row with William, 309, 316; financial insecurity, 330; wanderings, 330–1; and Dora's death, 332, 333; help in biography of William, 341

Quillinan, Rotha, 284

Racedown Lodge (Dorset), 348; William and Dorothy's first home together, 75, 85–8, 89; visitors, 87, 88, 145, 320; first meeting of Coleridge with William and Dorothy, 88

Radnor, William Pleydell-Bouverie, third Earl of, 268

Ratzeburg, 99

Rawnsley, Canon H. D., 321, 322, 333

Ray, Martha, 75

Recollections of the Lake Poets (De Quincey), 202–3, 204, 210, 225, 226, 265

Reed, Henry Hope, 336, 341; William's letters to, 321, 323, 327, 334

Reform Act (1832), 306, 323, 324

Reminiscences of Wordsworth among the Peasantry of Westmorland (Rawnsley), 321–2

Reynolds, John Hamilton, 274, 275

Rights of Man, The (Paine), 64

Robespierre, Maximilien Marie Isidore, 54, 55

Robinson, Henry Crabb, 207, 224, 238, 276, 279, 287, 322, 337, 341; close friendship with William, 221–2, 334; in Lake Poets circle, 262, 264; told of Annette, 269; at William's meeting with Annette and Caroline, 272; fury at Hazlitt's criticism of William, 277; Dorothy's letter to, 301; Italian tour with William, 307, 320, 328, 355; William's letters to, 312, 316; Christmases at Rydal, 334; and biography of William, 342

Robinson, Mary, 155, 156

Rogers, Samuel, 326; William's letters to, 238, 239, 297; negotiates between William and Murray, 297

Rousseau, Jean Jacques, 43

Rydal Mount, 349; move to, 214–16; furnishing of, 215–16, 219; as tourist attraction, 280, 295, 326; visitors and neighbours, 283–5, 315–19, 324, 326, 334, 336–7; settled life at, 294–6, 336; Dora's field, 295; illness at, 302; Dora's honeymoon at, 310; seventy-fourth birthday party at, 321; only royal visitor to, 326; shower bath for Dora's use, 331; Dora's death at, 332; Christmasses at, 334; William's death at, 338

Rydal Water, 112, 114, 182, 296

Salisbury Plain, 69

Sandwich, John Montagu, fourth Earl of, 74

Sandys, Edwin, Archbishop of York, 18

Scafell Pike, Coleridge's ascent of, as first recorded climb, 120

Scotland: 1803 tour, 154–62; 1831 tour, 289, 304

Scott, Sir Walter, 170, 173, 180, 181, 195, 264, 289, 293, 315; shows William the Border country, 160–1; visits Lakes, 161, 167, 283; popularity of, 178, 239, 279, 287; concern over William's new school of poetry, 188; donation to Green appeal, 188; refuses Laureateship, 220; his poetry deprecated by William, 238–9; bust displayed by William, 281; at Hampton Court, 286–7; bankruptcy, 298, 304; last meeting with William, 304; death, 304

Scrambler, Mr (Grasmere doctor), 210, 255

Sedbergh School, son John at, 254, 257, 291

Selincourt, Ernest de, 21, 133

Shelley, Mary Wollstonecraft, 74

Shelley, Percy Bysshe, 138, 262; visits Southey, 266–7; skit on 'Peter Bell', 275; acknowledges William as 'great poet', 277; death, 325

Sheridan, Richard Brinsley, 92

Shrewsbury, 105

Silver Howe, 114, 194

Simplon Pass, 47

Skiddaw, 6, 122, 152; Waterloo celebration on, 265–6

Smith, Adam, 77

Smith, Charlotte, 151

Smith, Sydney, 125, 319

Sockbridge (Cumberland), Wordsworth family estate, 7, 8

Sockburn on Tees, 107, 144

Southey, Mrs (mother of Robert), 80, 82

Southey, Cuthbert, 264

Southey (formerly Fricker), Edith, 81, 83, 88, 262, 264, 265, 310; marriage, 84; mental decline and death, 311

Southey, Herbert, 263–4

Southey, Isabel, 310, 311

Southey, Kate, 311, 312, 315

Southey, Robert, 101, 117, 119, 156, 163, 179, 198, 225, 238, 239, 279, 315; and Pantisocracy, 78, 79, 80–82, 84, 267; early life and radicalism, 79–80, 267–8; friendship with Coleridge, 79, 80–84; differences with him, 82, 83, 84; lectures, 82–3; meets William, 83; marriage to Edith Fricker, 84; William's unfavourable impression of, 87; occasional contacts with Coleridge, 88; Dorothy's poor opinion of, 93; reviews *Lyrical Ballads*

Southey, Robert—*contd.*
unfavourably, 102, 123, 261; renewed friendship with Coleridge, 122; move to Lakes, 122, 124, 262; at Greta Hall, 167–8, 261, 263, 266, 295; revised opinion of *Lyrical Ballads*, 124; as one of Lake Poets, 129, 188, 189, 220, 243; William more favourable to, 161; revulsion against France under Napoleon, 164, 173, 268; on Lakes tour with Scott, 167; comforts William on brother John's death, 170; bitter comment on William's social success, 178; on choice of name for second Wordsworth son, 180; on reviewers, 191; William's letter to, on Tom Wordsworth's death, 211–12; as Poet Laureate, 219–20, 261, 278, 312; visits Owen's factory, 231; hurt by attacks on *Excursion*, 242–3; closer relations with William, 261, 265, 269; reputation as poet, 262, 274; other literary activities, 262–3; his household, 263–4; his 'three wives', 264–5; De Quincey's description of, 265; celebration of Waterloo, 265–6; visitors and correspondence, 266–7; row with Byron, 267; high-Toryism, 267, 268; embarrassed by publication of early republican play, 267–8; meets Annette and Caroline, 269; 'Peter Bell' dedicated to, 276; Hazlitt's praise of, 278; bust displayed by William, 281; declines baronetcy, 310; mental decline and death of wife, 311; re-marriage, 311; his own mental decline and death, 311–12; on William's dormant sense of smell, 320; grave, 349
Spedding family, 69, 70
Spedding, John, 37
Spedding Mary, 37
Stafford, Marchioness of, 178
Stair, ninth Earl of, 19
Stephen, J. K., 343
Stuart, Daniel, 234, 271; as *Morning Post* editor, 121, 149, 196; and teasing paragraph on William's marriage, 149; William's letter to, 218
Swinburne, Algernon, 336

Taylor, Henry, 288
Taylor, William (Hawkshead headmaster), 30
Tennyson, Alfred, Lord, 326; William's praise of, 327; rise to fame, 342; on William's 'thick-ankled' element, 343
Thackeray, William Makepeace, 343; at Cambridge, 32, 34
Thalaba (Southey), 128
Thelwall, John, 94, 95
'Three Bears, The' (Southey), 312
Times, The, 262, 275

Tintern Abbey, 69, 83, 106, 109
Trevelyan, G. M., 29
Tyler, Miss (Southey's aunt), 79, 84
Tyler, Wat, Southey's dramatic poem about, 81, 267–8
Tyson, Ann, 16; William boarded with while at school, 17, 19, 21; as mother figure, 17–18; identification of her cottage, 21, 348; fits William out for Cambridge, 29; William's summer vacations with, 35–6; shuts up shop, 45
Tyson, Hugh, 16, 17, 19, 21

Ullswater, 20, 112, 114, 134, 157, 181; purchase of property on, 182–3

Vallon, Annette, 132, 137; William's affair with, 53–9, 61, 65, 67, 137, 174; birth of Caroline, 54; William's plan to marry, 55, 58; her letters, 55–7, 140, 141, 250; secrecy over, 55, 204, 250, 269, 342; William's uncles told of, 62–3, 68; William's disentanglement from, 139–42; later contact with, 269–70; visited by Southey, 269; marriage of Caroline, 271; first meeting with Mary, 272; death, 340
Vallon (later Baudouin), Caroline, 56, 57, 63, 142; birth, 54; christening, 141; William's sonnet to, 141, 273; reveals story to Southey, 269; engagement and marriage, 269–71; William's annual payments to, 271; his final settlement on, 272, 340; children, 272; meeting with William, 272; last meeting with him, 307; death, 341; descendants, 341
Vallon, Paul, 141
Victoria, Queen, William presented to, 326–7

Wadsworth (Yorks), 7
Walsh, G. (Home Office secret agent), 94–5
Walter, John, 263
Waterloo, Battle of (1815), 265, 270
Watson, Richard, Bishop of Llandaff, 32; William's invective adressed to, 64–5; William's changed attitude to, 222
Wedgwood, Josiah, 95, 96, 98
Wedgwood, Tom, 95, 96, 98
Weekly Entertainer, William's only signed letter to newspaper in, 86
Weeks, Shadrach, 82
West, Thomas, 37
Westminster School, 79
Westmorland, 1818 election in, 232–6
Westmorland Gazette, 234; De Quincey as editor of, 236–7
Whitehaven, 8, 9, 69, 70; Paul Jones raid on, 11

Whitwick (Leics), John Wordsworth's curacy at, 292, 300–301

Wight, Isle of, 56, 88

Wilberforce, Barbara, 283

Wilberforce, William, 31–2, 66, 127; impressed by Dorothy's class for poor children, 41; at Rydal Mount, 283

Wilkinson, Rev. Joseph, 289

William Wordsworth and Annette Vallon (Legouis), 271

Williams, Helen Maria, 51–2

Wilson, John: fan letter to William, 128, 201; move to Lakes, 201; godfather to Willy, 205; leaves Lakes, 224, 226; helped by William despite offending him, 283

Windermere, 20, 35, 37, 38, 111, 136, 323

Windsor, 66, 179

Windy Browe (Calvert farm), 69, 70–71, 349

Wordsworth, Ann (mother), 6, 9, 11; character, 10; illness and death, 13, 14

Wordsworth, Catherine (daughter), 254; birth, 195; De Quincey's devotion to, 204; death, 210–11, 212; 'Surprised by joy' written in memory of, 212, 213

Wordsworth, Charles (nephew), 281

Wordsworth, Christopher (brother), 6, 23, 93, 180, 259; character, 10, 25, 66, 285; at Cambridge, 34, 66, 83, 117, 280; engagement, 117; allowance to Dorothy, 145; successful Church career, 179, 258; marriage, 258; closer relationship with William, 258; William's letter to, 306; death, 332

Wordsworth, Christopher (nephew), 281; as biographer, 55, 143, 197, 313, 320, 341, 342

Wordsworth (later Quillinan), Dora (daughter), 251, 286, 327, 336; birth, 166; as William's favourite, 181, 254, 256, 284, 292, 308; on walk to Patterdale and Ullswater, 181–2; character, 254–6, 292–3; education, 255; ill health, 257, 293, 302, 331, 332; on Napoleon's escape from Elba, 270; first meeting with Quillinan, 284; travels with William, 287, 289, 293, 304, 328; given field adjoining Rydal Mount garden, 295; last meeting with Scott, 304; marriage to Quillinan, 307, 308–10, 316; wandering with him, 330–1; return to Lakes, 331–2; death, 332, 334; grave, 333

Wordsworth, Dorothy (sister), 93, 110, 121, 172, 180, 221, 223, 258; birth, 6; early sensitivity, 9, 15; with Penrith grandparents, 11, 12, 14; with Halifax relatives, 14, 23; and father's death, 22; regrets separation from brothers, 23; return to Penrith, 24; reunion with brothers, 24–6; as letter-writer, 24, 41, 49, 55, 66, 67, 71, 85, 89, 90, 100, 133, 152–

3, 165, 166, 167, 168, 215–16, 241, 242, 256, 263, 270, 271, 283, 298; her pen-portraits of brothers, 25, 66–7; insulted by guardians, 25–6; concern over William's opting out of Tripos course, 39; with uncle in Norfolk, 40–41, 43, 65–8, 70; fantasy of future life with William, 41, 42, 63, 67, 68, 75–6, 108, 112; absence of boy friends, 41, 132; worry over William's future, 42; William's letters to, 46, 47, 69, 111, 112; hint of jealousy over girls, 49, 58; told of William's affair with Annette, 55, 62, 68; corresponds with Annette, 55, 56, 63, 132, 141, 270; her criticisms of William's poems, 61–2; forbidden to see or mention him, 66; recognition of his faults, 67; secret reunion with him, 69; 'elopement' with him to Lakes, 70–71; as his amanuensis, 71, 87, 134; leaves Norfolk for ever, 75; joins William at Racedown, 75, 85–8; influence on him, 88, 131–3, 134–5; move to Alfoxden, 89; Coleridge's impression of, 90; independent spirit, 90; in Germany, 98–101; her *Journals*, 100, 133–6, 137, 138, 139, 145–6, 150, 151; possible part-original of Lucy, 101, 136; with Hutchinsons, 107; move to Dove Cottage, 112–14; domestic life, 114–16, 118–19, 135; devotion to William, 131, 135–9; involvement in his poetry, 132–3, 136; poetic gift, 133, 134, 240; intensity of relationship with William, 135–9, 143; striking physical presence and strong emotions, 137, 303; theory of incest, 138–9, 143, 245; meeting with Annette, 139–40, 142; and William's marriage, 144–6, 149, 301; continues to share his home, 144, 146, 148, 150 *et seq.*; domestic routine, 150–1, 246; cessation of *Journals*, 151; delight in William's children, 152–4, 181–2, 254; Scottish tour (1803), 154–8, 160–1; heartbroken at brother John's death, 169, 170; financial loss, 171; on Coleridge's return from Malta, 188; urges William to publish again, 192; writes pamphlet on deserving family, 198; on Allan Bank discomforts, 198; irritation with Coleridges, 199–200, 206; fondness for De Quincey, 204, 224; at Parsonage, 209; and Catherine's death, 210–11; move to Rydal Mount, 215–16; passes on gossip about De Quincey, 224; and 1818 election, 234–6, 248; on poor sales of *Excursion* and *White Doe*, 241, 242, 243; changed relationship with William after his marriage, 245–8; care of friends and relatives, 246, 247, 258, 284, 292, 293, 295, 300; disappointed in John, 253; finds Dora a handful, 254–5; on William's spoiling of Willy, 256–7; and Caroline's

Wordsworth, Dorothy—*contd.*
wedding, 270, 271; foreign tour (1820), 286; Scottish holiday, 295; forced to wear dentures, 295–6; on Scott's bankruptcy, 298; serious illness, 301–2; mental decline, 303, 306, 320, 328; locals' impression of, 322; death, 340

Wordsworth, Fanny (wife of Willy), 332

Wordsworth, Isabella (wife of son John), 307; death, 332

Wordsworth, Jane (wife of brother Richard), 223

Wordsworth, Jane (grand-daughter), 334

Wordsworth, John (father), 8–9, 14, 17, 18; as Lowther agent, 6, 7, 8, 228; death, 21–2; William's rare reference to, 171

Wordsworth, John (brother), 6, 112, 119, 137, 149; character, 10, 25, 116; naval career, 41, 70, 116, 151; joins William on Lakes tour, 108, 116; visits Dove Cottage, 116–17, 118; Yorkshire trip with William, 136, 144; allowance to Dorothy, 145; last voyage, 168–9; death, 169–72, 259; effect of death on William, 169–70, 171, 174, 177, 212; possibility of marriage to Sarah Hutchinson, 170, 302

Wordsworth, John (son), 153–4, 204, 210, 211, 308, 310; birth, 152; Latin lessons with De Quincey, 223; at Ambleside school and Sedbergh, 252–4; academic slowness, 252–3, 254, 256, 257, 291; at Oxford, 291–2; enters Church, 292; Leicestershire curacy, 292, 300–301; Cumberland living, 301, 307, 332; marriage to Isabella Curwen, 307; officiates at Dora's wedding, 309

Wordsworth, John (nephew), 281

Wordsworth (formerly Hutchinson), Mary (wife), 75, 89, 154, 166, 177, 204, 221, 241, 265, 282, 290, 304, 305, 320; early playmate of William, 12; later friendship, 24, 41–2, 142–3, 144; visits Racedown, 86; visits Dove Cottage, 117, 188; family background, 143–4; marriage to William, 144–6, 148–9, 301; domestic life, 150, 151, 245–6; birth of children, 152, 166, 180, 195, 205, 245; and John's death, 168; and purchase of Ullswater property, 183; death of children, 210–12, 246; at Rydal Mount, 215, 216; more active part in William's public life, 246, 247; happiness of marriage, 247, 249, 252, 295, 336; *White Doe* dedicated to, 247–8; Dorothy's veiled criticism of, 248; alteration in traditional view of, 249–50, 335–6; passionate letters between William and, 249–52; domestic bliss, 252, 295, 335–6; meets Annette, 272; inspiration of Duddon sonnets, 278, 299; travels abroad

with William, 285–6; in London, 286, 301, 327; on choice of profession for John, 291; and Dora's health, 293, 331; concern over Willy, 294; late blossoming, 295; and Dora's wedding, 309; and Fenwick and Martineau friendships, 315, 316, 318, 321; locals' impression of, as 'plain and stiff', 322; last Lakeland tour with William, 328; and Dora's death, 332, 334–5; greater part in William's creative work, 335; appearance, 335; kindness, 335; and William's last days and death, 337–8; sends *Prelude* to publisher, 340; and biography of William, 341–2

Wordsworth, Richard (grandfather), 6–7

Wordsworth, Richard (uncle), 9; as guardian, 22; death, 72

Wordsworth, Richard (brother), 6, 14, 41, 52, 144, 169; character, 10, 25; at Hawkshead school, 17, 19; as lawyer, 26, 39, 161; handles family affairs, 51, 54, 73, 151, 168, 171, 206, 258; cautions William over radical associates, 64; helps Dorothy, 70, 145; godfather to John, 152; unseemly marriage, 223, 258; illness and death, 258–9

Wordsworth, Tom (son), 210; birth and choice of name, 180–1; death, 211–12

Wordsworth, William: obsession with his childhood, 1–2; ancestry and birth, 5–9; earliest memories and interest in literature, 9–10; unusual freedom, 10, 17–18, 19, 26; at school in Cockermouth, 10–11; with Penrith grandparents, 11–14; his first visionary 'spot of time', 12–13; death of mother, 13; Hawkshead schooldays, 16–24; night-and-day wanderings, 19–20, 23; rural activities, 20, 27, 36–8; death of father, 21–2; poverty and guardianship of uncles, 22–3, 25–6, 30; social life, 23–4; first poetry, 24; early visions, 24, 26; reunion with Dorothy, 24–6; at Cambridge, 26, 28–35, 38–40, 42–4, 48, 50–51, 316; first sight of 'abandoned women', 29, 58; happy start to university life, 29–31, 35, 36; disillusion and dropping of honours course, 31–5, 38–40, 43, 45, 51; summer vacations, 35–8, 43; resumes writing verse, 36; his method of composing, 36, 105, 166; social life, 36–8; realization of himself as 'Dedicated Spirit', 38, 43, 65; own pattern of study, 38–40; first trip to France, 40, 45–8; early friendship with Mary, 41–2; fantasy of joint home with Dorothy, 41, 42, 68, 74, 75, 108; takes degree, 42, 48; effect of Cambridge on, 44; effect of French Revolution, 48, 50, 52–3, 54–5, 61, 103, 229; London idleness, 48–9; contemplates becoming a tramp, 50; tentative preparations for ordination, 50–51, 62; second and momentous trip to France, 51–5; passionate affair with Annette, 53–9, 61, 65, 67, 137, 174; leaves her in Orleans, 54, 56; plan to marry her, 55, 58; confesses to Dorothy, 55; first published verse, 61–2; aimlessness and uncertainty over career, 62–4, 65, 71; based in London, 63, 64–5, 74; involved in radical politics, 64–5, 68, 74; West Country tour with Calvert, 68–9; secret reunion with Dorothy, 69; 'elopement' with her to Lakes, 70–71; as companion to R. Calvert, 71–4; anxiety over legacy, 72–3; criticism of Lakes, 74; move to West Country, 75–6, 83–5; meets Coleridge and Southey, 83, 84–5; at Racedown, 85–8, 89; resumes writing, 85–6; Dorothy's importance to, 88, 131–3, 134–5; move to Alfoxden, 89; 'communal' life with Coleridge, 89–92, 117–19; his play rejected, 92–3; concentration on poetry, 93–4, 96, 100–101; suspected as French spy, 94–5; German visit, 96, 98–101; decides to return to North of England, 101, 107–8, 110; and reception of *Lyrical Ballads*, 101–7; move to Lakes, 108, 110–17; concern over changes there, 111; domestic life with Dorothy, 113–16, 135; interest in local life, 115–16; and new edition of *Lyrical Ballads*, 123–9; his definition of poetry, 126–7; first fan letter, 128, 201; grouped with Coleridge and Southey as 'Lake Poets', 129; devotion to Dorothy, 136–7; theory of incest, 138–9, 245; disentanglement from Annette, 139–42; marriage to Mary Hutchinson, 142–6, 148–9; domestic life with Mary and Dorothy, 150–1, 166, 173, 245–6, 252, 294–6; secures patronage of Beaumont, 152; Scottish tour, 154–8, 160–1; joins Volunteers, 164, 165; reaction from early republicanism, 164–5, 173–4; seeks tax advantages, 168; grief at brother John's death, 169–70, 171; financial worry, 170–1, 216–18; changes in personality in middle years, 172–5; effect of marriage, 173; obsessed by money, 177; sobering effect of John's death, 174, 177; rare piece of light descriptive writing, 174–5; social and literary success in London, 177–80; his portrait drawn, 179; teasingly referred to as 'Dear William', 181; purchase of Ullswater property, 182–3; more serious approach to religion, 186; visionary experience in Fleet Street, 187; peak of last great creative phase, 188; hurt by hostile reviews, 191–2, 196; move to Allan Bank, 192, 194–5; concentrates on prose, 196–7; humanitarian campaigns, 197–8; estranged from Coleridge, 205–9; their importance to each other, 208–9; early deaths of children, 210–12; move to Rydal Mount, 214–16, 219; meagre income from poetry, 216–17; seeks help from Lowthers, 217–18; first job, as Distributor of Stamps, 216, 218–19, 220, 230; new young writers disappointed in, 221, 222; growing reactionary attitude, 222–3, 226, 228–36; and 1818 election, 232–6; new volume of poetry after seven years, 237–43; modest public relations campaign, 241; hurt by fresh attacks, 242–3; changed relationship with Dorothy, 245–8; happiness of marriage, 247, 249, 252, 295, 336; passionate letters between Mary and, 249–52; problems of children's health and education, 252–7, 291–4; renewed contact with Annette and Caroline, 269–72; change in critical attitude towards him, 276–80; recognized as great poet, 277–8; penalties of fame, 280–3; piracy of works, 280–1; has bust sculpted, 281; tittle-tattle, 281–2; new friends and neighbours, 283–5, 315–19; foreign tours in 1820 and 1823, 285–6; whirlwind Irish tour, 288–9; 1831 Scottish tour, 289; writes guide to Lakes, 289–90; worry over sons' careers, 291–2, 293–4, 302; better financial state, 296–8, 313; deaths of contemporaries, 303–5, 306, 312, 325; inactive muse, 305, 313; gloom over state of nation, 306; Italian trip (1837), 307, 320, 328; misery over Dora's marriage, 307–10, 316, 330; accepts Laureateship after first refusing, 312, 313; other honours, 312; Civil List pension, 313; dictates memories of background to poems, 317; regarded as eccentric by locals, 319; seventy-fourth birthday party, 321; lost contact with peasantry, 322; campaign against railway, 322–3, 329; mellowing, 323–5; and summer visitors, 326; contacts with royalty, 326–7; London social round, 327; last Lakeland tour (1844), 328; grief at Dora's death, 332, 333, 334–5; last days, 333–8; comfort in grandchildren, 334; last trip outside Lake District (1849), 337; death, 338; biography, 341–2; his 'Two Voices', 343

Appearance: 46, 67, 91–2, 179, 287–8; dress, 91–2, 287, 319, 321; legs, 203, 225; Roman nose, 92, 153, 256; rusticity, 287, 288, 289

Characteristics and interests: absent-mindedness, 180; abstemiousness, 35, 93, 116, 296; anti-clericalism, 39–40; ardent feelings, 53, 66, 137–8, 250–2; arrogance, alleged, 225, 226, 238; books, lack of care for, 225; children, delight in, 181, 321, 334; dancing, 23, 36; depressions, 86, 177, 306–7; dogmatism,

Wordsworth, William—*contd.*
  Characteristics and interests—contd.
221, 222, 286, 288; egotism, 288, 336; emo-
tionalism, 197; fishing, 20, 114, 278; frugality, 173, 183, 282, 318; humour, sense of,
61, 135, 174–5, 186, 336, 337; landscape
gardening, 186, 216, 290; monologue, tendency to, 195, 285, 288, 326; moodiness, 10,
14, 26; moralizing tendency, 174, 196, 222,
227, 290; patriotism, 164, 165; pontifical
manner, 221, 222; puritanism, 65, 174, 223;
radicalism, 64, 68, 74, 84, 85, 90, 94–5, 173–
4, 232; reationary attitude, 222–3, 226, 228–
36, 261, 267, 268, 306; rebelliousness, 10, 13–
14, 26, 38–40, 53, 256; republicanism, 65,
164; reserve, 46, 67, 91, 112; rural sports, 20;
skating, 20, 114, 168, 203, 296; smell, lack
of sense of, 320; sociability, 23, 34, 36–7, 38,
178–9, 285, 327; speech, 92, 94, 286;
stability, 208; travel, 261, 285–6, 288–9, 328;
violent temper, 10, 26; visionary experiences, 12–13, 24, 69, 93, 161, 187; walking,
24, 114, 166, 289, 296, 338
  Health, 100, 296; eye trouble, 252, 286,
289, 296, 319, 320; hearing, 320; pains in
chest and side, 100, 152, 252; teeth, 295, 319
  Opinions and attitudes: aristocracy, 50, 127,
178, 183, 217–18, 228–9, 231, 282; Catholic
Emancipation, 306; Church of England, 62,
166, 306; critics, 102, 191–2, 238, 241–2, 243,
319; education, 197, 253, 323–4; French
Revolution, 45, 48, 50, 52–3, 54–5, 173–4,
229, 230, 232, 287; Industrial Revolution,
230; London, 60–61; manufacturers, 231;
money, 168, 171, 173, 297–8; moral freedom, 324; poetry, 102–3, 107, 126–7; political reform, 230–1, 306, 323, 324; property
classes, 231–2; railways, 322–3, 329; religion, 92, 186, 306; Tories, 165, 228, 231,
233–6, 267, 268; tourism, 111, 322–3; war,
65, 165; women, 203–4
  WRITINGS:
'Advice to the Young', 196, 201
'Among all Lovely Things', 188
'Another year, another deadly blow', 190
Borderers, The, 244; sole attempt at play, 86;
  rejected by Covent Garden, 93
'Brothers, The', 124
Collected Poems (1815), 238, 240, 272
Convention of Cintra, The, 196–7, 237
'Daffodils', 128, 188, 191; two best lines cre-
  dited to Mary, 250; quoted, 134, 250
Descriptive Sketches, 47, 54, 64, 138; first
  published verse, 61–2; praised by
  Coleridge, 83
Duddon sonnets, 278; quoted, 299

Ecclesiastical Sonnets, 279
Evening Walk, An, 36, 37, 43; first published
  verse, 61–2; praised by Coleridge, 83;
  dedicated to Dorothy, 132
Excursion, The, 192; writing of, 93; publica-
  tion, 237; William's first (and longest)
  long poem, 237, 240; unfavourable
  reviews, 239–40, 241–3, 274; high price
  and low sales, 241, 242
'Expostulation and Reply', 105; quoted, 97
'Extempore Effusion upon the Death of
  James Hogg', 305; quoted, 314
Guide to the Lakes, 289–91, 323
'Happy Warrior, The', 190
'Idiot Boy, The', 103, 128; quoted, 104
'Intimations of Immortality', 128, 188;
  quoted, 176
'It is a Beauteous Evening', quoted, 273
'Leech-gatherer, The', 132
'Lines composed a few Miles above Tintern
  Abbey', 106; quoted, 109
'Lucy' poems, 101, 124; quoted, 129–30
Lyrical Ballads (with Coleridge), 101–7, 133,
  171, 190, 201, 222, 278; compilation of,
  96, 106–7, 208; publication, 101–2, 107;
  poor reviews, 102, 122, 261; conversational style, 102–3; considered shocking, 103–4; rustic topics, 103–5; ridicule
  of, 104–5; better reviews, 122–3; new two-
  volume edition, 123–8, 169; limited but
  warm acclaim for, 124, 127–8; Lamb's
  opinion, 124–5; reprintings, 125, 128,
  177; William's 'conceited' Preface, 125–7,
  128, 188; middling critical coverage, 189;
  rearranged in *Collected Poems*, 240; first
  appearance in America, 336; quoted, 97,
  104, 105, 109, 129–30. *See also individual
  poems*
'Michael', 124
'Moods of my own Mind', 190
'My Heart leaps up', 188
'Nutting', 101, 124
'Ode to Duty', 174, 181, 188; quoted, 227
'On the Projected Kendal and Windermere
  Railway', quoted, 329
'On seeing Miss Helen Maria Williams weep
  at a Tale of Distress' (first published
  work), 51
'Peter Bell': Keats's and Reynolds's parody
  of, 274, 275; Shelley's skit on, 275; Byron's
  satire on, 275; publication, 276
Poems in Two Volumes (1807): publication,
  188; hostile reviews, 188–91; quoted, 227,
  260. *See also individual poems*
Prelude, The, 6, 20, 24, 33, 39, 47, 240, 316;
  as basic source of knowledge of early years,

1–2, 10, 21, 53, 57–8; first recorded 'spot of time' in, 12–13; identification of people in, 20; Cambridge attacked in, 31, 40, 42, 43; joyful Hawkshead sections, 36; anticlericalism in, 40; Vaudracour and Julia interlude, 57–8; London passages, 60, 61, 76; rare humour in, 61, 186; begun at Goslar, 101; self-analysis, 126; planned for posthumous publication, 128; completion of, 165, 174, 305; publication, 340, 342
'Recluse, The', 93, 238, 263, 305, 335
'Salisbury Plain', 69, 71
'She was a Phantom of Delight', 188; quoted, 260
'Solitary Reaper, The', 157, 188; quoted, 162
'Strange fits of passion', 124
'Surprised by joy', 212; quoted, 213
'Tables Turned, The', 105, 163; quoted, 97
'Thorn, The', 303; quoted, 104
'To a Butterfly', 15, 339
'To the Cuckoo', quoted, 339
'To the Daisy', 188
'To HC, Six Years Old', 333

'To the Spade of a Friend', 191
'We are seven', 105
'Westminster Bridge', 140, 188; quoted, 147
White Doe of Rylstone, The, 192, 238, 239, 274; dedicated to Mary, 248; quoted, 244, 248
'World is too much with us, The', quoted, 193
Wordsworth, Willy (son), 210, 214, 241, 301, 324; birth, 205; ill health, 246, 257, 293; academic slowness, 256, 257, 293–4; spoiling of, 256–7; idleness, 257, 293, 295; problem of career, 293–4, 302, 313; gives Dora away, 309; succeeds father as Distributor of Stamps, 313, 332; marriage to Fanny Graham, 332
Wordsworth, a Reinterpretation (Bateson), 138
'Wordsworth upon Helvellyn' (E. B. Browning), 327
Wrangham, Francis, 181

Yarmouth, 99, 101
Yarnell, Ellis, 336–7
York, Frederick, Duke of, 66